MORALITY AND CONVICTION IN AMERICAN POLITICS

A Reader

Editors

Martin Slann *Clemson University*

Susan Duffy *California Polytechnic State University*

Contributing Editors

Bernard K. Duffy
Lois L. Duke
Charles W. Dunn
Loch K. Johnson
John C. Koritansky
William Lasser
Peter A. Lawler
Richard W. Leeman
William D. Pederson
Bernard Schechterman
Stephen A. Smith
Mary Thornberry
Stephen Wainscott

Prentice Hall Englewood Cliffs, New Jersey 07632

Library of Congress Cataloging-in-Publication Data

Morality and conviction in American politics: a reader/[edited by]
Martin Slann, Susan Duffy.
p. cm.
Includes bibliographies and index.
ISBN 0-13-600891-7 : $17.00
1. Political ethics—United States. I. Slann, Martin W.
II. Duffy, Susan
JK468.E7M67 1990 88-34424
172—dc19 CIP

To our spouses: Ruth and Bernard

and to our children: Elizabeth Liat Tal Guy

Editorial/production supervision and
interior design: Cyndy Lyle Rymer
Cover design: Photo Plus Art
Manufacturing buyer: Peter Havens

A Division of Simon & Schuster
Englewood Cliffs, New Jersey 07632

Printed in the United States of America
10 9 8 7 6 5 4 3 2 1

ISBN 0-13-600891-7

Prentice-Hall International (UK) Limited, *London*
Prentice-Hall of Australia Pty. Limited, *Sydney*
Prentice-Hall Canada Inc., *Toronto*
Prentice-Hall Hispanoamericana, S.A., *Mexico*
Prentice-Hall of India Private Limited, *New Delhi*
Prentice-Hall of Japan, Inc., *Tokyo*
Simon & Schuster Asia Pte. Ltd., *Singapore*
Editora Prentice-Hall do Brasil, Ltda., *Rio de Janeiro*

CONTENTS

FOREWORD

By Bernard K. Duffy

Some social critics would claim that the time has come when, in the prophetic words of William Butler Yeats, "The best lack all conviction, while the worst are full of passionate intensity." Others would argue that relativism has so overtaken society that it risks losing its moral foundation. Ronald Reagan's presidency was noted for its identification with conservative religious groups and its strong ideological moorings, while his predecessor, Jimmy Carter, ran on a platform of restoring morality to government. Following suit, George Bush told the nation in his Inaugural Address that "America is never wholly herself unless she is engaged in high moral principle. We as a people have such a purpose today. It is to make kinder the face of the nation and gentler the face of the world." Politicians find they must establish moral agendas as well as court groups with strong ideological and moral convictions.

This is by no means a new phenomenon. United States political history reveals the influence of transcendent beliefs on the actions of government. An ideological belief in Manifest Destiny and no small degree of missionary zeal led to bitter struggles for territory in the American West and an arrogant imperialism in the Far East. In the 1950s preachers like Billy Sunday linked fundamentalist religious beliefs with an anticommunist foreign policy, and the communist witchhunt created by Joseph McCarthy had a strong religious and moral undercurrent. Richard Nixon and other "Cold Warriors" rose to prominence by rhetorically dividing the world between godless communists and Christian capitalists. Those who took the nonideological, intellectual highroad such as Adlai Stevenson quickly fell by the wayside. Each generation of politicians has discovered the utility of appealing directly to the biases of large groups with readily identifiable and largely inflexible moral convictions. The supposed clout of Richard Nixon's "great silent majority" was replaced by the political pieties of "the Moral Majority" identified in the rhetoric of the Reverend Jerry Falwell and North Carolina Senator Jesse Helms. The tides of politics are increasingly determined by the gravitational pull of satellites, dense in opinion and belief, that orbit the larger political sphere.

Reason rarely leads to strong conviction among the masses. Passion runs deeper and unifies, while reason invites intellectual dissent and divides. Hitler railed against the parliamentary disputes of Vienna and proposed that the German people find him with their hearts, not their minds. Passionate belief leads to solidarity among political confederates and to the inflexible positions that characterize much of the political debate of the last several decades. The mass media exploitatively bombard audiences with sensationalistic images of the problems that beset the nation. Each day brings new stimuli that either numb further those who are already desensitized or arouse strong emotions in those still capable of responding. Ideological, religious, and political convictions give meaning to the myriad events that make up the news. Strongly felt convictions lead one to know with certainty if Colonel Oliver North is guilty or innocent, if the bombing of Libya was right or wrong, if the Soviet Union is indeed an "evil empire" or a peace loving nation committed to *Glasnost*, if Theodore Bundy was put to death justly, if Governor Michael Dukakis stands with the angels on the abortion question, and so on through the countless issues that knit the brows of philosophers and social theorists and are made simple by prime-time preachers, tub-thumping politicians, tabloid newspapers, and investigative television reporters.

Passion is a great leveler. While conviction may be the product of inquiry and reason, intellect is not required to take a position and stand four square upon it. Education requires us to recognize our own fallibility, and to suspend our convictions as we consider the viewpoints of others. The human quality of emotional empathy allows us to survey the landscape of another's passions, to inspect the world from an alternative vantage point and to return to our own windows on reality with new understanding. The consideration of other points of view helps liberate us from the prejudices and tendencies that our social and economic positions in the culture dictate. We understand our own perspectives better by examining those that we do not share. At a time when relativism itself has been called into question by conservative intellectuals like Allan Bloom, author of *The Closing of the American Mind*, it is admittedly controversial to assert the importance of the capacity to see one's own beliefs as culturally and socially determined.

This book invites the reader to compare ways of seeing the world. It considers the morally involved issues that have excited some of the nation's most intense and persistent political struggles. To be unaware of these issues is not to know American politics. But the discussions of political issues that fill these pages are not meant solely for students of politics, because they are also materials for other kinds of analysis. Students of written and oral argumentation and composition, of logic, and of critical thinking may fruitfully inquire into how the proponents of such causes as capital punishment, creationism, free speech, abortion, and human rights have used the resources of language to persuade the electorate. The essays, speeches, and editorials reprinted in this book are a rich repository of argument types, emotional appeals, political posturing, and public relations strategies.

The editors delegated to contributing editors the task of selecting appropriate material for each unit considered in the book. The selections are preceded by the contributing editors' introductions intended to set the stage for the readings and to focus attention on important issues that students might wish to consider. The contributing editors were asked to use their professional judgment in selecting readings that would reveal the nature of the controversies they were assigned and to feel no obligation to conceal their own views. The result is a reader that acknowledges the controversial nature of the issues that are represented. This book addresses in terms that cannot fail to stimulate interest, the morally involved, value-laden character of political discussion and debate in the United States. In examining politics at the level of the sensibilities and passions of the electorate, this book reveals the human dimension of American politics.

PREFACE

Our work on this reader was prompted by our desire to encourage active class discussion and participation in American Government courses as well as in courses in Argumentation, Critical Thinking, and Persuasion. Our different academic disciplines, Political Science and Speech Communication, offered us very different perspectives about the influence of bias and strong ideological convictions on American politics. There is the long history of American political oratory with its demagogues, zealots, statesmen, and political saints. And there is the equally long history of foreign and domestic policies, virulent campaigns, pork barrel politics, political action committees, and special interest groups who wield enormous influence in the political arena. Though we share a common ground we approach the subject from different directions. However, very early on in our work on this book we perceived that our students in both disciplines need to be able to do four things:

1. They need to be able to recognize bias, ideology, and the various uses of evidence to support an abstract belief.
2. They need to critically assess the credibility of positions espoused in public debate and the credibility of the speakers or groups who attempt to persuade them.
3. They need to be able to articulate their positions about values and competing value systems.
4. They need to come to understand how these values affect public policy and their role as educated voters.

We felt that a reader which supplied a sampling of articles evidencing strong moral, philosophical, ideological, or pragmatic positions affecting

American politics and its citizenry would be most effective in meeting this goal.

We invited fifteen scholars from the disciplines of Political Science and Speech Communication to select readings on current topics that spawn heated debate: the Congress, the Presidency, the Law, the Bureaucracy, the Media, Abortion, Capital Punishment, the Evolutionist/Creationist Debate, Homosexuality, Human Rights, Censorship, Nuclear Arms, Totalitarian and Authoritarian Governments, Foreign Aid, and Terrorism. We were delighted with the creative and scholarly responses we received from each of the contributing editors. Each article reprinted here articulates a strong position that necessitates critical analysis. We hope that each will engender animated and critical class discussions and provide students with the opportunity to take a position, support it, and challenge each other and their professors.

We started this project in 1987 when Ronald Reagan was President, Gary Hart's presidential campaign was bogged down in the "character" issue, and the Iran-Contra Hearings were about to get into full swing. As we finish it in 1989, George Bush is President, Congress is embroiled in a controversy about voting itself a substantial pay raise, and there has been a tragic terrorist attack on a Pan American jetliner over Scotland. Other value-laden issues continue to surface in the newspaper each day.

We are grateful to all the authors and editors who granted permission for us to reprint the articles contained here. We hope the students who read these essays will be moved to consider the arguments, form new ones, and enjoy the intellectual exercise. More than that, we hope the students who use this volume will come to be informed and articulate citizens, not because of the material it contains, but because they evaluated, criticized, and scrutinized the positions it outlines. It is important to us that they grow to be individuals who participate in our democratic process responsibly and intelligently; who listen with an ability to separate truth from falsehood, and who speak to political and social issues vigorously and ethically.

Susan Duffy
Martin Slann

Acknowledgments

We wish to thank those who helped us in the developmental phases of this book and who continued their support throughout this project. Karen Horton, editor for Prentice Hall, was most helpful in all stages of the project, as was Cyndy Rymer, the production editor, and Martha Williams, the copy editor. Bernard Duffy was instrumental in helping us decide on the format of the book that would include contributing editors for each chapter. For his suggestions, criticisms, and help with proofreading, we offer our warm thanks.

Most importantly, we would like to thank all the contributing editors to this volume: Bernard Duffy, Lois Duke, Charles Dunn, Loch Johnson, John Koritansky, William Lasser, Peter Lawler, Richard Leeman, William Pederson, Bernard Schechterman, Stephen Smith, Mary Thornberry, and Stephen Wainscott. These scholars, representing the fields of political science and speech communication, have made this an exciting and gratifying project. Without exception they have been extraordinarily cooperative in writing essays to reflect the intent of the project, submitting the essays on time, securing the permissions for each of the articles reprinted in their respective chapters, and accepting our suggestions for revisions with graciousness and good humor. To them we offer our most heartfelt thanks, for without them this project would still be a dream.

We would also like to thank the Clemson University political science department secretary, Debra Whitfield, for her constant and good-natured assistance and Janet Leach, the Cal Poly Speech communication department secretary, for her help with the index.

Finally, we would like to thank the readers of this volume in its various stages: Prof. Joseph Mikyska, Illinois Valley Community College; Prof. Richard J. Bloss, Chicago State University; Prof. Paul N. Chardoul, Grand Rapids Junior College. We are grateful for their suggestions and criticisms and hope that they will see their suggestions have been incorporated into this volume.

INTRODUCTION

In the United States the relationship between morals and politics is an old and largely undefined one. Today's speakers in political, educational, and even religious arenas face audiences whose beliefs are heterogeneous. No longer are the Bible and the Constitution the moral constants they once were for millions of Americans. And although we pride ourselves collectively on our patriotism and work ethic, we are no longer a nation of people whose beliefs are homogenous or who share a value system that dictates right or wrong, good or evil. Our interest in how various ethical and ideological belief systems influence American public policy led us to the title of this reader—*Morality and Conviction in American Politics.*

The purpose of this book is not so much to define this relationship between and among morality, personal ethics, ideology, and politics, but to provide a forum in which students can identify, and ultimately come to understand, various moral and ideological positions that shape American politics. We do not ask you to agree or disagree with these positions, only to recognize that they exist and are influential in the democratic process.

Many of today's issues, such as abortion, the death penalty, public school prayer, homosexual rights, and censorship—issues examined in this book—lead to absolutist arguments based on religious or moral justification. Americans seek to fill the need for permanence, a sense of coherence, and order in their lives by adopting various ideological positions. Although many would agree that our leaders should not be ideologues, we as a nation have repeatedly elected ideological proponents to the Congress, and even the presidency. They, in turn, have appointed others, often with equally strong ideological positions, to cabinet posts, the courts, and to crucial governing bodies, such as the Federal Communication Commission. How these individuals have shaped public policy, and how they have responded to the phenomenon of single-issue interest groups and their respective political action committees is central to this project.

From the beginning we found that the book naturally divided into three sections:

I. American Political Institutions: Individual Freedoms and Political Stability
II. Individual Issues: Value Systems and Law
III. Global Issues: American Foreign Policy and International Morality

Each section is divided into five chapters. Each chapter reflects many of the concerns held by American voters and politicians and contains readings that emphasize representative schools of thought on issues of both moral and political import.

By examining the diverse, and sometimes extreme, positions that national debates in each of these areas have spawned, we hope to demonstrate that morality, personal ethics, ideology, and religion are inextricably bound in the political process in the United States. In the end it is public opinion that determines much of the morality as well as the content of politics. Ortega y Gasset's observed that "never has anyone ruled on this earth by basing his rule on any other thing than public opinion." No elected or appointed governmental official is completely immune to the pressures of public opinion.

Many of today's issues are fraught with religious, moral, ethical, and ideological overtones. Issues such as abortion, the death penalty, public school prayer, homosexual rights, and censorship are not easily resolved. Moral concerns have been part of political considerations in the United States since the formation of the republic.

Differing religious and moral stances over church and state still remain a source of discomfort for American politicians. This is due to the prescriptive nature of most religions, and the absolutism of some. By their nature religiously oriented issues can produce inflexible and polarized positions that spill over the pulpit into the political rostrum. This is not a new phenomenon in American politics.

The very issues that this volume considers readily precipitate extremist justifications. We did not set out to present "both sides" of an issue, although many of the chapters do that. Our intention is to present positions that have strong ideological, moral, or ethical arguments that in turn influence, or try to influence, American politics.

For better or worse, our political and social institutions reflect and characterize our entire society. When we evaluate them, we also indulge in the frequently unpleasant task of evaluating ourselves. In a world that cynics often consider amoral, the United States remains a nation whose activities are often monitored, if not often restrained, by some concept of morality. The electorate, for example, still shuns political candidates whose personal conduct is less than impeccable. There may be a strong degree of hypocrisy in all of this, but the very fact that lip service is given to moral behavior is an indication of our willingness to embrace some ethical standard as a nation. If traditional morality did not retain its hold on millions of Americans, homosexuality, abortion, and the death penalty, would undoubtedly be debated quite differently. The intensity, fervor, and zeal that are hallmarks of American political debate remind us that politics is the product of human passion rather than divine reason.

1

CONGRESS AND MORALITY: REPRESENTING A DEMOCRACY

Richard W. Leeman and Lois L. Duke

For the legislative body in a representative democracy, morality is a question of product and process. The product—the legislation—is presumed to be moral itself and to enforce morals. Whether moral or not, elaborate arguments are constructed to show that it is, as the slavery debates of the previous century illustrate. The morality of the product is the substance of much of this book, and it is better discussed in chapters devoted exclusively to specific topics. Our concern in this chapter is with the process: What constitutes ethical representation of the body politic? Our discussion can be divided somewhat artificially into two areas, elections and legislation. The distinction is artificial because, as will become apparent, the two halves stand in a symbiotic relationship with one another.

Because we live in a representative democracy, the process begins with the election of someone to represent us for the purpose of making law. Problems with the selection process have existed since the beginning. "Treating" was a colonial practice by which the candidate supplied free hard cider for his constituents on the Election Day holiday. Many early American newspapers were owned and operated by political parties; their penchant for publishing any scandalous rumor available about an opponent explains the *New York Times'* motto "All the News That's Fit to Print." The word "gerrymander"—meaning to redraw legislative districts to give one candidate an advantage over another—comes from Governor Gerry of Massachusetts doing just that in the early nineteenth century. Dead voters throughout this century have cast many a ballot long after becoming deceased. The problem common to all four examples is that of ensuring that the person elected to Congress is the one who *ought* to be elected, and not simply the one who buys, begs, borrows, or steals the election.

Modern Congressional elections are plagued by two major problems: money and what that money buys. Former congressman Richard Bolling's essay "Money in Politics" laments the tremendous amount of money now required to run for office. In 1984, he points out, the average candidate for the House of Representatives spent $205,000. Some critics hold that this huge amount of money considerably decreases the political field. Only the very wealthy or those with the backing of the special interests are likely to run, they argue, thus undercutting the ideal of public service. Bolling is more concerned with the effects of money on Congress and "its ability to govern effectively." He charges that special interest money—in the form of Political Action Committees (PACs)—distorts and blocks legislation, skews representation away from the common good and towards the monied interests, and undermines public confidence in Congress. He accurately defines the major argument advanced by the supporters of PACs, that ours is a pluralistic system of competing special interests. Bolling, however, argues that not all "interests" can compete on the same level financially, and so found himself "serving in the most gutless Congress I had ever seen." Controlling the "pernicious influence of money in politics," he writes, "is essential to the survival of our democracy."

While Bolling's concern is that the search for election money thwarts the goals of governance, others are alarmed that money now taints the electoral process itself. Of particular concern recently has been the rise of political consultants and the use of the media by those consultants. Some, like David Altman, are concerned that consultants emphasize imagery over substance. Modern media advertising is "an open invitation to the demagogue, a path to elective office for the incompetent but glib candidate."[1] Altman's fears seem confirmed when political consultants like Bob Goodman reveal that he "strive[s] for...an emotion, not a position" because "feelings decide it all. We must *like* this human being to vote for him."[2]

The controversy, however, is not simply that consultants emphasize image over substance; it includes the *kind* of images they sell. Because image advertising is grounded in one's emotions, "media consultants do not package candidates so much as they package voters' prejudices."[3] Prejudices may be either for or against, but candidates are finding that negative prejudices are frequently stronger, and therefore potentially more powerful. Initially leery of negative advertising, media managers now believe it more effective than originally thought and find themselves using it more and more. Negative advertising has several ethical dimensions to it, including the damage done to the reputations of candidates, the use of false charges, and the potentially detrimental effects on the electorate. Ginsberg and Weissberg, among others, have argued that negative campaigning encourages a negative attitude towards the electoral process itself.[4] Most consultants believe that negative advertising is simply part of the process, and contend that as a marketplace the system regulates itself. Writes Joe Napolitan, "You know that you've got to come back next year, and the years after that, you know that you must survive on your reputation, and if the reputation stinks you're not likely to get clients."[5] Some, though, agree with Charles Guggenheim's assessment at the end of the *Washington Post* article included here: "It's not a very good profession."

Once in office, the question becomes not who will represent the electorate, but how the electorate will be represented. To some, the answer is "not very well." Money, they charge, corrupts the process of representation, but the money these critics worry about is for personal gain, not reelection. The *Wall Street Journal,* for example, finds it curious that Congress has exempted itself from the Ethics in Government Act. The motive for passing the act was not to clean up government, the *Journal* argues, but to aggrandize more power for the House and Senate. The law is not so much an enforcer of ethics as it is a "political weapon." One can speculate, however, that the *Journal's* argument is less ethical than political. The *Journal* berates Congress for "belaboring the executive branch," and implies several times that Congressional investigations have wasted time, money, and effort. Then, however, it proposes that Congress apply "the same level of oversight" to itself.

Money can intrude on the political process for purposes other than political action committees or personal gain. For example, some argue that Congress plays "pork-barrel politics" in order to curry favor with the folks back home. Former Treasury Secretary William Simon made this point when discussing the inability of the government to solve its budget deficit problem. "[The problem is] not only the president, it's Congress. Congress under Democrat and Republican alike, it makes no difference. They're a bunch of hypocrites who have one credo, and that credo is 'more.' All they give a damn about is being reelected. They don't care about the long term. The long term to the Congress is the next election. Period."[6] Similarly, Nobel economist James Buchanan has argued that Congress will always vote in their self-interest, and reelection is their primary self-interest. If true, one commentator poses an interesting moral dilemma. "As the moral philosophers tell us, ought implies can: To say the government should do X is to say that it can do X. By casting doubt on whether it can [act in the interest of the common good], Buchanan challenges the idea that it ought to try."[7]

Two essays illustrate the practical effects of this problem. Tom Morganthau's article "The Year of the Gimmick" suggests the lengths to which Congress may go to camouflage the "hypocrisy." The article presents the moral dilemmas involved in sacrificing the future for the short term, doing the "easy things," or being less than honest by using "smoke and mirrors" to hide the actual deficit. The ethical concerns expressed here emerge in legislative debate about issues like the line-item veto and the Gramm-Rudman "abdication of responsibility." Director of the Office of Management and Budget (OMB) James Miller raises both of these issues in his speech, believing it an "inherent" part of the legislative process that Congress will be fiscally irresponsible. Miller invests the executive branch with greater responsibility and moral force because the president is the only representative in this democracy elected by *all* the people.

These two essays provide a transition to the final question addressed in this chapter. Is Congress elected to reflect the will of the people? Or is it elected to *lead* the public? The *America* editorial reflects the conflicting answers Americans tend to give in response. Early in the essay, Congress is depicted as the representative of the people's will. Legislators are urged to cut off funds to the contras because only 28 percent of Americans approve of the funding. The rest of the article, however, implies that Congress has a moral duty to cut off funding *regardless* of public opinion polls. Contra funding is "immoral, illegal, and unwise." On each count, funding should be rejected, presumably regardless of the popularity involved.

The moral dilemmas raised in these essays are inextricably intertwined. Who should be elected to represent us, and what should that electoral process be like? How can we ensure that the electoral process influences the legislative process, but not in a way that results in smoke, mirrors, and pork-barrels? Or can it? Should Congress reflect the public's will, or mold it? These questions are important for all American citizens, because Congress is only half of the equation in a representative democracy. If one finds fault with the morals of Congress, perhaps Pogo's famous admonition applies: "We have met the enemy, and he is us."

NOTES

1. David R. Altman, "Political TV Spots Should be Banned," *New York Times* (6 August 1978), p. F14.
2. As quoted in Larry J. Sabato, *The Rise of Political Consultants* (New York: Basic Books, 1981), p. 145.
3. Ibid.
4. Benjamin Ginsberg and Robert Weissberg, "Elections and Mobilization of Popular Support," *American Journal of Political Science* 22 (1978), pp. 31–55.
5. Joseph Napolitan, *The Election Game and How to Win It* (New York: Doubleday, 1972), p. 4.
6. William Simon, "The MacNeil-Lehrer Newshour," PBS-TV, 20 October 1987.
7. David Henderson, "Buchanan's Prize," *National Review* (31 Dec. 1986), p. 20.

Money in Politics

Richard Bolling

It is well established, I suppose, that those, like Thoreau or Dante, who spend time in strange or distant or eye-opening places are obliged to report back on what they have seen and learned. This article reports on some of what I have seen during my years in another eye-opening place, the U.S. Congress. While I found it less idyllic than Walden Pond, fortunately I also found it less hellish or populated with sinners than the Inferno.

I am, in fact, an ardent fan of the institution of the U.S. House of Representatives, but these days I am also extremely concerned about the Congress and its ability to govern effectively. My concern does not stem from the magnitude or complexity of the issues that confront Congress. During my 34 years there, my colleagues and I with some success addressed a number of the most difficult and deep-rooted problems this country has known, such as civil rights and poverty, education and health care; and of course, none of these jobs is ever completed. Today's problems may be difficult, but they certainly will and can be faced and dealt with.

Rather, I am concerned because one basic problem is undermining the ability of Congress to address any other issues effectively. That problem is the corrosive, pervasive, and too often invisible influence of special interest money. Most damaging to the Congress is the recent explosion in campaign contributions from political action committees (PACs), which are formed by corporations, unions, trade associations, and ideological groups in order to exercise influence by contributing money to election campaigns. There are other forms of special interest money, however, that are also increasingly corroding the integrity of Congress, such as speaking fees, known as honoraria, and the undisclosed, multimillion-dollar lobbying efforts of various industries and interest groups.

I would like to discuss where the problem of special interest money came from; how severe it is, and what we, collectively, can do about it.

Richard Bolling, "Money in Politics," *American Academy of Political and Social Science Annals* (February 1986), pp. 77–85. Reprinted with permission of the author. Adapted from a speech delivered by Richard Bolling at Boston College, Chestnut Hill, Massachusetts, in September 1983.

THE SOURCE OF THE PROBLEM

Why has special interest money become such a threat to the Congress? There are two developments that I witnessed during my years in politics that I believe combined to produce the current crisis.

The first was the exponential growth in campaign costs. When I was first elected to Congress in 1948, I could raise only $2500. Money was hard to find, but campaigns were cheap. Some radio was used, and really no television. The average campaign cost for the House was probably less than $10,000. In 1984, in contrast, candidates for the House of Representatives on average spent $205,000. In other words, while the cost of living has increased over fourfold since I first ran for Congress, the cost of staying alive in politics has increased, on the average, by much more than 20 times.

The second development I witnessed that has contributed to the current crisis was that, as congressmen increasingly needed campaign money, interest groups increasingly wanted congressmen. Over the last 15 or so years, as the public demanded government protection and regulation in more areas, such as the environment, consumer products, and job safety, labor and corporate interest groups expanded their efforts to shape the resulting laws. Thus, as the regulatory budget of the federal government increased fivefold since the early 1970s, so did the number of corporate and labor PACs.

Interest groups also began seeking more influence over Congress, perhaps because Congress became the easiest and most productive place to seek it at the federal level. In 1974, Congress passed major amendments to the Federal Election Campaign Act, which had been passed three years earlier. Those amendments established that presidential candidates would have the option of financing their campaigns principally with public funds in the primaries and exclusively with public funds in the general election. Since virtually all the candidates have opted for public financing, the new public financing system has effectively prohibited private contributions in presidential general elections and reduced the role of private money in the presidential nominating process.[1] Unfortunately, however, Congress declined to adopt that reform for itself. With the role of special interest campaign contributions somewhat curtailed in presidential campaigns, and no public financing for congressional races, many special interest groups turned their attention—and much of their money—to Congress.

[1]Elizabeth Drew shows, however, that large sums of money are being spent that clearly evade the intent, if not the letter, of the law. See Drew, *Politics and Money* (New York, Macmillan, 1983).

Over the years, as interest groups developed a greater desire to use their money to influence congressional policy-making, they also became dangerously sophisticated in how to do it. They learned to target their contributions to reach the chairmen and members of congressional committees and subcommittees with jurisdiction over highly prized tax breaks or subsidies or contracts. In the 1984 election, not surprisingly, members of two of the most powerful House committees—the Ways and Means Committee and the Energy and Commerce Committee—received on average more PAC contributions than members of any other House committee. Ironically, the same technologies that made campaigns so expensive—such as polling and direct mail—allowed these groups to target their contributions, their honoraria, and their lobbying efforts to produce the maximum influence.

At this point I would like to make it clear that to corrupt or to influence greatly outcomes in congressional committees or subcommittees usually does not require obtaining the services of many members. Congressional committees are often narrowly divided to begin with, and one or two subservient individuals may make a great difference in the outcome on very important legislation. The system is so fragile and vulnerable that real purity is essential to consistent success for the public interest.

THE EXTENT OF THE PROBLEM

As congressmen needed more campaign funds and as interest groups desired more influence in Congress, the result was an alarming growth in special interest money. It only requires a few figures and examples to see how alarming that growth has been. Consider the most corrosive source of special interest money, PACs. In 1974, there were 608 such committees. Today there are nearly 4000. In 1974 PACs gave $12.5 million to congressional candidates. By the 1984 elections their contributions exceeded $104 million, an eightfold increase in just 10 years.[2] Most disturbing, the dependence of congressmen on PAC funds has increased steadily. In 1974 PAC money accounted for only about 14 percent of the funds for an average campaign in the House of Representatives. By 1984, however, House candidates on average were receiving 38 percent of their funding from PACs; 20 of 27 current committee chairs and House leaders got more than half of their campaign funds from these interest groups. In the last two elections, four Senate candidates received over $1 million each from PACs.[3]

[2]*People v. PACs: Common Cause Guide to Winning the War against Political Action Committees* (Washington, DC: Common Cause, 1983).

[3]"House Incumbents Get 44c of Every Campaign Dollar from PACs in 1984 Election" (Press release, Common Cause, 1985); "1984 Senate Candidates Raised $146 Million, Spent, $137 Million and Received $28 Million from PACs" (Press release, Common Cause, 1985).

Interest groups are pouring increasing sums of money into Congress through other channels as well, such as honoraria. In 1984, for instance, members of Congress received $5.2 million in honoraria.[4] Undoubtedly, some honoraria are modest payments for bona fide speaking engagements. But in other cases, congressmen are receiving $1000 or $2000 for merely having coffee with a handful of an interest group's executives. In many cases, the interest groups that are paying these honoraria are the same groups whose PACs are making substantial contributions. In 1984, members of the two congressional tax-writing committees received over $1 million in honoraria from special interest groups, and members of these two committees received over $16 million from PACs in their most recent election.[5] But unlike campaign contributions, honoraria are going directly into the pockets of members of Congress.

Special interest groups are also buying influence through undisclosed grass-roots lobbying efforts. Certainly there is nothing objectionable about grass-roots lobbying itself, but a number of interest groups are currently spending millions to influence legislation while disclosing few of these expenditures under federal lobbying regulations. For example, in 1983, the banking industry mounted a multimillion-dollar campaign to repeal one of the most needed parts of the 1982 tax act, that concerning withholding on interest and dividends. Banks ran scores of newspaper advertisements and enclosed millions of mini-harangues and preprinted congressional letters in their customers' monthly statements. Within weeks, Congress was inundated with letters urging repeal of withholding. Yet, because few of the trade associations and none of the banks had disclosed their massive expenditures, the withholding provision was all but repealed before Congress knew how much of the uproar had been purchased by the industry.

THE DAMAGE DONE BY SPECIAL INTEREST MONEY

All this special interest money is, in a number of ways, threatening Congress's ability to govern.

First, in many cases, the money is distorting or blocking legislation. In 1982, for example, the Federal Trade Commission proposed the used-car rule, which would have required used-car dealers to tell customers about any known defects in the cars they were about to buy. The used-car dealers

[4]"Senators and Representatives Received $5.2 Million in 1984 Honoraria; Members of Tax Writing Committees Got $1 Million of Total; Tobacco Institute Top Giver at $129,691" (Press release, Common Cause, 1985).

[5]"Business PACs Gave $11 Million to Congressional Tax-Writers" (Press release, Common Cause, 1985).

opposed the rule and, with their PAC money, persuaded Congress to veto it. The 69 senators who voted down the used-car rule received, on the average, twice as much in PAC contributions from the automobile dealers as those who voted against the auto dealers. In the House, the ratio was five to one. A recent study presented to the American Political Science Association concluded that, even accounting for party affiliation and ideology, the more than $1 million contributed by the auto dealers' PAC made a significant—and in some cases decisive—difference in the congressional votes on the rule.

There is an embarrassment of similar cases. Whether it is agricultural subsidies or health care costs or environmental protection or tax loopholes, special interest money is buying too much—and at the public's expense.

The influence of special interest money in these cases is rarely in the form of an explicit quid pro quo. Rather, this money—and especially PAC money—distorts legislation through a more subtle and ongoing process. PACs know that most congressmen run for reelection and will be periodically in need of their money. PACs also know that they will have the power to keep that money flowing to a member of Congress or to cut it off, depending on the congressmen's votes in the years between elections. Because members of Congress know they will need that money, they are hesitant to vote in ways that might offend the PACs....

Second, the torrent of special interest money is drowning out representation. Our representative democracy is founded on the principle that elected officials will freely vote their consciences while earnestly working in their constituents' best interests and actively listening to what those interests are. But a member of Congress may not feel free to vote his or her conscience when that Congress member must depend on special interest groups to provide a third or half of his or her campaign funds. Furthermore, the congressman cannot even know what his constituents' interests are when their letters are being prompted—and in some cases, printed, stamped, and mailed—by some interest group's undisclosed lobbying efforts. The result is that some congressmen are voting for legislation that bears less relation to their constituents' interests than to the special interest money they have been receiving. In other cases, special interest money simply throws Congress into deadlock, and legislation that would have been in almost everybody's interest fails to pass.

Of course, some dispute that all this special interest money erodes representation. They cite James Madison's arguments about pluralism from *The Federalist* and argue that the pressures from the PAC funds of competing groups will cancel each other out. But this argument assumes that there will always be a PAC for each of the countervailing interests. In fact, as Senator Robert Dole of Kansas has observed, "poor people don't make campaign contributions. You might get a different result if there were a Poor-PAC up here."[6] An example is the issue of the used-car rule. The only interest not represented by PAC funds in that fight were the interests of consumers and the general public. At a time like this, when the Congress is deciding crucial questions about the course of the economy, about social equity, and about the proper role of government, we cannot afford to have policies that represent only one side—the side with the money and the PACs.

Finally, the explosion in PAC funds and other forms of special interest money is undermining public confidence in the institution of Congress, and for good reason. It may sound idealistic, but I know from experience that Congress must have and must appear to have integrity in order to retain the public's confidence. More and more, the public suspects that at least a portion of the Congress is no longer pure. The cause of this suspicion is that the public sees legislation that, to ever greater extents, looks like special interest wish lists. What the public increasingly discovers is that interest groups are buying the sort of access they as voters could never dream of, and what the public increasingly hears is members of Congress and former members like myself sounding the alarm.

The public justifiably loses faith in the Congress when it hears my former colleague from Missouri, Senator Thomas Eagleton, saying the present campaign-financing system

> virtually forces Members of Congress to go hat in hand, begging for money from special interests whose sole purpose for existing is to seek a *quid pro quo.* The scandal is taking place every day and will continue to do so while the present system is in place.[7]

The public justifiably loses faith in the Congress when it hears former Congressman James Shannon of Massachusetts saying that

> the problem of money in politics hasn't been an obsession of mine, but it's becoming one now.... What's bothering me is when you start seeing guys acting against what you know are their philosophies and constituencies and instincts.... There are some here who say that PACs don't influence public policy. That's baloney.[8]

And the public justifiably loses faith in the Congress when it hears Senator Dole saying that

[6]Albert Hunt, "Cash Politics," *Wall Street Journal,* 26 July 1982.

[7]Statement of Senator Thomas Eagleton, in U.S., Congress, Senate, Committee on Rules and Administration, *Hearings on Campaign Finance Reform Proposals of 1983.* 98th Cong., 1st sess., 1983, p. 52.

[8]Drew, *Politics and Money,* p. 51.

> when these political action committees give money they expect something in return other than good government. It is making it much more difficult to legislate. We may reach a point where if everybody is buying something with PAC money, we cannot get anything done.[9]

In sum, during my service in Congress, I witnessed congressmen's needs for funds and interest groups' desire for influence increase and combine in a way that steadily began to undermine policy, representation, and the institution of Congress. I remember that as we moved through the sixties and through the Johnson administration, there developed an undefinable feeling on Capital Hill and in Washington—an odor, if you will—that the amount of money flowing in was becoming enormous and that there were some situations developing very rapidly that were just ripe for corruption. During the Nixon administration, as the Watergate scandal broke open, that odor became a stench. By the time I retired, the corruption of special interest money had infected the legislative branch, and, partly as a result, I found myself serving in the most gutless Congress I had ever seen. What I fear today is that special interest money is damaging Congress to the same scandalous degree that it damaged the executive branch during Watergate; the only difference is that the means now being used appear to be sanctioned.

THE FRAMEWORK FOR A SOLUTION

I believe that there is a way out of this problem, and I think an examination of how we have dealt with special interest money in the past gives some guidance for where we should go in the future. Basically, it seems that in the past we have tried, to varying degrees, to reduce the undue influence of special interest money by making it visible, reasonable, and resistible.

The first reaction to special interest money typically has been to make it visible. Thus the key provisions of the first major piece of campaign-finance legislation to pass Congress in recent times, the Federal Election Campaign Act of 1971, required disclosure of contributions to federal campaigns and required PACs to register with the government. Similarly, Congress first attempted to make lobbying more visible by requiring that interest groups report such expenditures, and the Senate initially tried to cope with honoraria by requiring that they be disclosed.

Effective disclosure laws are essential to curbing the excessive influence of special interest money. In the area of campaign finance, for example, disclosure has enabled the press and groups like Common Cause to

[9]Hunt, "Cash Politics."

become effective watchdogs over PAC spending. Of course, the fact that PAC contributions continue to corrupt Congress demonstrates that visibility is not always enough, but in other areas, such as lobbying, effective disclosure is likely all that is necessary or warranted.

The second step toward curbing special interest influence has been to make special interest money reasonable. By this I mean that special interest money must be limited to amounts that are reasonable relative to other sources. That was the step Congress took following Watergate; as it limited the allowable size of contributions from individuals and political parties, it also limited the allowable size of PAC contributions.

That was also the step Congress ultimately took with regard to honoraria. House members limited outside earned income like honoraria to 30 percent of their salaries and—after a tough fight that the late Senator Henry Jackson led in 1983 with courage and wisdom—the Senate ultimately followed suit.

In late December of 1985, however, Congress increased the honoraria limit for Senators—as a regrettable Christmas stocking stuffer. Senators can now receive up to $30,000 in honoraria per year; for House members the limit is $22,000.

Finally, to make special interest money less corrosive, we have tried some measures to make it resistible. That is, Congress tried to wean candidates and elected officials from their dependency on fat-cat donors and interest-group money by providing them with alternative means of support. This was the philosophy behind the provisions in the 1974 laws that established public financing and expenditure limits for presidential campaigns. By providing an alternative source of campaign funds, the laws at least partially freed presidential candidates from the sort of influence-seeking funds that loomed so large in Watergate.

Originally, those laws also specified expenditure limits for congressional candidates. These limits sought to make special interest money more resistible by making campaigns less expensive. Unfortunately, in the 1976 case of *Buckley v. Valeo,* the Supreme Court struck down the congressional expenditure limits by ruling that such limits could exist only in conjunction with public financing.[10]

The desire to make special interest money resistible has also been evident in past efforts to control honoraria. Many have argued for adequate congressional salaries in conjunction with limits on honoraria. The reasoning is clear: it is preferable to make Congress beholden to the public than to exclusionary monied interests.

[10]*Buckley v. Valeo,* 424 U.S. 1 (1976).

If the solution lies in making special interest money visible, reasonable, and resistible, then there is still much to be done. Lobbying expenditures, for example, are still not visible. The only lobby disclosure law on the books—the 1946 Federal Regulation of Lobbying Act—is weak, loophole ridden, and unenforced. Few corporations or trade associations disclose their grass-roots lobbying expenditures. Moreover, in flagrant disregard of the existing law, many fail to file any disclosure reports whatsoever.

A great deal also needs to be done to keep the flow of special interest money reasonable. In the area of campaign finance, one urgently needed remedy is a limit on the total amount of PAC money that a congressman may accept during a campaign. It is clearly not reasonable to expect that candidates will accept over $1 million from PACs and not be influenced by that money. It is clearly not reasonable to expect that some candidates will accept over half of their campaign money from PACs and still hold the interests of their constituents to be foremost. In the Ninety-eighth Congress, Wisconsin Congressman David Obey and over 150 cosponsors introduced legislation that would limit a candidate's aggregate PAC receipts to $90,000 in House campaigns. In the Ninety-ninth Congress, Senators David Boren and Barry Goldwater and a broad bipartisan coalition have proposed similar PAC limits for both House and Senate candidates. Such legislation deserves active support.

Last, we must continue efforts to make special interest money more resistible. I believe that the overwhelming majority of representatives and senators would more faithfully represent the interests of their constituents if they could afford to do so. Therefore we must look for ways to make it *easier for them to say no to PACs, to say no to the interest groups offering honoraria, and to say no to hidden lobbying pressures.* The best way we can help members of Congress say no is to provide some form of public financing of congressional campaigns.[11] Although public financing of presidential campaigns has not been trouble free, and even though it also needs improvement, it has been undeniably successful in helping presidential candidates resist special interest money. Watergate demonstrated that, in 1972, the presidency was on the special interest auction block. By contrast, PAC money now accounts for less than 2 percent of presidential campaign funds. In fact, in the 1984 presidential contest, three candidates declared that they would not accept any PAC funds. We need to provide that kind of flexibility to members of Congress, and public financing is the best way to provide it.

Professor Merton C. Bernstein and I have proposed a variation on the idea of public financing for congressional campaigns. We proposed that

[11]See Charles McC. Mathias, Jr., "Should There Be Public Financing of Congressional Campaigns?" *The Annals* of the American Academy of Political and Social Science, 486, July 1986.

public funds be made available that would match PAC contributions and other PAC campaign expenditures dollar for dollar. These funds would be given to the PAC beneficiary's opponent. While at first this sounds expensive, such a program would diminish and perhaps, in time, eliminate the incentive for PACs to make contributions or for candidates to accept them. If a PAC contribution or expenditure buys the favored candidate no advantage because of matching public funds to his or her rival, PAC contributions would soon lose their purpose.

PAC contributions overwhelmingly favor incumbents. In 1984 House elections, for example, of every PAC dollar, S.78 went to incumbents. Therefore present members of Congress might be expected to resist enactment of a campaign financing program that reduces their ability to draw on PAC money. I think that many members of Congress would prefer, however, to reclaim their political fate—and perhaps their souls—from PACs. But even if they remained unmoved by such a morally tempting prospect, we are confident that challengers could adroitly exploit their opponents' continued support of the status quo.

A program of matching public funds to PAC funds could be modeled on the presidential campaign financing laws, under which the Federal Election Commission makes public money available once a candidate receives a sufficient number of individual contributions under a given amount. Each congressional candidate would be required to obtain a minimum number of contributors before qualifying for public funds. There would also be a maximum limit—say $100—on each contribution. Once a PAC made contributions or expenditures on behalf of a candidate above that amount, the candidate's opponent would receive public funds equal to the direct contributions from the PAC and other PAC expenditures, such as the purchase of television time.

In time, I would expect PACs to diminish or disappear—and with them, the need for substantial public outlays. This proposal presents no curb on free speech, and it promises to remove PAC pollution.

It is neither naive nor idealistic to try to control the pernicious influence of money in politics. It is essential to the survival of our democracy. I remember what people said about some of the legislation we successfully ushered through Congress in those 34 years I served. They said there was no way to pass a civil rights act, but we passed not one, but several. They said there was no way to pass a budget act, but we passed it. If they say there is no way to pass lobby disclosure or PAC limits or public financing of congressional campaigns, then, I say, let them be wrong again. I also remember that when I ran for reelection in 1964, I had every party organization and many special interest groups in my district rally against me in the primary. I was able to prevail, however, and part of the reason was that I had a phrase that turned out the volunteers and stirred up the voters. I said that it was going to be "the folks against the factions." Now that may sound naive, but it was true, and it took, and it is why we won.

These reforms to campaign financing are needed. I understand the way special interest money is hobbling the Congress that I served in for many years, and I am worried. I see that the public is not getting the legislation and the representation it deserves, and I am angered. And I hear the public asking if we can make those reforms a reality. I answer not only that we can, but that we must.

Found: The Attraction of Detraction

***Martin Schram*, Washington Post Staff Writer**

More than ever, the candidates in this year's election campaigns have presented themselves by putting their best fist forward.

The rule of political etiquette this year: if you can't say something nice about your opponent, say something scurrilous:

In Tennessee, GOP Senate candidate Robin Beard tried to depict Sen. Jim Sasser as soft on Castro by showing an actor made up to look like Castro light his cigar with an American bill and sneeringly say, "Muchas gracias, Señor Sasser."

In Massachusetts, Republican Rep. Margaret Heckler attacked Rep. Barney Frank, her opponent in a hard-fought House race, by running an ad that showed a picture of Frank with the words "Prostitution" and "Pornography" emblazoned across his face.

In California, Gov. Edmund G. (Jerry) Brown Jr., the Democratic candidate for the Senate, attempted to portray his Republican opponent, San Diego Mayor Pete Wilson, as opposed to a freeze of nuclear weapons by juxtaposing a film clip of a nuclear explosion with shots of a child saying, "I want to go on living."

Negative political advertising is the standard fare nation-wide. The word from national Republican and Democratic campaign strategists went

---

Martin Schram, "Found: The Attraction of Detraction," *The Washington Post,* 30 October 1982; A1 and A3. Staff writers David S. Broder, Bill Peterson, Helen Dewar, and Paul Taylor contributed to this report. Reprinted with permission of *The Washington Post.*

out early to the candidates: attack. Negative Ads work. This is partly because they match the national mood.

"The country is basically down," said New York media expert David Garth. "People are mad at the politicians, and taxes, and the budget, and unemployment. But the question for all of us is how you use the negative spots—and when do you go into overkill?"

A memo distributed last June by National Republican officials to GOP candidates advised: "The candidate who attacks generates a positive vote intention on the electorate to vote for the attacking candidate." Democrats got similar counsel from their party strategists.

"One of the very significant things this year is that we have seen much more negative advertising by incumbents who were already running ahead of their opponents," said Jay Bryant, of Bishop, Bryant & Associates, coauthor of the memo with pollster Lance Tarrance. They called it "inoculation advertising" in their memo.

"This had always been considered bad strategy before. Now I think that has been changed forever.

Adds Democratic pollster Patrick Caddell: "They [the Republicans] used negative advertising against us a bit in 1978—and it worked. And then we used it against them a bit more in 1980 [Jimmy Carter vs. Edward M. Kennedy]—and it worked. And now everybody is using it in 1982."

Now that the floodgates are open, the pros are watching to see who survives because of it. So far the results are mixed.

The moderate and proper Heckler set out to have Frank banned in Boston. One of her television ads shows a picture of Frank and a voice says he voted to allow legalized prostitution and pornography in every town in the state. Across his face are the words "Prostitution" and "Pornography." Frank backed a bill that sought to keep prostitution and pornography from spreading into residential neighborhoods in every town by limiting adult entertainment operations to a single "combat zone."

Frank counterattacked with a television ad that also featured his picture. A voice says: "Barney Frank knows that your image gets messed up at election time..."—and a hand pencils a mustache and goatee on him—"...but this is going too far." Soon the face is a mess of red magic marker.

"There is a word for that kind of tactic," the voice continues. The screen finally was filled with the single word: "Smear."

Heckler trails Frank by 11 percentage points in the latest *Boston Globe* poll.

In California, Brown's controversial ad sought to depict his Senate race against Wilson, a moderate Republican, as a matter of life or death with Brown being on the side of life.

It ends with the voice-over: "Pete Wilson opposes the nuclear arms freeze. Jerry Brown supports it. Vote for your life. Elect Jerry Brown to the U.S. Senate."

In 1964 Lyndon B. Johnson ignited an explosion of outrage with a similar television ad depicting a girl picking daisies as a countdown ticks off and culminates in a nuclear mushroom cloud. It was intended to show what Johnson's Republican opponent, Barry Goldwater, might do as president. The ad was yanked after one showing. Brown's ad lasted about a week.

In a number of states, the tone of negative ads was set not by Republicans or Democrats, but by such conservative ideological organizations as the National Conservative Political Action Committee (NCPAC).

In Montana, NCPAC aired 1,000 commercials charging that Sen. John Melcher, a moderate Democrat who voted with President Reagan on his tax and budget cuts, is "out of step with Montana."

Melcher lost a 27-point lead and trailed Republican Larry Williams until he cut an ad that had two cows do the talking for him. The cows tell the voters that outsiders have been coming into the state trying to influence the race, but that they have been "stepping in what they have been trying to sell." Melcher's talking cows helped carry him back in the lead. Democrats have made social security, Reaganomics and double-digit unemployment their major themes. An ad circulated to Democratic candidates by the national committee shows a scissors snipping a Social Security card into tiny pieces, suggesting that Republicans are trying to destroy the program.

In Ohio Rep. Clarence J. Brown, the Republican gubernatorial candidate, sought to deflect these issues by running ads accusing Democrat Richard Celeste of having voted, as a state legislator, for handgun control and advocating policies that would have doubled the state income tax.

Celeste, who retains a significant lead, responded with an ad saying that Brown showed up to vote on only 20 percent of the roll calls in Congress this year. Only eight congressmen in history have had so poor a record, the ad says—"and seven of the eight were sick, dead, or indicted."

The Republicans' favorite theme is to try to tar their opponents with the traditional charge that Democrats are big spenders. Many have been effective, but there have been instances of wretched excess such as Beard's ads against Sasser in Tennessee.

One depicted a wooden crate labeled "Foreign Aid" with hands grabbing stacks of money from it as a voice says: "When it comes to spending taxpayers' money, Sen. James Sasser is a master. Take foreign aid. While important programs are being cut here at home, Sasser has voted to allow foreign aid to be sent to committed enemies of our country. Vietnam, Laos, Cambodia, Marxist Angola and even Communist Cuba. You can bet James Sasser is making a lot more friends abroad than there in Tennessee."

An actor portraying Fidel Castro lights a cigar with a $100 bill and sneeringly laughs: "Muchas gracias, Señor Sasser."

The ad was pulled, but not before the *Nashville Banner* withdrew its endorsement of Beard.

"The Beard stuff will live in history," said Bob Squier, who does media work for Sasser and other Democratic candidates. "That commercial cost that young man 10 points. We had him beaten, but that ad did him in."

A benchmark of sorts has occurred in the Virginia 8th Congressional District race, where former Democratic representative Herbert Harris is trying for a comeback against the man who beat him two years ago, Rep. Stanford Parris.

Each has filled the local television screens with unflattering accounts of his opponent's record. The result: Harris and Parris both lost support. Parris' pollster, Lance Tarrance, attributed the decline of both candidates to their negative ads.

A wry way of dealing with such tactics was crafted by the Buckley-Rothstein political consulting firm for a quiet Democratic incumbent, Sen. Quentin N. Burdick of North Dakota, who was charged with being a big spender.

Burdick's responding television ad opened with a voice: "Some people say this man is a big spender. Quentin Burdick a big spender?"

This was followed by a videotape of Republican Gov. Allen I. Olsen, ridiculing Burdick at a roast: "The fact is he's cheap. When [President] Reagan went after the school lunch program, you thought our Democratic senator would be concerned. He was worried about where he was going to have lunch next week. Quentin has viewed Jack Benny as a role model throughout his life and he's the only guy who thought Scrooge was really on the right track."

Not all the negative ammunition has been fired at members of the other party.

In New York's hotly contested Democratic gubernatorial primary, Mayor Edward Koch put some heavy fire on Lt. Gov. Mario Cuomo, who won the primary. One, designed by Garth, began by telling viewers they had 20 seconds to think of a single thing Cuomo had done as lieutenant governor. What followed was a clock that ticked away the 20 seconds for what seemed like an eternity.

Garth has had second thoughts.

"The ticking clock was based on fact," he contended. "But it certainly was a heavy spot—one that might have gone across the border as being too heavy."

That may also have been true of the latest ad for Republican Sen. Harrison H. Schmitt of New Mexico by GOP media expert Roger Ailes. Schmitt watched his once-commanding lead over state Attorney General Jeff Bingaman dwindle to nothing.

Schmitt aired an Ailes ad charging that Bingaman played a major role in "freeing a convicted felon" by recommending a "pardon" for a man who had been on the FBI's most-wanted list.

What it did not say was that U.S. Justice Department had requested that the man be released in its custody as the key witness in another trial, for the murder of a judge in Texas. When the governor requested a legal opinion on whether this could be done, Bingaman reported that a conditional parole—not a pardon—could be arranged.

Ailes had based the Schmitt ad on an incorrect article in *The Albuquerque Tribune,* a story that the newspaper later retracted.

"There is nothing false in those spots," said Ailes. "We relied on a press report."

In another ad, Schmitt charged that Bingaman refused to prosecute inmates responsible for a prison riot in which 33 prisoners died. Actually, Bingaman had spoken out repeatedly at the time promising that the inmates would be prosecuted, but it was the task of local district attorneys.

"He [Bingaman] tried to take advantage of the New Mexico prison riot for his own political advantage," said Ailes. "So it's fair game."

What would Ailes be saying if he were on the other side of the ads?

"Oh, I'd scream foul," Ailes quickly replied. "But my responsibility ends with the act. Maybe folks can say I am an unethical guy. But it's not my job to make his [Democrat Bingaman's] case."

Charles Guggenheim, who authored some mild media for Sen. John C. Danforth (R-Mo.), said: "I don't like negative ads and neither does the candidate. But...we are beginning to get blips in our direction. Since they've been running. It's awful that you have to do this."

He hesitated and then added: "It's not a very good profession."

Hypocrisy in Government

The other day House Speaker Jim Wright challenged President Reagan's offhand comment that he saw no evidence of lawbreaking in the Iran-Contra testimony. The speaker even offered a list of laws that were broken, including, for example, the National Security Act and the Arms Export Control Act.

"Hypocrisy in Government," *The Wall Street Journal,* 10 August 1987, 26 (Eastern Edition).

About the same time our Brooks Jackson took a close look at the speaker's own financial affairs. In addition to his salary of $100,000. The speaker reported outside income of $129,000 to $291,000 last year. This included income from his partnership with Fort Worth developer George Mallick in a company that makes investments and imports gems.

Mr. Mallick, as it happens, has also been one of the promoters of an effort to develop the Fort Worth stockyards as "the Williamsburg of the West." (However, his efforts to gain a major stake in the development have recently gone sour.) The project has received an $11.8 million federal grant from the Economic Development Administration, though the EDA reports it has yet to receive an application for the funds from any Forth Worth officials. Speaker Wright's office, however, boasted it had once again delivered for the folks back home.

With the speaker pushing his business partner's project, there clearly is an "appearance of impropriety." So why don't we have a special prosecutor to pore over the Wright-Mallick relationship, investigating whether support for the stockyards project was a payoff for Mr. Mallick's help in building the speaker's personal wealth? We're sure that with his punctiliousness about ethics and the law, the speaker would be glad to turn over all his office records about his support for the stockyards project, all correspondence with Mr. Mallick and any memos of phone conversations with him. Maybe if the prosecutor searched the U.S. code, he might even find a law that might arguably have been broken—"conspiracy to defraud the United States" perhaps.

We would like to make clear that we believe special prosecutors are unconstitutional. The Wright-Mallick dealings need to be investigated only if they meet the usual tests a prosecutor would apply to any two citizens in the routine course of enforcing the law. Anyway the problem in Congress is not illegal corruption but legal corruption, such as the very idea of giving $11.8 million to a stockyards boondoggle—or for that matter having the EDA piggy bank to begin with.

We do, however, oppose double standards. And if the speaker were in the executive branch, a special prosecutor would surely be named and Mr. Wright would immediately be sentenced to spending a major share of his time dealing with the detailed investigation. That's what the Ethics In Government Act is all about. One of the special prosecutors investigating Attorney General Meese, for example, spent months trying to find some evidence that Mr. Meese's wife's purchase of 200 shares of stock violated the insider-trading laws. Why don't we apply the same standard to Speaker Wright and other members of Congress?

Because Congress has exempted itself from major provisions of the Ethics in Government Act, that's why. To put it bluntly, Congress doesn't give a whit about ethics in government. If it did, it would apply the same standards to itself. But here we have Michael Deaver indicted for perjury about his lobbying after leaving the White House, but any former member of Congress has a right to visit the congressional floor to press his lobbying. The Ethics in Government Act is not about ethics: it is about belaboring the executive branch to increase the power of the legislative branch. Let's rename it: The Hypocrisy in Government Act. It is coming up for renewal this fall. A president with some sense of protecting the presidency should demand that the same rules apply to all three branches of government, and veto any extension that singles out the executive.

Congress is supposed to police itself, the theory being that an independent branch of government should keep its own house. But consider what it lets itself get away with:

Mr. Mallick's involvement with Mr. Wright goes back to 1979 when the two men and their wives incorporated an investment company called Malightco. House rules require that members disclose underlying holdings in such closely held entities that do no public reporting of their own. Mr. Wright doesn't and an aide says, "He isn't much interested in doing that."

GOP Rep. Newt Gingrich points out that it was those kinds of disclosure omissions that led to a 1981 investigation of Rep. George Hansen, a maverick Republican. Rep. Hansen was convicted of failure to disclose some of his wife's financial dealings and is now in federal prison. Rep. Gingrich says one degree of congressional scrutiny seems to apply if the accused is a member in good standing of the Congressional Club and another if the person is—like Mr. Hansen—an outsider who wants to shake up Washington.

Democratic Banking Committee Chairman Fernand St Germain is no congressional outsider. On Wednesday, the House voted 291–111 not to have the Ethics Committee reopen its investigation into charges of financial misconduct against him.

In April, the Ethics Committee had concluded that Rep. St Germain had violated a House rule by accepting transportation from a savings and loan. However, it ruled the violation did not suggest "a pattern of improper acceptance." The committee also noted financial disclosure violations including the undervaluing of Mr. St Germain's assets by more than $1 million. In neither case was disciplinary action taken.

Now there are disturbing signs that the committee may have given Mr. St Germain a gentleman's wink. Brooks Jackson also reported last month that the Justice Department has begun a criminal investigation of some entertainment bills of Mr. St Germain's that were allegedly paid for by a savings and loan industry lobbyist. Ethics Committee staffers are said to have tried to interview the lobbyist but "backed off" when the U.S. League of Savings Institutions protested.

In 1985 Rep. Bill Boner of Tennessee became the focus of charges that he had accepted nearly $50,000 in bribes and had used $300,000 in campaign funds for his personal use. The House Ethics Committee suspended an investigation of Rep. Boner in April 1986 because the Justice Department was launching its own inquiry, even though many of the allegations were separate from the Justice investigation. Early this year, Justice ended its inquiry, but the Ethics Committee has since failed to move its own investigation forward.

Tennessee political observers point out that Mr. Boner is in a runoff election for mayor of Nashville, and they believe the Ethics Committee is stalling in hopes that he will soon leave the House and allow the committee to wash its hands of the matter. They also note that Speaker Wright, the man who appoints Ethics Committee members, is a friend and supporter of Mr. Boner. Last year Mr. Wright said Mr. Boner was a victim of a vendetta while he campaigned for him during a heated primary contest.

Common Cause, a good government lobby, notes that ethics panels rarely discipline members. The House Ethics Committee failed to recommend any punishment for Rep. Mary Rose Oakar of Ohio, Rep. Dan Daniel of Virginia and former Rep. James Weaver of Oregon, despite its findings that all had violated House rules. The committee noted that all three had taken steps to remedy the violations—although only after they were publicized. Fred Wertheimer, the president of Common Cause says, "The message this sends to the public, and to the members of the House, is that ethics rules may be violated with impunity."

A chance to take another step toward ending hypocrisy in government came in June when Rep. Gingrich and others proposed that a special commission suggest reforms in how congressional corruption charges are investigated. The measure lost 297–77 with a majority of Republicans and all but one Democrat voting against it. There may no longer be bipartisan foreign policy, but there is still a bipartisan approach to congressional ethics: See no evil, speak no evil, hear no evil.

The Ethics in Government Act, born out of Watergate, has become a political weapon against whatever administration is in office, ensuring a permanent Watergate. Members of the executive branch are subjected to a degree of scrutiny rarely leveled at Congress or the judiciary, dignifying every allegation and ensuring constant investigations. Given human frailty, such scrutiny will produce enough real mistakes and misjudgments to fuel the process. But with only one branch constantly forced to bare its dirty linen, this creates yet another imbalance of power, and a further unconstitutional eroding of the power of the presidency.

If Congress expects to renew this act, it owes it to the nation to clean up its own act, starting by taking the power to appoint House Ethics Committee members away from Speaker Wright, whose reporting violations clearly do need scrutiny. If Congress isn't willing to apply to its own members the same level of oversight it demands of the executive, the office of special prosecutor and most of the rest of the Ethics in Government Act should be scrapped. And to protect his office, the president should use his veto to this end.

The Year of the Gimmick

Tom Morganthau

The federal government will end its fiscal year this week some $230 billion in the red—which is a bottom-line indicator that 1986, once billed at "the year of the budget," has become the year of the gimmick, instead. Congress, rushing toward adjournment and preoccupied with tax reform, the war on drugs and appropriating money to keep the federal government in business, ran smack into the budgetary wall erected by the Gramm-Rudman deficit-reduction law last year. Facing a Sept. 30 deadline and a projected 1987 deficit of $168 billion, the House and Senate voted budget-reconciliation bills designed to reach the Gramm-Rudman deficit target of $154 billion. But critics charged that both bills were full of "smoke and mirrors"—budgetary devices that appeared to cut spending and raise revenues without actually doing much of either. "We did the easy things, and maybe in an election year that was the best we could do," Sen. Phil Gramm said philosophically. But others, like Republican Rep. John Porter of Illinois, called it an example of "Washington at its worst: you get yours, I get mine—and the kids get the bill."

The legislation would, for example, rely heavily on the one-time, $11 billion tax windfall that would be created if tax reform, which easily passed the House and Senate last week, goes into effect in 1987. It also raises revenue by "privatizing" some of the federal government's more salable assets, such as the Conrail freight system and loan portfolios now underwritten by the Small Business Administration, the Rural Electrification Administration and the Export-Import Bank. All told these sales should net the Treasury an estimated $7 billion—though critics challenged the wisdom of fending off the deficit with a potpourri of one-time gains. "I know we can sell the

---

Tom Morganthau, "The Year of the Gimmick," *Newsweek*, 6 Oct. 1986; 24.

Washington Monument," joked Democratic Senator Ernest Hollings. But, Hollings added, "next year we are going to run out of smoke and mirrors and we are going to have to raise revenues."

Slight of hand: Other examples of dubious fiscal policy included a projected $3.3 billion increase in federal tax collections due to enhanced enforcement by the IRS and a $1.8 billion "user fee" on imports—which administration officials said probably violated international agreements on trade and tariffs. But the prize winner was the House's sleight of hand on general revenue sharing. Trying to reduce the 1987 deficit, the House voted to distribute $680 million in aid to states and cities before Sept. 30 so it could be charged against the deficit for 1986. "Using that kind of logic, we could 'balance' [the 1987] budget," scoffed Republican Rep. Robert Walker. "All we'd have to do is take the whole defense budget out of 1987 and bring it back to 1986." That would raise the 1986 deficit to over $500 billion, Walker added sarcastically, "but who cares? That's history."

It was not, as House Budget Committee chairman William Gray delicately observed, "a perfect package." For one thing, the White House was hinting at a veto if some features of the House bill survive during negotiations with the Senate. Ronald Reagan was said to be perturbed by the House's move to spend more on Medicare and less on defense, among other things. Even worse, the '87 budget rests on questionable economic forecasts. Both Congress and the Reagan administration are assuming, for example, that the economy will grow by at least 3.2 percent next year and that inflation (which raises tax revenues) will be 3 percent. Few independent forecasters see it that way, and some are warning of recession. That could mean a 1987 deficit of $200 billion or worse—and real budget battles for years to come.

The Need to Say No

The Pork Barrel Tag to Important Bills

James C. Miller, III, Director, Office of Management and Budget

...Today, with your permission I'd like to speak to a different issue—one that reflects my new responsibilities in the Reagan Administration, but one, nevertheless, that I hope you'll agree is most important. It has to do with the role of the Office of Management and Budget (OMB)—from one administration to the next—in saying "no" to pleas for excessive spending and bad policies. In short, it has to do with the role of OMB, in the words of one of my predecessors, Jim Lynn, in being the "Abominable No-Man."

Since all of you are probably better read than I, you no doubt remember well your Dickens. Well, in Dickens I've found another good shorthand description of my office. In *David Copperfield* there is that wonderful character, Mr. Micawber, who, you will recall, is always looking for something to turn *up*. OMB, ladies and gentlemen, is an "inverted Micawber"—we are always looking for something to turn *down!*

Aware of this and the "Abdominable No-Man" analogies, I was not surprised last month to read an article about me in the *New York Times* whose headline read:

> THE MILLER LEXICON:
> NO, NO, NO, NO, NO

The article began as follows:

> "After more than [five] months as director of the White House Office of Management and Budget, James C. Miller 3d is leaving his mark on Capitol Hill. Somewhat like Zorro, he is zapping his adversaries with an 'N', as in 'no'."

While I don't necessarily enjoy the role of nay-sayer, I will not take serious exception to the *Times'* characterization. Indeed, inherent in our political system is the requirement that someone—usually the President or his representative—take on the role of the "Abominable No-Man" or inverted Micawber. I would like to explore with you today the reasons why this is so.

James C. Miller, III, "The Need to Say No," address to the Detroit Economic Club, Detroit, Michigan, 1 April 1986, *Vital Speeches of the Day* (15 May 1986), 467–469.

Why is it seemingly necessary always to be in the posture of saying "no"? Essentially, the answer has two parts.

First, there is an inherent propensity of legislatures to overspend. It stems from the fundamental nature of modern industrial democracies, in which to each group the advantage always appears in favor of spending rather than restraint. Numerous Congressmen recognize and acknowledge this problem; indeed, it is a major reason for passage of the Gramm-Rudman-Hollings legislation last year with its maximum deficits and automatic features—a recognition that by itself Congress seems incapable of significantly curbing spending.

Given this propensity, and given our dangerously large budget deficits, it will naturally fall to the executive branch, and in particular to the Budget Director, to be constantly on guard against excessive spending and having a firm resolve to say "no." It's amazing the many ways the extra spending comes at you—from North, South, East, and West, up from the floors and down from the ceilings, as obscure provisions in appropriations bills and technical provisions in reconciliation bills, in riders barring reductions of personnel or the closing of Federal offices. Just about every day a new threat in some current piece of legislation is brought to my attention, and their variety and the chutzpa represented by their authors never cease to amaze me. A couple of dozen of such provisions are incorporated in a current supplemental appropriations bill—and you probably haven't read a word about them in the press because, by Washington standards, they are too small or too complicated to be noticed.

The second part of the answer is the inherent tension, in our unique form of democratic government, between the legislature and the executive. My job is to advance and defend the priorities of the President, and it is obvious there are lots of people in Congress who do not share his priorities. When they insist on doing things their way, it is my job to say "no." If I didn't, the people would be cheated, because they are the ones who elected the President—the only official apart from the Vice President elected by *all* the people.

I'd like to give you some examples of why my job is so often to say "no," and I'll start with the second category—the clash of priorities. The best place to begin is the budget resolution currently being considered in the Senate.

With the Gramm-Rudman-Hollings law on the books—and it will remain on the books even if the Supreme Court declares unconstitutional the mechanism which triggers the automatic spending cuts—all parties to the budget debate must now live with maximum deficit ceilings, year by year. There is no escape from political deadlock through higher deficits. As on occasion I have put it, there's no longer a big pot of red ink to dip into and write with if everything else fails.

Given maximum deficits, and given the clear fact that actual deficits will exceed the maximum deficits in every year unless deficit-reducing actions are taken, there are only three ways to comply with the new law—raise taxes, cut defense still further after major slashes in the last two years, or prune domestic spending (the last category, I should note, includes not only spending cuts but also such things as user fees and sales of assets that do not involve reductions in programs).

The President is paid to make choices, and he has made them. Higher taxes are not the right way to reduce the deficit for a number of reasons—not the least of which is he took this position in the 1984 election, and voters in 49 out of 50 states agreed with them. That was about as close to a national referendum on a single issue as we are likely to see. Higher taxes risk curtailing our current economic expansion, and they carry hidden costs that offset some of the revenue effects. Our revenues, as a share of GNP, are running right at the historical average of about 18.5 percent; the problem is not lack of revenues but excessive spending.

The President has also determined that defense cannot any longer be the place to look for big savings. Few Americans realize the magnitude of the erosion of the planned defense program that has taken place in the last two years. To give you just one figure, estimated outlays for defense in FY 1987 in the budget we submitted in February are $66 billion below what we planned for FY 1987 two years earlier, in the FY 1985 budget. This is a huge reduction—more than double all the proposed domestic cuts put together. The President reluctantly has accepted the lower level of defense spending forced upon him by Congress. But further reductions clearly raise serious dangers.

Given these two entirely rational choices, what remains is for us to address marginal domestic spending programs with a firm resolve. We have calculated that we can get on the Gramm-Rudman-Hollings deficit track with actual programmatic spending reductions in FY 1987 of only $22.4 billion—just five percent of the budget excluding defense, interest, and Social Security. This is in no sense a devastation of the Government's social spending. Nor is it a declaration of war on the cities or the other dreadful things that some have alleged. These reductions, including terminations of some 40 programs that are no longer warranted, are supplemented by user fees, asset sales, and minor revenue items—such as having the Internal Revenue Service collect more of the taxes actually due to achieve the $38 billion of deficit reduction needed to meet FY 1987's Gramm-Rudman-Hollings target.

Well, a lot of members of the House and Senate—in both parties, I must acknowledge—don't like these choices. They would rather raise taxes or slash defense, or both, than do the pruning of domestic spending that we advocate and think is fully justified. Often the reason is not that the individual

Member of Congress really believes in these spending programs, but rather than he or she doesn't want to take the heat from those constituents affected by eliminating or reducing or charging for them.

I can understand their problem. But that does not mean I should agree automatically and immediately to their calls for "negotiation." For what does negotiation mean in this context? If it means anything, it means erosion of the President's choices. It means more taxes, less defense, and very little reduction in domestic spending. When I say "no" to major concessions as the game is barely beginning, I am not being stubborn but simply using my best judgment as to how best to defend the position of the President. He will not prevail if I am constantly yielding.

Let me give you a recent example of where saying "no" yielded excellent results. Unlike the maneuvering over the FY 1987 budget, which is just beginning, in this drama the last act is over. The title was "reconciliation."

As part of the budget process last year, for FY 1986 Congress mandated in its budget resolution certain revenue increases and outlay savings that were to be achieved by changes in permanent law, many of them involving entitlement programs that are not controlled by the appropriations process. The legislation in question is called an omnibus reconciliation act, and it certainly is omnibus. Like a stone gathering moss, this legislation, while achieving remarkably little by way of real budget savings, picked up from various committees scores of provisions that had never been envisioned in the first place, many of them actually increasing outlays. Some of these provisions, such as a revised tobacco program and the sharing with coastal states of offshore oil revenues that had been tied up in court, were of great political interest to some Members of Congress. So, there was a sense of urgency about passing this legislation, even though it achieved rather little in the way of deficit reduction.

Looking at its provisions as a whole, we in the Administration stood firm, suggesting the President would veto the bill unless a list of particularly egregious items were removed or modified. After literally months of discussions—in which, to be sure, we made a few concessions on our side, though not many—the Senate finally adopted something we could live with. The House, after rejecting this version once, finally accepted it on March 20th, amid much moaning and groaning during floor debate about the role of OMB. What we got was a bill that makes some real savings, though modest in amount, and avoids all of the worst giveaways, new taxes, and the like. This result tells me that standing firm can pay real dividends.

In any case, the reconciliation drama was but one more skirmish in the constant struggle against excessive spending. Let me cite a few more things that have come along in the past few years, most of which ultimately succeeded, because they were attached to "must" legislation, and without the power of line item veto the President was forced to accept them. These examples of what can only be termed "pork" run the gamut from defense to education.

—Last year Congress added $33.4 million to the Interior appropriations bill to purchase an additional 60,000 acres as an *enlargement* of a National *Park* which lies off the West Coast. The land consists of remote islands some 25 miles offshore, making it virtually impossible for most people to visit. Moreover, the land has no special national significance.

—An Anadromous Fish Research Center will be built in the Northeast at a cost to taxpayers of between eight and 10 million dollars, even though from the Federal point of view it is wholly unnecessary. Existing private, State, or Federal facilities could easily be used for the same purpose!

—A school in a Southern state is slated to receive nearly a quarter of a million dollars for dairy goat research. The language inserted into the FY 1986 appropriations bill was crafted so as virtually to assure that the school in question is the only one in the country that can qualify.

—Each year a number of low-priority military construction projects are attached to appropriations bills by Members of Congress trying to curry local favor. FY 1986 saw as many as 15 of these added, costing taxpayers roughly $50 million. The single most costly project—$11.4 million—was new officers' living quarters at a Southern base, where new suites will replace existing quarters which, while not luxurious, are entirely adequate.

—A city in a Southern state has a new Federally funded subway and a nearly-completed "people-mover" system which has cost taxpayers over three quarters of a billion dollars. Its ridership is only about 25,000 per day—about one tenth that originally projected. Its fare box is expected to cover only 25 percent of its operating costs; the city's own local press calls it a "white elephant"; and a county referendum rejected by two-to-one a penny increase in the local sales tax to help finance its construction and operation.

—An Institute of Government in an East Coast City has received $2.22 million in the last four years to train teachers in the principles of government—concepts which presumably teachers are supposed to know before they graduate from college.

—More than $270 million has been larded into the budget over the last three years to build a variety of university science facilities. Many of the university beneficiaries had no detailed plans for their new programs. They were funded nonetheless, through direct intervention by powerful Congressional committee members, in a free-for-all spirit devoid of any scientific evaluation of merit.

So much for these examples of "pork"—and I assure you they are typical, not egregious.

We say "no" whenever and wherever we can be at all effective, but we don't always win. Is there no occasion, then, for a Budget Director to say "yes"? Of course there is.

It is time to say yes when Congress shows evidence of making hard choices instead of trying to escape them.

It is time to say yes when budgetary decisions are based on the national interest—including the national interest in a lower level of total spending and a lower deficit—rather than the ever-present parochial interest of the region, the district, or the interest group.

It is time to say yes when Congress—while in no sense being a rubber stamp—begins to give reasonable deference to the priorities of a President who has a record level of public approval and who won an overwhelming electoral victory.

Until those things happen—and they do happen occasionally—it will remain necessary for me to say "no." It is not the way to be popular, but then the President didn't promise me a rose garden. Nor, as I've come to learn, has anyone ever erected a monument to a Budget Director.

Thank you very much!

"Sleazy" Is the Word for It

On March 18, by a close vote (52 to 48), the Senate declined to cut off military funding for the Nicaraguan contras. The money in question amounted to $40 million still to be expended from the $70 million appropriated last year for contra arms. A shift of only two votes could have changed things—and only one vote if Nebraska Democrat Edward Zorinsky, an opponent of contra aid, had not died only to be replaced by Republican David Karnes voting in favor of it. In any case, this outcome is extremely disappointing, and the American people have a right to be astonished that the Senate votes to continue a funding operation that polls show only 28 percent of Americans approve. Sen. Robert J. Dole (R., Kan.) saw the vote as "a new opportunity to convince the American people what we're doing is right." The American people have had five years to be convinced, and naturally they are now less convinced than they were when this sorry policy started.

The Senate vote was on a question of principle, really, since the President has vowed to veto any cut-off of this year's funds. By a vote of 230 to 196, the House recently succeeded in passing a somewhat different, if less principled, cut-off bill that places a moratorium on further funding until previous contra expenditures are adequately accounted for. Even if the Senate later approves its own version of this House bill, that approach, too, will surely be vetoed by the President. In any case, an attempt to pass such a moratorium in the Senate might be blocked by a filibuster so as to prevent the President from having to use his veto.

Even though defeated and tactically less successful, therefore, than the moratorium proposal that passed in the House, this March 18 Senate vote "on principle" at least addressed the issue squarely. After all, it is not as though contra funding would be a fine idea if only past expenditures were all accounted for, as the House moratorium implies. Nor is it the case that contra funding might be a good idea farther down the road after the contras had a "chance to prove themselves," as a moratorium might allow. Suppositions like those—that we should be happy if the contra money were all counted (or in any case not diverted from Iran), or even happier if the contras were more disruptive of Nicaragua than they already are—represent a gross misunderstanding of the fundamental problem with the proxy war the United States is sponsoring in Nicaragua. Namely, the war is immoral, illegal and unwise—immoral because we are using our wealth to procure a bloody conflict that we are unwilling to engage in ourselves, illegal because we are trying to overthrow the duly elected Government of a nation with which we are not at war, unwise because we are arousing suspicion and hostility up and down Latin America.

In the words of Sen. Lowell P. Weicker Jr. (R., Conn.), at whose insistence the Senate vote was pushed through, it is truly a "sleazy policy." The response of Sen. Ernest F. Hollings (D., S.C.) that war is "always sleazy" was fudging. In the first place, a just war can be honorable, though this one is neither just nor honorable. In the second place, this is a war that we are buying and yet not taking full responsibility for. We are not suffering its ill effects, but are imposing those sufferings on others. That is what is sleazy. It is literally a shame that the Senate passed up an opportunity to do the right thing and instead chose to temporize. That the Senate was temporizing was made clear enough by its voices that said, "Wait till next time." By this they meant that, when the President asks for even more contra funding next fall, he will not get it. If contra funding were stopped next fall, that would indeed be encouraging, but also late. Meanwhile, just as the Senate was deciding not to take a stand, news broke that the C.I.A. is providing the contras with plans and blueprints of bridges, dams and communications systems that the United States helped build in Nicaragua in the pre-Sandinista days. This will allow the contras to destroy them more easily. As Ronald Reagan used to say of the Panama Canal, when he was protesting President Carter's negotiation of a Canal Treaty: "We bought it, we paid for it, it's ours."

DISCUSSION QUESTIONS

1. Should senators and representatives be permitted to accept money from political action committees? Should they be allowed to receive honoraria for speaking engagements while they are in office?
2. Do congressional representatives have a moral/ethical obligation to vote the way they are directed by their constituents, or is it that being privy to information not known to "the folks back home" allows them to vote as they see fit rather than how the people see fit?
3. What changes, if any, should be made in political campaign financing?
4. What are the controversies that the Congress now finds itself embroiled in on ethical issues?

2

LAW AND MORALITY

William Lasser

The connections between law and morality are old and extensive. The two subjects even share a common vocabulary; among the words we use in both their legal and moral senses are "justice" and "injustice," "duty," "obligation," and "rights." In early societies—and for many nonwestern societies even today—the distinctions between the legal realm and the moral realm were blurry or even nonexistent; the ancient Hebrews, for example, had a common source of both legal and moral rules and treated the two as inseparable parts of a single whole.

For traditional societies, therefore, law and morality worked hand in hand to regulate the behavior of individuals and to improve the character of the citizens. Government was concerned not merely with the physical protection and safety of the citizenry, but also with their moral and spiritual development. Governments were expected to legislate both morality and religion.

In modern democratic societies, however, law and morality do not fit together so neatly. The United States, for example, was founded on the principle that the government was created and exists to allow individual citizens the right to "life, liberty, and the pursuit of happiness." Part of the individual's "pursuit of happiness" is his or her right to choose freely and practice his own religion and moral code. In other societies it might be acceptable for the government to impose the morality and religion of the majority on all citizens, but under the American theory of government such a practice would undermine the very purpose of the government itself.

Because government exists to secure the rights of individuals to pursue their private interests as they see fit, law and morality are frequently in tension in the United States. This tension expresses itself in two ways. First, there is a strong argument to be made that law and morality should be kept separate; that it is neither practical nor desirable for the society (acting through the government) to impose its moral code on all citizens. In the past, and in other societies, it was thought perfectly proper for the law to prescribe appropriate and inappropriate sexual conduct, drinking habits, and family relationships. Increasingly, however, courts have struck down such laws as unconstitutional, finding that they violate the constitutional guarantees of liberty and privacy. The courts' actions in these areas have, in turn, produced a strong feeling among many groups that the legislation of morality is not only constitutional but also vitally necessary.

Of course many laws embody moral principles. We have laws against murder and stealing, for example, both of which derive from the Ten Commandments and other moral or religious formulations. No one doubts that, at least in such contexts, society is justified (and, perhaps, is required) to impose its view of morality on all persons within its jurisdiction. Such laws are necessary for the preservation not only of society, but also of its members. The question, then, is where to draw the line between the permissable and impermissable imposition of morality through legislation.

Law and morality are in tension in another area as well. When the Supreme Court (or a lower court) seeks to determine whether a particular law is constitutional or not, to what extent can the judges look to principles of morality in making their decision?

Over the years the courts have been shy about striking down acts of Congress or the state legislatures because they violate a particular conception of morality. The Constitution, as Justice Oliver Wendell Holmes wrote about economic policy, "is made for people of fundamentally different views." The debate between Justices Iredell and Chase (*Calder* vs. *Bull* reading) focuses precisely on this question, and Justice Iredell won; since very early in the nineteenth century, the Supreme Court has struck down laws only if they conflict with a specific constitutional provision.

Focusing only on the Constitution does not solve the judges' problem, however, for moral considerations can still be introduced through the interpretation of specific constitutional provisions. Many constitutional provisions are vague, or, as lawyers say, "open-ended." The Constitution, for example, guarantees that "life, liberty, or property" will not be taken away without "due process of law," and prohibits the imposition of "cruel and unusual punishments." But just what does "due process of law mean"? Is the death penalty by nature "cruel and unusual"? Are the judges justified in looking to contemporary or historical conceptions of morality in answering these questions?

Over the years the judges have tried many approaches to the difficult question of interpreting the Constitution's open-ended provisions, and many, ultimately, depend on conceptions of morality. Laws violate the due process clause, various justices have said at various times, when they violate "a principle of justice so rooted in the traditions and conscience of our people as to be ranked as fundamental"; when they violate basic values "of the very essence of ordered liberty"; when they violate "fundamental principles of liberty and justice which lie at the heart of all our civil and political institutions"; or when they "offend those canons of decency and fairness which express the notions of justice of English-speaking peoples." However formulated, the judges have always had some recourse to some sense of morality or higher justice. In fact, it is probably impossible for judges to function without incorporating some conception of morality into their decision making. The political philosophy on which the Constitution is based embodies a clear conception of natural law and natural right, and the very idea of limited government (and of judges enforcing the limitations on government) implies a certain conception of morality to begin with.

The connection between law and morality, then, comes down to two questions. First, is society justified in using the law to impose its view of morality on all citizens? And second, are the judges of the U.S. Supreme Court (and of the lower courts) justified in imposing some particular view of morality on the lawmakers, whether their own moral code or the moral principles they find embodied in the Constitution?

For practical purposes, as this essay has already suggested, the answer to both questions is at least a partial yes. And that raises a third question: When the morality of the Constitution (or, depending on your point of view, of the judges' interpretation of the Constitution) conflicts with the morality of the people as expressed through their representatives, which should prevail? This is not as easy a question as it might seem, for the textbook answer—namely, that the law of the Constitution is "higher" law and thus controls the law of the statute—has not always proved acceptable to the American people. In the famous *Dred Scott* case of 1857, the Supreme Court's decision that the Constitution sanctioned slavery and prohibited congressional interference with the rights of slave-holders prompted Abraham Lincoln to declare that "the candid citizen must confess that if the policy of the Government upon vital questions affecting the whole people is to be irrevocably fixed by decisions of the Supreme Court, the instant they are made in ordinary litigation between parties in personal actions, the people will have ceased to be their own governors, having to that extent practically resigned their Government into the hands of that eminent tribunal." In the end, of course, the Court's decision helped to bring about a bloody civil war.

The readings that follow address these three questions. The selections from Justice Oliver Wendell Holmes, Judge Robert Bork, and the legal philosopher H. L. A. Hart address the first question, namely, to what extent is society justified in imposing its morality through law. The selections from *Calder* v. *Bull* and *Griswold* v. *Connecticut*—two Supreme Court cases handed down 150 years apart—address the second question, whether judges are justified in imposing their conception of higher law on the people. The final selection, from a book by the constitutional scholar Alexander Bickel, looks at the final question, and attempts a reconciliation of apparent irreconcilables.

The Path of the Law

Oliver Wendell Holmes, Jr.

...I think it desirable at once to point out and dispel a confusion between morality and law, which sometimes rises to the height of conscious theory, and more often and indeed constantly is making trouble in detail without reaching the point of consciousness. You can see very plainly that a bad man has as much reason as a good one for wishing to avoid an encounter with the public force, and therefore you can see the practical importance of the distinction between morality and law. A man who cares nothing for an ethical rule which is believed and practised by his neighbors is likely nevertheless to care a good deal to avoid being made to pay money, and will want to keep out of jail if he can.

I take it for granted that no hearer of mine will misinterpret what I have to say as the language of cynicism. The law is the witness and external deposit of our moral life. Its history is the history of the moral development of the race. The practice of it, in spite of popular jests, tends to make good citizens and good men. When I emphasize the difference between law and morals I do so with reference to a single end, that of learning and understanding the law. For that purpose you must definitely master its specific marks, and it is for that that I ask you for the moment to imagine yourselves indifferent to other and greater things.

Oliver Wendell Holmes, Jr., "The Path of the Law," *Harvard Law Review* (1897), 459–62.

I do not say that there is not a wider point of view from which the distinction between law and morals becomes of secondary or no importance, as all mathematical distinctions vanish in presence of the infinite. But I do say that that distinction is of the first importance for the object which we are here to consider,—a right study and mastery of the law as a business with well understood limits, a body of dogma enclosed within definite lines. I have just shown the practical reason for saying so. If you want to know the law and nothing else, you must look at it as a bad man, who cares only for the material consequences which such knowledge enables him to predict, not as a good one, who finds his reasons for conduct, whether inside the law or outside of it, in the vaguer sanctions of conscience. The theoretical importance of the distinction is no less, if you would reason on your subject aright. The law is full of phraseology drawn from morals, and by the mere force of language continually invites us to pass from one domain to the other without perceiving it, as we are sure to do unless we have the boundary constantly before our minds. The law talks about rights, and duties, and malice, and intent, and negligence, and so forth, and nothing is easier, or, I may say, more common in legal reasoning, than to take these words in their moral sense, at some stage of the argument, and so to drop into fallacy. For instance, when we speak of the rights of man in a moral sense, we mean to mark the limits of interference with individual freedom which we think are prescribed by conscience, or by our ideal, however reached. Yet it is certain that many laws have been enforced in the past, and it is likely that some are enforced now, which are condemned by the most enlightened opinion of the time, or which at all events pass the limit of interference as many consciences would draw it. Manifestly, therefore, nothing but confusion of thought can result from assuming that the rights of man in a moral sense are equally rights in the sense of the Constitution and the law. No doubt simple and extreme cases can be put of imaginable laws which the statute-making power would not dare to enact, even in the absence of written constitutional prohibitions, because the community would rise in rebellion and fight; and this gives some plausibility to the proposition that the law, if not a part of morality, is limited by it. But this limit of power is not coextensive with any system of morals....

The confusion with which I am dealing besets confessedly legal conceptions. Take the fundamental question, What constitutes the law? You will find some text writers telling you that it is something different from what is decided by the courts of Massachusetts or England, that it is a system of reason, that it is a deduction from principles of ethics or admitted axioms or what not, which may or may not coincide with the decisions. But if we take the view of our friend the bad man we shall find that he does not care two straws for the axioms or deductions, but that he does want to know what the

Massachusetts or English courts are likely to do in fact. I am much of his mind. The prophecies of what the courts will do in fact, and nothing more pretentious, are what I mean by the law.

Take again a notion which as popularly understood is the widest conception which the law contains;—the notion of legal duty, to which already I have referred. We fill the word with all the content which we draw from morals. But what does it mean to a bad man? Mainly, and in the first place, a prophecy that if he does certain things he will be subjected to disagreeable consequences by way of imprisonment or compulsory payment of money. But from his point of view, what is the difference between being fined and being taxed a certain sum for doing a certain thing?...Leaving the criminal law on one side, what is the difference between the liability under the mill acts or statutes authorizing a taking by eminent domain and the liability for what we call a wrongful conversion of property where restoration is out of the question? In both cases the party taking another man's property has to pay its fair value as assessed by a jury, and no more. What significance is there in calling one taking right and another wrong from the point of view of the law? It does not matter, so far as the given consequence, the compulsory payment, is concerned, whether the act to which it is attached is described in terms of praise or in terms of blame, or whether the law purports to prohibit it or to allow it. If it matters at all, still speaking from the bad man's point of view, it must be because in one case and not in the other some further disadvantages, or at least some further consequences, are attached to the act by the law. The only other disadvantages thus attached to it which I ever have been able to think of are to be found in two somewhat insignificant legal doctrines, both of which might be abolished without much disturbance. One is, that a contract to do a prohibited act is unlawful, and the other, that, if one of two or more joint wrongdoers has to pay all the damages, he cannot recover contribution from his fellows. And that I believe is all. You see how the vague circumference of the notion of duty shrinks and at the same time grows more precise when we wash it with cynical acid and expel everything except the object of our study, the operations of the law.

Nowhere is the confusion between legal and moral ideas more manifest than in the law of contract. Among other things, here again the so called primary rights and duties are invested with a mystic significance beyond what can be assigned and explained. The duty to keep a contract at common law means a prediction that you must pay damages if you do not keep it,—and nothing else....But such a mode of looking at the matter stinks in the nostrils of those who think it advantageous to get as much ethics into the law as they can....

Tradition and Morality in Constitutional Law

Robert H. Bork

We are entering, I believe, a period in which our legal culture and constitutional law may be transformed, with even more power accruing to judges than is presently the case. There are two reasons for that. One is that constitutional law has very little theory of its own and hence is almost pathologically lacking in immune defenses against the intellectual fevers of the larger society as well as against the disorders generated by its own internal organs.

The second is that the institutions of the law, in particular the schools, are becoming increasingly converted to an ideology of the Constitution that demands just such an infusion of extraconstitutional moral and political notions. A not untypical example of the first is the entry into the law of the first amendment of the old, and incorrect, view that the only kinds of harm that a community is entitled to suppress are physical and economic injuries. Moral harms are not to be counted because to do so would interfere with the autonomy of the individual. That is an indefensible definition of what people are entitled to regard as harms.

The result of discounting moral harm is the privatization of morality, which requires the law of the community to practice moral relativism. It is thought that individuals are entitled to their moral beliefs but may not gather as a community to express those moral beliefs in law. Once an idea of that sort takes hold in the intellectual world, it is very likely to find lodgment in constitutional theory and then in constitutional law. The walls of the law have proved excessively permeable to intellectual osmosis. Out of prudence, I will give but one example of the many that might be cited.

A state attempted to apply its obscenity statute to a public display of an obscene word. The Supreme Court majority struck down the conviction on the grounds that regulation is a slippery slope and that moral relativism is a constitutional command. The opinion said, "The principle contended for by the State seems inherently boundless. How is one to distinguish this from any other offensive word?" One might as well say that the negligence standard of tort law is inherently boundless, for how is one to distinguish the reckless driver from the safe one? The answer in both cases is, by the common

---

sense of the community. Almost all judgments in the law are ones of degree, and the law does not flinch from such judgments except when, as in the case of morals, it seriously doubts the community's right to define harms. Moral relativism was even more explicit in the majority opinion, however, for the Court observed, apparently thinking the observation decisive: "One man's vulgarity is another's lyric."* On that ground, it is difficult to see how law on any subject can be permitted to exist.

But the Court immediately went further, reducing the whole question to one of private preference, saying: "We think it is largely because governmental officials cannot make principled distinctions in this area that the Constitution leaves matters of taste and style so largely to the individual." Thus, the community's moral and aesthetic judgments are reduced to questions of style and those are then said to be privatized by the Constitution. It testifies all the more clearly to the power of ideas floating in the general culture to alter the Constitution that this opinion was written by a justice generally regarded as moderate to conservative in his constitutional views.

George Orwell reminded us long ago about the power of language to corrupt thought and the consequent baleful effects upon politics. The same deterioration is certainly possible in morality. But I am not concerned about the constitutional protection cast about an obscene word. Of more concern is the constitutionalizing of the notion that moral harm is not harm legislators are entitled to consider. As Lord Devlin said, "What makes a society is a community of ideas, not political ideas alone but also ideas about the way its members should behave and govern their lives." A society that ceases to be a community increases the danger that weariness with turmoil and relativism may bring about an order in which many more, and more valuable, freedoms are lost than those we thought we were protecting.

...It is well to be clear about the role moral discourse should play in law. [Richard John] Neuhaus is entirely correct in saying

> whatever else law may be, it is a human enterprise in response to human behavior, and human behavior is stubbornly entangled with beliefs about right and wrong. Law that is recognized as legitimate is therefore related to—even organically related to, if you will—the larger universe of moral discourse that helps shape human behavior. In short, if law is not also a moral enterprise, it is without legitimacy or binding force.

To that excellent statement I would add only that it is crucial to bear in mind what kind of law, and which legal institutions, we are talking about. In a constitutional democracy the moral content of law must be given by the

*The reference is to Justice John Marshall Harlan's opinion for the Court in *Cohen v. California* (1971).

morality of the framer or the legislator, never by the morality of the judge. The sole task of the latter—and it is a task quite large enough for anyone's wisdom, skill, and virtue—is to translate the framer's or the legislator's morality into a rule to govern unforeseen circumstances. That abstinence from giving his own desires free play, that continuing and self-conscious renunciation of power, that is the morality of the jurist.

Law, Liberty and Morality

H. L. A. Hart

...Is the fact that certain conduct is by common standards immoral sufficient to justify making that conduct punishable by law? Is it morally permissible to enforce morality as such? Ought immorality as such to be a crime?

To this question John Stuart Mill gave an emphatic negative answer in his essay *On Liberty* one hundred years ago, and the famous sentence in which he frames this answer expresses the central doctrine of his essay. He said, "The only purpose for which power can rightfully be exercised over any member of a civilised community against his will is to prevent harm to others." And to identify the many different things which he intended to exclude, he added, "His own good either physical or moral is not a sufficient warrant. He cannot rightfully be compelled to do or forbear because it will be better for him to do so, because it will make him happier, because in the opinions of others, to do so would be wise or even right."

...Mill's principles are still very much alive in the criticism of law, whatever their theoretical deficiencies may be. But twice in one hundred years they have been challenged by two masters of the Common Law. The first of these was the great Victorian judge and historian of the Criminal Law, James Fitzjames Stephen. His criticism of Mill is to be found in the sombre and impressive book *Liberty, Equality, Fraternity,* which he wrote as a direct reply to Mill's essay....It is evident from the tone of this book that Stephen thought he had found crushing arguments against Mill and had demonstrated that the law might justifiably enforce morality as such or, as he said, that the law should be "a persecution of the grosser forms of vice."

H. L. A. Hart, *Law, Liberty and Morality* (Stanford, CA: Stanford University Press, 1963), 4, 15–16, 48–52, 75–77.

Nearly a century later, on the publication of the Wolfenden Committee's report, Lord Devlin, now a member of the House of Lords and a most distinguished writer on the criminal law, in his essay on *The Enforcement of Morals* took as his target the Report's contention "that there must be a realm of morality and immorality which is not the law's business" and argued in opposition to it that "the suppression of vice is as much the law's business as the suppression of subversive activities."

THE MODERATE AND THE EXTREME THESIS

When we turn...to the positive grounds held to justify the legal enforcement of morality it is important to distinguish a moderate and an extreme thesis, though critics of Mill have sometimes moved from one to the other without marking the transition. Lord Devlin seems to me to maintain, for most of his essay, the moderate thesis and Stephen the extreme.

According to the moderate thesis, a shared morality is the cement of society; without it there would be aggregates of individuals but no society. "A recognized morality" is, in Lord Devlin's words, "as necessary to society's existence as a recognized government," and though a particular act of immorality may not harm or endanger or corrupt others nor, when done in private, either shock or give offence to others, this does not conclude the matter. For we must not view conduct in isolation from its effect on the moral code: if we remember this, we can see that one who is "no menace to others" nonetheless may by his immoral conduct "threaten one of the great moral principles on which society is based." In this sense the breach of moral principle is an offence "against society as a whole," and society may use the law to preserve its morality as it uses it to safeguard anything else essential to its existence. This is why "the suppression of vice is as much the law's business as the suppression of subversive activities."

By contrast, the extreme thesis does not look upon a shared morality as of merely instrumental value analogous to ordered government, and it does not justify the punishment of immorality as a step taken, like the punishment of treason, to preserve society from dissolution or collapse. Instead, the enforcement of morality is regarded as a thing of value, even if immoral acts harm no one directly, or indirectly by weakening the moral cement of society. I do not say it is possible to allot to one or other of these two theses every argument used, but they do, I think, characterise the main critical positions at the root of most arguments, and they incidentally exhibit an ambiguity in the expression "enforcing morality as such." Perhaps the clearest way of distinguishing the two theses is to see that there are always two levels at which we may ask whether some breach of positive morality is harmful. We may ask first, Does this act harm anyone independently of its repercussion on the shared morality of society? And secondly we may ask, Does this act affect the shared morality and thereby weaken society? The moderate thesis requires, if the punishment of the act is to be justified, an affirmative answer at least at the second level. The extreme thesis does not require an affirmative answer at either level.

Lord Devlin appears to defend the moderate thesis. I say "appears" because, though he says that society has the right to enforce a morality as such on the ground that a shared morality is essential to society's existence, it is not at all clear that for him the statement that immorality jeopardizes or weakens society is a statement of empirical fact. It seems sometimes to be an *a priori* assumption, and sometimes a necessary truth and a very odd one. The most important indication that this is so is that, apart from one vague reference to "history" showing that "the loosening of moral bonds is often the first stage of disintegration," no evidence is produced to show that deviation from accepted sexual morality, even by adults in private, is something which, like treason, threatens the existence of society. No reputable historian has maintained this thesis, and there is indeed much evidence against it. As a proposition of fact it is entitled to no more respect than the Emperor Justinian's statement that homosexuality was the cause of earthquakes. Lord Devlin's belief in it, and his apparent indifference to the question of evidence, are at points traceable to an undiscussed assumption. This is that all morality—sexual morality together with the morality that forbids acts injurious to others such as killing, stealing, and dishonesty—forms a single seamless web, so that those who deviate from any part are likely or perhaps bound to deviate from the whole. It is of course clear (and one of the oldest insights of political theory) that society could not exist without a morality which mirrored and supplemented the law's proscription of conduct injurious to others. But there is again no evidence to support, and much to refute, the theory that those who deviate from conventional sexual morality are in other ways hostile to society.

There seems, however, to be central to Lord Devlin's thought something more interesting, though no more convincing, than the conception of social morality as a seamless web. For he appears to move from the acceptable proposition that *some* shared morality is essential to the existence of any society to the unacceptable proposition that a society is identical with its morality as that is at any given moment of its history, so that a change in its morality is tantamount to the destruction of a society. The former proposition might be even accepted as a necessary rather than an empirical truth depending on a quite plausible definition of society as a body of men who hold certain moral views in common. But the latter proposition is absurd. Taken strictly, it would prevent us saying that the morality of a given society had changed, and would compel us instead to say that one society had disappeared and another one taken its place. But it is only on this absurd criterion of what it is for the same society to continue to exist that it could be asserted without evidence that any deviation from a society's shared morality threatens its existence.

The extreme thesis has many variants, and it is not always clear which of them its advocates are concerned to urge. According to some variants, the legal enforcement of morality is only of instrumental value: it is merely a means, though an indispensable one, for preserving morality, whereas the preservation of morality is the end, valuable in itself, which justifies its legal enforcement. According to other variants, there is something intrinsically valuable in the legal enforcement of morality. What is common to all varieties of the extreme thesis is that, unlike the moderate thesis, they do not hold the enforcement of morality or its preservation to be valuable merely because of their beneficial consequences in securing the existence of society.

...To use coercion to maintain the moral *status quo* at any point in a society's history would be artificially to arrest the process which gives social institutions their value.

This distinction between the use of coercion to enforce morality and other methods which we in fact use to preserve it, such as argument, advice, and exhortation, is both very important and much neglected in discussions of the present topic. Stephen, in his arguments against Mill, seems most of the time to forget or to ignore these other methods and the great importance which Mill attached to them. For he frequently argues as if Mill's doctrine of liberty meant that men must never express any convictions concerning the conduct of their fellow citizens if that conduct is not harmful to others. It is true that Mill believed that "the state or the public" is not warranted "*for the purposes of repression or punishment*" in deciding that such conduct is good or bad. But it is not true that he thought that concerning such conduct or "the experiments in living" which it represents "no one else has anything to say to it." Nor did he think that society could "draw a line where education ends and perfect moral indifference begins." In making these ill-founded criticisms Stephen not only misunderstood and so misrepresented Mill, but he showed how narrowly he himself conceived of morality and the processes by which it is sustained. For Mill's concern throughout his essay is to restrict the use of coercion, not to promote moral indifference. It is true he includes in the coercion or "constraint" of which he disapproves not only legal enforcement of morality but also other peremptory forms of social pressure such as moral blame and demands for conformity. But it is a disastrous misunderstanding of morality to think that where we cannot use coercion in its support we must be silent and indifferent. In Chapter 4 of his essay Mill takes great pains to show the other resources which we have and should use:

> It would be a great misunderstanding of this doctrine to suppose that it is one of selfish indifference which pretends that human beings have no business with each others conduct in life and that they should not concern themselves about the well-doing or well-being of one another unless their own interest is involved....Human beings owe to each other help to distinguish the better from the worse and encouragement to choose the former and avoid the latter.

Discussion, advice, argument—all these, since they leave the individual "the final judge," may according to Mill be used in a society where freedom is properly respected. We may even "obtrude" on another "considerations to aid his judgment and exhortations to strengthen his will." We may in extreme cases "warn" him of our adverse judgment or feelings of distaste and contempt. We may avoid his company and caution others against it. Many might think that Mill here comes perilously near to sanctioning coercion even though he regards these things as "strictly inseparable from the unfavorable judgments of others" and never to be inflicted for the sake of punishment. But if he erred in that direction, it is certainly clear that he recognised the important truth that in morality we are not forced to choose between deliberate coercion and indifference.

Judicial Response to Philosophical Limitations on Governmental Power: *Calder* v. *Bull*

[In finding no constitutional or other basis for interfering with state legislative action that set aside a refusal to probate a will and granted a new hearing at which the probate court approved the will,[1] two of the opinions expressed conflicting views concerning limitations on governmental power.]

CHASE, Justice. [Whether] the legislature of any of the States can revise and correct by law, a decision of any of its courts of justice, although not prohibited by the constitution of the State, is a question of very great importance, and not necessary NOW to be determined; because the resolution or law in question does not go so far. I cannot subscribe to the omnipotence of a State legislature, or that it is absolute and without control; although its authority should not be expressly restrained by the constitution, or fun-

[1]The Court viewed the ex post facto clause of the Constitution as applicable only to criminal cases.

Excerpts from *Calder* v. *Bull* citation, 3 U.S. (3 Dall.) 386, 1 L.Ed. 648 (1798) in William B. Lockhart, Yale Kamisar, Jesse H. Choper, and Steven H. Shiffrin, eds., *Constitutional Law: Cases, Comments, Questions*, 6th Ed. (St. Paul Minn.: West Publishing Co., 1980), pp. 378-379. Reprinted with permission from West Publishing Co.

damental law of the state. The people of the United States erected their constitutions, or forms of government, to establish justice, to promote the general welfare, to secure the blessings of liberty, and to protect their persons and property from violence. The purposes for which men enter into society will determine the nature and terms of the social compact; and as they are the foundation of the legislative power, they will decide what are the proper objects of it. The nature and ends of legislative power will limit the *exercise* of it. This fundamental principle flows from the very nature of our free republican governments, that no man should be compelled to do what the laws do not require; nor to refrain from acts which the laws permit. There are acts which the federal, or state, legislature cannot do, without exceeding their authority. There are certain vital principles in our free republican governments, which will determine and overrule an apparent and flagrant abuse of legislative power; as to authorize manifest injustice by positive law; to take away that security for personal liberty, or private property, for the protection whereof the government was established. An act of the legislature (for I cannot call it a law), contrary to the great first principles of the social compact, cannot be considered a rightful exercise of legislative authority. The obligation of a law in governments established on express compact, and on republican principles, must be determined by the nature of the power on which it is founded. A few instances will suffice to explain what I mean. A law that punished a citizen for an innocent action or, in other words, for an act, which, when done, was in violation of no existing law; a law that destroys, or impairs, the lawful private contracts of citizens; a law that makes a man a judge in his own cause; or a law that takes property from A and gives it to B: It is against all reason and justice, for a people to intrust a legislature with SUCH powers; and therefore, it cannot be presumed that they have done it. The genius, the nature, and the spirit, of our State governments, amount to a prohibition of such acts of legislation; and the general principles of law and reason forbid them. [To] maintain that our Federal, or State legislature possesses such powers, if they had not been expressly restrained, would, in my opinion, be a political heresy, altogether inadmissible in our free republican governments....[2]

IREDELL, Justice. [If] a government, composed of legislative, executive and judicial departments, were established, by a constitution which imposed no limits on the legislative power, the consequence would inevitably be, that whatever the legislative power chose to enact, would be lawfully enacted, and the judicial power could never interpose to pronounce it void. It is true, that some speculative jurists have held, that a legislative act against natural justice must, in itself, be void; but I cannot think that, under such a government any court of justice would possess a power to declare it so.

[2]Professor Ely interprets Chase, J.'s, opinion as a philosophical, not a constitutional, argument. See Ely, *On Discovering Fundamental Values*, 92 Harv. L. Rev. 5, 26–27 n. 95 (1978).

[I]t has been the policy of all the American states, which have, individually, framed their state constitutions, since the revolution, and of the people of the United States, when they framed the federal constitution, to define with precision the objects of the legislative power, and to restrain its exercise within marked and settled boundaries. If any act of Congress, or of the legislature of a state, violates those constitutional provisions, it is unquestionably void. [If], on the other hand, the legislature of the Union, or the legislature of any member of the Union, shall pass a law, within the general scope of their constitutional power, the court cannot pronounce it to be void, merely because it is, in their judgment, contrary to the principles of natural justice. The ideals of natural justice are regulated by no fixed standard: the ablest and the purest men have differed upon the subject; and all that the court could properly say, in such an event, would be that the legislature (possessed of an equal right of opinion) had passed an act which, in the opinion of the judges, was inconsistent with the abstract principles of natural justice....

Griswold v. *Connecticut*

[The question for the Supreme Court was whether a Connecticut statute making the use of contraceptives illegal (and also making it illegal for any person to assist, abet, or counsel another in the use of contraceptives) was constitutional. The Court ruled that the Connecticut statute was unconstitutional. Justice Goldberg's concurrence follows:]

Mr. Justice GOLDBERG, whom THE CHIEF JUSTICE and Mr. Justice BRENNAN join, concurring.

I [join the Court's opinion]. Although I have not accepted the view that "due process" as used in the Fourteenth Amendment includes all of the first eight Amendments, I do agree that the concept of liberty protects those personal rights that are fundamental, and is not confined to the specific terms of the Bill of Rights. My conclusion [that] it embraces the right of marital privacy though that right is not mentioned explicitly in the Constitution is supported both by numerous decisions [and] by the language and history of the Ninth Amendment [which] reveal that the Framers of the Constitution believed that there are additional fundamental rights, protected from governmental infringement....

The Ninth Amendment [was] proffered to quiet expressed fears that a bill of specifically enumerated rights could not be sufficiently broad to cover

---

Excerpts from *Griswold* v. *Connecticut*, 381 U.S. 479 (1965), footnotes deleted. In William B. Lockhart, Yale Kamisar, Jesse H. Choper, and Steven H. Shiffrin, eds. *Constitutional Law: Cases, Comments, Questions*, 6th Ed. (St. Paul, Minn: West Publishing Co., 1980), pp. 461-463. Reprinted with permission from West Publishing Co.

all essential rights and that the specific mention of certain rights would be interpreted as a denial that others were protected....

While this Court has had little occasion to interpret the Ninth Amendment, "[i]t cannot be presumed that any clause in the constitution is intended to be without effect." [To] hold that a right so basic and fundamental and so deep-rooted in our society as the right of privacy in marriage may be infringed because that right is not guaranteed in so many words by the first eight amendments to the Constitution is to ignore the Ninth Amendment and to give it no effect whatsoever....I do not mean to imply that the Ninth Amendment is applied against the States by the Fourteenth [nor] to state that the Ninth Amendment constitutes an independent source of rights protected from infringement by either the States or the Federal Government. Rather, the Ninth Amendment shows a belief of the Constitution's authors that fundamental rights exist that are not expressly enumerated in the first eight amendments and an intent that the list of rights included there not be deemed exhaustive. [T]his Court has held, often unanimously, that the Fifth and Fourteenth Amendments protect certain fundamental personal liberties from abridgment by the Federal Government or the States. [I] do not see how this [interpretation of the Ninth Amendment] broadens the authority of the Court; rather it serves to support what this Court has been doing in protecting fundamental rights.

[While] the Ninth Amendment—and indeed the entire Bill of Rights—originally concerned restrictions upon *federal* power, the subsequently enacted Fourteenth Amendment prohibits the States as well from abridging fundamental personal liberties. [In] sum, the Ninth Amendment simply lends strong support to the view that the "liberty" protected by the Fifth and Fourteenth Amendments from infringement by the Federal Government or the States is not restricted to rights specifically mentioned in the first eight amendments.

In determining which rights are fundamental, judges are not left at large to decide cases in light of their personal and private notions. Rather, they must look to the "traditions and [collective] conscience of our people" to determine whether a principle is "so rooted [there] [as] to be ranked as fundamental."..."Liberty" also "gains content from the emanations [of] specific [constitutional] guarantees" and "from experience with the requirements of a free society." *Poe* (dissenting opinion of Douglas, J.).

I agree fully with the Court that, applying these tests, the right of privacy is a fundamental personal right, emanating "from the totality of the constitutional scheme under which we live." Mr. Justice Brandeis, dissenting in *Olmstead v. United States*, 277 U.S. 438, 48 S.Ct. 564, 72 L.Ed. 944 (1928), comprehensively summarized the principles underlying the Constitution's guarantees of privacy: "The protection guaranteed by the [Fourth and Fifth] amendments is much broader in scope. The [Framers] sought to protect Americans in their beliefs, their thoughts, their emotions and their sensations. They conferred as against the government, the right to be let alone—the most comprehensive of rights and the right most valued by civilized men."...

I agree with Mr. Justice Harlan's statement in his dissenting opinion in *Poe:* "[The] integrity of [family] life is something so fundamental that it has been found to draw to its protection the principles of more than one explicitly granted Constitutional right. [Of] this whole 'private realm of family life' it is difficult to imagine what is more private or more intimate than a husband and wife's marital relations."

The entire fabric of the Constitution and the purposes that clearly underlie its specific guarantees demonstrate that the rights to marital privacy and to marry and raise a family are of similar order and magnitude as the fundamental rights specifically protected.

[Surely] the Government, absent a showing of a compelling subordinating state interest, could not decree that all husbands and wives must be sterilized after two children have been born to them. Yet by [the dissenters'] reasoning such an invasion of marital privacy would not be subject to constitutional challenge because, while it might be "silly," no provision of the Constitution specifically prevents the Government from curtailing the marital right to bear children and raise a family. [I]f upon a showing of a slender basis of rationality, a law outlawing voluntary birth control by married persons is valid, then, by the same reasoning, a law requiring compulsory birth control also would seem to be valid. In my view, however, both types of law would unjustifiably intrude upon rights of marital privacy which are constitutionally protected.

In a long series of cases this Court has held that where fundamental personal liberties are involved, they may not be abridged by the States simply on a showing that a regulatory statute has some rational relationship to the effectuation of a proper state purpose. "Where there is a significant encroachment upon personal liberty, the State may prevail only upon showing a subordinating interest which is compelling," *Bates v. Little Rock,* [Ch. 9, Sec. 3]. [The] State, at most, argues that there is some rational relation between this statute and what is admittedly a legitimate subject of state concern—the discouraging of extra-marital relations. It says that preventing the use of birth-control devices by married persons helps prevent the indulgence by some in such extra-marital relations. The rationality of this justification is dubious, particularly in light of the admitted widespread availability to all persons [in] Connecticut, unmarried as well as married, of birth-control devices for the prevention of disease, as distinguished from the prevention of conception. But in any event, it is clear that the state interest in safeguarding marital fidelity can be served by a more discriminately tailored statute, which does not, like the present one, sweep unnecessarily broadly, reaching far beyond the evil sought to be dealt with and intruding upon the privacy of all married couples....

Finally, it should be said of the Court's holding today that it in no way interferes with a State's proper regulation of sexual promiscuity or misconduct. As any Brother Harlan so well stated in his dissenting opinion in *Poe:* "Adultery, homosexuality and the like are sexual intimacies which the State forbids [but] the intimacy of husband and wife is necessarily an essential and accepted feature of the institution of marriage, an institution which the State not only must allow, but which always and in every age it has fostered and protected. It is one thing when the State exerts its power either to forbid extra-marital sexuality [or] to say who may marry, but it is quite another when, having acknowledged a marriage and the intimacies inherent in it, it undertakes to regulate by means of the criminal law the details of that intimacy."...

The Least Dangerous Branch

Alexander Bickel

[The constitutional scholar Alexander Bickel, after surveying various objections to the idea of judicial review, concluded that it was necessary to find a justification for judicial review "on principle, quite aside from supports in history and the continuity of practice." In a section entitled, "The Moral Approval of the Lines: Principle," Bickel wrote:]

...The search must be for a function which might (indeed, must) involve the making of policy, yet which differs from the legislative and executive functions; which is peculiarly suited to the capabilities of the courts; which will not likely be performed elsewhere if the courts do not assume it; which can be so exercised as to be acceptable in a society that generally shares Judge Hand's satisfaction in a "sense of common venture"; which will be effective when needed; and whose discharge by the courts will not lower the quality of the other departments' performance by denuding them of the dignity and burden of their own responsibility. It will not be possible fully to meet all that is said against judicial review. Such is not the way with ques-

---

Alexander Bickel, *The Least Dangerous Branch: The Supreme Court at the Bar of Politics* (New Haven, CT: Yale University Press, 1986), 24–28. Excerpts reprinted with permission of Yale University Press.

tions of government. We can only fill the other side of the scales with countervailing judgments on the real needs and the actual workings of our society and, of course, with our own portions of faith and hope. Then we may estimate how far the needle has moved.

The point of departure is a truism; perhaps it even rises to the unassailability of a platitude. It is that many actions of government have two aspects: their immediate, necessarily intended, practical effects, and their perhaps unintended or unappreciated bearing on values we hold to have more general and permanent interest. It is a premise we deduce not merely from the fact of a written constitution but from the history of the race, and ultimately as a moral judgment of the good society, that government should serve not only what we conceive from time to time to be our immediate material needs but also certain enduring values. This in part is what is meant by government under law. But such values do not present themselves ready-made. They have a past always, to be sure, but they must be continually derived, enunciated, and seen in relevant application. And it remains to ask which institution of our government—if any single one in particular—should be the pronouncer and guardian of such values.

Men in all walks of public life are able occasionally to perceive this second aspect of public questions. Sometimes they are also able to base their decisions on it; that is one of the things we like to call acting on principle. Often they do not do so, however, particularly when they sit in legislative assemblies. There, when the pressure for immediate results is strong enough and emotions ride high enough, men will ordinarily prefer to act on expediency rather than take the long view. Possibly legislators—everything else being equal—are as capable as other men of following the path of principle, where the path is clear or at any rate discernible. Our system, however, like all secular systems, calls for the evolution of principle in novel circumstances, rather than only for its mechanical application. Not merely respect for the rule of established principles but the creative establishment and renewal of a coherent body of principled rules—that is what our legislatures have proven themselves ill equipped to give us.

Initially, great reliance for principled decision was placed in the Senators and the President, who have more extended terms of office and were meant to be elected only indirectly. Yet the Senate and the President were conceived of as less closely tied to, not as divorced from, electoral responsibility and the political marketplace. And so even then the need might have been felt for an institution which stands altogether aside from the current clash of interests, and which, insofar as is humanly possible, is concerned only with principle. We cannot know whether, as Thayer believed, our legislatures are what they are because we have judicial review, or whether we have judicial review and consider it necessary because legislatures are what they are. Yet it is arguable also that the partial separation of the legislative and judicial functions—and it is not meant to be absolute—is beneficial in any event, because it makes it possible for the desires of various groups and interests concerning immediate results to be heard clearly and unrestrainedly in one place. It may be thought fitting that somewhere in government, at some stage in the process of law-making, such felt needs should find unambiguous expression. Moreover, and more importantly, courts have certain capacities for dealing with matters of principle that legislatures and executives do not possess. Judges have, or should have, the leisure, the training, and the insulation to follow the ways of the scholar in pursuing the ends of government. This is crucial in sorting out the enduring values of a society, and it is not something that institutions can do well occasionally, while operating for the most part with a different set of gears. It calls for a habit of mind, and for undeviating institutional customs. Another advantage that courts have is that questions of principle never carry the same aspect for them as they did for the legislature or the executive. Statutes, after all, deal typically with abstract or dimly foreseen problems. The courts are concerned with the flesh and blood of an actual case. This tends to modify, perhaps to lengthen, everyone's view. It also provides an extremely salutary proving ground for all abstractions; it is conducive, in a phrase of Holmes, to thinking things, not words, and thus to the evolution of principle by a process that tests as it creates.

Their insulation and the marvelous mystery of time give courts the capacity to appeal to men's better natures, to call forth their aspirations, which may have been forgotten in the moment's hue and cry. This is what Justice Stone called the opportunity for "the sober second thought."[1] Hence it is that the courts, although they may somewhat dampen the people's and the legislatures' efforts to educate themselves, are also a great and highly effective educational institution. Judge Gibson, in the very opinion mentioned earlier..., highly critical as he was, took account of this. "In the business of government," he wrote, "a recurrence to first principles answers the end of an observation at sea with a view to correct the dead reckoning; and, for this purpose, a written constitution is an instrument of inestimable value. It is of inestimable value also, in rendering its principles familiar to the mass of the people....[2] The educational institution that both takes the observation to correct the dead reckoning and makes it known is the voice of the Constitution: the Supreme Court exercising judicial review. The Justices, in Dean Rostow's phrase, "are inevitably teachers in a vital national seminar."[3] No other branch of the American government is nearly so well equipped to conduct

[1]H. F. Stone, "The Common Law in the United States," 50 *Harvard Law Review* 4, 25 (1936).

[2]*Eakin* v. *Raub*, supra n. 23, at p. 354.

[3]E.V. Rostow, "The Democratic Character of Judicial Review," *66 Harvard Law Review* (1952) at 208.

one. And such a seminar can do a great deal to keep our society from becoming so riven that no court will be able to save it. Of course, we have never quite been that society in which the spirit of moderation is so richly in flower that no court need save it.

Thus, as Professor Henry M. Hart, Jr., has written, and as surely most of the profession and of informed laity believe; for if not this, what and why?—thus the Court appears "predestined in the long run, not only by the thrilling tradition of Anglo-American law but also by the hard facts of its position in the structure of American institutions, to be a voice of reason charged with the creative function of discerning afresh and of articulating and developing impersonal and durable principles. . . ."[4] This line of thought may perhaps blunt, if it does not meet, the force of all the arguments on the other side. No doubt full consistency with democratic theory has not been established. The heart of the democratic faith is government by the consent of the governed. The further premise is not incompatible that the good society not only will want to satisfy the immediate needs of the greatest number but also will strive to support and maintain enduring general values. I have followed the view that the elected institutions are ill fitted, or not so well fitted as the courts, to perform the latter task. This rests on the assumption that the people themselves, by direct action at the ballot box, are surely incapable of sustaining a working system of general values specifically applied. But that much we assume throughout, being a representative, deliberative democracy. Matters of expediency are not generally submitted to direct referendum. Nor should matters of principle, which require even more intensive deliberation, be so submitted. Reference of specific policies to the people for initial decision is, with few exceptions, the fallacy of the misplaced mystics, or the way of those who would use the forms of democracy to undemocratic ends. It is not the way in which working democracies live. But democracies do live by the idea, central to the process of gaining the consent of the governed, that the majority has the ultimate power to displace the decision-makers and to reject any part of their policy. With that idea, judicial review must achieve some measure of consonance.

Democratic government under law—the slogan pulls in two opposed directions, but that does not keep it from being applicable to an operative polity. If it carries the elements of explosion, it doesn't contain a critical mass of them. Yet if the critical mass is not to be reached, there must be an accommodation, a degree of concord between the diverging elements. Having been checked, should the people persist; having been educated, should the people insist, must they not win over every fundamental principle save one—which is the principle that they must win? Are we sufficiently certain of the per-

[4]H. M. Hart, Jr., "Foreword: The Time Chart of the Justices," 73 *Harvard Law Review* 84, 99 (1959).

manent validity of any other principle to be ready to impose it against a consistent and determined majority, and could we do so for long? Have not the people the right of peaceable revolution, as assuredly, over time, they possess the capacity for a bloody one?

The premise of democracy is egalitarian, and, as Professor Herbert J. Muller has written, every bright sophomore knows how to punch holes in it. Yet, as Mr. Muller goes on to say, there is "no universal standard of superiority," there are no sure scales in which to weigh all the relevant virtues and capacities of men, and many a little man may rightly claim to be a better citizen than the expert or the genius. Moreover, and most significantly, "all men are in fact equal in respect of their common structure and their common destiny." Hence, to repeat the insight of Judge Hand, government must be their common venture. Who will think it moral ultimately to direct the lives of men against the will of the greater number of them? Or wise? "Man's historical experience should sober the revolutionaries who know the certain solution to our problems, and sober as well the traditionalists whose solution is a return to the ancient faiths, which have always failed in the past.[5]

To bring judicial review into concord with such presuppositions requires a closer analysis of the actual operation of the process in various circumstances. The preliminary suggestions may be advanced that the rule of principle imposed by the Court is seldom rigid, that the Court has ways of persuading before it attempts to coerce, and that, over time, sustained opinion running counter to the Court's constitutional law can achieve its nullification directly or by desuetude. It may further be that if the process is properly carried out, an aspect of the current—not only the timeless, mystic—popular will finds expression in constitutional adjudication. The result may be a tolerable accommodation with the theory and practice of democracy.

THE MYSTIC FUNCTION

This inquiry into a general justification of judicial review cannot end without taking account of a most suggestive and perceptive argument recently advanced by Professor Charles L. Black, Jr.[6] It begins by emphasizing that the Court performs not only a checking function but also a legitimating one, as Mr. Black well calls it. Judicial review means not only that the Court may strike down a legislative action as unconstitutional but also that it may validate it as within constitutionally granted powers and as not violating

[5] H. J. Muller, *The Uses of the Past* (New York: Oxford University Press, 1957), pp. 364–65, 367.
[6] C. L. Black, Jr., *The People and the Court* (New York: Macmillan, 1960), pp. 34 *et seq*.

constitutional limitations. Mr. Black contends, further, that the legitimating function would be impossible of performance if the checking function did not exist as well: what is the good of a declaration of validity from an institution which is by hypothesis required to validate everything that is brought before it? This is plainly so, though it is oddly stated. The picture is accurate, but it is stood on its head. The truth is that the legitimating function is an inescapable, even if unintended, by-product of the checking power. But what follows? What is the nature of this legitimating function, and what the need for it?

With a relish one can readily share, Mr. Black cites the story of the French intellectual who, upon arrival in New York harbor, exclaims: "It is wonderful to breathe the sweet air of legitimacy!" He contends essentially that what filled the Frenchman's lungs, what smelled to him so different from the succession of short-lived empires and republics endemic to his homeland, was the sweet odor of the Supreme Court of the United States. But I think it much simpler and nearer the reality of both the American and the French experience to begin with the proposition that legitimacy comes to a regime that is felt to be good and to have proven itself as such to generations past as well as in the present. Such a government must be principled as well as responsible; but it must be felt to be the one without having ceased to be the other, and unless it is responsible it cannot in fact be stable, and is not in my view morally supportable. Quite possibly, there have been governments that were electorally responsible and yet failed to attain stability....

DISCUSSION QUESTIONS

1. Do states have a right to pass laws which prohibit certain sexual acts—even among married couples? Is this not imposing a morality on the citizenry?
2. How does one justify varying state laws and punishments for the identical crime such as capital punishment, or for the identical controversial procedure such as abortion or euthanasia? Is there one code of ethics that governs the nation—or many?
3. Are Supreme Court justices justified in imposing their conception of law on the people? Should laws be put to a public vote in regular elections?

3

THE PRESIDENCY

Charles W. Dunn

Religion, morality, and presidential ethics spark heated debates among many people of all political persuasions. This chapter's essays address the volatile issue of personal morality and convictions controlling the American presidency. In them one finds discussion focused on three important questions:

1. To what extent should presidential leadership be morally based?
2. Do morality and religion influence too much or too little the exercise of presidential leadership in this country?
3. To what extent should political issues be posed as religious and moral questions?

Religion and morality have long been part of the history of American politics. For example, could either the abolitionist movement in the nineteenth century or the civil rights drive of the 1960s have been successful without their religious and moral bases of support? More recently, could the anti-abortion, pro-school prayer, anti-ERA, and other similar movements have made a major impact on public debate, and ultimately on the election of a president, without religious and moral leadership from a variety of Protestant and Roman Catholic leaders? The answer, of course, is a resounding "no" to both questions.

Increasingly, presidential campaigns are stamped with religious and moral issues as avowed religious leaders become candidates and the "character" issue becomes more of a litmus test of the morality of candidates.

Should religious leaders like Jesse Jackson and Pat Robertson be allowed to inject their personal morality into presidential politics as candidates for the nation's highest office? Jackson considers it very moral to oppose the contras in Nicaragua while Robertson believes his support for the contras is highly moral. Right religion and correct morality are in the eyes of the beholder. What is religious and moral to one person may be irreligious and immoral to another.

The American presidency is the single most powerful political office in the world. It thus offers an illustrative example of the influence of religion, or one might contend, personal ethics, in international politics. Accordingly, it is important here to pose and answer two questions: How are religion and morality used by presidents? How are presidents influenced by religion and morality? Answering each is a difficult task. By and large American Presidents have been religious, or have professed to be religious. This is documented in John Sutherland Bonnell's study *Presidential Profiles* that states of the presidents:

> Several of them had seriously debated entering the...ministry. One was...a preacher when he was elected. Three were sons of ministers. Five had married daughters of clergymen. Two had served as military chaplains without ordination. One had read the Bible through three times before the age of fourteen....One compiled a scholarly selection of the moral teachings of Jesus which was widely read at the time and is found in libraries today.[1]

Religion is no longer the issue it once was for election to the presidency, but morality is. As demonstrated in 1988, the American electorate holds candidates to a very high standard of personal morality.

Politically, there is an ideological tendency to equate morality or immorality with conservative or liberal positions depending on one's stance. But conservatives and liberals usually differ not only ideologically, but also religiously or theologically. Conservatives and liberals dramatically divide on the following issues that have serious religious or moral overtones.

Conservative	*Issue*	*Liberals*
Pro	Prayer in Schools	Anti
Pro	Star Wars Defense	Anti
Pro	Contra Aid	Anti
Anti	Abortion	Pro
Anti	ERA	Pro
Anti	Nuclear Freeze	Pro

Figure 1 contains another helpful way to analyze presidents, presidential candidates, and other leading political figures by presenting quadrants into which political personalities and presidents may be categorized based upon their religious beliefs and political or ideological convictions. The horizontal line represents the religious division between conservative and liberal while the vertical line represents the political or ideological division between conservative and liberal.

FIGURE 1. The Ideological and Theological Tendencies of Presidents F.D.R.–Reagan[2]

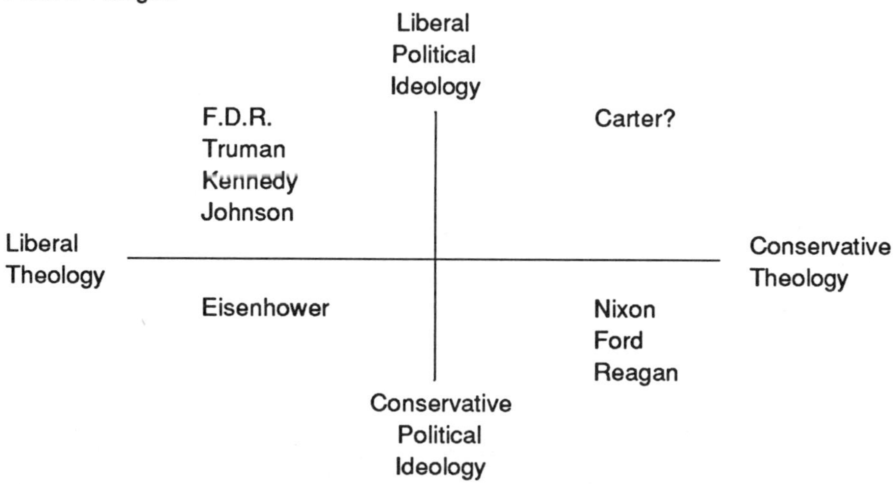

It is important to note that there are degrees of difference between and among political personalities in a given category and that political views may change. Looking at the conservative quadrant, for example, Reagan is more conservative than Ford. In seeking to win conservative religious support some presidential candidates, like George Bush, appeared to modify both their religious and ideological convictions, thus making them more conservative. Bush is a member of a liberal, mainline protestant denomination, the Episcopal Church, but he does not hold to all of his church's views either theologically or ideologically. He opposes abortion, for example.

Presidents and presidential candidates have had to step carefully to avoid political fatality from issue-landmines set by religious and morally-based groups. President Carter, while personally opposed to abortion, refused to attack the Democratic Party's platform plank in favor of abortion. President Reagan, though personally supportive of tax-exempt status for parochial schools even when their religious convictions require them to adopt policies in conflict with public policy, backed down from his position when opponents charged his position was racist.

Presented here are three approaches to the relationships between religion, morality, and the presidency. In the first, Charles W. Dunn shows how and why presidents respond to religious issues. In the second, James Ceaser offers thoughts on the most recent "presidential affair," as the "scandolgists" are calling the Iran-contra Hearings. He notes the constitutional framework and the ethical arena in which participants engaged in "moral fable" spinning, and comes to the conclusion that the hearings were useful in that they put the Congress as well as the president on trial. In the third essay, Hadley Arkes argues that presidents have gradually been denuded of their moral clothing and that this seriously threatens American constitutional democracy.

In this country the president's role is seen purely as a political leader. The president does not assume titular leadership of any religious denomination as do British monarchs. The American public has become more accepting of personal choices of presidents; divorce and religious affiliation are no longer issues that will prevent a candidate from being elected. Yet the electorate still shuns political candidates whose personal conduct is less than impeccable and is critical of presidents for the indiscretions of their staff members. Reagan was duly criticized for his political appointments, and nominations for appointments when those individuals faced allegations of questionable ethical activities.

How the president retains and incorporates personal morality and how he surrounds himself with moral or unscrupulous advisors is of great significance to the people of the United States and the people of the world. The matter of personal morality cannot be underestimated even in a country that provides for separation of church and state, and that has instituted a system of checks and balances to ensure that the president will not wield all the power.

NOTES

1. John Sutherland Bonnell, *Presidential Profiles: Religion in the Life of American Presidents* (Philadelphia: Westminister Press, 1971), pp. 14–15.
2. Charles W. Dunn, ed., *American Political Theology* (New York: Praeger Publishers, 1984), p. 169.

The Theological Dimensions of Presidential Leadership: A Classification Model

Charles W. Dunn

> Americans treat America as a religion. Hatred for political opponents waxes theological. Like separate islands, the political religions of the land are connected through a single office. The president is the one pontiff bridging all.[1]
>
> ***Michael Novak***

While the ideological dimensions of presidential leadership are generally obvious, the theological dimensions, though less obvious, are no less important, especially as they relate to the ideological. It is naturally and properly assumed with clear historical support that a president's ideology affects how he performs in office. To wit, using some obvious examples, Lyndon Johnson from a liberal ideological background, contrasts sharply with Ronald Reagan from a conservative background with respect to a variety of aspects of presidential leadership, but especially public policy. The basic policy approach of a liberal president tends to increase while a conservative president tends to reduce, or at least desires to do so, the size and scope of the national government.

IMPORTANCE OF PRESIDENTIAL THEOLOGY

The importance of a theological understanding of presidential leadership may be established in several ways. First, the presidency quite often is referred to in theological terms, such as "faith in the presidency," "trust in presidential leadership," "a sacred office," "confidence in presidential leadership," or "saving the presidency."

Second, leading presidential analysts, observers, and presidents themselves have used theological analogies, metaphors, and similes to describe

[1]Michael Novak, *Choosing Our King* (New York: Macmillan, 1974), p. xv.

Charles W. Dunn, "The Theological Dimensions of Presidential Leadership: A Classification Model," *Presidential Studies Quarterly* 14, no. 1 (Winter 1984), 61–72. Reprinted with permission of *Presidential Studies Quarterly*, Center for the Study of The Presidency, New York.

the presidency. Theodore Roosevelt referred to the office as a "bully pulpit" while Franklin Roosevelt said it is "preeminently a place of moral leadership." Richard Nixon said:

> To a crisis of the *spirit*, we need an answer of the *spirit*. We can build a *great cathedral* of the *spirit*. We have endured a long night of the American *spirit*. But as our eyes catch the dimness of the first rays of dawn, let us not curse the remaining *dark*, let us gather the *light*. Our destiny offers not the *cup* of despair, but the *chalice* of opportunity.[2] (emphasis supplied)

New York *Times* journalist James Reston concluded that "the White House is the pulpit of the nation and the president is its chaplain."[3] Then perhaps presidential scholar Clinton Rossiter rose or stooped to the highest or lowest use of theological terminology, depending on one's perspective, when he said of Lincoln that he was "the martyred Christ of democracy's passion play."[4]

Campaigns for the presidency offer a third reason for understanding the theological dimensions of presidential leadership. The 1976 and 1980 presidential campaigns present excellent verbal as well as visual examples of theological symbol manipulation by presidential candidates. In 1976, candidate Jimmy Carter said he was "born again," a not-so-subtle code word from John 3 designed to woo the substantial segment of the American electorate that claims to be "born again." And the Sunday immediately prior to election day, President Ford, an Episcopalian, was prominently pictured shaking hands with the Southern Baptist Convention's best known conservative preacher, W. A. Criswell, while entering the front door of the First Baptist Church, Dallas, Texas. In 1980 candidate Ronald Reagan appeared before a theologically conservative meeting hosted by the Religious Roundtable in Texas where he proclaimed his faith in the Genesis account of creation and expressed support for prayer in the public schools.

Still a fourth reason for expanding our understanding concerns the use of theological rhetoric in support of public policy aims. Lincoln's Gettysburg Address, his Second Inaugural and his earlier "house divided" speech are replete with numerous theological themes. But perhaps more than any other president, William McKinley's policy toward the Philippines reveals the significant relationship between theology and public policy.

> The truth is I didn't want the Philippines, and when they came to us a gift from the gods I did not know what to do with them...I sought counsel...I walked

[2]1969 Inaugural Address.

[3]As cited in Thomas E. Cronin, "The Textbook Presidency and Political Science," in *The Congressional Record*, October 5, 1970, p. S17106.

[4]Clinton Rossiter, *The American Presidency*, revised edition (New York: New American Library, 1960), p. 239.

the floor of the White House night after night until midnight, and I am not ashamed to tell you gentlemen, that I went down on my knees and prayed to Almighty God for light and guidance more than one night. And late one night it came to me this way—I don't know how it was but it came...there was nothing left for us to do but to take them all, and to educate the Filipinos, and uplift and civilize and Christianize them, and by God's grace do the very best we could by them as our fellowmen for whom Christ died.[5]

As he entered the presidential office during the Depression, Franklin Roosevelt used biblical terminology when he declared that "the money changers have fled from their high seats in the temple of civilization."[6] In defense of his voting rights bill in 1965, President Johnson stated before Congress:

...should we double our wealth and conquer the stars and still be unequal to this issue, then we will have failed as a people and as a nation.

For with a country as with a person, '*What is a man profited, if he shall gain the whole world, and lose his own soul?*'

Above the pyramid on the great seal of the United States it says in Latin, 'God has favored our undertaking.'

God will not favor everything we do. It is rather our duty to divine His will. I cannot help but believe that He truly understands and that He really favors the undertaking that we begin here tonight.[7] (emphasis supplied)

Fifth, a substantial body of scholarship, particularly among sociologists, theologians, and historians, documents a civil religion replete with its own terminology generally considered inoffensive to a broad theological spectrum. As Conrad Cherry has pointed out:

Throughout their history Americans have been possessed by an acute sense of divine election. They have fancied themselves a New Israel, a people chosen for the awesome responsibility of serving as a light to the nations, a city set upon a hill. This preponderating self-image, in its original form as well as in its myriad mutations, has served as both a stimulus of creative American energy and a source of American self-righteousness. It has long been, in other words, the essence of America's motivating mythology.[8]

While William McKinley's Philippine statement may be considered outside the accepted boundary lines of the civil religion, both conservative and liberal presidents on the whole have drawn liberally from biblical and theological terminology to establish the credibility of their political aspirations and policy objectives. Many of the most famous of all political slogans

[5]As cited in Novak, p. 154.

[6]Presidential Address, March 4, 1933.

[7]Presidential Address, March 15, 1965.

[8]Conrad Cherry, *God's New Israel* (Englewood Cliffs, N.J.: Prentice Hall, 1971), p. viii.

have biblical and theological overtones, such as "the white man's burden" and "manifest destiny," that helped presidents and others inspire the populace.

Although probably no president excelled Lincoln in the use of the terminology of civil religion, Jefferson may have come close. For example, he proposed that the seal of the United States portray "the children of Israel in the wilderness led by a cloud by day and a pillar by night."[9] In his second inaugural, he declared: "I shall need...the favor of that Being in whose hands we are, who led our fathers, as Israel of old, from their native land and planted them in a country flowing with all the necessities and comforts of life."[10] Perhaps President Eisenhower best summed up the impact of civil religion when he said: "Our government makes no sense unless it is founded in a deeply felt faith—and I don't care what it is."[11]

Sixth, in at least some instances, religious or theological advice has been sought and given to presidents, including Reinhold Niebuhr to Franklin Roosevelt, Billy Graham to several presidents, such as Kennedy, Johnson, and Nixon and Jerry Falwell to Ronald Reagan. Sometimes their advice has been received both substantively and symbolically as when Presidents Kennedy, Johnson, and Nixon publicly announced and had pictures taken of their public policy discussions with Billy Graham.

Seventh, presidents cannot ignore, except at their own potential political peril, political movements with a theological base, such as the abolitionist movement prior to the Civil War that existed principally because of theological forces and the Nuclear Freeze and Moral Majority movements of today. The abolitionist movement with its uncompromising theologically based opposition to slavery kept "the feet of presidents to the fire" in the prosecution of their cause. The Nuclear Freeze movement whose troops are sprinkled liberally with persons of liberal theological convictions has forced President Reagan to acknowledge their presence by counter-attacking on this issue. The Moral Majority, an umbrella for many conservative theological personalities, similarly served as a lightning rod for President Reagan's social and theological agenda on such issues as ERA, school prayer and abortion.

Church joining, if not faithful attendance, is an eighth reason for understanding the impact of theology and religion on presidents. Perhaps the best example of this occurred in 1952 when the Democratic candidate Adlai Stevenson, a Unitarian, became a Presbyterian, and a nonchurchmember, General Eisenhower, also became a Presbyterian. ...[P]residents tend to be

[9] As cited in Perry C. Cotham, *Politics, Americanism and Christianity* (Grand Rapids, Mich.: Baker Book House, 1976), p. 51.

[10] Ibid., p. 52.

[11] In Robert N. Bellah, *Beyond Belief* (New York: Harper & Row, 1970), p. 170.

members of, or attend, the safe or mainline denominational churches, such as Methodist, Presbyterian, Episcopalian, and Baptist. President Nixon took the unusual course of holding Sunday morning worship services in the White House with leading clergy from several denominations presiding.

The moderating influence of the safe or mainline churches on presidential behavior suggests a ninth reason. Or it could be said that politics itself tends to moderate the theological and religious convictions of presidents. Except for perhaps William McKinley and possibly Jimmy Carter, conservative and fundamental convictions appeared to have waned either before or during the presidencies of those presidents from such backgrounds like James A. Garfield and Warren Harding. With respect to Jimmy Carter one must wonder about how conservative or fundamental his theological and religious convictions were. Superficially they were deeply rooted if one remembers his Sunday School attendance with Bible in hand; however, his favorite theologians were liberal, and he did not appear to insist upon White House staff behavior consistent with his apparent personal convictions, Hamilton Jordan being the prime example of the prodigal. Although wooing conservative theological groups in his 1980 campaign, President Reagan generally tended to modify his statements and behavior during his presidency apparently in response to a broader American constituency.

The essential point is that like their political ideology, the theology of most Americans tends to be in the middle, i.e., neither hot nor cold. Thus, the middle of the electorate, we may reasonably argue, pressures presidents to conform to them.

Finally the national party platforms, particularly in recent years, present a contrast between conservative and liberal theological convictions perhaps best shown in the 1980 platforms wherein they differed sharply on such issues as school prayer, abortion, ERA (equal rights amendment for women) and others. That presidents feel the theological pressure from these platforms may be shown with respect to Jimmy Carter, who though personally opposed to abortion for theological reasons, would not take a stand against the mainstream of his party on this issue. Also, in 1980 George Bush had to agree to support the Republican Platform that contained several theologically based planks which he opposed.

Not only do these ten reasons offer sufficient justification for examining the relationships between presidential behavior and theological convictions, but they also begin to unveil differences between and among presidents. It is here that efforts have been made to classify presidents based upon religious and theological considerations. Our purpose now is to review these efforts and then to offer another classification scheme that shows relationships between theological and ideological aspects of presidential behavior.

...[T]he ideological and theological components tend to reinforce one another. Liberal presidents ideologically also tend to be liberal presidents theologically while conservative presidents ideologically tend to be theologically conservative.

Second, one cannot always determine which came first, the "chicken or the egg," that is, whether a president is liberal primarily because of ideology or theology. Superficially, the safe conclusion would be that theology tends to reinforce ideology more than the other way around, but then we do not have sufficient evidence to conclude that firmly. One principal support for this conclusion is that presidents generally speak more about their ideology than their theology.

Third, some presidents appear never to give serious thought to their theological convictions, such as Harry S. Truman and Dwight David Eisenhower. In such instances theology would definitely tend to reinforce more than to direct their ideological positions.

Fourth, what cannot be shown are the degrees of conservatism and liberalism. To wit, Walter Mondale is clearly more liberal ideologically and theologically than Jimmy Carter, and Ronald Reagan is more conservative than Richard Nixon.

Fifth, those in the conservative-conservative quadrant [See Figure 1 in introduction to chapter] are more likely to be Republicans and those in the liberal-liberal quadrant are more likely to be Democrats. This adds further evidence to the conclusion that theological liberals are more comfortable in the Democratic Party and theological conservatives are more at ease in the Republican Party.

Sixth, since Lyndon Johnson all presidents have either symbolically or substantively (or both) professed to be conservative theologically. This is at least a thread of evidence that strengthens the claim of ideological conservatives that there is a conservative resurgence in the nation. Another way to look at it is that from Nixon through Reagan, presidents have tended to go beyond the trappings of inoffensive civil religion to show the nation more clearly and dramatically their personal theological and religious convictions.

Seventh, the difficulty in placing Jimmy Carter also helps to reveal why he had difficulty governing. He made much use of theologically conservative symbols in capturing the Democratic nomination for president in 1976 and also in winning the office. Ironically the Democratic Party with a theologically liberal base in its platform and majority in Congress somewhat put President Carter in a vise between two irreconcilable points of view. He, a person of at least symbolically conservative theological convictions, had difficulty leading a party of definite liberal theological and ideological convictions.

Eighth, while conservative ideological and theological presidents dominated the presidency from Washington through Hoover, those of a liberal persuasion dominated from Franklin Roosevelt through Lyndon Johnson. This pattern conforms to the historical theological pattern as conservative theology dominated most of American history until the 1930s. Now after a period of liberal theological domination, there has been a conservative theological resurgence that at least to some extent is reflected among the presidents as our most recent presidents have made greater efforts to appear more conservative theologically, evidently in response to a latent arousal of grassroots theological conservatism.

GENERALS OR FOOTSOLDIERS

The evidence tends to suggest that presidents are not generals on the theological battlefield. In a democratic sense as elected officials, they generally respond more to public pressures on theological issues than they lead the public. Then too as individuals they tend not to have strong theological convictions. The political experience, if not the presidency itself, evidently has the effect of moderating strongly held theological convictions among presidents. In an effort not to be offensive, presidents usually identify with mainline churches and use inoffensive language often called the language of the "civil religion" that attracts, but does not alienate, a cross-section of the religious among the electorate.

Presidents are not immune, however, to theological pressures for a variety of reasons. For example, theologically based political movements, such as liberally oriented ones on the Vietnam War and the nuclear freeze issues and conservative ones on issues like ERA and abortion, force presidents to respond. Party platforms with theologically based planks may also substantially influence presidential leadership.

In theological warfare over public policy then, presidents are important figures on the battlefield, but in rank they are probably somewhere between generals and footsoldiers.

Saying Good-bye to a Nice Affair: Thoughts on the Iran-Contra Hearings

James Ceaser

From conception to term, the first phase of the Iran-Contra affair ran almost exactly nine months. During this gestation period, it claimed a larger share of media attention than any other subject, with the possible exception of AIDS. For its length and staying power, Iran-Contra is a strong candidate for inclusion among the major presidential affairs of this century, a surprising result in view of the many pundits who initially wrote it off as insignificant. It was an affair that, to borrow a phrase from presidential campaign politics, ran far better than expected.

For students of affairs and scandals, Iran-Contra has provided an abundance of material. Although scandology is still in its infancy, the discipline has made remarkable progress in delineating its subject matter. A presidential affair, scandologists now concur, can be defined as a blunder, impropriety, or illegality—or related series of the same—plus a possible cover-up, which is charged to the president or to high administration officials and which puts the presidency on the defensive in the eyes of the nation. Many would add that an affair must also unfold so that what occurred and why it occurred is not thought to be known in full. This opens the door to a lingering sense of suspicion and a steady stream of revelations (the so-called "dribble-out" effect).

A genuine affair, in other words, is best tasted and savored without being swallowed too quickly. It is for this reason that in applied scandology or affair management, those who manage the president's case are eager to appear to get all the facts out as quickly as possible. Those who oppose the president adopt a posture of scrupulous deliberateness, praising official disclosures but cautioning on the need for an open mind on the "many questions" yet to be studied. In this rhetorical joust between feigned candor and studied judiciousness, the advantage seems to lie with the president's opponents. The mere charge of "yet another" revelation works to the detriment of the executive by calling into question the very premise of candor. Indeed, no effective shield has yet been developed to defend against a sound strategy of attack. Once the momentum of an affair is under way, the best a president

---

James Ceaser, "Saying Good-bye to a Nice Affair: Thoughts on the Iran-Contra Hearings," *Public Opinion* 10, no. 3 (September/October 1987), 7–8, 55–56. Reprinted with permission of The American Enterprise Institute.

can hope for, other than a blunder by his accusers, is that, having made all the requisite gestures of contrition, his public spanking will be administered quickly.

A sound grasp of affair management skills is clearly at a premium today. Getting over affairs has become a vital part of contemporary politics, and the history of recent presidencies can be written in no small measure by how they have fared in dealing with affairs. Affairs are a modern parody of the institutional system of checks and balances. To the extent that a president's public standing is a measure of his power or authority, an affair successfully prosecuted is a weapon to weaken and erode that authority. The aim is not just to correct a specific evil, but to alter the political balance. Affairs are the stuff by which presidencies are made or broken.

THE SUPPLY SIDE

The study of any affair requires both a supply- and demand-side analysis. On the supply side, which deals with the blunder itself, an investigation of the Iran-Contra affair leaves a good deal of puzzlement about why it attained such robustness. To cite the alleged stupidity and incompetent execution of the Iran arms sale does not suffice, for there have been other presidential decisions, no better conceived or executed, that have escaped such rigorous condemnation. Nor is it evident that the alleged illegalities and irregularities of the NSC's Contra supply effort, of which the funds diversion was only a small part, could have provoked the crisis, for there have been other instances of illegalities and runaway operations without so dramatic an effect. Each foul-up by itself would thus seem to have lacked the punch to create this affair. The Iran arms sale, widely judged to be stupid, was not in the main illegal, while the Contra aid program, widely judged to be illegal, does not appear especially stupid. It was, then, the combination of the two blunders, with its peculiar marriage in the public mind of the stupid and the illegal, that gave this event its special force.

Many of the political paradoxes of this affair can be understood only by bearing in mind its strange parentage. Recall that for Ronald Reagan's traditional detractors, his principal sins had been inflexibility, a lack of compassion, and a harebrained disposition to employ military means, as in the attack on Libya. Had the late scandal been confined to the Iran arms deal, one might have expected Reagan's detractors at some point to have pulled their punches. They must have felt somewhat uneasy ridiculing an act born of compassion, or a little guilty for using the hostage families as pawns to embarrass the president, or at least reluctant to push the country to the right by making the president's softness their grounds for condemnation. Indeed, if someone had wanted to end the possibility of dealing with terrorists, no better strategy could have been devised than to sell arms to Iran and allow the story to be leaked.

It was the Contra aid dimension that freed Reagan's critics from any conflict and allowed them to follow their natural inclination to attack the administration's militarism and condemn the inherent evil of executive secrecy and discretion. By the same token, for some of the fervent friends of the president who might have been displeased with the Iran initiative, the Contra aid effort served as a rallying point, lending the passion of anti-Communism to their fight against the tag team of the media and Congress.

MAKING DEMANDS

No account of this affair is adequate, however, without also considering the demand side. The American political system, as many foreign observers have remarked, possesses a built-in capacity for generating affairs because of the existence of a coordinate body (Congress), fully as much the government as the president, that is capable of investigating administration policies. This capacity is energized when the two institutions are controlled by different parties, a condition that has now become the rule more than the exception. Even on the charitable assumption that the majority party in Congress operates without partisan motives, any partisan split still leaves the government without the normal instinct to protect itself from political damage or to handle embarrassing matters of state with a modicum of discretion and dispatch.

Demand is also bid up by the press, which reaches the zenith of its power during affairs. Still, it would be a mistake to think the press could exercise such power by itself, for to serve as the primary affair manager eventually stretches the media's supply lines too far. The press operates most effectively in cases where it has an official news story to cover in Congress and when its various revelations serve either to scout out targets for Congress to attack, or to mop up after a congressional assault has been made. Congressional procedures are clearly assisted by the media, and Congress, which enjoyed weeks of TV exposure during the hearings, is scarcely the public relations ingenue that many have supposed. Yet to label the alliance between Congress and the press a conspiracy, as many do today, is absurd. A conspiracy is something secret, whereas the press's debt to the separation of powers for its extraordinary influence in national politics is one of the most well-known facts about American government.

A STUDY GUIDE

The Iran-Contra affair "worked" on so many different levels in so many different ways that no one can hope to reconstruct—or deconstruct—all of its meanings. Still, it is important to develop concepts for analyzing this and other presidential affairs. Probably the greatest mistake is to view an affair statically as a single artifact; rather, it must be seen as a process—an evolving work added to and created at each step along the way. It is a kind of elementary school class mural fingerpainted by the power holders who struggle all the while for control of its artistic direction. The work is held together by a thematic thread on which are hung different scenes or episodes, each of which holds center stage for a brief moment. These scenes or episodes are as much a part of the affair as the affair itself.

Iran-Contra gave birth to scores of such episodes. Most were matters chiefly of interest to those in Washington. For example, there was the changing of the so-called "prime ministers"—from Don Regan to Howard Baker (Regan, much maligned in January, enjoyed a late-July comeback as an avuncular master of the one-liner). There was the bid of the State Department to use the affair to assert hegemony over the conduct of foreign policy (Shultz's version of "I'm in control here"). And there was the effort to implicate the Attorney General (the purest case of an affair within an affair).

The episode that clearly made the greatest public impression was the testimony of Lt. Colonel North, who burst on the scene like a meteor in a display so singular that it promises to keep students of public opinion occupied for many years. North's "hero for a week" status has been widely compared to the public's embrace of General MacArthur after he was fired by President Truman. But the cases are hardly parallel, for MacArthur had been a hero before his return from Korea, whereas North, if he had a reputation at all before the hearings, suffered from notoriety.

It in no way diminishes the virtuosity of North's performance to observe that the anti-administration affair managers had set the stage for his triumph by committing perhaps the only significant blunder they could have made: overplaying their hand. The strategy for the hearings had been to lead public opinion by the hand to reexperience the shocking details of the Iran-Contra decisions, with a vague hope of uncovering a smoking pistol along the way. North was to be the key "witness" in this script, the one to be brought in and layed low, with some congressional careers being advanced in the process. Indeed, North's testimony was so crucial to the hearings that this gave him, paradoxically, leverage to negotiate the conditions of his appearance before the committee (North refused to testify privately in advance). It was almost as if the committee had become hostage to its hostage.

Even for many who may have been dismayed at North's unusual activities and alarmed at what he, along with CIA Director William Casey, planned to put on his little shelf, there must have been a certain delight in seeing the committee's script unravel. Few, after all, could fail to remark on the spectacle of non-elected committee lawyers dressing down the non-elected lieutenant colonel while lecturing the American public on the authoritative meaning of the Constitution. Committee affairs managers found themselves suddenly confronted with a naughty public opinion that threatened to overwhelm the well-behaved public opinion they had been so assiduously cultivating. Yet to condemn this unwelcome invasion of mass sentiment was impossible. After all, it was not Colonel North who had made public opinion the "coin of the realm." North merely took this process to its exquisite extreme, piling up the currency of yellow telegrams in a display that might have been considered crass if it had not been so effective.

At the symbolic level, the rest of the hearings consisted of the effort of affair managers to cage runaway public opinion. Moral fables were spun of the stuff that makes a national hero, with many committee members scurrying to offer up their own *bona fides*. The final twist, for anyone still paying attention, was the hasty effort to build up George Shultz as an alternative role model and replacement hero. Shultz's tell-all frankness, which turned his testimony into a national T-group session, won widespread praise for courageousness, even as it made the administration look contemptible. Although President Reagan had kept Shultz and fired North, and although Shultz's story of what Reagan knew perfectly corroborated the president's version, it was no longer clear who exactly was helping whom. In this state of confusion, with Reagan's critics praising Shultz's integrity while doubting his account of what the president knew, and with Reagan's strongest supporters sniping at his best witness, it was clearly time to wind things up.

WHO'S IN CHARGE?

Is there in the hearings some deeper meaning and teaching that goes beyond the lessons of poor judgment and mismanagement learned after the Tower Commission report? Certainly many think so, for the hearings ended with solemn reminders of the Bicentennial of the Constitution and self-congratulatory declarations on the lessons of 1787.

Yet if Iran-Contra reached the celestial heights of a constitutional affair, it is not so clear what lessons have been learned. In fact the most unexpected result of the hearings is that they reopened an important constitutional debate on how foreign policy should be made. This result is unexpected because neither the legislative branch nor the executive branch approached the event intending to engage in a true debate. Most members of the committee saw the hearings as an occasion for vindicating interpretations of the Constitution represented in legislation like the Boland Amendment; and the administration, whatever its deepest thoughts, had no stomach for a constitutional fight, especially since its own performance had been so poor. Nevertheless the issue of the president's rightful role in foreign policy did emerge during the hearings, and this debate may carry over to the next presidential campaign.

For the majority on the committee, in a view that may be called the New Whigism, there is no constitutional limit to the use of the lawmaking power in the conduct of foreign affairs outside of interference with the few specific powers granted to the president. Congress's spending power, for example, can be used not just in its ordinary sense to control the assignment of funds or properties, but to curb the discretion of the president by limiting the activities of members of the executive branch in how they might use intelligence or conduct diplomatic matters. Such limitations are justified on the grounds that since salaries and expenses are paid from appropriated funds, all activities of these employees can be reached by law. The New Whigism is predicated on the idea that the Constitution intended all the major powers in the executive and legislative branches to be shared, with legislation determining in each instance the portions of the shares.

The other view, championed by Colonel Alexander Hamilton long before Colonel Oliver North, is that Article II, by vesting the president with the "executive power," gave a grant or claim to a broad discretion in the conduct of foreign affairs and latitude to act except where a power specifically given to or shared with Congress is involved. In this view, the use of the legislative powers to limit the president's discretion to direct his subordinates in their activities might be resisted by the president as an intrusion into his constitutional power. This power was granted by the Framers because they understood that in a dangerous world a discretionary authority to act in quick and unusual ways is essential to promote the nation's interest. The Constitution is based in the first instance on a separation of powers, after which certain specific powers, like the making of treaties, are shared. The existence of checks and balances results from the need to coordinate the will of separate powers to accomplish most broad policy objectives, as in following up a president's diplomatic initiative with legislation providing concrete aid. This is hardly the equivalent of making legislation the arbiter of the fundamental powers.

The final point involves how constitutional powers should be maintained. For many today, the Constitution is seen primarily as a legal document whose meaning is to be trusted to legal experts and decided by judges. Yet on the most fundamental constitutional questions in history, this has not been the case. The Constitution is not an ordinary statute, but a document that partitions powers among levels of governments and among institutions, giving each institution certain grants of power and certain instruments to use for the protection of those powers. The enforcement of the Constitution must rest in the first instance with the institutions themselves. If there is something that the hearings taught many complacent proponents of the president's power, it is that instead of just complaining about congressional intrusions, a president must be vigorous in protecting his constitutional authority, even if it means vetoing desired policies.

Where the two institutions cannot resolve their differences by the usual means, another forum may be needed. yet except in certain limited instances, that forum is not appropriately the Supreme Court. One of the greatest contemporary misunderstandings of our form of government is that which identifies the Constitution with constitutional law and which supposes that the only resolution of a constitutional question is a Supreme Court decision. In fact, the most important constitutional struggles are resolved politically by the American people exercising a constitutional judgment. In this sense the Iran-Contra hearings may have served a useful function, for they put Congress as well as the president on trial. A verdict has yet to be rendered.

On the Moral Standing of the President as an Interpreter of the Constitution: Some Reflections on Our Current "Crises"

Hadley Arkes, Amherst College

We know that the abuse of power may cause an erosion of authority, but I would suggest that the current "crisis" over Iran and the Contras confirms a notably different lesson: It is the erosion of authority, or the denial to the president of his rightful, constitutional powers, which has produced a stream of factitious crises. The "scandals" are generated by the prospect of an uncontained president, who is seeking to evade the restraints of the law, in

Hadley Arkes, "On the Moral Standing of the President as an Interpreter of the Constitution: Some Reflections on our Current 'Crises'," *PS* (Summer 1987), 637–642. Reprinted with permission of *PS*, American Political Science Association.

order to deploy the instruments of violence in foreign policy. But the president appears to be bent on a course of lawlessness, he seems persistently to be threatening a "constitutional crisis," only if one accepts the premise that these statutory restraints on the president are eminently reasonable and constitutional. If they are not, then there is no pattern of lawlessness on the part of the president, no scandal, no crisis.

One commentator has recently remarked that the War Powers Act and the Boland amendment have been parts of a design to "criminalize" differences in policy between Congress and the president.[1] A president who took seriously his responsibilities under the Constitution, or a president who sought to exercise the powers that his predecessors have routinely exercised, would be compelled to steer around these restrictions. When he does, he will be charged with putting himself "above the law." The opposition party, and its allies in the media, will express their outrage and declare the presence of another "scandal." There will be calls for a special prosecutor, for a select congressional committee to hold extended hearings—in short, the whole script and the stage directions for Watergate, called into play once again. We now have a part of the political class, in government and the media, who have made "deploring" into a vocation: Their main competence has been cultivated in the art of investigating and holding long, debilitating hearings, with the object of bringing down the Administration or rendering the government of the day ineffectual. This part of the political class is incapable itself of governing or managing a foreign policy. Their mission in our politics is to make it virtually impracticable to administer a serious foreign and military policy in the sense that was understood by the Founders: They are not prepared to say that the forces threatening this country from abroad are sufficiently grave that it may be necessary at times for an executive to act with secrecy and vigor—which is to say, without stopping to consult with a plural body of legislators and their staffs. They seem to find more danger in the power of the American president than in the power of the Soviet bloc. At any rate, they seem to suggest that the American regime would not be worth preserving if it could be preserved only by trusting an elected president to commit military forces, outside the supervision of Congress and the review of courts. But to say that is to say that an important faction in our current politics no longer accepts the understanding of the Founders about the nature of the executive and the place of the presidency within the American Constitution.

When the Lincoln Administration blockaded the Southern ports, Richard Henry Dana presented the brief for the government before the Supreme Court, and he took the occasion to remind the judges of this elemen-

[1]See Mark Helprin, "The Imperial Congress," *The Wall Street Journal*, April 9, 1987, p. 32 (editorial page).

tary point: "War is *a state of things,* and not an act of legislative will."[2] Adversaries are not always so decorous as to confront us with this "state of things" when Congress happens to be in session. It could hardly be supposed that the government would stand without any legal claim to defend the country until the Congress could be assembled. It made far more sense to suppose, with Lincoln and Dana, that the power to deploy the military and defend the nation could be exercised by the one branch of the government that is *never out of session,* never out of town. Years later, in the famous *Curtiss-Wright* case,[3] Justice Sutherland would point out that these powers to act in defense of the country were the "necessary concomitants of nationality"; they would exist in any national government: These powers were not strictly dependent on the Constitution, because they were older than the Constitution. As Sutherland remarked, "The Union existed before the Constitution."[4] These powers of defense existed before our current, or second Constitution; and they would exist quite apart from the form we imparted to our government with any new Constitution. As Sutherland went on to explain, these powers were never exercised by the states or the legislature; they were, at all times, solely in the hands of the executive. In this field, the president was not merely a ministerial officer, carrying out the policies of a sovereign Congress; he was, himself, a source of law. As Sutherland put it, in that highly quoted passage; the president exercised a "plenary and exclusive power...as the sole organ of the federal government in the field of international relations—a power which does not require as a basis for its exercise an act of Congress."[5]

Sutherland went on to explain that the courts must accord to the president, in this field, "a degree of discretion and freedom from statutory restriction which would not be admissible were domestic affairs alone involved." And so if it is legitimate to counter the menace of Libya by freezing Libyan assets or staging a resistance by American planes in the Gulf of Sidra, it seems to be understood that these moves could not achieve their effects if they had to be advertised in advance, placed on the calendar of Congress, and made the subject of extended hearings. As Chief Justice Taney once recognized, in one of those rare moments when he managed to get something right, certain kinds of acts must be carried out quickly and decisively if they are to be carried out at all. In these instances, he remarked, "the interposition of the [government] must be prompt, or it is of little value."[6] And the authority that is constituted to act in that way under the Constitution is, distinctly, the authority of the executive.

[2]*The Prize Cases,* 67 U.S. 635 (1862).

[3]*U.S. v. Curtiss-Wright Export Corp.,* 299 U.S. 304 (1936).

[4]*Ibid.,* at 317.

[5]*Ibid.,* at 320.

[6]See Taney in *Luther v. Borden,* 48 U.S. 1 (1849), at 44.

In any event, there seems to be little question today that the president may act, with a large measure of discretion, in moving planes and warships, without the approval of Congress, to forestall an attack on American ships in the Persian Gulf or on American bases in Beirut. Presumably, we would also concede the authority of the president to use techniques of electronic surveillance, as those devices were used in the summer of 1985 to trace the movement of the terrorists who had hijacked the Achille Lauro.

Let us suppose for a moment that, in gathering intelligence abroad, our government became aware of a connection, in Greece, between the PLO and the Sandinista regime in Nicaragua. What if the government took the steps that were aptly measured to break this connection and disrupt a project that may be hostile to our interests? Would a move of this kind have violated the Boland amendment because it would have fed, indirectly, into the politics of Nicaragua? The president was enjoined by that amendment from doing anything that would directly or indirectly support the Contras. Was this a mandate that any president could practicably have honored? The branch of government that is never out of session, the branch that receives our foreign and military intelligence in an ongoing way, can rarely blind itself to these webs of connection among our adversaries and our interests abroad. And if it would preserve the freedom it must preserve, in dealing with projects directed against us, it cannot be constrained by the kinds of formulas that Congress may produce in provisions like the Boland amendment. This effort on the part of Congress to "micromanage" our foreign policy must be doomed to futility. But it acquires a certain mischievous quality from the fact that the legislation itself serves to inspire the inventiveness of our adversaries: The Congress may seek to bind the executive to the Boland amendment, but it cannot bind the Sandinistas. When the Congress forbids the executive to resist the current regime in Nicaragua, it provides a respite that may be used to strengthen the hold of the regime, and it permits that government to turn more of its tools, and its peculiar genius, to the project of intimidating its neighbors. As Henry Kissinger recalled, his negotiations on Cambodia were brought to a virtual end in 1973 after Congress mandated a halt to the use of bombing in that country by the middle of the year: "At that point," wrote Kissinger, "certain of victory, the Khmer Rouge lost all interest in negotiations," and the American government lost whatever leverage it might have had to restore Prince Sihanouk.[7]

An earlier generation of jurists understood that the powers of the executive could be abused, and yet they recognized that power could be abused by legislators and judges; that certain kinds of crises could not be met with the procedures that governed legislatures and courts. But the willingness to

[7]See Kissinger, *The White House Years* (Boston: Little, Brown, 1979), p. 1415.

trust to the responsibility of the executive was rooted, also, in the recognition that the president is a *constitutional* officer of this government: He has an authority to reach judgments about constitutionality in shaping the course of his own decisions, and his commitment to the Constitution cannot be presumed to be any less faithful or earnest than the commitment of any judge.

And yet, our current crises have been deepened precisely because there is an unwillingness to recognize in the president a constitutional standing that was articulated by Jefferson, Jackson, and Lincoln: viz., that the president must have the authority to act, within his own sphere, as an interpreter of the Constitution, and his judgments need not always yield to the judgments of the courts. When President Reagan ordered the invasion of Grenada in 1983, Senator Gary Hart noted with alarm that Mr. Reagan did not accept the constitutionality of the War Powers Act of 1973. Senator Hart admonished the president that he was nevertheless bound to obey the law, until it could be "tested in the Supreme Court."[8] Apparently, for Senator Hart, the Supreme Court held an exclusive and preeminent authority in settling these questions of constitutionality, and the president could not claim the freedom to honor his own judgment that the law was unconstitutional.

Hart expressed here the orthodoxy that has become common in our own day, but it is quite at odds with the understanding held by Jackson, Lincoln, and the Founders. In fact, the understanding reflected in Hart has become so dominant in our own time that it might be hard for us to conceive just what the alternative might be. We might begin to get at the matter in this way: Let us suppose that the president were faced with an act of Congress that provided military conscription only for people of a minority race in this country. Would he be obliged to consider only the "utility" of this measure as he weighed the possibility of a veto? Would he be obliged to consider only whether the policy was likely to "work," or would he be bound also to consider whether the legislation was incompatible with the principles that underlie the American Constitution? To take that latter possibility seriously is to remind ourselves that the president must bear a responsibility, no less than that of any congressman or judge, to consider whether his acts are compatible with the principles of constitutionalism.

But what if the president reaches a judgment on this matter that is at odds with the judgment of the Supreme Court? This was precisely the case with Lincoln: It was part of the mission of Lincoln and his party to resist and overturn the decision brought forth by the Supreme Court in the case of *Dred*

[8]*Congressional Record*, October 28, 1983, S 14869.

Scott v. Sandford. In that infamous case, the Court "established" that blacks could not have the standing of citizens to sue in the courts, and that no man could be deprived of his property in slaves, even if he brought that property into territories in which slavery had been forbidden by Congress. Lincoln's position here was that he was willing to respect the process of law by respecting the disposition made by the Court in settling the fate of Dred Scott in *that* particular case. But he and his party would "oppose that decision as a political rule which shall be binding on the...members of Congress or the President to favor no measure that does not actually concur with the principles of that decision."[9]

To put it another way, Lincoln was willing to accept the judgment of the case as it bore on the conflict between two litigants. What he was not obliged to accept was the *principle* or the broader rule of law that the Court was trying to create in the case. And the Lincoln administration came to discover very early just how far the executive branch under President Buchanan had been willing to apply the principle of the *Dred Scott* decision. In two notable cases arising from Boston, a black student had been denied a passport to study in France and a black inventor had been denied a patent on a new invention. Since the court had decided, in *Dred Scott*, that blacks were not citizens, the local agents of the federal government now reasoned that blacks could not carry the passports of American citizens and they could not receive patents under the laws of the United States.[10] I would point out that the circumstances in these cases bore little resemblance to the situation described in *Dred Scott*. There was no one, in these cases, litigating over property in slaves or the authority of Congress to legislate for the territories of the United States. The cases revealed two agencies of the federal government, simply applying in their own spheres, even in cases quite removed from the circumstances of the *Dred Scott* case, a more general rule or principle which they thought had been articulated in that case.

The Lincoln administration reversed both decisions. The attorney general announced that the Administration would be guided by its own understanding: that free blacks born in the United States were citizens of the United States. And a year later Lincoln would sign new legislation that banned slavery from the territories of the United States, as the president affirmed, again, that in the decisions which came under his hand, he would

[9]*The Works of Abraham Lincoln*, ed. Roy P. Basler (New Brunswick, N.J.: Rutgers University Press, 1953), Vol. III, p. 255.

[10]The record of these cases can be found in *The Works of Charles Sumner* (Boston: Lee & Shepard, 1880), Vol. 5, pp. 497–98; Vol. 6, p. 144.

not be bound by the "principles" declared by the Supreme Court in a litigated case brought by two private parties.[11]

I would submit that these decisions of the Lincoln administration can be regarded as defensible only on the understanding that was held by Lincoln and the Founders about the separation of powers and the responsibility of each branch to interpret the Constitution. That is not the understanding held by former Senator Hart—the understanding that is critical today to the continuing crises and to the charge that our presidents have been putting themselves "above the law." But if we return for a moment to Senator Hart, we might notice an omission rather embarrassing to his argument. As Hart counseled the president to respect the law until it was tested before the Supreme Court, he seemed to overlook the fact that, four months earlier, in a major, sweeping decision, the Court had declared all varieties of the "legislative veto" to be unconstitutional. In one stroke, the Court had swept away an arrangement which had been incorporated in nearly 200 statutes, including, very notably, the War Powers Act. The design of the legislative veto was central to that Act, because it confirmed the initiative of the president in deploying troops, while leaving to the Congress the power to overturn the judgment of the president by withholding its assent. If the legislative veto was unconstitutional, then the War Powers Act had to come under the most serious constitutional doubt. And yet, none of that doubt was reflected in the commentary of Senator Hart. He introduced a resolution to invoke the War Powers Act in relation to Grenada, and so we would gather that he and his colleagues persisted in regarding that Act as constitutional, quite apart from the judgment of the Supreme Court in *Immigration and Naturalization Service v. Chadha.*[12]

Hart and his colleagues in the Senate were evidently unwilling to extend to the War Powers Act the objection that the Court had declared in principle to the legislative veto in all of its applications. Hart was apparently asserting the authority of the Congress to reach a judgment on the constitutionality of its own legislative acts quite apart from what the Court may have to say. Or, Hart preferred to confine the judgment of the Court to the problem of immigration that was dealt with in the *Chadha* case, rather than

[11]For a fuller treatment of this question, see Arkes, *First Things* (Princeton: Princeton University Press, 1986), pp. 418–22. Lincoln attended closely to the writings of John Marshall, and he had no reason to expect that the position he staked out here was inconsistent in any way with the understanding articulated by the Chief Justice in *Marbury v. Madison*. The misunderstanding has now become diffused, among lawyers and politicians, that the same case which established the authority of the Court to interpret the Constitution also established the Court as the *sole*, authoritative interpreter of the Constitution. But no claim of that kind is put forth in *Marbury v. Madison;* in fact, Marshall claimed nothing for the judges that could not have been claimed for any other officer of the government. Again, see Arkes, above, for a more extended discussion.

[12]77 L. Ed. 2d 317 (1983).

applying the broader principle of that judgment to matters as distant from that case as the engagement of the War Powers Act in Grenada.

But Hart could not take these positions, of course, without replicating precisely the understanding held by Lincoln about the authority of the president and Congress in interpreting the Constitution. That understanding worked, in this case, to support Mr. Reagan's position, and, in its final irony, to render vacuous the very argument that Hart was leveling against the president. With that move, Mr. Hart attained a position that was at least uncommon, if not entirely novel, in American public life: He had produced an argument whose very assertion stood as proof of its falsity.

We cannot pretend that the recent trend of our politics and law marks anything other than a serious reduction in the constitutional standing of the presidency. This reduction of the president has proceeded with the approval, by and large, of the press and the academy, and even large portions of our political class. Their cheerful acquiescence in this reduction arises from their moral rejection of the president's claims and the uses that have been made of the powers of the presidency in recent years. But it is a benign illusion that the president can continue to fulfill the description of the office contained in the Constitution—that he can continue to act, with unimpaired capacity, in preserving a constitutional government from its enemies, or in securing the conditions of domestic justice—that he can continue to do these things without the fuller reach of his moral claim as an officer, and an interpreter, of the Constitution. The melancholy question for us is whether a president stripped of that moral claim can be adequate to the ends of the presidency as they were understood by the Founders. But that is merely another way of asking whether the president, in this diminished state, can be adequate to the responsibilities that are preeminently his own and whether he is in a position any longer to fulfill the design of the American Constitution.

DISCUSSION QUESTIONS

1. The last presidential campaign had several candidates drop from the race because of what has been called the "character" factor. Should the past and present personal lives of candidates and their families be an issue in a presidential election?
2. What are the "religious land-mines" that the president must avoid today?
3. Does the president provide moral/ethical guidance to the nation as well as political guidance? Should he be expected to?
4. Do morality and religion influence too much or too little the exercise of presidential leadership?

4

BUREAUCRACY AND MORALITY

William D. Pederson

Although bureaucracy has come to mean delay, red tape, and pettiness in popular usage, a literal definition of the term is quite different. A bureaucracy is an organization with a large number of persons to achieve a goal. Rather than a negative image, professional administrators view it as the most rational type of organization to accomplish a task involving many people. On the other hand, Max Weber, the turn-of-the-century German social scientist (1864–1920) and "father of bureaucracy," initially considered it an ideal social system, but later worried about its possibilities as an "iron cage" for human beings.

Bureaucracy has four main characteristics: (1) a hierarchy with superior and inferior relationships; (2) a division of labor that encourages the need for specialists rather than generalists; (3) an emphasis on formal rules and records to accomplish tasks; and (4) impersonal decision making justified on the basis of maintaining fairness. These similar characteristics are found in large public (governmental) and private (corporate) organizations.[1]

Management approaches to bureaucracies are crucial to whether they develop pathological symptoms of aggressiveness, growth for growth's sake, and sheer "busy work." The traditional approach, known as "Theory X," stresses unequal relationships, excessive specialization and rules, as well as neutral decision making. Critics of this approach regard it as an effort to impose a narrow economic model on workers that encourages authoritarian managers and apathetic workers. Morality (or the lack of it) is imposed from the top.

"Theory Y" is the main alternative approach to large-scale organizations. Abraham H. Maslow developed a psychological model to motivation fundamentally different from the economic model in "Theory X." Maslow's "Theory Y" suggests that human beings have a set of innate needs (physiological, safety, socioaffectionate, esteem, and self-realization) that requires satisfaction before psychological health is possible. Organizations are likely to remain dysfunctional until these needs are satisfied. Fulfillment of them is likely to encourage empathy between employees and employers, rather than apathy or hostility. The self-actualization model tends to encourage democratic values and practices (openness, informality, and equality). Higher levels of morality are likely to increase as formal management tends to dissolve in the self-actualization model. Individuals become responsible for their actions.

Although "Washington fat-cat bureaucrats" are an easy target, most federal bureaucrats live outside Washington, D.C., in the fifty states. In fact, state and local bureaucracy has grown at a faster rate than the federal government. In proportion to employment, civilian governmental employees (federal, state, and local), amounted to only 15 percent of all nonfarm employees in 1960 and 17 percent by 1980.[2] Nonetheless, American government has tended to move from participatory to bureaucratic government regardless of level or function.[3]

The president is the manager of the largest bureaucracy in the country. There are three million civilian employees in the federal executive branch of government. The former Department of Health, Education and Welfare used to have a larger budget than any nation in the world except the Soviet Union and the United States. On the other hand, some multinational corporations rival the size of governmental units. In many cases, government lags behind. In response to executive branch expansion, the Congress has responded with an "iron law of emulation." There are now 17,000 employees on Capitol Hill. The judicial branch has shown administrative growth too.

The selections for this chapter illustrate the problems and issues confronting modern bureaucracy. The first, "The Prince and His Courtiers" by Russell Baker and Charles Peters, puts American bureaucracy in a cross-cultural and longitudinal context. The development of the White House staff into a bureaucracy over the past fifty years epitomizes the problems that political leaders have faced throughout history. Political and corporate leaders set the tone for their bureaucracies and how they are managed (or mismanaged).

The second selection, "But Albert Speer Was a Great Manager" by Paul Greenberg, expands on the background of one of the most "successful" bureaucrats of modern times. Albert Speer was Hitler's alter ego. Readers may find some disturbing parallels between Speer and the "moral neuters" involved in the Watergate and Gippergate (Iran-contra) affairs. Although the United States has never experienced a Holocaust, it did have "relocation centers" during World War II. One wonders what kind of bureaucrats might have emerged in the relocation centers for Japanese Americans, if American bureaucrats had been imbued with a revolutionary ideology as were their German counterparts. In other situations, the United States has produced some amazingly successful "public entrepreneurs" (for example, Hyman Rickover, J. Edgar Hoover, and Robert Moses), whose bureaucratic empires rivaled elected officials.[4]

The third selection, "Justice, Texas Style" by David Maraniss, concerns the phenomenon of the maverick in modern organizations. William Wayne Justice is a federal district judge in east Texas who has sometimes been referred to as "the real governor of Texas." At the cost of local ostracism, he has used his judicial position to bring Texas up to national standards in the areas of school integration, juvenile justice, and prison reform. His judicial activism requires the largest number of law clerks working for a federal district judge in the United States. His changing moral convictions reminds one of the changes of Earl Warren who once interned Japanese American citizens and later led a judicial revolution on the U.S. Supreme Court, as well as his colleague Hugo L. Black who once belonged to the Ku Klux Klan and later became a champion of the Bill of Rights.

The fourth selection, "Morality and Education" from *Manas,* returns to the classical concern for justice. Despite enormous pressures to conform in modern organizations, some individuals resist the "banality of evil." Lawrence Kohlberg's stage theory of morality is presented in the article as a possible explanation for differences in morality. Questions of morality and conviction are likely to become even more frequent as long as modern life remains on a bureaucratic path.

NOTES

1. William D. Pederson, "Bureaucracy," in Archie P. MacDonald, ed., *Encyclopedia USA,* vol. 8 (Gulf Breeze, Fla." Academic International Press, 1986), pp. 68–71.
2. David Nachmias and David H. Rosenbloom, *Bureaucratic Government USA* (New York: St. Martin's Press, 1980).
3. John E. Schwarz, *America's Hidden Success* (New York: W.W. Norton and Co., 1983), pp. 97–98.
4. Eugene Lewis, *Public Entrepreneurship: Toward a Theory of Bureaucratic Political Power* (Bloomington: Indiana University Press, 1980).

The Prince and His Courtiers: At the White House, the Kremlin, and the Reichschancellery

Russell Baker and Charles Peters

The analogy between the modern presidency and the royal European court, bewigged, bejeweled, and beset with intrigue, is not original with George Reedy, but he is the first to alarm us with notice that court government is undergoing a 20th-century rebirth in the White House. This renaissance of the princely court, Reedy insists, is breeding immense danger for American government, for much the same reason that the 17th- and 18th-century courts of Western Europe contributed to the development of violent revolutions.

In both France and England, our immediate political forebears, kings lost their heads because they had become unable to sense or hear the intent and passion of their peoples through the barriers of courts erected to glorify and, ironically, to protect them. Reedy suggests that the presidency is in somewhat the same danger, and for essentially the same reasons.

The president, needing "access to reality" in order to govern effectively, too often has access, instead, only to a self-serving court of flunkeys, knights, earls, and dukes in business suits, whose best chances of advancing their separate fortunes usually lie in diverting reality before it can reach the president. The result is a dangerous presidential isolation, which may be compounded in its peril because court life works to persuade the president that he is more closely in touch with reality than anyone else in the realm.

Thus, we had those repeated assertions from Lyndon Johnson that only the president had all the facts on which to base decisions about Vietnam, when in truth he lacked the first fact that was most essential of all for a leader and easiest to learn outside the White House court: to wit, that his people were not behind him as he waded deeper and deeper into the quagmire. This isolation from reality kept Lyndon Johnson and Richard Nixon obsessed with Southeast Asia as a prime problem of government at a time when very few among the people could sustain more than a flickering interest in it, and then only when aroused by White House theatrics.

Russell Baker and Charles Peters, "The Prince and His Courtiers: At the White House, the Kremlin, and the Reichschancellery," *Washington Monthly* 4 (February 1973), 30–39.

Reedy suggests that the presidency may be confronted, if not with the headsman or guillotinist, with an institutional arteriosclerosis no less fatal at a time when the interests of government seem increasingly alien to the interests of the governed.

When Reedy's book was first published, its importance as a work of political science was discounted by some reviewers on grounds that Reedy, as a member of the Johnson staff, had based his treatise on a singularly peculiar presidency, one in which parallels to the Sun King were ludicrously easy to draw.

Reedy's discussion of courtiers insulating the president against reality was taken by many readers as sour grapes, a subtle intellectual's way of taking his vengeance upon the cleverer players of the court game who had eased him into retirement. John Roche, who stayed with President Johnson's staff to the end, refers with mild contempt to the notion that presidential staff aides can seriously be likened to royal courtiers.

Members of the Kennedy circle—that strange, apparently indissoluble court in search of a king—contend that Johnson was, of course, susceptible to royal isolation by slick courtiers. But not their man, not Jack. The court analogy had no validity when applied to a president of superior competence.

And yet.... And yet....

There were signs, not altogether superficial, that the development of something remarkably like court life had been rapidly accelerating at the White House since the arrival of Franklin Roosevelt. With Roosevelt, the presidency—for reasons not too difficult to understand in an era that was dotting the rest of the earth with strutting Caesars—entered a period of apotheosis. There had been strong presidents before, but now we were embarked on the time of the strong presidency, a time which is still with us.

THE TRAPPINGS OF COURT

In sheer body density alone, the insulation around the presidency has thickened rapidly. Herbert Hoover had a staff of only 42 persons. A generation later, General Eisenhower, who prided himself on taut administration, had more than 2,000. Under Kennedy and Johnson, foreign-policy management groups were moved into the White House, and institutional divisions between domestic- and foreign-policy barons began to develop. In the Nixon White House, an expanding foreign policy dukedom was established under Henry Kissinger with a staff of his own moving in independent orbit around Kissinger, who simultaneously maintains a great-lord's orbit around the president in the larger White House universe.

The trappings of court began, simultaneously, to multiply. The custom-built carriages, magnificently engineered automobiles built expressly for the White House. Great ocean-spanning jets kept constantly at the ready. Special helicopters. Presidential appearances were preceded and surrounded by the inevitable, ineffectual showing of the private presidential bodyguard. Security at the White House thickened. First, there were the gates through which ordinary mortals might not step. Inside, the lobbies swarmed with hangers-on, most especially the press, waiting for some emanation to filter out from the ruler burrowed deep behind offices occupied by gentlemen of ascending importance. The elite might have entree to the Oval Room, equivalent of the Royal Bedchamber. For the sub-elite there were certain Presence Chambers where the Presidential Magnificence might be seen in the flesh, might indeed grant the boon of a smile, of a casual "Hi, there!" to the fortunate. And there was the White House Mess, where the etiquette of who might eat at what table was of an intricacy that would surely have bemused Louis XIV.

American fears of monarchy at the head of government are familiar to schoolboys—the debate at the beginning about how the leader of the new country should be styled, the fears of the more republican founders that the president might develop into a king and that the seat of government might develop into a court.

These fears survived from memories of the abuses of the English court of the 17th and 18th centuries, at which people and Parliament were frequently dealt with according to the advice of some royal favorite, whose grasp of statecraft ended with a mastery of sycophancy. The most notoriously inept of the courtiers whimsically given power by kings was perhaps the Duke of Buckingham, who seems to have bewitched King James I with his male beauty and skills at flattery and royal companionship. Buckingham survived James to continue incompetent government into the reign of King Charles I. When Buckingham was eventually murdered, all England lit bonfires to honor his murderer. The experience of such government, repeated in differing degrees in the reigns of Charles II and James II and later under the Hanovers, was part of the intellectual heritage of the men who founded the Republic. Hence, the distaste for courts.

Reedy's thesis holds that the time the Founders feared may have arrived at last, unnoted under all the mock-serious political uproar about kings, tyrants, and courtiers that has been part of the currency of political campaigning throughout American history. Reedy, in fact, gives us a full-length portrait of the courtier's life at the modern presidential court.

And what is a courtier's life like at the White House? Why, surprising to tell, not terribly different from court life at the Reichschancellery in the reign of Adolf Hitler, where a courtier's life was surprisingly like life in the Kremlin, at the court of Josef Stalin.

SERVILITY BECOMES ENDEMIC

By an extraordinary publishing coincidence, Reedy's memoir appeared in the same year (1970) that Albert Speer and Nikita Khrushchev gave us their memoirs of life at the top in Germany and Russia.* Neither the Speer nor Khrushchev book concerns itself consciously with court life under Hitler and Stalin; yet, when they are read in context with Reedy, we are startled to discover that the styles of government being described by all three are remarkably alike.

At each court, for example, we find the leader, or prince, treated with a deference approaching reverence, which must inevitably tempt all but the humblest souls (who are rarely to be found running large aggressive states) to assume they possess a superiority bordering on divinity. In time, the man treated with such distinction begins to expect it as his due. The sycophantic Buckingham repeatedly signed his notes to the king, "Your faithful slave and dog," and James seems never to have told him that a friend's groveling was embarrassing to the king. Jack Valenti, who knew his man as well as anyone in Washington, knew that Lyndon Johnson would not bridle if Valenti told the world he slept better for knowing Johnson was in the White House. Princes, whether monarchist, fascist, communist, or democratic, become accustomed to feeling like very special people.

Reedy writes of the White House:

> There is built into the presidency a series of devices that tend to remove the occupant of the Oval Room from all of the forces which require most men to rub up against the hard facts of life on a daily basis. The life of the White House is the life of a court. It is a structure designed for one purpose and one purpose only—to serve the material needs and the desires of a single man....
>
> He is treated with all the reverence due a monarch. No one interrupts presidential contemplation for anything less than a major catastrophe somewhere on the globe. No one speaks to him unless spoken to first. No one ever invites him to "go soak your head" when his demands become petulant and unreasonable.

Speer found a similar condition under Hitler. He writes:

> There is a special trap for every holder of power....His favor is so desirable to his subordinates that they will sue for it by every means possible. Servility be-

**The Twilight of the Presidency* by George E. Reedy—World Publishing, 197 pages. *Inside the Third Reich*, Memoirs by Albert Speer—The Macmillan Company, 675 pages. *Khrushchev Remembers*, translated and edited by Strobe Talbott—Little, Brown and Company, 618 pages.

comes endemic among his entourage, who compete among themselves in their show of devotion. This exercises a sway over the ruler who becomes corrupted in turn.

And in Moscow, at about the same time Speer and colleagues were competing to persuade the Fuehrer of his surpassing excellence, Khrushchev and comrades in Moscow were busily laboring to show Stalin that there was no duty more vital for them than humoring his whims. At the end of a brutally exhausting day, Khrushchev recalls:

> We would meet either in his study at the Kremlin or, more often, in the Kremlin movie theater. Stalin used to select the movies himself.... When a movie ended, Stalin would suggest, "Well, let's go get something to eat, why don't we?" By now it was usually one or two o'clock in the morning. It was time to go to bed.... But everyone would say, yes, he was hungry, too. This lie was like a reflex. We would all get into our cars and drive to the dacha.

UNCOMFORTABLE TRUTHS

The prince, having become accustomed through the assurances of the courtiers to the sensation of being an extraordinary human being, becomes more difficult to deal with at certain times. One such time is the moment when an uncomfortable truth is delivered at the palace door. A courtier's first instinct is to protect the prince, and there are rationalizations for doing so in the unwritten court protocols, as Reedy notes:

> It is felt that this man is grappling with problems of such tremendous consequence that every effort must be made to relieve him of the irritations that vex the average citizen.

It vexes the average citizen, fully aware of his own incompetence, to be forced to dwell upon the fact that in life, things frequently don't work out. Imagine, then, the difficulty of having to confront a prince, conditioned to believe in his peculiarly excellent superiority, with the fact that his policy is failing. There must be many of Lyndon Johnson's dukes and earls who, remembering the Vietnam years, would find it possible to sympathize with Hermann Goering's lines in an anecdote by Speer.

About to board his train to leave Berlin, Goering was visited by General Adolf Galland. Goering took the occasion to reprimand Galland for having told Hitler that American fighter planes had penetrated German territory. Galland said they would soon be flying even deeper into Germany. "Fantasies!" Goering said. Galland said American fighters had already been shot down at Aachen. "Impossible!" said Goering. And yet, Galland insisted, the downed planes were at Aachen.

> Goering finally declared: "What must have happened is that they were shot down much farther to the west. I mean, if they were very high when they were shot down they could have glided quite a distance farther before they crashed."
> Not a muscle moved in Galland's face. "Glided to the east, sir? If my plane were shot up...."
> "Now then, Herr Galland," Goering fulminated, trying to put an end to the debate, "I officially assert that the American fighter planes did not reach Aachen."
> The General ventured a last statement. "But, sir, they were there!"
> At this point Goering's self-control gave way. "I herewith give you an official order that they weren't there! Do you understand? The American fighters were not there! Get that! I intend to report that to the Fuehrer."

It can't happen here? After the Sontay raid failed to discover a single American prisoner of war, much less rescue one, Secretary of Defense Laird went to the White House. What was this? A failure? Not at all, Laird explained. It had been a triumph for American intelligence.

Communism occasionally has the bad news problem, too; and apparently deals with it just as fascists and democrats do.

Khrushchev tells a story that had been told to him by Mikoyan. Demchenko, a member of the Ukrainian Politburo, called on Mikoyan in Moscow.

> Here's what Demchenko said: "Anastas Ivanovich, does Comrade Stalin—for that matter, does anyone in the Politburo—know what's happening in the Ukraine? A train recently pulled into Kiev loaded with corpses of people who had starved to death. It had picked up corpses all the way from Poltava to Kiev. I think somebody had better inform Stalin about this situation."
> You can see what an abnormal state of affairs had developed when someone like Demchenko, a member of the Ukrainian Politboro, was afraid to go see Stalin himself.

Actually, according to the evidence of our three memoirists, it wasn't abnormal at all. Rather than disturb the prince by becoming the delivery agent for bad news, and thus perhaps lose favor, the courtier elects to withhold from him information essential to realistic policy decisions. Or, to put it more bluntly, his own interests are placed above the interests of the prince and the state he professes to serve.

Experienced courtsmen may find it naive that anyone should expect them to behave otherwise. The rationale has been finely worked out; it has been articulated many times by men explaining why they chose not to voice their dissent from the Johnson war policy. Open dissent ends one's chance to exercise his benign influence within the government, and creates job openings to be filled by less high-minded men. In brief, he who runs away shall live to run away another day.

THE KEYS TO THE KINGDOM

Reedy, Khrushchev, and Speer give us comparable pictures of the advancing corruption created in the courtiers by their impulse to establish and protect their intimacy with the leader.

The White House assistants, writes Reedy, constitute "the greatest of all barriers to presidential access to reality." For them:

> ...there is only one fixed goal in life. It is somehow to gain and maintain access to the President. This is a process which resembles nothing else known in the world except possibly the Japanese game of *go,* a contest in which there are very few fixed rules and the playing consists of laying down alternating counters in patterns that permit flexibility but seek to deny that flexibility to the opponent. The success of the player depends upon the whim of the President. Consequently, the President's psychology is studied minutely, and a working day in the White House is marked by innumerable probes to determine which routes to the Oval Room are open and which end in a blind alley.

This world sounds remarkably like the court of King James I, at which the Catholic faction, finding the King between favorites and knowing his weakness for handsome young men, kept thrusting a lovely young man of their choosing across the King's path, in hopes of obtaining the keys to the kingdom.

In Johnson's White House, the technique at least must have been rather duller. The basic method, Reedy reports, was "to be present either personally or by a proxy piece of paper when 'good news' arrives and to be certain that someone else is present when the news is bad."

Speer found precisely the same principle at work around Hitler. Writing of Martin Bormann, his *bête noire,* he states:

> Bormann followed the simple principle of always remaining in closest proximity to the source of all grace and favor. He accompanied Hitler to the Berghof and on trips, and in the Chancellery never left his side until Hitler went to bed in the early morning hours....
>
> The powerful men under Hitler were already jealously watching one another like so many pretenders to the throne. Quite early there were struggles for position among Goebbels, Goering, Rosenberg, Ley, Himmler, Ribbentrop, and Hess.... But none of them recognized a threat in the shape of trusty Borman. He had succeeded in representing himself as insignificant while imperceptibly building up his bastions.

"To be close to Stalin," Khurshchev remembers, "this seemed to be the crowning moment of my career."

And elsewhere, "I believed that everything Stalin said in the name of the party was inspired by genius, and that I had only to apply it to my own life." As this comment suggests, the courtier may, at some early stage in the relationship, develop such a psychological identity with his particular prince that he will abandon his own judgment and, like a lover, submerge his identity in that of the prince. The sweet delirium of ecstasy is produced when the prince returns the worship with some small gesture of recognition.

"For me to speak with the idol of a nation," writes Speer, "to discuss building plans with him, sit beside him in the theater, or eat ravioli with him in the Osteria" was simply "overwhelming."

"Now I was completely under Hitler's spell, unreservedly and unthinkingly held by him. I was ready to follow him anywhere."

On occasion, when Speer would greet Hitler with, "Heil, Mein Fuehrer!" Hitler would reply with, "Heil, Speer!" At such moments, Speer recalls, he felt "as if a medal had been conferred upon me.... All the intrigues and struggles for power were directed toward eliciting such a word, or what it stood for."

YES MR. PRESIDENT, I AGREE

Receiving the recognition and approval of the leader becomes a pleasure so powerful that the strongest of courtiers find it difficult to deny themselves. The empty-headed thrills which the younger Khrushchev and Speer derived from the notice of their leaders may be dismissed as the natural response of innocence in the presence of a celebrity. But what are we to make of the account of a National Security Council meeting under Lyndon Johnson, as recounted by Chester Cooper in *The Lost Crusade?* Cooper writes:

> The President, in due course, would announce his decision and then poll everyone in the room—Council members, their assistants, and members of the White House and NSC staffs. "Mr. Secretary, do you agree with the decision?" "Yes, Mr. President." "Mr. X, do you agree?" "I agree, Mr. President." During the process I would frequently fall into a Walter Mitty-like fantasy: When my turn came I would rise to my feet slowly, look around the room and then directly at the President, and say very quietly and emphatically, "Mr. President, gentlemen, I most definitely do *not* agree." But I was removed from my trance when I heard the President's voice saying, "Mr. Cooper, do you agree?" And out would come a "Yes, Mr. President, I agree."

The courtier's need to please his leader often has disastrous consequences for the people on the other end of royal decisions. When the Russians surrounded Hitler's Sixth Army at Stalingrad, at a critical moment in World War II, a black reality began to threaten the Fuehrer's notion that the Wehrmacht could not be defeated. At the timed suggestion of a general, he was even considering an effort to save the Army by breaking out into a retreat until Reichsmarshal Goering entered the room:

> Depressed, with a beseeching note in his voice, Hitler asked him: "What about supplying Stalingrad by air?" Goering snapped to attention and declared solemnly: "My leader! I personally guarantee the supplying of Stalingrad by air. You can rely on that."

His delusion of invincibility thus restored, Hitler would hear no more talk of retreat. He ordered the Sixth Army to stay and fight it out in Stalingrad, where it slowly faced extinction when Goering's promise proved totally fabricated—as everyone on the General Staff knew it would. Finally, a group of generals persuaded Chief of Staff Keitel to recommend to Hitler an evacuation of the Army's helpless survivors. It was the only sane thing to do, and Keitel promised that he would. The courtier's instinct, however, overwhelmed him at the critical moment, as Speer recounts:

> But at the situation conference, when Hitler once again stressed the necessity of holding out in Stalingrad, Keitel strode emotionally toward him, pointed to the map, where a small remnant of the city was surrounded by thick red rings, and declared: "Mein Fuehrer, we will hold that!"

It is enough to make one sympathize with a tyrant, for the determination of his courtiers to deceive him for their own personal ends—if he is aware of it—confronts him with problems as baffling as those posed by an enemy state's diplomacy.

Rarely is combat among the courtiers pursued to much political purpose in these 20th-century courts. Old scores are settled. There is intrigue, jealousy. One may win prerogatives that can be gloated upon. There is the satisfaction of public recognition, of being written about with awe in the press, and other small chaff. On great issues, however, the court is rarely a court in the Elizabethan sense, but rather more like that self-applauding cheering section which modern American politicians like to call a "team." Members are permitted to work out personal rivalries behind the arras, but on issues of substance every man must shape up, and work with the team.

With court struggle fought out along petty personal lines, the courtiers are inevitably reduced to demeaning little maneuvers to protect their backs, while working into good knife position vis-à-vis their immediate opponents.

Bormann, Speer recalls, avoided long business trips and vacations for fear another would insinuate himself during the absence into Bormann's place. "The man with the hedge clippers," Speer calls Bormann. "He was forever using all his energy, cunning, and brutality to prevent anyone from rising above a certain level."

Speer himself was not without skill at the struggle. Hitler often explained the elimination of important men on grounds that they were in ill health. Politicians, therefore, "pricked up their ears" when they heard of Hitler's associates being "sick." And so, to keep his profile discreetly low,

Speer, even when he became "really sick," deemed it "advisable to remain as active as possible."

Khrushchev, referring to personal competition for favor in the Kremlin, describes Stalin's men as "tearing at each other's throats." Indeed, as his version of the Beria story reveals, Khrushchev himself, by the time of Stalin's death, had become superbly adept at tearing throats.

"The life of a courtier," Reedy comments, "is to be Sammy Glick or to fight Sammy Glick."

KENNEDY AND O'DONNELL

This composite portrait of the new courts which seem to flourish around great political power in our century explains a great deal about why things go wrong in modern governments. The court imbues the prince with both religious and nationalistic characteristics that make him a figure of awe. ("I support the president," Americans will say, on most issues in which they have no immediate financial or blood interest. It is closely akin to saying, "I support the flag.")

The courtiers tend to identify the prince with the state. ("What is good for Josef Stalin is good for the Soviet Union," to paraphrase the young Khrushchev in American.) To help the state, the courtier must reach a position of intimacy with the prince, and to do this he must block or eliminate other courtiers moving toward the same goal. Above all, he must please the prince. And a prince who has been conditioned to consider himself a quasi-divine blend of flag, cause, and country is most unlikely to be pleased at being exposed too frequently to reality.

The danger becomes obvious, and Reedy has stated it. Our leaders, whatever their ideology, may very possibly be out of touch with the world that the rest of us live in. That hostile grille fence which keeps us away from the White House has two sides. The other seals off the president from the country he thinks he is governing.

As all this suggests, the courtier-prince relationship is almost inevitably corrupting to both parties. Consider the relationship of John Kennedy and one of his finest courtiers, Kenneth O'Donnell. In his memoirs published (last year) in *Life*, O'Donnell stated that Kennedy planned in 1963 to end the Vietnam war in 1965, after his reelection had been assured. O'Donnell, with his courtier's tendency to identify prince with state and place the welfare of ruler above all, saw nothing morally wrong, and to this day apparently fails to see anything out of order, with Kennedy's willingness to let men continue dying through 1963 and 1964 because it was politically awkward to end the war before assuring his own reelection.

What motivates the courtier? Money has something to do with it. Throughout history, the non-rich have tended to seek the patronage and protection of the rich. But money is far from the whole story. Another factor is the need to function, the opportunity the courtier gets to use his talents, to prove his mastery of special skills. Men wielding the pen or the brush naturally gravitate to the castle. Italian artists, for example, were given liberal use of church walls and domes to turn their talents to issues of ethereal importance in return for ignoring the rapacity and decadence of the princes who gave them their chance. Likewise, Albert Speer was able to blur away Hitler's final solution for the Jews as he focused on his own job performance. "I often ask myself what I would have done if I had recognized Hitler's real face and the true nature of the regime he had established," Speer said. "The answer was...my position as Hitler's architect had become indispensable....I was in accord with the system so long as it permitted me to function effectively."

But the need to function is not the whole story, either. Note that Speer did not say "my position as architect," but rather, "my position as *Hitler's* architect" (our emphasis). This is finally what is most depressing of all: the compulsion of men to seek their identities in the gaudier identity of someone they perceive to be greater than they. It is the religious impulse perverted so that one's allegiance is to LBJ rather than to an idea of what the president should be.

THE PRINCE-SUBSTITUTE

Of course, most of us do not have a real prince to have faith in. We have evolved something like a prince-substitute, however, in the governmental and corporate bureaucracies; the universities, organized labor, foundations, with which so many of us are so unhappily familiar. Here we see working most of the same principles which animate life at the great political courts. Speer's willingness to overlook Hitler's mass murders as irrelevant to his specialty is similar to Khrushchev's position on Stalin's purges, as Khrushchev recalls:

> A list was put together of the people who should be exiled from the city. I don't know where these people were sent. I never asked. If you weren't told something, that meant it didn't concern you.

And although these examples are perhaps more dramatic, the attitudes are identical to those of today's corporate specialist—say the advertising men at General Motors, who didn't feel responsible for the unsafe cars produced by their company. Modern institutions remind us in other ways of the court—the elevation of the organization to suprahuman importance, the minuet of the courtiers, the increasing difficulty of perceiving reality.

The universities, for example, are still puzzled about "what the kids really want." AT&T is still trying to figure out why it didn't anticipate a rising demand for phone service in New York. Penn Central executives are still amazed that there was no one around the office who knew how to run a railroad. The unions are irritated because blacks excluded from jobs by union policy accuse them of racism. And so on, and on, and on. The organization man has already become the characteristic man of our time, the man who shapes our destiny after the princes have finished reciting their ghost-written (by organization men) speeches.

A prophetic article in *The Observer* of London, written about Speer in 1944, is worth recalling, for what it says about our own time.

> Speer is, in a sense, more important for Germany than Hitler, Himmler, Goering, Goebbels, or the generals. They all have, in a way, become the mere auxiliaries of the man who actually directs the giant power machine—charged with drawing from it the maximum effort under maximum strain....In him is the very epitome of the "managerial revolution."
>
> Speer is not one of the flamboyant and picturesque Nazis. Whether he has any other than conventional political opinions at all is unknown. He might have joined any other political party which gave him a job and a career. He is very much the successful average man, well dressed, civil, noncorrupt, very middle class in his style of life, with a wife and six children....[He] symbolizes a type which is becoming increasingly important in all belligerent countries: the pure technician, the classless bright young man without background, with no other original aim than to make his way in the world and no other means than his technical and managerial ability. It is the lack of psychological and spiritual ballast and the ease with which he handles the terrifying technical and organizational machinery of our age, which makes this slight type go extremely far nowadays....This is their age; the Hitlers and Himmlers we may get rid of, but the Speers, whatever happens to this particular special man, will long be with us.

And so they are, the new courtiers, rising at their most efficient to heights where they seem very close to becoming the organization, but never quite. One day, we are surprised that the organization has sloughed off one brilliant young man and found another immediately to replace him.

In a thousand conference rooms, where the smell of moral sterility is as strong as ether in a hospital corridor, the new courtiers do their minuet each day and the organizations slip further and further from reality.

> How many of us [Reedy asks] have sat without protest through meetings where glorified nonentities expounded profound platitudes in the non-thought and the "innovative" non-proposal? How many of us have writhed in secret agony while "dedicated" mediocrities have responded with the organization man's

> version of Alleluia: "That grabs me. Run it up the flagpole and I'll salute it"?
> These obscenities have become the condition of life in the modern world—in business, in labor, in liberal and conservative organizations, in publishing, in education, and even in our churches. And when they reach government, where decisions are life and death for hundreds of millions of people, they reach the ultimate of the intolerable....
> Somehow this thing must be made human again. Somehow we must learn to govern our people from an office that is secular and not from a court that is sanctified. If our destruction comes, it will be because we placed our faith—our unquestioning faith—in institutions that were only brick and wood and in men who were only flesh and blood and this seems to be the condition of the last half of the twentieth century.

Speer's personal lament may already apply to thousands who have never dreamed of Nazism and serve as epitaph for generations to come. "Years later, in Spandau," he writes, "I read Ernst Cassirer's comment on the men who of their own accord threw away man's highest privilege: to be an autonomous person.

"Now I was one of them."

But Albert Speer Was a Great Manager

Paul Greenberg

ALBERT SPEER was the most educated and civilized, the most articulate and interesting, and in his judgments and writings perhaps the fairest of the Nazi war criminals tried at Nuremberg. If one could understand Albert Speer, one might be able to understand the tragedy of modern Germany. Most nations have produced their demagogues and demons, their Hitlers and Himmlers, but how explain why, in the Germany of this century, the "decent" people, the supposedly educated and civilized, not only followed their demons, but aided and abetted them? Yes, to understand Albert Speer would be to understand modern Germany.

But how understand Herr Speer? Here was an administrative genius, a wizard at production who seemed indifferent much of the time to how those products would be used. He was, in the phrase of British historian H. R. Trevor-Roper, a "moral neuter." He went from being Adolph Hitler's per-

---

Paul Greenberg, "But Albert Speer Was a Great Manager," *Shreveport Journal*, 12 September 1981. Reprinted with permission of Paul Greenberg.

sonal architect to minister of armaments and then of the whole German war economy—without betraying any sign of the fanatic. He stood out in Hitler's coterie like a calm executive in a menagerie of zealots.

In the midst of the war, the *London Observer* produced a profile of Albert Speer that may still be the best description of his type, and why it is so important to understand it:

"Speer is, in a sense, more important for Germany today than Hitler, Himmler, Georing, Goebbels, or the generals. They all have, in a way, become the mere auxiliaries of the man who actually directs the giant power machine—charged with drawing from it the maximum effort under maximum strain...In him is the very epitome of the 'managerial revolution.'

"Speer is not one of the flamboyant and picturesque Nazis. Whether he has any other than conventional political opinions at all is unknown. He might have joined any other political party which gave him a job and a career. He is very much the successful average man, well dressed, civil, noncorrupt, very middle-class in his style of life, with a wife and six children. Much less than any of the other German leaders does he stand for anything particularly German or particularly Nazi. He rather symbolizes a type which is becoming increasingly important in all belligerent countries: the pure technician, the classless bright young man without background, with no other original aim than to make his way in the world and no other means than his technical and managerial ability. It is the lack of psychological and spiritual ballast, and the ease with which he handles the terrifying technical and organizational machinery of our age, which makes this slight type go extremely far nowadays....This is their age; the Hitlers and Himmlers we may get rid of, but the Speers, whatever happens to this particular special man, will long be with us."

Albert Speer made a point of jokingly showing Hitler a translation of the article in the *Observer* before any of his rivals in that mad court could present it as evidence of his un-Nazi demeanor. Der Fuehrer read it all the way through, then handed it back, according to Albert Speer, with great respect. It was the tribute to one generation of the Nazi revolution to the next, the tribute of ideologue to technocrat. Hitler might as well have handed over a fistful of ashes, for that is all that would remain of the New Germany he and his architect were going to construct together.

Albert Speer should have suspected as much from Der Fuehrer's taste in architecture; his boss always wanted young Speer to design buildings that would make magnificent ruins. That was the essence of Hitler's idea of architecture. The ruins came soon enough; the thousand-year Reich lasted little more than a decade.

How did Albert Speer get suckered? How did he sucker himself? Why did he join the Nazi Party almost frivolously, on a whim, without studying party programs or political questions? He would never have approved an ordinary blueprint so casually. Later, he would be given 20 years to think on the question. And in his memoirs, he would conclude:

"As an intellectual I might have been expected to collect documentation with the same thoroughness and to examine various points of view with the same lack of bias that I had learned to apply to my preliminary architectural studies. This failure was rooted in my inadequate political schooling...not, given my education, to have read books, magazines, and newspapers of various viewpoints: not to have tried to see through the whole apparatus of mystification—was already criminal."

The next time one hears it said that not everyone need study politics, particularly to become only a technician, or an executive, or a mere voter...think on Albert Speer. Think on Germany. Herr Speer's memoirs, like his other products, were detailed, efficient, and craftsmanlike. They remain highly useful to students of the period. And yet they are more analytical than profound. They peel off layer after layer of description and explanation, revealing an emotional emptiness at the core. At the news of his death, one wondered: Was he ever alive?

Only Albert Speer's technocracy seems profound. As late as 1944, when he was doubtless the biggest employer of slave labor on the European continent, and when hundreds of thousands of human beings were being worked to death at his direction, Herr Speer could write this memorandum to his Fuehrer: "The task I have to fulfill is an unpolitical one. I have felt at ease in my work only so long as my person and my work were evaluated solely by the standard of practical accomplishments."

The full grotesquerie of his attitude would not strike him until after the war; he had allowed the work ethic to drive out all other ethics, or morality. As he would write later: "I did not see any moral ground outside the system where I should have taken my stand." His was a terrifying kind of innocence. Despite all their differences in age, education, times, and sophistication, one can't help comparing him with, yes, our own Lt. Calley.

Despite the plethora of formal confessions, and a post-facto high-mindedness exceptional in the literature of Nazidom, Albert Speer's memoirs remain unmoving. They are formal, correct, perceptive, instructive, and hollow. His writing is as effective, and as soulless, as his administration was. And as successful; his books were best sellers. Albert Speer was able to make even confession a successful enterprise.

Even after all his words, Albert Speer remains at least as mysterious, and as inhuman in his own way, as Adolf Hitler. And the thought occurs that the Speers may be far more numerous than the Hitlers, and far more dangerous in an age of technology. It is an age in which vast projects may be launched and seemingly miraculous inventions employed without very many thinking to inquire: To what end?

Justice, Texas Style

David Maraniss

Tyler, Tex.—Justice in Texas is not an abstraction, but flesh and blood and, as only real life can render it, a federal judge. William Wayne Justice is chief judge of the eastern district of Texas, where the piney woods, catfish ponds, rebel flags, roadside barbecue shacks, pillared mansions, idioms and manners all speak of the Deep South.

This judge named Justice is not so simply defined by title and geography. His courtroom in Tyler, where the necks are said to be redder than the roses, has served as an unlikely forum for many of the major civil liberties issues of modern America.

As the judge who ended racial segregation in east Texas schools, ruled that children of illegal immigrants should not be charged tuition for public education, directed Texas to stop abusing juveniles at state detention centers, ordered junior colleges to reinstate male students expelled because of their long hair, mandated bilingual education in elementary schools and directed an overhaul of the Texas prison system, Justice not surprisingly provokes superlatives—and expletives.

He has been called the most hated man in Texas, the most powerful man in Texas and the real governor of Texas. Civil libertarians view him as a courageous figure unafraid to force bureaucracies to adhere to the Constitution. Many Texas politicians, who consider their state a republic unto itself, regard him as the symbol of federal intervention. Conservative scholars say his orders are costly and impractical, that he has a misguided notion of a judge's role in the balance of powers.

Justice, an unassuming man who has lived all of his 67 years in east Texas (except for service in India during World War II), is a self-proclaimed populist who defines his mission as "to provide equal justice for poor and rich, and to try to follow the law." As he enters his 20th year on the federal bench, he has assumed his normal position—smack in the thick of things.

That was assured on the final day of 1986, when he issued another order in the massive and seemingly endless prison case *Ruiz v. Estelle.* Six years after ordering the state to clean up its prisons, Justice cited Texas for contempt of court, saying it had not sufficiently improved conditions in the system, the second most populous in the nation, behind California's. Unless progress is made by April 1, Justice will fine the state $800,00 a day.

David Maraniss, "Justice, Texas Style," *The Washington Post*, 28 February 1987, G1–3. Reprinted with permission of *The Washington Post.*

In the days following the order, the postman delivered the expected smattering of hate mail to the judge's chambers.

Postmark Rosenberg: *Mr. Justice, What's the matter with you anyway? Do you honestly believe that the citizens of Texas want prisoners who have murdered back out on the street just because you don't want two-bed cells? I certainly hope it's your family instead of mine that the scum decide to violate the next time they get out.*

Postmark Houston: *Dear Judge Justice, Please send me your home address so that we might furnish each and every one of the convicts with it so that they might come by and thank you personally. Hopefully they all might like Tyler so much that they will stay there as well.*

Postmark Dallas: *Dear Judge, Based on what I hear and read you are the most despised man in Texas. What do you think your children and grandchildren think of you? Have you thought of them? The state of Texas cannot afford the prisons we have now—not to think of what it will cost after all your ideas are completed. How about a suggestion—retire!*

The contempt finding coincided with word that the prisons had reached the state-mandated population limit—38,377, 95 percent of capacity—and briefly might have to turn away new inmates. That happened for a week in 1982, and sheriffs, stuck with unwanted prisoners for a few extra days, lambasted Justice, who first set capacity standards to prevent unconstitutional overcrowding. Once again, some sheriffs vowed to haul prisoners to the state prison at Huntsville and leave them handcuffed to the gates.

Bill Clements, the gruff Dallas oil man who defeated Mark White for the governorship in November, made an unusual pilgrimage to Tyler to meet Justice a few days before his inauguration. He told the judge that he welcomed the air. He also said that he had a plan to get the needed money—perhaps $400 million—to improve prison conditions, and that in the meantime he wanted to put up barracks-type housing on the prison grounds.

Although Justice was interested in action, not words, the meeting marked a turning point. William Turner, the lead attorney for the prisoners, said that beforehand he thought the meeting would be silly, but that it took on great symbolic weight.

"For the first time the state was not attacking Judge Justice," Turner said. "Equally important, a governor was finally taking personal responsibility for the prisons. Instead of the usual distance and deniability, Clements in effect said, I'm going to take over here. I'm responsible, finally, the symbol of the conservative Republican governor going to make peace with the populist federal judge was fascinating. It was like Nixon going to China."

To many Texans, Justice has seemed as foreign as China. In the letters that flow into his office, he is often told to go back to where he came from, but that trip would be a short one. He was born and reared in Athens, the Henderson County seat, about 35 miles southwest of Tyler.

Athens and Tyler represent the extremes of east Texas society. Tyler, in Smith County, was founded by slave owners who cleared the land for cotton and later grew rich on the black gold of the nearby oil fields. Athens had neither cotton nor oil, just peanuts and black-eyed peas. Ralph Yarborough, the former senator from Texas who for decades led the liberal wing of the state Democratic Party, grew up in Henderson County. He looks on the bright side to the economic divide.

"You've heard, 'Where wealth accumulates, men decay'?" Yarborough once said. "Well, our theory for Henderson County is that wealth didn't accumulate and men didn't decay."

Yarborough was a close friend of the judge's father, Will Justice, a lawyer of skill and flair, of whom it was said: "There is no justice in east Texas but Will Justice." As a prosecutor, he went to juries with 156 cases and got convictions on all but one. As a defense attorney, he handled more than 200 capital cases, and the worst sentence a client ever received was 40 years.

When William Wayne was 7, Will Justice made him partner. He changed the stationery and the nameplate above his office door to "W.D. Justice and Son." The son's reverence for this father was such that he gladly accepted this predetermined role, saying, "I always felt that I ought to do what he intended for me to do."

As Justice learned it from his father, the law was more than a job. He remembers how his dad would come home every night from his courthouse square office, sit down in bed after dinner, his head propped up by a few pillows, a big cigar in his mouth, a box of kitchen matches at his side, and read his files and case law for hours on end.

That memory is one of three that resonate among his childhood recollections.

Another is of the freight trains that rumbled through Athens several times a day during the Depression, with hungry, jobless men "hanging on the boxcars as thick as flies." Some of those men would knock on the Justices' back door, one of the places in town where they could get some food. The third memory is of playing with black kids and white kids in the back alley and hearing a white friend's mother scold her son for mixing with the other race.

What other people remember about Justice during his early days is less vivid. He was an unexceptional student at the University of Texas. After the war, when he returned to Athens to practice law at Justice & Justice, his manner was conventional and unassuming, revealing a sharp mind but none of his father's flamboyance.

The first case they tried together was a lesson in style. It involved two junk dealers accused of selling stolen property and young Justice thought they had no case. When his father asked, "Wayne, would you like to make the final arguments for us?" he said no way. The father laughed, slapped him on the back, strolled toward the jury and began an irrelevant appeal to passion and prejudice. The jury went out and returned in 10 minutes with an acquittal. "I learned from that," Justice said, "that there is always something that can be said—and should be said."

Justice became a small-town stereotype—an overweight, cigar-smoking Rotary Club president whose career ascent was based on political patronage. Yarborough, the old family friend, was chiefly responsible for his appointment as U.S. attorney in 1962. Six years later, after going to the White House and cutting a deal with fellow Texan Lyndon B. Johnson, Yarborough got Justice the federal judgeship.

By then, Justice's father had died, he himself had quit smoking, started running and working out, and lost 50 pounds. He felt at peace with himself, free to follow his instincts and the law, protected from the vagaries of politics and public opinion by a lifetime appointment.

Justice began his judgeship two months after the Rev. Martin Luther King, Jr. was assassinated in Memphis. In Tyler, he found a city literally divided by railroad tracks. Blacks lived on the north side and attended Emmett Scott High School. Whites lived south of the tracks. They had two high schools: John Tyler, where most of the students were from working-class families, and Robert E. Lee, the rich kids' school.

Nearly 15 years had passed since the courts began desegregating southern schools, but in Tyler change came slowly. The first step was taken in 1963, when students were allowed to switch schools voluntarily. In 1966, the school board chose four black teachers from Scott to teach at Robert E. Lee.

Dorothy Pendleton, who grew up in north Tyler and was educated at all-black schools through her college years, was one of those four black teachers. It was her first experience in an integrated setting, and she remembers feeling "like an animal at the zoo, always stared at." The white teachers, she recalls, tended to be nice to her when they were alone, but "when there were other whites around, it was as though they couldn't see you."

In 1970, as part of an agreement worked out in Justice's court, Scott was closed and the two white high schools were fully integrated. Martin Edwards, who had just been elected the first black member of the Tyler school board, sat in the courtroom during hearings. Since his viewpoint differed from that of the white school board members, he was forced to retain his own lawyer, at his own expense.

"I shall never forget the day that the decision was ultimately reached," Edwards said. "When I came out of the courtroom and approached the elevator in the federal building, this white man came up to me accompanied by others, and said, 'If anything happens to my girls, I'm coming after you.' I'm going to tell you that scared the hell out of me."

The racial tension worsened in the spring of 1971, with Justice taking the heat. At John Tyler, black students rebelled during a quota-rigged cheerleaders election and staged a walkout. More than 200 blacks were expelled by the school board, which set strict standards for readmission. When a lawyer took the case to Justice's court, the judge viewed it as a situation where the white school board was "tickled and eager to get rid of black students." He ordered the board to readmit them immediately.

At Robert E. Lee, black students were enraged by the school's Confederate symbols—the rebel flags that lined the campus walkways, the "Rebel nickname, the "Rebellette" cheerleaders. The school colors were red and white, and one day the football coach gave a pep rally speech that ended. "Always remember to be proud of the red and *white*." Black kids stormed out and started ripping down the Rebel flags.

Debby Magee, a student at Robert E. Lee that year, remembers that her father, like many parents in Tyler, blamed the turmoil on Judge Justice. "Justice was blamed for everything," said Magee, who now works in Justice's office and had been disowned by her dad. "You would go home and the parents would talk about this sonuvabitch trying to degrade their children. That's when the 'Impeachment Judge Justice' bumper stickers got real hot."

After school, white teen-agers circled the courthouse on Erwin Street, waving Confederate flags and cursing the judge. One of his clerks remembers that a barber stopped his haircut in midshear when he revealed that he worked for Justice. The judge's wife Sue had to drive back to Athens to get her hair done. The painters who were working on the Justices' house walked off the job. His secretary, Marcelle Simmons, read every piece of hate mail and listened, politely, to every irate telephone call.

"I never hung up on anyone," Simmons said. "I always listened and said, 'I'll pass the message on to the judge.' I would not use their language, however. Many times they called him a nigger lover. I'd get angry, but the judge has the greatest ability to handle it. He'd say, 'I have to do what I think is right. I can't pay any attention. They have a right to criticize.' "

Justice has been ostracized in Tyler ever since. He and his wife are rarely invited to social functions. When the judge dines at the Petroleum Club, he usually sits alone or with his law clerks. When the city honored the great tailback Earl Campbell, who went from John Tyler High School in the mid-'70s to win the Heisman Trophy at the University of Texas, Justice, an avid

Longhorns football fan, the man who made it possible for Campbell to attend an integrated high school, was not invited.

"My white coworkers still hate him," said Dorothy Pendleton, entering her 22nd year as a business teacher at Robert E. Lee. "Any time his name comes up, they start moaning. But I love him. His name, it is so fitting."

In the long-running confrontation between Judge Justice and the State of Texas, the first key figure was a Mexican American girl from El Paso named Alicia Morales.

As the oldest child in the large family headed by a drunken, unemployed father, Alicia worked after school and on weekends starting when she was 12, and she gave all but $5 of her weekly earnings to her father. One day, when she asked him whether she could keep $8, her father became enraged, beat her with a broom, dragged her to the local detention center and asked to have her sent away. Without a lawyer, without a hearing, Alicia Morales was sent to the state home for girls in Gainesville for nearly four years.

In 1970, Steve Bercu, a public interest lawyer in El Paso, discovered that scores of young boys and girls like Alicia were being sent to state homes without due process. He filed suit in state court and obtained a discovery to talk with some of the incarcerated youths. When he arrived at Gainesville, the long-haired Bercu was told that the state did not want him to speak to his clients. Since Gainesville was in Justice's district, Bercu made the journey to east Texas and got an injunction from the federal judge ordering the state to let him in.

In his first interviews at the juvenile homes, Bercu heard horrifying stories not only of how these children were being sent away, but of what was happening to them there: of youths being tear-gassed while locked in their cells; of scores of them being chained together and forced to move in unison across a field, picking the earth with sharp hoes; of skinny and effeminate boys being placed in the same units with bullies and rapists. With help from 200 law students at Texas and Southern Methodist University, Bercu and his associates interviewed all 2,700 youths in the state homes. They went to trial in Justice's court with a class action suit charging the state with denial of due process and cruel and inhuman punishment of children.

The state not only defended the system but argued that it was a national model. Its strategy was to deny, resist, threaten witnesses and attack the judge. One day Justice and his law clerk, Richard Mithoff, drove over to the boys' home in Gatesville for a firsthand look at the facility.

"I remember how terribly moved the judge was by what he had seen," Mithoff recalled. "By young children being locked up in solitary confinement. He was dismayed that the state would deny it was happening rather than try to change it."

Near the end of the trial, one of the state's four attorneys, Max Flusche, realized that he was arguing a bad case and closed his cross-examination with the words, "I better quit while I'm behind." But the state did not quit, and after Justice ruled for the plaintiffs and directed the state to make sweeping changes in the system, the attorney general's office began an appeals process that dragged on for 12 years. In the middle of that process, the Texas House of Representatives voted to place a youthful offenders facility next to Justice's home in Tyler.

"Anybody who wants to understand why Justice issues such detailed remedial orders and insists upon compliance ought to go back and study that Morales case," said Otis Carroll, a Tyler attorney. "What the state was doing then would be universally scorned today, yet the legislature supported it and and public either didn't know or didn't care. Justice did what he had to do to get their attention."

The Texas prison case began in the early 1970s when Justice had his law clerks inventory hundreds of inmate *habeas corpus* writs and letters that complained of cruel and unusual punishment in the state prisons, and then recruited a lawyer to develop them into a civil action suit. It was in many respects a replay of the Morales case on a larger scale.

The state not only denied that there were problems in the corrections system but insisted that its prisons—which had two doctors for every 17,000 prisoners, where 2,000 inmates slept on the floor and where inmate trusties known as building tenders essentially ran the cell blocks through bullying, coercion, rape and blackmail—were the best in the nation. The basic approach of state officials was to drag out the case and blame Justice for any violence in the prisons after he ruled against them.

Today, some state officials acknowledge that their past behavior, not the activism of the federal judge, was the central issue.

"Our attitude has changed dramatically from when this was first filed," state Attorney General Jim Mattox said last week at a news conference where he discussed he state's response to Justice's recent contempt finding. "There was a time when the state was probably not acting in good faith. Some of the evidence that was put forth was not truthful and honest. We are not taking that approach anymore."

That confession was another sign of how profoundly Texas has changed during Justice's 20 years on the bench. When he started, the Texas mystique was of a place apart, suffused with its own myths and symbols and ways of doing business, which no outsider, especially not a federal judge, could challenge. The Texas way was the right way. Period. It was a place with an enormous contradiction—built on the ethic of rugged individualism and yet denying individual liberties to groups at the bottom of its power structure.

As the frontier myths faded with urbanization, as economic decline brought a certain humility, as the population grew more black and Hispanic, conflict—and change—became inevitable. To an extraordinary degree, that conflict and change was played out in a federal courtroom in Tyler.

Justice's critics, such as University of Texas law professor Lino Graglia, argue that the judge became the instrument of that change, and in so doing misused his authority. "The role of the judge is to interpret the law." Graglia said. "Not to make the law, not to change the social policies that the legislature has established by passing the law."

There is another way of looking at it.

"You know the Harper Lee Book 'To Kill a Mockingbird,' " said Richard Mithoff, the former Justice clerk who is now a successful Houston trial attorney.

"Every trial lawyer knows that story of the lawyer—played by Gregory Peck in the movie—who defends a black man accused of raping a white woman in a small southern town. There is that marvelous scene where the lawyer's little girl, Scout, asks the lady next door why it is that her father has been chosen to defend this man. Why her father? And the woman tells Scout, 'There are just some men in this world who have to do the unpleasant work that no one else will do, and your father is one of those rare men.'

"I think Judge Justice is one of those men. I think he is doing what many judges and lawyers would rather not do. He is ruling in the tough cases in the areas that are breaking new ground in constitutional law and doing it with courage and fairness and grace."

Moral Development and Education

In his seventh epistle, to the friends and companions of Dion of Syracuse, Plato explained why, in his youth, he gave up his active interest in politics and the attempt to take part in government. He found politics hopelessly corrupt and determined to spend his life in an inquiry into the best philosophy for ordering human affairs, and then into education of the young in that philosophy. By this means he hoped to alter both the ideas and the

---

"Moral Development and Education," *Manas* 35, no. 9, pp. 1–2; 7–8. Reprinted with permission of Henry Geiger, president, Manas Publishing Company.

ways of the people of his time, so that, eventually, they might originate a truly good community. The fruit of Plato's effort may be briefly indicated by the remark of Alfred North Whitehead to the effect that all subsequent philosophy has been but footnotes to Plato. It is notable that he not only taught men how to think, but how to think nobly. The keynote of Plato's philosophy is found in the question: Can virtue be taught? His dialogues revolve around this question.

There is ample evidence that today this Platonic—or basically human—inquiry needs to be deliberately renewed. Some quotations will make this clear. First, then, from the humanistic psychologist, A. H. Maslow:

> The state of valuelessness has been variously described as anomie, amorality, anhedonia, rootlessness, emptiness, hopelessness, the lack of something to believe in and to be devoted to.... We too are in an interregnum between old value systems that have not worked and new ones not yet born.... We need a validated, usable system of values, values that we can believe in and devote ourselves to because they are true rather than because we are *exhorted* to "believe and have faith."

Next, from Louis Halle's *The Search for an Eternal Norm:*

> What is basic to human life, as distinct from all other life is a discrepancy between a normative order in men's minds and the existential circumstances in which they actually find themselves.... When it comes to conduct that is not purely instinctive, each of us has to have a normative order in his mind on which to base it. He has no other way of deciding what he ought to do and how he ought to do it.

Then, Bruno Bettelheim in *Harper's* for last October:

> What our society suffers from most today is the absence of consensus about what it and life in it ought to be. Such consensus cannot be gained from society's present stage, or from fantasies about what it ought to be. For that, the present is too close and too diversified, and the future too uncertain, to make believable claims about it.

From Erich Kahler's *Out of the Labyrinth:*

> Entangled in such gigantic mass relationships, the individual sinks into hopeless insignificance, impotence and ignorance.... Through the rapid communication and interaction of events, everything occurs much faster than before.... Who can be aware and keep abreast of all this?... What single man, even in our governments and parliaments, has a comprehensive view even of the momentary situation, let alone of what is looming up from the depth and breadth of daily events to form the future?...
>
> This trend implies a decline of morals, a moral degeneration. For morality is nothing else but the attitude toward the whole—positive or negative, further-

> ing or hindering and disturbing. When knowledge of and orientation in the whole are no longer possible, then the individual must, in his consternation, be carried away by the nearest wave of impulse or opportunity. To whomever human history and events are no longer a living whole and a oneness, to him the brotherhood of man cannot have any meaning.

Finally, from a great educator, Arthur Morgan:

> In a country like the United States, there has been a truce among competitive theologies, resulting in tacit agreement that 'the church' shall convey 'the meaning of life' as determined by tradition, while public education shall instruct in practical ways and means. This cultural failure to relate ends and means has meant uncritical reliance on biological drives, emergence of vacuum-filling cultural tendencies, and acceptance of residues of traditional belief—a policy of drift balanced somewhat by free, critical inquiry. But unless strong concern for purpose and significance introduces an ordering principle for both life and education, sustained effort will be lacking, and there will be a tendency to lapse into biological hedonism.

In our skeptical yet morally hungering age, certain questions need immediate answer. What, for one, does "moral" mean? Can there be moral standards which are more than the customs which vary around the world? How would it be possible to teach morals without "indoctrination"? Can, indeed, morality be taught at all? What has science to say about this idea? Can science contribute, or should it remain silent because morals are outside the ranges of competent scientific method?

Fortunately, there is now a book which examines and develops all these questions. It does not settle them, but shows what may be involved in obtaining acceptable answers, and evaluates the various conclusions that have been reached and the means of reaching them. This book is the first in a series of three volumes called *Essays in Moral Development*, of which volume I is titled *The Philosophy of Moral Development*. The author is Lawrence Kohlberg, professor of psychology in the graduate school of education at Harvard University. Kohlberg has been working on the theme of this series of books for about twenty years, starting in 1958 with a study of seventy-five boys in a school in Chicago, tracing their "moral development" over a period of twelve years, from the time they were ten to sixteen years old to when they were from twenty-two to twenty-eight. His fundamental conclusion, later confirmed by research with other children in other cultures, is that these youngsters went through six developmental stages of moral attitude—changes which he speaks of as "natural," although not inevitable. Not all reach the higher stages.

This book is considerably more than an account of the twelve year experiment with some schoolboys. The author engages in justification of the theory of moral development and debates extensively with his critics in academic terms. All this is no doubt necessary—in order to wear away at scholarly prejudice and to expose the futility of value free science in relation to human beings—yet one cannot help wishing that the author would provide a simple, affirmative account of his thinking, with the general public for his audience. (Perhaps this will come later.) Meanwhile, Dr. Kohlberg is openly Platonic and his education and lifework have fitted him to introduce the idea of a morality such as Maslow described—"a validated, usable system of values, values that we can believe in and devote ourselves to because they are true rather than because we are *exhorted* to 'believe and have faith'."

Following Plato, Kohlberg's conception of moral values or principles is both intuitively and rationally grounded, and he believes that the scientific spirit is essential in verifying intuition in experience. He ends his preface:

> This is not the first time in which the weakening of traditional morality has led to serious dialogue about moral education. The first time was the Athens of Socrates, Plato, and Aristotle. I hope that these volumes serve some purpose in reviving the dialogue in contemporary North America and Great Britain.

In his introductory chapter, Dr. Kohlberg adopts "the implications of Socratic dialogue as an approach to moral education":

> Socrates was not impelled only by an 'inquiry learning' approach to values. For him, Socratic dialogues rested on a sense of some personal virtue in himself that was displayed not by preaching but by implicit convictions of belief and action. These convictions were:
>
> - *First,* virtue is ultimately one, not many, and it is always the same ideal form regardless of climate or culture.
> - *Second,* the name of this ideal form is justice.
> - *Third,* not only is the good one, but virtue is knowledge of the good. He who knows the good chooses the good.
> - *Fourth,* the kind of knowledge of the good that is virtue is philosophical knowledge or intuition of the ideal form of the good, not correct opinion or acceptance of conventional beliefs.
> - *Fifth,* the good can then be taught, but its teachers must in a certain sense be philosopher-kings.
> - *Sixth,* the reason the good can be taught is because we know it all along dimly or at a low level and its teaching is more a calling out than an instruction.
> - *Seventh,* the reason we think the good cannot be taught is because the same good is known differently at different levels and direct instruction cannot take place across levels.
> - *Eighth,* then the teaching of virtue is the asking of questions and the pointing the way, not the giving of answers. Moral education is the leading of people upward, not the putting into the mind of knowledge that was not there before.

If *justice* is to be taken as the basis of all moral thinking, then what is Justice? Kohler gives a discussion-definition:

> I appeal to the reader's intuitions by discussing dilemmas in which there is a conflict between the principle of utility as the greatest good for the greatest number and the principle of justice as respect for individual human dignity. I claim that justice as reversibility (moral musical chairs) resolves these dilemmas by recognizing utility within a framework of respect for individual dignity expressed as the willingness to trade places with others; that is, the Golden Rule.

We might expand on this by suggesting that justice means supplying, as best we know, the sort of experience each one needs in order to learn or grow. Since actual justice remains obscure, the intent to do this sort of justice is about all we can hope to achieve. Yet the *intent*, even if imperfectly carried out, may accomplish more than we think. Humans are at least able to understand and appreciate the attempt to do justice, if it is truly sincere. Plato believed that to be treated like humans, fairly, is all that anyone with his own instinct for justice is likely to ask. This is the "reversibility" Kohlberg speaks of.

He begins the chapter on moral education—for "justice"—by comparing the Socratic approach with that of two schools of modern psychologists:

> It is usually supposed that psychology contributes to moral education by telling us appropriate methods of moral teaching and learning. A Skinnerian will speak of proper schedules of reinforcement in moral learning, a Freudian will speak of the importance of the balance of parental love and firmness that will promote superego identification, and so on. When Skinnerians or Freudians speak on the topic of moral education, then, they start by answering yes to Meno's question, 'Is virtue something that can be taught?' and go on to tell us how. In *Walden Two*, Skinner not only tells us that virtue comes by practice and reinforcement but also designs an ideal republic that educates all its children to be virtuous in this way.
>
> My own response to these questions was more modest. When confronted by a group of parents who asked me, 'How can we help make our children virtuous?' I had to answer, as did Socrates, 'You must think I am very fortunate to know how virtue is acquired. The fact is that, far from knowing whether it can be taught, I have no idea what virtue really is.' Like most psychologists, I knew that science could teach me nothing as to what virtue is. Science could speak about causal relations, about the relations of means to end, but it could not speak about ends or values themselves. If I could not define virtue or the ends of moral education, could I really offer advice as to the means by which virtue should be taught? Could it really be argued that the means for teaching obedience to authority are the same as the means for teaching freedom of moral opinion, that the means for teaching altruism are the same as the means for teaching competitive striving, that the making of a good storm trooper involves the same procedures as the making of a philosopher-king?

This indeed, is the core problem for one who contemplates the project of moral education.

Dr. Kohlberg seems to have been able to extricate himself from this dilemma after encountering the *fact* of the stages of moral development in the population of boys. There are three main stages, each divided into two, making six, with possibly a transcendent seventh. The three are called Preconventional, Conventional, and Postconventional. The other three are intermediate or halfstep transitional stages.

One could think of these stages as each embodying one set of ideas about the locus of power, and about the authority which defines obligation. Where is the power or authority to which one must answer? Is it inside or outside the self? At the preconventional stage, it is always outside. You do what you ought to do because God says so. You are subject to Divine Command, and you'd better not try to *reason* about it—as Galileo was angrily instructed by the Pope and the Inquisition. You do what you do to avoid pain and enjoy pleasure, and to get what you need. In this sense, plain power from the outside runs your life, dictating moral decision. I do what is right because I'll be whipped if I don't. If I please my friends, they'll be nice to me.

At the conventional level there is a kind of generalized projection of good/bad categories of behavior, requiring conformity and loyalty to the expectations of the group. "Right behavior consists of doing one's duty, showing respect for authority, and maintaining the given social order for its own sake."

Stages five and six belong to the postconventional level. Here the movement is toward principled decision with reference to moral ideas. Constitutional government illustrates this level, with emphasis on the "legal point of view." The obligation is to the law, although the law may be improved upon through inspection of its working in terms of social utility.

Stage six recognizes in Conscience a higher authority than man-made laws, and the principles of behavior here are self-chosen, independent of external claims.

Tentatively proposed is a seventh stage, where conduct has a religious quality or sanction. For illustration Kohlberg offers Marcus Aurelius:

> We choose him partly because he is outside the Judeo-Christian tradition, which helps define universals in religious thinking. And we choose him partly because in the world of the Roman empire, in which absolute power corrupted absolutely, this man with absolute power was the only man who was absolutely incorruptible, absolutely principled. In days that at times seem like the decline of the American empire, in which there are so many examples of power corrupting, we need to look at universal foundations of integrity.

Marcus starts with the conviction that the universe is "lawful, knowable, and evolving," and he does not separate God from Nature. He said in his *Meditations:*

> You yourself are part of that universe. Remember always what world-nature is and what your own nature is and that your nature is such a small fraction of so vast a whole. Then you will recognize that no man can hinder you from conforming each word and deed to that nature of which you are a part.

In short, by thinking like the universe we become moral. In stating this cosmic perspective, Dr. Kohlberg proposes, Marcus Aurelius "succeeds in illuminating how, in any culture, a person without special gifts or inner light, but with the courage and thoughtfulness to think through the human condition, can achieve moral and spiritual maturity." Spinoza, another example of the seventh stage, declares that moral achievement or wisdom or love "involves the discovery of the union of the mind with the whole of nature." Kohlberg comments:

> The pains of life are caused by the disappointments or losses in our loves of particular people or aims. But if we are aware of the relationship of all people and all things to the whole of Nature or to God, then we continue to love the whole in spite of the disappointments or losses. And if we love life or nature, we are even able to face our own death with equanimity, because we love life more than our own particular and finite life. The demand for our survival can be met only by identification or union with something more eternal. The knowledge of, and love of, Nature or God are a form of union. In a sense, half-poetic, half-logical, but never supernatural, our mind is part of a whole, Spinoza claims, and if we know and love the eternal we ourselves are in some sense eternal.

It is needful to go from these sublime considerations—which are nonetheless necessary as foundation for the structural development of Dr. Kohlberg's thesis—to the lower levels where most of us live. It was here, and especially in the transition stages, that the psychologist saw the boys he was studying—and later many other subjects—*move,* however uncertainly, from one stage to the next. The progressive development in moral attitude was so clear, and repeated so many times, that it became for him a scientific fact. This, he says, is the natural role of science in such studies. It provides confirmatory facts in actual experience, and also introduces necessary qualifications. Thinking about what is right *needs* the checks of experience, the settings provided by life. Science is indispensable as critic. Moral development, then, involves intuitive, cognitive, and scientific thinking.

It became apparent to Kohlberg that no stage could be skipped. An individual might stop for the rest of his life at stage three or four, but he could not get to four without going through and assimilating the values of stage three. Yet he could think about the next stages before reaching them. This is how development takes place.

Dr. Kohlberg's most important contention may be that morality is not derivative in essence. It is a unique realm of independent thinking, no matter how interlaced with other modes of inquiry. Humans, then, have, express, and develop moral intelligence, and this intelligence is not reducible to any other way of thinking about ourselves.

Lawrence Kohlberg's book may help to start a wave of thinking along these lines. He has had great forerunners and he will have great successors, yet this work (and doubtless the other two volumes to come) stands in our time as a pioneering contribution to a change that may be finally recognized as prerequisite to all the other achievements we long for, and are working hard to reach.

DISCUSSION QUESTIONS

1. How can ethical standards be upheld in governmental bureaucracies?
2. Who are some famous "whistle blowers" in local, state, and national bureaucracies?
3. Do the ethical concerns of the people get through the bureaucratic red tape to the leaders in a position to effect change?
4. Do "decent" citizens like Speer in Greenberg's article find their way into the bureaucratic morass and lose their sense of ethics—their morality? If so, how does this happen?
5. Identify one bureaucratic group that is inherently moral and succeeds in its mission. How does it do this?

5

THE MEDIA

Susan Duffy

The single most influential factor affecting the perceptions that Americans have of our leaders and our political process is the media. It is they who social critics claim have reduced our world to a global village. Since the Vietnam war the media have assumed the role of the nation's conscience. The film coverage of Vietnam, which brought the horrors of war into our homes and showed Americans dying on television, shocked us. It was the first "living room war" and the first time that the media were able so powerfully to influence public sentiment. The effect was profound. The media brought us to a position of moral outrage.

Close on the heels of Vietnam came Watergate and again, we were led by the media to moral indignation. Today the problems are just as emotionally charged. The media present terrorist activities, war, racism, violence in South Africa and the Middle East, and catastrophes at home in graphic detail. We see the carnage and the bodies on the nightly news. Implicitly the media ask us to judge right and wrong, good and evil. Whether we have been angered, shocked, saddened, or even bored by the deluge of information, we have known. We are an informed nation.

Yet the question remains, is a free press a responsible press? Is there a morality that controls the powerful media, or does it amorally and dispassionately present facts for public consumption? Issues involving the media are particularly volatile and often give rise to moral and ideological justifications. Both print and broadcast journalists are governed by a code of ethics. The presumption is these are honorable, ethical men and women whose job is to keep the public informed about the issues and people who affect our lives, and to do so objectively and truthfully. But at what point does personal morality, the individual's sense of what is right or wrong, impinge on journalistic objectivity and professional ethics? This has been an important question for journalists struggling with running a story that contains "classified" information, or showing film of someone committing suicide or being gunned down in an airport.

As a nation we would like to think that our leaders are equally honorable and moral. But how do we know this? The media tell us. We watch our political leaders on television, read their speeches and comments in newspapers and magazines, and through this very limited exposure, we judge their character. In assessing our leaders the media serve as our eyes and ears. We are constantly reminded that the impression we have of our leaders is one that has been carefully structured for the media.

Because of this arguable claim that image making dominates American politics, and unfortunately, because of the tarnished images of some men and women in power, the public has become more cynical about our politicians. We have come to trust them less. We suspect they are less than ethical. Every election challenges voters to peek behind the masks of the candidates and the media are encouraged and expected to expose inconsistancies, errors in judgment, and character flaws of those aspiring to power. Today the media have taken to heart Thomas Jefferson's comment: "When a man assumes a public trust he should consider himself a public property."[1] The media have been criticized for being confrontational. At times they have been, but justifiably so. The love/hate relationship between American politicians and the press corps is well documented. Each administration deals with the media differently—but never ambivalently.

It is not so much this persistent delving into personal backgrounds that gives Americans pause about the media. Most recently the concern has been focused on the potential threat to national security with the publication or broadcasting of stories containing classified information. As Lyle Denniston asserts in *The Quill* "...since Vietnam, the press has been casting off its willingness to remain in the joint enterprise of keeping the military's secrets."[2] This is an ethical concern for both the public and journalists. When the United States invaded Grenada in 1984 the Reagan Administration imposed a news blackout. The media were outraged, claiming that war correspondents had never jeopardized the security of a military operation and that the people's right to know had been violated. Though later polls indicated a majority of the public felt the press should have accompanied invading troops, the initial public response was overwhelmingly against the media. This shocked American journalists. Something was fundamentally wrong. In its efforts to serve the public, the media had come to alienate it. To use an analogy offered by Carl Sessions Stepp, "...the press, casting itself as David, had managed to leave the crowds cheering for Goliath."[3]

Despite its support of freedom of the press, the American public has grown uneasy with the power wielded by the press. The media and the government are cast in adversarial roles, each with a moral mandate to serve the people. But the press, being neither elected nor appointed, does not wear the same mantle of public approval. It is not perceived as the equal to the President, the Congress, the Senate or the Supreme Court. In several instances the press has exposed governmental excesses, wrong-doing and even contributed to the political demise of prominent individuals.

Yet, as the nation has applauded the courage and fortitude of its free press, it has denounced the subsequent self-righteous muscle-flexing by the media as arrogant and unacceptable. What Alexander Solzhenitsyn said at Harvard in 1978, that "the press has become the greatest power within Western countries, exceeding that of the legislature, the executive and the judiciary," has been repeated in a variety of ways.[4] As a nation we reject this.

The media illicit strong reactions from individuals and groups on both sides of current issues. The speeches and articles reprinted here exemplify various ideological positions. Anthony Marro's article, "When the Government Tells Lies," addresses the nettlesome moral question of political leaders telling the complete truth and the concomitant moral responsibility of the media to uncover the truth when it is kept from the public. Are there circumstances in which it is morally acceptable for the government to lie? His conclusions reflect the liberal position that the press should be even more aggressive in its political coverage.

On the other hand, in a speech before the Society of Professional Journalists, William T. Casey chastised the media for disclosing sensitive information and invoked a Supreme Court decision that would impose criminal penalties on anyone publishing information on communications intelligence.

In 1987, Gary Hart withdrew from the presidential campaign because the media made a case against his character. Whether or not the media have a right or obligation to play "vice cop" as Nicholas von Hoffman portrays them, is a salient issue that must be addressed. That same year a distraught Pennsylvania bureaucrat under criminal investigation, called a news conference and committed suicide before the assembled press corps as the cameras rolled. The fact that this incident was seen live by men, women, and children has serious implications. "What Did Mr. Dwyer Do, Daddy?" examines the ethics of filming such an occurrence while "One from the Heart" chronicles one executive news producer's decision to edit the footage to cut the actual shooting. Finally, Earl R. Hutchinson looks to the heart of the matter in his speech "To Kill a Messenger: The Ethics of Journalism" and concludes that "...the press simply cannot afford any major ethical lapses."

As I write this Lt. Col. Oliver North is a media "hero," some might say "product" because of coverage of the Iran-contra hearings. But as you read this Oliver North will most probably be a distant memory with another public figure replacing him under the critical eye of the national press corps. Each year brings new successes and new scandals—and through it all we know.

Our morals, our convictions, and our politics are reflected in, and affected by the media. Although we may be alarmed by what we see, or pained by the incisive glimpses into the soul of the nation, nonetheless, we believe in the press. We will not deny the media's right to print or broadcast fact and opinion. A free press is a responsible press, but it is not amoral. It is the responsibility of a free citizenry to be an educated citizenry, one that recognizes ideological proselytism, moralization, and bias in the written or spoken word and then filters this information through a personal belief system. In this country the media are faithful, albeit vicious, guardians. We accord them trust and free movement. In return we ask for objectivity and the truth.

NOTES

1. Thomas Jefferson to Baron Von Humbold, 1807. In John Bartlett, *Familiar Quotations,* 14th ed. (Boston: Little, Brown and Company, 1968), p. 472.
2. Lyle Denniston. "Planning for Future Grenadas," *The Quill* (January 1984), p. 12.
3. Carl Sessions Stepp. "In the Wake of Grenada," *The Quill* (March 1984), p. 12.
4. Alexander Solzhenitsyn. "A World Split Apart," *Vital Speeches of the Day* (1 Sept. 1978), p. 681.

When the Government Tells Lies

Anthony Marro

NOVEMBER 25, 1957—Dwight Eisenhower, sixty-seven years old and recently recovered from both a heart attack and abdominal surgery, is in his office. He tries to pick up a document, and can't. He tries to read it, and fails. The words, he later says, "seemed literally to run off the top of the page." He

Anthony Marro, "When the Government Tells Lies," *Columbia Journalism Review* (March/April 1985), 29–41. Edited version reprinted with permission of the *Columbia Journalism Review* and Anthony Marro.

tries to get up, and nearly falls down. He tries to tell his secretary what is wrong, but she can't make any sense of what he is saying. His physician realizes almost immediately that Eisenhower has suffered some sort of a stroke.

The president has developed "a chill," the press office tells reporters. It is not until twenty-four hours later that the nation is told that its president is seriously ill.

DECEMBER 7, 1971—Henry Kissinger is briefing the press on the government's position on the India-Pakistan war. "First of all, let's get a number of things straight," he begins. "There have been some comments that the administration is anti-Indian. This is totally inaccurate." A briefing paper has been handed out at the start of the session. The first sentence reads: "The policy of this administration towards South Asia must be understood. It is neither anti-Indian nor pro-Pakistan."

A month later, Jack Anderson publishes the transcript of a meeting attended by Kissinger on December 3, just four days before the briefing for the press. "I am getting hell every half-hour from the president that we are not being tough enough on India...," Kissinger is quoted as saying. "He wants to tilt in favor of Pakistan."

APRIL 22, 1980—Jody Powell, President Carter's chief spokesman, is talking with Jack Nelson, Washington bureau chief for the *Los Angeles Times*. No military operation is being planned to rescue the hostages in Iran, Powell tells him. A blockade might be feasible, somewhere down the road, but a rescue mission just wouldn't make any sense.

The newspapers with Nelson's story, which says that the Carter White House considers a rescue operation impractical, are still scattered around in living rooms all over Los Angeles when the members of Delta Team board airplanes for the raid on Teheran.

OCTOBER 24, 1983—Larry Speakes, the White House spokesman, is asked by reporters whether U.S. troops have landed on Grenada. He checks with a member of President Reagan's national security staff, and relays the response. "Preposterous," he says, and goes on to deny that any invasion is planned.

The landing takes place the next day.

For starters, Stephen Hess probably is right. The Brookings Institution scholar, who has studied both Washington reporters and government press operations, says that most government spokespersons don't like to lie. For one thing, telling the truth is official U.S. government policy. For another, they prefer telling the truth. To lie, he says, is to "fail to play fair with reporters and the public, to diminish their self-esteem, and to complicate their work."

But complications and crises are of the essence of government, and trying to put the best face on a sensitive situation also is part of the job. Political posturing, face-saving, honest error, bad judgment, and legitimate national security concerns also play a role, and so, to different degrees in different administrations, do arrogance, deceit, disregard for the public, high-handedness, and attempts to cover up stupidity and criminal conduct. The result is that reporters have come to accept some level of deception as part of the routine, and to expect, as Hess delicately phrases it, "less than full candor" on the part of their government.

In fact, Washington reporters over the years have had to deal with a steady barrage of deceptions, half-truths, and outright lies—deceptions about national security operations that were so sensitive that they probably wouldn't have published the information even if they had been able to obtain it, and deceits so petty that they wondered why anyone would bother to lie in the first place.

There was the time in 1960 when Lincoln White tried to explain away the crash of the U-2 airplane in the Soviet Union. It had been on a weather mission and had just strayed off course, the State Department's chief spokesman said. "Now, our assumption is that the [pilot] blacked out. There was absolutely no — N-O, no — deliberate attempt to violate Soviet air space. There never has been." Within days it became clear that the pilot, Francis Gary Powers, was alive, that the Soviets had him, and that he was talking. The principal attachment to the airplane was not a thermometer but a camera, and its mission was not weather reconnaissance but spying.

There was the time in 1966 that Lyndon Johnson claimed that one of his great-great-grandfathers had died at the Alamo (not true), and the time in 1971 that the White House claimed that Tricia Nixon's wedding cake had been based on an old family recipe (it apparently had been created by a White House chef).

There was the time in 1975 when FBI Director Clarence Kelley said that while there had been some warrantless break-ins by FBI agents in the past, they had been confined by and large to foreign espionage and counterintelligence matters, and had been ended by J. Edgar Hoover in 1966. In truth, there had been thousands, all of them illegal, most of them against American citizens, many of them against people never charged with any crime, and some as recently as 1972. Kelley's aides were left to explain that the head of the nation's most sophisticated police agency had been misinformed.

There was the time in 1954 when Henry Cabot Lodge, ambassador to the UN, described fighting in Guatemala as "a revolt of Guatemalans against Guatemalans," despite the fact the uprising was being orchestrated, in large part, by Frank Wisner, the deputy director for plans for the CIA. There was the time in 1981 when the Reagan administration released a white paper on

Central America that attributed authorship of key documents to several guerrilla leaders who clearly had not written them. There was the time, during the Bay of Pigs invasion, when the government lied in saying that the bombings were being conducted by defectors from Castro's own air force, and then, when reporters discovered the lie, groused because the reporters did not create lies of their own to help protect the government's lie.

There was the time in a televised debate last October when President Reagan insisted that more people were receiving food stamps than ever before (actually the number had dropped by about 400,000 since he had become president), and when Walter Mondale claimed that Reagan had sought to "terminate" a housing program for the elderly (in fact, the Reagan administration had made major cuts in the program, but hadn't tried to abolish it).

There was the time that John Mitchell, the former attorney general, was indicted for lying about Watergate, the time that Richard Helms, the former head of the CIA, was indicted for lying about Chile, and the time that Rita Lavelle, a former official with the Environmental Protection Agency, was indicted for lying about the EPA's handling of toxic waste.

There was the time that Ron Nessen, President Ford's press secretary, began a response to a question by saying "To tell you the truth..." only to be overwhelmed by sarcastic applause.

THE MANIFOLD FORMS OF DECEPTION

I. F. Stone has said that "Every government is run by liars, and nothing they say should be believed."

James Deakin, who covered the White House for many years for the *St. Louis Post-Dispatch,* pretty much agreed with Stone, but worded it differently. "Every government is run by people who seek to wield and retain power," he wrote in *Straight Stuff,* his brilliantly witty book on Washington journalism. "To do this, they must convince the public of certain things: That their policies are correct. That their facts and explanations should be accepted. That they are in control of events and situations. That sounds nicer [than Stone]. And it comes out at the same place.

To achieve these things, it's necessary not only for governments to deceive, but also to hype, slant, tilt, and gloss over, trying at the same time to present a situation in its most favorable light, while hiding, or hedging on, or deflecting reporters away from any information that might conflict with its version. Indeed, Stephen Hess has written, "It is hard to find a discussion of modern government's relations with the press that does not include the words 'manage,' 'manipulate,' and 'control.' "

It probably is a fool's errand to try to measure degrees of deception from one administration to the next, or to try to show whether Democrats are more or less deceptive than Republicans. Clearly, much misinformation was produced by the Reagan administration during its first four years, on such matters as the invasion of Grenada, revolution in Central America, its concern for the handicapped, and its commitment to civil rights. But there is no way of assessing how it compares with, or whether it's even in the same league with, the massive amounts of misinformation put out by the Johnson administration during the Vietnam War, for example, or by the Nixon administration during the Watergate years.

For one thing, it often takes years for deceptions to surface. It took congressional hearings, criminal prosecutions, and serious reporting by people like Nicholas Horrock and John Crewdson, both then working for *The New York Times*, to expose the degree to which the FBI had been staging illegal break-ins against American citizens. And even in 1985, fifteen years after the fact, we were still learning in the libel trial of General Westmoreland against CBS about the degree to which key officials in the Johnson administration knew that, despite their public statements to the contrary, there wasn't any light at the end of the tunnel.

For another thing, there is the question of degree, and the issue of whether, and at what point, numerous small deceptions begin to equal major ones.

There was a time, early in the Reagan administration, when the president's aides argued that it didn't matter whether some of his stories were literally true—his numerous misstatements of fact, his confusion about detail, and his repeated anecdotes about supposed welfare cheats that no one was ever able to confirm, for example—because they contained a larger truth.

"We've been dealing with four years of an administration that freely states—and stated early—that literal truth was not a concern," says Bill Kovach, the Washington news editor of *The New York Times*. "This is the first time I've heard that literal truth is not important to the presidency."

There also is the matter of attitude. "This administration is much more arrogant with the press," says one career government official who has served through several administrations. "The attitude is, 'Screw you, we don't need you. The Reagan administration is going to be successful despite the editorials in *The Washington Post* and *The New York Times*, and the cartoons in the *Los Angeles Times*.' "

And Morton Halperin, the director of the left-leaning Center for National Security Studies, says that many key officials in the Reagan administration have a philosophy of government that doesn't include public discussion and debate. "These guys came here straight out of nineteen forty-six," he says. "They came out of World War Two, when the government lied all the time, and it was all right to lie. The whole Normandy invasion, and the covert operations that surrounded it, are an important part of that mindset.... They still think fundamentally that foreign policy should be left to the executive branch and that people shouldn't even try to find out what they're up to."

Deceptions by government officials take many forms, and it's not always easy to show what they amount to. They can include simple face-saving, such as Geraldine Ferraro claiming she felt "vindicated" by a House report critical of her failure to disclose her husband's financial interests, and routine political posturing, such as the White House announcing full support for people like Anne Burford and James Watt, when both had clearly become major liabilities and were on their way out of the government. And there is the endless, predictable attempt by administrations to portray themselves in the best light, as Reagan did in a speech to the National Council of Negro Women in July 1983. "We have authorized for filing three school desegregation cases, more than were authorized by the previous administration during its first thirty months in office," he said.

At first blush, this looks like a simple statement of fact. But when James Nathan Miller took a look at the numbers, he concluded in an article in *The Atlantic* on Reagan's civil rights record that "This seemingly straightforward twenty-four-word sentence contains three carefully crafted semantic deceptions."

To begin with, Reagan's administration hadn't actually filed more cases than Carter's. His Justice Department had filed only one, while Carter's had filed two. Secondly, while Reagan seemed to be saying that he had filed more cases, he hadn't really said that. What he had said was that his administration had *authorized* that the suits be filed. And thirdly, while he implied that he was talking about his record and Carter's on the same terms, in truth he was using an apples and oranges comparison of legal suits his people had authorized (but not yet acted on), with suits that Carter actually had taken to court.

The fact that it took Miller about twelve hours' worth of digging just to deal with that one sentence gives some notion of the problem at hand.

...In *The Other Side of the Story,* his book on his years as President Carter's press secretary, Powell argues that there are two reasons why the government can, and sometimes should, lie. The first is that the "government has a legitimate right to secrecy in certain matters because the welfare of the nation requires it." The second is that the press, for the most part, has a right to print what it knows. Freedom of the press is so important to democracy, he says, that when there is a conflict with legitimate national security needs, it is probably better for the government to simply lie to the press than to try to limit it, censor it, or restrict it through prior restraint.

But Powell admits to at least one other lie that had nothing to do with national security or life-and-death matters. It was a question that, as Powell put it, "involved the personal life of a colleague and that of his family." Powell says he decided to lie because to respond with the truth would have resulted in "great pain and embarrassment for a number of perfectly innocent people." And, besides, he didn't think that the matter was of any legitimate public interest to begin with. Powell thus goes a step beyond Sylvester, and argues that it is sometimes permissible for a government to lie to protect the privacy of public figures, as well as to protect the security of the nation.

Powell, now a Washington columnist, says he has come to understand more clearly than he used to why it is that "journalists get so damn skeptical about what people [in government] tell them." He says he has no doubts at all that he acted properly in the Iran situation, but has mixed feelings about the second lie. "That's harder to defend without getting into the details, which I won't do," he says, adding that he would probably lie again in that situation, too.

"The minimal line you can draw there is that you can absolutely say that lying to cover up your own embarrassments is not permissible," says Powell. "Once you get past that, you get into areas where, unfortunately, things tend to be mixed. Then you have to weigh in the sort of long-term impact, not just in terms of the credibility of a particular administration, but the credibility of the government over the long haul. If you contribute to the idea that people can't believe anything their government tells them, that's awful. It's also dangerous."

In his book, Powell cites other cases in which he thinks a government sometimes might have a right to lie, including protection of intelligence sources and methods, protection of an innocent person whose name had cropped up during a Justice Department investigation, and a pending decision by the Treasury Department that could have major financial consequences to individuals and to the nation.

And it is here that he runs into conflict with many others, including Hess, who argue that there is a big difference between lying to protect legitimate national security matters and lying to protect anything less. "It's very easy to slop over into other areas...and I'm less sympathetic when it does," says Hess. "Just because something might concern the 'public good,' that isn't enough" to justify government lying. "It has to be to save lives, as in the Iranian hostage thing, or similar wartime activities."

But while many people in government and in the media agree that, in some circumstances, the government has a right to lie, they also agree that the people have a right to know what their government is really up to. And they argue that a chief reason that the government gets away with as much deception as it does is that the press, for all of its bluster and all its professed skepticism, is far too willing to take the government at its word.

Sylvester, for example, placed much of the blame for misinformation about government activities on the laziness and ineptitude of reporters, saying that they relied too much on handouts and failed to ask the right questions." Every sophisticated [reporter] knows the federal government puts its best, not its worst, foot forward...," he said. "That being so, it is [the reporter's] function to penetrate this protective coloration behind which all men attempt to mask their errors. If there is a credibility gap, it measures the failure of newsmen to do their job."...

FOUR KINDS OF LIES— AND THE PROBLEMS THEY POSE FOR THE PRESS

Not all deceptions are equal, of course. There is a big difference between a Joe McCarthy making harsh, and often groundless, charges of treason, and the sort of political posturing that causes a president to defend an aide who has done something dumb. After several years of studying the press-government relationship from both sides, Hess has concluded that some reporters tolerate, even welcome, minor deceptions, because exposing deceptions helps them to display their skills. While studying the State Department press operations during Reagan's first term, he says, he found many examples of deception, most of them minor, and didn't detect much outrage on the part of the reporters there. "It is only the Big Lie, the deliberate and consistent pattern of misstatement on a matter of importance, that turns Washington reporters into inflamed civil libertarians," Hess writes in *The Government/Press Connection.*

Hess cites four broad categories of government deceptions. On a scale of decreasing acceptability to the press, he says, are so-called "honest lies," inadvertent lies, half-truths (which include many forms of political posturing and selective release of data), and flat-out lies. An "honest lie," for Hess, is a legitimate national security matter, such as Powell lying about the raid on Teheran. Even if they don't approve of such a lie, most reporters can understand the need for it, he says.

Reporters also tend to forgive inadvertent lies, because they know from their own work that mistakes happen when things are done in a hurry. Bill Beecher, a former Defense Department information officer and now a reporter for *The Boston Globe,* has said that "half the initial internal reporting within government in a crisis is wrong."

It is with half-truths, a specialty at the State Department, that some reporters begin to get resentful. The chief technique here is for a press officer to define the question as narrowly as possible and then answer it that way. Here are two examples Hess cites in *The Government/Press Connection*. Both, he said in an interview, are real examples, with the facts altered just slightly "to protect the guilty."

> Q—Has the assistant secretary of state been invited to China?
> A—No. (Meaning: He will go to China as an adviser to vice president. It is the vice president who has been invited. Therefore, I am not lying. Rationale: I have to say this because protocol requires that the Chinese must first publicly extend the invitation.
>
> Q—Will the ambassador-at-large go to Egypt?
> A—No decision has been made. (Meaning: A "decision" is made when the Secretary of State signs the cable. The cable will be signed tomorrow. Therefore, I am not lying. Rationale: I do not have the authority to give a premature confirmation.)

In the Reagan administration, examples of all four types of deception can be found in the invasion of Grenada. Larry Speakes himself may not have known that he was telling a lie when he said that it was "preposterous" to think U.S. forces had invaded, and that no invasion would take place. But Rear Admiral John Poindexter, who told Speakes it was preposterous, knew that the landing would take place the next day, and kept Speakes and other press aides in the dark about it. Speakes did not respond to a request for an interview, but Hess and Powell and a number of the journalists interviewed for this article argued that, even if he had known and then told the lie, it might have been justifiable.

The initial claim by the government that there were no civilian casualties appears to have been inadvertent. The Pentagon says that it didn't know about the bombing of the mental hospital by a Navy plane (at least seventeen persons were killed) until several days after it occurred, and no one has yet proven otherwise.

The claim by the administration that leaders of other Caribbean countries urged it to take action appears to be in the nature of a half-truth. The administration said that the urging from other leaders came after the assassination of Maurice Bishop, the Marxist prime minister of Grenada, on October 19. But Stuart Taylor, Jr., in a lengthy piece in *The New York Times* on some of the misinformation put out by the U.S. government during and immediately after the invasion, quotes the prime minister of Barbados as saying that U.S. officials had been talking about possible action at least as early as October 15, four days before the killing.

And while it's hard to determine whether the government was telling an outright lie when it said it had prevented reporters from accompanying the troops because of concern for the safety of the journalists, subsequent comments by Secretary of State George Shultz seem to give some sense of the real reason for the ban. "These days, in the advocacy journalism that's been adopted, it seems as though the reporters are always against us and so they're always trying to screw things up," he said. "And when you're trying to conduct a military operation, you don't need that."

It is difficult to know whether some of the most important misinformation was deliberate or inadvertent because the degree of the deception depends on whether there was any intent to deceive. Reagan, in a television speech to the nation, said there were an estimated 400 to 600 Cubans on the island, and that they were "a military force," rather than construction workers. The next day, Admiral Wesley L. McDonald said that captured documents showed that there were at least 1,100 Cubans on Grenada, and that they were all "well-trained professional soldiers."

Eventually, the State Department said that the Cuban government's own figure probably was right—that there had been 784 Cubans on the island. Still later, U.S. military authorities on Grenada said that, after interrogating them, they had concluded that most of the Cubans really had been construction workers, and that only about 100 had been combatants. "Thus, over three days the Pentagon estimate of the number of Cuban fighters who had met the invading force seems to have plunged from more than 1,000 to fewer than 200, including the estimated 30 to 70 Cubans who were killed," Taylor wrote.

What difference does it make whether there were 784 Cubans on Grenada or 1,100, and whether they were "well-trained professional soldiers," as Admiral McDonald insisted, or construction workers, as the Cuban government claimed? One answer, of course, is that one version suggests an attempt to take over a country and perhaps export revolution (which the Reagan administration said was the case), while the other version suggests that Cuba might only have been providing economic aid to a government that it considered an ally.

The inflation of the number of Cubans, and the initial characterization of them as a military force, was a part of the data that were used by the Reagan administration to argue that a Cuban takeover was at hand, that American students were in danger, and that, as many newspapers repeated in their headlines, "We got there just in time."

Grenada also highlighted a major problem in trying to counter deception and misinformation. The president was able to give his version on national television, to a huge audience, and was backed up by carefully selected and edited television film clips. The challenges to the official version came over a period of days and weeks, and they were fragmented and uncoordinated. One paper would challenge one statement, a second paper would challenge a second one, and a television report would challenge a third. A large number of Americans heard the president say, "We got there just in time." But it was only in a disjointed and scattershot way, over a period of weeks following the invasion, that the press raised the two immediate and obvious questions, neither of them yet fully answered.

Did we?

In time for what?

This issue arose again during the presidential campaign, when George Bush claimed in his television debate with Geraldine Ferraro that Mondale had said that the American Marines who had died in the bombing of the embassy in Beirut had died in "shame." Mondale denied this; and pressed Bush for a retraction. And in the process Peter Teeley, Bush's press secretary, brought the whole problem into focus.

"You can say anything you want in a debate, and eighty million people hear it," he told reporters. "If reporters then document that a candidate spoke untruthfully, so what? Maybe two hundred people read it, or two thousand or twenty thousand."

Which makes the point that, particularly in the television age, reporters need to be aggressive in documenting and pointing out deceptions, half-truths, and outright lies, unless governments and officials are going to be allowed to lie with impunity....

THE NEED FOR A MORE AGGRESSIVE PRESS

It is not necessary to challenge every statistic to make a point, and readers of most major newspapers have been told repeatedly that the Reagan administration has a philosophy about enforcement of civil rights laws that is very different from that of most recent administrations. But Miller nonetheless has a point when he says that for reporters to accept such numbers on their face is to allow themselves and their readers to be manipulated and deceived.

The challenge is likely to become greater as Reagan, immensely popular and recently swept back into office by a landslide, moves ahead with his stated goals for limiting the flow of information to the public. Already, his administration has supported bills that would exempt the Secret Service, the CIA, and most FBI activities from the Freedom of Information Act, and has imposed a rule at the Defense Department that any person with access to classified information must submit to lie detector tests whenever asked to. It has reversed the Carter administration policy and now allows the FBI and CIA to infiltrate the media if the attorney general finds it in the interest of the national security to do so, and has set regulations that allow the FBI to infiltrate and monitor domestic groups, including the press, while conducting investigations of organized crime or terrorism. It has slashed the budget of the indexing staff of the National Archives, meaning that access to historical records, including the Nixon tapes, will be delayed for years. It has created mechanisms for monitoring contacts between White House staffers and reporters, and has issued guidelines telling officials handling FOIA requests to be stingy in giving fee reductions to journalists, scholars, and authors. It has rewritten the classification system to insure that more, rather than less, information will be classified. And it has made proposals—already implemented in some agencies—that would require all officials who have had access to classified information to come back to the government for the rest of their lives and submit for prior censorship any speeches, letters to the editor, news articles, or works of fiction.

Nick Horrock, of *Newsweek,* who has worked in Washington for most of the past two decades, says that some of the changes are atmospheric, and not entirely caused by Reagan. "There has been a shift back to an atmosphere much more like it was in the early 1960s," Horrock says. "During the Vietnam War and Watergate, a lot of dissidents were in the government, and they were quick to speak out, to tell reporters that things weren't working the way they should. Now, there aren't so many dissidents. It's not popular to take risks. Being a whistle-blower is no longer popular."

In a recent article, William Greider, the former assistant managing editor for national news at *The Washington Post* and now national editor of *Rolling Stone* magazine, argued that the press, too, seems to be in retreat. "It seems to be pulling in its lances, taking fewer risks, avoiding the hard and nasty confrontations it would have zealously pursued five or ten years ago…," he wrote. "The trend I see is deep and subtle—a shift toward 'hard news,' which means narrow splinters of unexamined fact, a turning away from more provocative explorations of subjects that have not been legitimized by official sources."

If he's right, and many in the media agree that he is, it is happening at a particularly bad time. The history of the press-government relationship since World War II shows that administrations have claimed a right to lie in some circumstances, and have been unable to resist the temptation to deceive in a great many others. And this particular administration, headed by a tremendously popular president, has made clear that it wants to make information about government operations harder to get, and, in terms of threats to their careers, more dangerous for civil servants to provide.

That means that the press needs to be even more aggressive, not less, if it is to follow the John Mitchell rule for covering government: Don't watch what we say. Watch what we do.

Our National Secrets: The Intelligence Community and the Press

William T. Casey

I am very pleased to speak to you this evening, officers, members and guests of the Society of Professional Journalists, about the extremely delicate and critical relationship between the press and the intelligence community. But I want to be very careful and precise in addressing this concern. Too frequently when I speak of the damage from publishing classified information, I find myself accused of wanting to demolish the First Amendment and trying to muzzle our free press.

To avoid any misunderstanding, let me say that I cherish the First Amendment and admire the diligence and ingenuity of the working press. I applaud your exposure of waste, inefficiency, and corruption. I salute and support your obligation to ferret out and publish the information the people need to be well informed about events around the world as well as the activities of their democratic government. In this, I speak from 40 years of experience as a friend, a supporter and a participant in the media.

Senator Durenberger told the National Press Club last June that 1985 will be remembered as the year of the spy, but that 1986 will be known as the year of the leak. He couldn't have been more correct. Our nation's security has literally been hemorrhaging as sensitive classified information continually appears in the world media.

And make no mistake about it. The publication of these secrets has caused great damage to our ability to collect intelligence about the intentions, plans and activities of those who work against our nation's interests—be they Soviets, terrorists, or drug dealers. It is vital that the press and the public understand what is going on, why it is happening, and what needs to be done about it.

William T. Casey, "Our National Secrets: The Intelligence Community and the Press," A speech delivered before the Society of Professional Journalists, Washington, D.C., Sept. 24, 1986. *Vital Speeches of the Day* (1 December 1986), 98–100. Reprinted with permission of Thomas Daly, managing editor, *Vital Speeches of the Day.*

Our country has invested many years of effort, the talent of hundreds of thousands of our citizens, and billions of dollars on intelligence. And the nation has gotten an excellent return on its investment. We have and continue to develop methods of collecting the information needed to assess missiles and other weapons aimed at us, determine the intentions and vulnerabilities of our adversaries so that we can respond with effective defenses and countermeasures, protect our citizens and installations around the world from terrorism, and assist our diplomats and policymakers by telling them the cold hard truth about events around the world that affect U.S. interests. Good intelligence is critical to our national security, critical to our hopes of effective arms control, and critical to the safety and liberty of our citizens.

For the past five years it has been my responsibility and my pleasure to direct and coordinate the intelligence effort that is our country's first line of defense. Our intelligence organizations collect information of interest to U.S. policymakers through sensitive dealings with people around the world who want to help us, sometimes at great risk, also through a variety of advanced technological systems, and also through the cooperative efforts of our allies. If the details of how we collect intelligence are publicized or can be deduced through the information these sources provide, the agents will be arrested and perhaps executed, our adversaries will take steps to neutralize our technical collection capabilities, and our allies as they lose confidence in our ability to protect their information will refuse to share it with us. Secrecy and confidentiality about how and through whom we collect information is essential to our effectiveness.

To protect our national security and our intelligence sources, we must classify and restrict the circulation not only of information about how and where we collect intelligence but of the reports and assessments based on that intelligence if they might reveal or compromise our sources and methods. The KGB and other hostile intelligence services each year spend billions of dollars trying to acquire this information. But the unauthorized publication of restricted information hands to our adversaries on a silver platter information that their spies, their researchers, and their satellites are working 24 hours a day to uncover and use against us.

We have clearly reached the point where we must address this risk to our fundamental security. The way to begin is to lay out what is happening in an unvarnished way. It is difficult to discuss the specific damage to this nation's ability to protect itself without confirming the accuracy of information which has been delivered through the media and removing any doubts that might remain in the minds of the KGB or the terrorists. I can say that some of our sources have not been heard from after their information has been published in the U.S. press. Others have decided that cooperating with us is too risky. Leaders and intelligence services of our closest allies have told us that if we can't tighten up, they will have to pull back on cooperation with us because they have had enough of reading the information they provide in the U.S. media.

How can we regain control of our national secrets? We must tighten discipline among U.S. government employees who use classified information. We must develop better cooperation between the media and the government on stories which put intelligence sources and methods at risk. We must establish that restrictions on the misuse of sensitive and properly classified information cannot be violated with impunity. We must enforce and perhaps tighten laws Congress has enacted to protect classified information.

The most effective way of preventing damage from leaks is to increase discipline within the government. The inability to control sensitive information is destructive of the morale of people who do keep secrets, as well as damaging to our security. The President has re-emphasized the special obligation federal workers have to protect the classified information with which they are entrusted. Efforts to uncover and discipline those who violate this trust need to be strengthened. New laws may be needed to deal with federal employees who decide on their own to disclose classified information.

The government official, military officer or contractor employee who has been cleared for access to classified material is responsible for keeping the secrets he is given. There is no room for doubt about this. Each person who is cleared must sign a nondisclosure agreement which spells out his or her responsibilities in significant detail. When these individuals discuss classified information with unauthorized persons, there is little likelihood that they do not understand what they are doing. Still, we have allowed an atmosphere to develop where many believe there is little risk and no penalty for violating the trust placed in them by their nation.

Within the government, the effort to stop and penalize the unauthorized disclosure of classified intelligence has been weak and fragmented. It needs to be tightened up and speeded up. Unauthorized disclosures need to be identified as soon as they are published. Investigations must be swift and thorough. Disciplinary action appropriate to the violation needs to be applied to deter others from similar violations.

Too much information is classified. We will work to reduce the body of classified information, but that can't be done overnight. It will take time. In acting against unauthorized disclosures we should focus on really damaging and critical disclosures.

Even as we improve discipline within the government, the media will continue to come into possession of information which, if published, can jeopardize lives, damage national security and the international relationships and the reputation for reliability of our nation. Many in your profession recognize a responsibility to weigh these dangers before rushing into print or onto the air waves. The task is to strike the very delicate and difficult balance between this responsibility and the obligation to provide the public the information it needs for self-government.

Media leaders recognize this as Katharine Graham did when she said recently: "When the media obtains especially sensitive information, we are willing to tell the authorities what we have learned and what we plan to report. And while reserving the right to make the final decision ourselves, we are anxious to listen to arguments about why information should not be aired. [The media] want to do nothing that would endanger human life or national security. We are willing to cooperate with the authorities in witholding information that could have those consequences."

Ben Bradlee, in an op-ed piece in the *Washington Post* of 8 June 1986 said: "We do consult with the government regularly about sensitive stories and we do withhold stories for national security reasons, far more than the public might think. The *Post* has withheld information from more than a dozen stories so far this year for these reasons." He then went on to say: "We don't allow the government—or anyone else—to decide what we should print. That is our job."

I agree that no one can tell a publisher what he must print. On the other hand, Congress has enacted legislation which makes it unlawful to disclose or publish certain categories of information and the media, like everybody else, must adhere to the law.

The First Amendment to the Constitution is cited to make the point that the media should be the sole judge of what should or should not be printed on national security matters. The public's right to know, however, is not absolute. Where national security and foreign policy are at issue, the First Amendment permits determinations by appropriate governmental authorities that certain information should not be released into the public domain. This is what the classification system is all about. When the sanctity of classified information is protected by a duly enacted criminal statute, those who would publish or otherwise disclose proceed at their own risk.

In the Pentagon Papers case, the Supreme Court ruled that the First Amendment outlawed prior restraint, but Justice Douglas and Justice White, in concurring opinions, supported the law imposing criminal penalties on the publication of information on communications intelligence.

This statute was passed shortly after World War II to protect classified information about communications intelligence from being "knowingly and willfully" published or in any other way made available to an unauthorized person. Congress carefully limited the application of this prohibition to communications intelligence, which it called "a small degree of classified matter, a category which is both vital and vulnerable to almost a unique degree." Our reading of Japanese and German communications had brought victory in World War II much earlier and saved many thousands of lives and Congress clearly regarded communications intelligence as one of our best chances to learn about other nations' military plans and of warnings of military attacks against us.

Today, as media disclosure deprives us of our best source of warning of terrorist and other threats, we cannot justify failure to use a statute enacted by Congress to protect this sensitive and irreplaceable information. Justice Byron White wrote in his concurring opinion on the controversial Pentagon Papers case in 1971 that the language in the communications statute is "precise." He warned that "newspapers are presumably now on full notice of the position of the United States and must face the consequences if they publish."

As unauthorized disclosures increasingly debilitate other sources of intelligence for which Senator Durenberger and his colleagues in the Congress appropriate billions of dollars to develop and maintain, I believe it will be necessary for them in their next legislative session to consider more explicit restrictions on unauthorized disclosure of other types of properly classified information.

In closing, I want to emphasize that I have been gratified by the readiness of many of you to carefully consider on occasion withholding publication of information which could jeopardize national interests or to present a story in a way that meets the public need yet minimizes potential damage to intelligence sources.

We respect and want to cooperate with your need and obligation to report on national security issues and the national security process. We are prepared to discuss our general policies and procedures. We may sometimes need to insist on the right to approve quotations or pre-publication review to ensure that nothing is inadvertently said that could jeopardize our sources. Our information and activities are too likely to be too closely related to sensitive sources or operations for us to hand out juicy items for journalistic scoops.

Let me relay some criticisms and suggestions from the intelligence community that may be of value to you in journalism who, like us, report and analyze and rely on sources. You have as much interest as we do, certainly, in the security of the country, and the capability of our intelligence organizations to deal with an increasingly dangerous and complicated world.

There are in our government people who think they can obtain favorable publicity for programs they support, encourage bad press for programs they oppose, make themselves look good in the media, settle a score with an adversary, or simply bask in the reflected glory of the media star with whom they cooperate. That's fair game, but not when they break the law by mishandling classified information. When they do so their actions are sometimes far more damaging than waste, fraud, and corruption. In the thousands of column inches devoted to editorials criticizing government abuses and inefficiencies, only a few have ever called to task those who betray classified information to the media. There is a double standard at work here which says a violation of trust that sells newspapers or attracts television viewers is not as serious as one which does not. We ask you to help us hold before government employees their obligation of trust and honor.

We, in the intelligence community, will be alert to your criticism and in turn work to benefit from it. We are making greater efforts to sanitize information which the public should have to understand the threats we all face.

We are eager to develop better understanding and closer cooperation between you in the working press, who perform such a vital function in our society, and the intelligence community, which plays an essential role in protecting this nation. America needs a free, vigorous press and it needs a superior intelligence service. We can have both as we serve our country in vital and fundamental matters.

Should the Press Play Vice Cop?

Nicholas von Hoffman

The interview was a first, of sorts, for journalism. Last month Representative Barney Frank called in a reporter from *The Boston Globe,* his home state's largest newspaper, and committed an act of pre-emptive confession. He told the reporter that he was gay.

To anyone who's been around Capitol Hill for more than a month, the news came as one of the year's biggest unsurprises. Whether it was news to the voters in Frank's district is problematic, but the reason Frank came out of the closet was plain enough: he wanted to make sure that those voters got the news from him and not from *The Miami Herald*, Ted Koppel or the other

---

Nicholas von Hoffman, "Should the Press Play Vice Cop?" *The Nation* (20 June 1987), 852–853.

gonadseeking practitioners of sex-snoop journalism. In the interview Frank said it was the dismemberment of Gary Hart that had forced his hand.

Frank, who is one of the smartest men in national politics, understood that what had been done to Hart did little to resolve the "character issues" in the contest for the Democratic presidential nomination but much for the cause of blackmail and those who practice the craft. Hart's destruction was a warning to every politician that the rules had changed in favor of the sex blackmailer.

Journalists agree that the rules have changed but contend that the shift is a reflection of changing values in society, and blah-blah-de-blah-blah. What has assuredly changed is that the establishment, non-porn press will now go with sex stories about famous people in general, and politicians in particular, that it wouldn't have touched a couple of years ago.

Before *l'affaire* Hart, the policy was not to print or put on the air anything having to do with politicians and sex unless the incident had been made part of the public record. Thus, when Representative Wilbur Mills was knocked out of politics because of his drunken association with fan dancer Fanne Fox, it made the papers only after the two had been caught by the police sloshing around in the tidal basin near the Jefferson Memorial. When Representative Wayne Hays's liaison with a popsy was exposed in the public prints, it was after she was discovered on the public payroll. The Ted Kennedy–Mary Jo Kopechne scandal came to light because it was entwined in a serious police matter. In these three famous stories, reporters did not play the part of voyeurs, house dicks or sex creeps.

Acting according to the same informal rule, the press would not print one famous political sex story. Even though Federal Bureau of Investigation agents offered a number of newspaper editors transcripts of the small sex orgy at the Willard Hotel that Martin Luther King Jr. had for himself, the story did not see the light of day. It had been a private affair and had never become part of any public record or official action.

With the Hart stakeout, the old guidelines for journalistic behavior vanished. After the Hart episode, a politician cannot be sure whether or not the media will go into print or on the air with personal sex material. The politician has to presume that an editor somewhere will decide that the public's right to know has been engaged and must be satisfied by names, dates and clinical details.

The public's right to know was invoked in regard to trapping Hart in the classic lies of the unfaithful husband. The people, it seemed, had a right to see that when pressed by reporters to answer yes or no, Did you or did you not cheat on your wife? Gary Hart didn't tell the truth. A more germane test for a person aspiring to the top might be to learn, when in a corner, how well he or she lies. After all, it can be argued that Eisenhower's greatest mistake in the U2 fiasco came when he stopped lying.

In any event, did the people also have a right to know the other woman's name? What office was Donna Rice running for? Nevertheless her name and face were disseminated across the globe by all known forms of communication, from smoke signal to satellite. The rest of her more or less unclad body was to be seen at every newspaper kiosk and on every television screen in the Free World. Doubtless this is the people's right to peep. How can we cast an intelligent vote in next year's primaries if we haven't seen Donna Rice nude?

The editors and reporters who knocked Gary Hart out of politics by kicking in his hotel-room door complained that Hart wasn't answering their questions about his life between the sheets. Then the candidate, failing to interest the press in foreign policy or the lightness of the dollar, got snappish and quit the race. Nevertheless, those same ladies and gentlemen will be heard next year complaining that the candidates aren't talking about the issues.

The issues, of course, are what the major media decide to play up. Thus, eight days after the defenestration of Hart, the remaining Democratic candidates, knowing that it is not they but journalism that sets the topics for debate in America, had picked up the cue. All of them were out on the hustings with their wives, their kiddlipoos and the family's old English sheepdog. Bright of face, clear of eye, there wasn't an adulterer in the crowd. Shortly thereafter a group in Iowa announced it was staging something akin to a beauty contest among the candidates' wives to choose who would make the best First Lady. If it were bovine rectitude and similar demonstrations of character that the media demanded, the candidates would be happy to delegate the secondary, life-and-death issues to their staffs.

Americans of a century ago had a grasp of what qualities were needed in a President. The choice was between Senator James G. Blaine, a doting husband and father but a politician corrupt enough to feel at home in the 1980s, and Grover Cleveland, a man of sterling probity in his public life but the father of an illegitimate child. The voters of 1884 sent Blaine home to his family, where he would do the most good, and Cleveland to the White House, where his qualities would best be employed. But then there was no *Washington Post* to come to Cleveland, as the paper allegedly did to Hart, and say that it would publish the name of another of his mistresses unless he got out of the race.

There is a smarminess about *The Washington Post*'s second-woman story that has not been penetrated. After days of rumors circulating about its source on this unhappy tale, *The Post* conceded that it learned about woman *numero dos* when certain reports of a private detective agency were placed in its hands. Who hired the detective agency? Gossip has it that it was a not-to-be-named ex-senator suspicious that his wife was trysting with Gary

Hart; gossip also has it that the reports were given to someone in Senator Joseph Biden's campaign who made sure they fell into the right hands. *The Post* has affirmed that a private detective agency was indeed involved. It has denied that the channel of transmission was a rival political campaign. But should we give a newspaper's denial any greater credence than a politician's?

The execution of candidate Hart was excused as a special, one-time-only demonstration of media power. Hart was selected for capital punishment because, they said, he stupidly denied that he was cheating on his wife and dared reporters to follow him around and try to catch him *in flagrante delicto.* One wonders what would have happened if he'd dared them to run him over with a Mack truck. Their fallback rationalization was that Hart has so many women and was so brazen about it that he fell into a unique category. Apparently, there is a finite, if not yet announced, number of adulteries permitted before the reporters gather round and stone the offending politician. It's not sin that's objected to, only satyriasis.

As Ohio Governor Richard Celeste can attest, a different standard was applied to him by the Cleveland *Plain Dealer,* which bannered a front-page story accusing him of having had three *liaisons dangereuses.* The besieged man's wife rushed to say that whatever he may have done, she forgave him; but that only gave rise to stories about her, and so it goes, on and on and on.

This is not, of course, the first time in human history that sexual intrigue has been part of a process of political advancement and the selection of leaders. Suetonius in The Lives of the Twelve Caesars depicts such a government, the end result being that power was placed in the hands of pimps, prostitutes, eunuchs, procurers, tale bearers, whoremasters, poisoners and perverts. If reporters are to play the role of sex cops, our political process will be made captive to the slimiest of moral tyrannies, one in which only the grandest hypocrites and the most adept fakirs can rise to the top. Nor can people out of politics escape when organs like *The Washington Post* begin printing on yellow paper.

Within days of Hart's retirement from politics the rules for covering the sex lives of the rich and famous were again adjusted to make underwear sniffing yet more permissible. As recently as a couple of months ago it would have been unlikely for the respectable media to publicize accusations of homosexuality concerning a TV evangelist or any other nonpolitical public figure unless it was also a police matter. In the past few weeks, however, ABC and Ted Koppel have blazed new trails in this important area of public inquiry. *Nightline* set viewer rating records with Koppel's discussions about whether Jim Bakker had had sex with some unnamed men in a steam bath. The accusations had nothing to do with the contested tax exemptions claimed for the neon Jesurama or Christathon Bakker runs in his South

Carolina theme park. Although the gender of people unlucky enough to be bedded by this yucky little minister has scant connection with politics, public policy or anything else relevant to ethical journalism, the subject has been at the top of the news night after night. Moreover, ABC reporters had no direct knowledge of the alleged acts; thus, Koppel and his network, with no independent investigation on their part, simply lent themselves to broadcasting sex-related charges made by Jerry Falwell and Bakker's other enemies. The people's right to pant had been well served.

Blackmailers were well served too. After what has been done to Bakker, no public figure, in or out of politics (other than Mother Teresa, perhaps) can any longer tell a blackmailer, "Do your damnedest, no decent newspaper, no reputable broadcaster, will touch filth like that." The Koppel/ABC message is that they'll not only touch it, they'll compete for it.

And the damage caused by the union of blackmail and crotch-centered journalism is invisible. The extortionist will exact the vote he wants on a key bill, will place his person in the important job; the blackmailer will get the military secret or the money or the influence, and no one will know.

"What Did Mr. Dwyer Do, Daddy?"

David B. Dick

The medium has become the madness, and this just won't do if we are to survive as anything resembling rational sensitive, caring human beings.

When R. Budd Dwyer, the treasurer of Pennsylvania, called a news conference January 22 in Harrisburg, ostensibly to announce his resignation before being sentenced for a fraud conviction, he talked for a while, pulled out a .357 Magnum revolver, stuck it into his mouth and pulled the trigger.

The subsequent news treatment of the incident became a terrifying example of Professor Harold D. Lasswell's "silver bullet" theory of mass communications.

The silver bullet zaps you before you have a chance to say, "Hell, no."

The question of what news people should do when a silver bullet strikes is often described as a "dilemma." But it is a continuing problem, and calling it a dilemma provides an unacceptable loophole through which

---

David B. Dick, " 'What Did Mr. Dwyer Do, Daddy?' " *The Quill* (March 1987), 18–20. Reprinted with permission of the author.

weak-willed, quick-and-dirty practitioners slip through too easily and too piously.

"A tough one to call," I hear them saying darkly in their newsrooms when a silver bullet strikes, meanwhile shouting to a colleague who has just walked in from another assignment, and who has therefore missed the really Big One: "Take a look at this!"

The fact is, in Pennsylvania a tormented human being blew his brains out, and for reasons known only to him did it not in the privacy of his garage but center stage before television cameras.

The matter should not have been ignored; but it should have been treated with a greater regard for TV viewers, the radio audience, and the readers of newspapers.

Before we rush to place the stamp of "insensitivity" on one news medium, TV, we should remember that radio and print journalists were also present at the news conference. *The Washington Post* and the *New York Daily News,* in fact, were among the papers that ran pictures of the final seconds of Dwyer's life.

There is no justification for naming television as the only bad guy in this bizarre Pennsylvania morality play. We journalists are all human beings first and journalists second. If journalists today are guilty, as some charge, of sometimes forgetting that maxim, then they have played a major role in the desensitizing of an entire generation with an unrelenting fusillade of silver bullets.

I've done my part in the desensitizing process. While a correspondent with CBS News, I was confronted with having to recommend whether or not to use footage of one human being killing another human being in the Baton Rouge airport. That was another silver bullet in the head. I now profoundly regret my recommendation to run the pictures.

It's time to recognize that we in the news media are part of the problem; it's time that men and women in the business had the moral courage to take a stand for a higher level of ethical conduct.

Forget the Dwyer suicide for a moment. I suggest that it's wrong as a general principle for one human being (an assignment editor, perhaps, or a news director) to say to another human being (a camera operator in the field): "You get the pictures; we'll decide whether to use them."

To be sure, the you-get-the-pictures business has been Standard Operating Procedure for many years. Perhaps media critic Ron Powers summed up the moral absurdity of it best when he quoted a photographer as having said: "I am a camera with the shutters open.... I am passive.... I don't think."

This handsomely paid passiveness serves the newsgathering process well—to a point. But every human being must have the option to turn the camera off and go to another human being's assistance when life itself has been placed in jeopardy.

Perhaps there was not time enough to help the state treasurer of Pennsylvania. Perhaps only in hindsight was there time enough to distract him and wrestle the gun from his hand.

But as one human being trying to be rational, sensitive and caring, I find no ethical justification for blindly broadcasting the tape of the suicide, to surrendering to the mindlessness of, "If we've got it, we ought to use it."

I think I hear some of my former professional colleagues saying something like, "Come off it, David. Now you're hiding behind your new-found academic gowns, preaching morality to us when in fact if *you* had staffed the Dwyer news conference, you would have expected your camera operator to have continued rolling, and you would have been disappointed if it had been any other way.

"After all, the Emmy sitting on your mantlepiece down on your retirement farm was won because cameraman Laurens Pierce kept rolling when George Wallace was gunned down in the Laurel, Maryland shopping center."

Partly true. The day Wallace was shot I agonized with everybody else at CBS News while the film was in the processor and I rejoiced with everybody else when it emerged with every frame in focus.

Nevertheless, there is a considerable difference between the attempted assassination of George Wallace and the suicide of R. Budd Dwyer.

And there certainly is a difference between the Dwyer pictures and the Abraham Zapruder footage of the assassination of President Kennedy, the CBS News footage of the murder of presidential candidate Robert F. Kennedy, and the attempted assassination of President Reagan.

Jack Ruby's shot into the stomach of Lee Harvey Oswald, and the sight of more than 900 bloated bodies at Jonestown are exceptional and unavoidable situations. Jim Jones fired a silver bullet, too, but the story was not that he, as an individual, committed suicide. The story was the tragedy of more than 900 humans led astray.

Edward T. Adams won a Pulitzer Prize and a Sigma Delta Chi Distinguished Service Award for his photo series of the Saigon chief of police's point-blank firing of a pistol bullet into the head of a Vietcong prisoner. The prominence of those involved did not determine the news value of the photos; the brutality of the war did. Likewise, footage of the murder of ABC Correspondent Bill Stewart in Nicaragua was the turning point of that civil war. Whether we are talking about George Wallace or the brothers Kennedy or Lee Harvey Oswald or the Vietcong prisoner or Bill Stewart or the members of the Jonestown cult, we are talking about *victims* of violence. They were acted upon, and because of who they were, or because of the context of their times, what happened to them was indeed newsworthy. That news people were present at the time of the event, or shortly thereafter, was a matter of coincidence.

The death of Budd Dwyer was newsworthy, and should have been reported. But he was both victim and victimizer, a deranged man who chose to make us all victims of his madness. The news media cooperated, as planned—unwittingly before the shot, and mindlessly after the shot. Journalists were parties to the act.

R. Budd Dwyer was hardly a household name anywhere outside Pennsylvania. What made Dwyer "newsworthy" was not so much his prominence as it was his insertion of the .357 Magnum revolver into his mouth and the pulling of the trigger.

Representatives of the few television stations that aired the entire suicide gave a nobler explanation of why they did so. Said one: "It's a historic event....It's a reflection of a very important man in Pennsylvania society and what he did." That's a peculiarly skewed definition of "historic," one that would fail any test of rigorous thought.

All right. Am I to understand that WPXI-TV in Pittsburgh and WPVI-TV in Philadelphia and other stations that carried it are comfortable with the knowledge that this gruesome, horrifying, brain-searing footage of one human being's death was seen in households where children, never mind "adults," were present?

"What did Mr. Dwyer do, Daddy?"

"Well, as you could see, he committed suicide, Darling."

Duty supersedes comfortableness. I know that. But do professional and ethical journalists (which is not, I hope, a contradiction in terms) have a *duty* to show the public in complete or nearly complete detail the self-destruction of another human being?

I think not.

So, what to do?

Don't show the footage involving the gun. Simply tell the story with the following explanation: "We choose not to show the public pictures that exceed the bounds of our concept of what is decent and proper and above all, humane."

That course was not widely followed. And, predictably, other journalists (including at least one former professional turned academic) had a field day evaluating the sorry state of affairs. The Louisville *Courier-Journal* ran a headline: "Graphic suicide photos put news executives in a quandary."

Is there anyone out there who wonders why anyone should have been in a quandary about something so evident to a reasonably discerning person?

But then, what is to be said about R. Budd Dwyer's "use" of the media? Mr. Dwyer had the option to take his own life many ways, of course.

But if we journalists, broadcast and print, don't exercise our right of refusing to scatter Dwyer's brain fragments from one end of Pennsylvania to the other, and possibly from one end of the nation to the other, all in the name of "he did it, and we have pictures," then we've sold our souls to a devil who insists that the public has a right to see everything, no matter how macabre.

Media critic Powers longs for "guidelines for the human soul," but there is the possibility that for quite some time, in the rush to tell it like it is and show it like it was, some journalists have simply given up on the idea of guidelines.

They see guidelines as self-righteous intrusions into their lives, and R. Budd Dwyer will fade from memory—until the next time a silver bullet comes along.

We ought to meet this media devil head-on with language he just possibly may be able to understand. Putting the Dwyer footage on the air (or on paper) is very much like saying, "We've got a suicide, y'all come."

Let Hollywood dally with the grotesque; professional journalists have no business wallowing in that swamp. The silver bullets increasingly have become the shots heard around the living rooms of our nation. It's time to remember the simple guideline that we are human beings first, journalists second.

Anything less than that will lead eventually to destruction of the human soul, and at that point it won't matter if passive journalists are there to report it. There won't be anybody left to watch.

One from the Heart: How a Tough Decision Was Made

Frederick L. D'Ambrosi

Is there any reason to show a man's head explode on TV? In the newsroom of WTAE-TV, the Pittsburgh station where I work as executive news producer, it took us less than a minute to say no to that question.

WTAE-TV, an ABC affiliate, wasn't staffing R. Budd Dwyer's press conference in Harrisburg when he put a .357 Magnum in his mouth and pulled the trigger. Pittsburgh's two other network-affiliated stations were.

By the time we got the story off the wire shortly after 11:00 a.m., WPXI-TV, the NBC affiliate, was already breaking into its regular programming. They did a phone interview with their reporter in Harrisburg, but didn't have any pictures.

The WTAE newsroom went into disaster mode. I alerted the studio crew and headed for the control room. Assignments Manager Jody Woznicki started scrambling crews and digging for information.

Reporter Jack Salvatore went to the studio and got on the air at 11:15 with the basics: State Treasurer Budd Dwyer had shot himself at a news conference; we don't know his condition.

Minutes later, Assistant News Director John Poister went to the editing room and News Director Joe Rovitto and anchor Sally Wiggin went to the studio. Wiggin took over the cut-ins from Salvatore, and News Director Rovitto became the final checkpoint for all information before it got on the air.

But at that point, we still lacked pictures.

Then word came from the desk: Our ABC sister station in Philadelphia, WPVI-TV, had been at the news conference, and it had been the first station to book time on the satellite uplink out of Harrisburg. It was going to feed the bird at 11:30. We could downlink the feed and use it, which would make us the first Pittsburgh station capable of airing pictures of the suicide.

When the feed came down, I watched it on a monitor in the control room. I could see Rovitto and Wiggin in the studio watching on another monitor. It was raw tape of the news conference, cued to about two minutes before the shooting.

Frederick L. D'Ambrosi, "One from the Heart: How a Tough Decision Was Made," *The Quill* (March 1987), 20–21. Reprinted with permission of the author.

We watched as Dwyer rambled on about the criminal justice system. He handed out letters to his aides. He grabbed a manila envelope and pulled out a gun.

The WPVI cameraman hung in there. His camera was on a tripod, and the picture was rock-steady. He even zoomed in for a tight shot of the gun as Dwyer waved it around.

I remember thinking, as if somehow giving directions to the cameraman: "Pull out! You're going to miss the whole thing!"

As if on cue, the zoom lens pulls back to a medium shot, showing Dwyer head to waist. Within seconds, the gun goes toward his mouth. There's the muffled sound of a shot and blood sprays across the curtain behind him.

Dwyer slumps against the wall and the camera follows him down, zooming in on his head as blood flows like a red waterfall down his face.

The photographer is in a perfect position to record everything. He is to Dwyer's right, and his shot isn't blocked by the podium or by the table Dwyer had carefully positioned to protect himself from potential saviors.

At that point, I turned away from the screen. In 10 years of watching raw video of every conceivable atrocity, I've never seen worse.

I can see Rovitto and Wiggin in the studio. Wiggin, a veteran street reporter, is upset, and Rovitto is trying to calm her.

I *know* that Rovitto is not going to let the gunshot get on the air. He has always said, after all, that I let too much operating room video get into our medical stories.

Meanwhile, Assistant News Director Poister is in the editing room, where he has two identical tapes running. One will be left as is; the other will be edited.

Poister tells an editor to stop one of the tapes and "black it" from the instant the gun begins to move toward Dwyer's mouth. The studio anchor will take over at that point.

Rovitto calls Poister and approves the decision that's already in motion. Then Rovitto calls to tell me about it. My approval is implied. Rovitto knows I'd argue if I disagreed.

Seconds later the tape is ready, cued to the final minute of Budd Dwyer's life. I tell the director to let the tape go to black, which is not the usual procedure. Ordinarily, we get out of a tape while there's still video on the screen. But in this case, I wanted the viewers to see the exact point where we'd made our black-out decision.

The station breaks programming. Wiggin talks. The tape rolls, and suddenly I get this sick feeling that we have the wrong tape loaded. Stranger things have happened in the confusion of a news crisis.

I call the playback room. It's the right tape.

The director overhears some of my conversation and gets nervous. He punchs back to Wiggin right after Dwyer starts waving the gun around. So much for editorial decisions. In TV, it's the guy with his hand on the button who has the final say.

We ran the same version of the shooting on the noon news.

Afterward, we met in News Director Rovitto's office to take a second look at our decision.

Everyone agreed we'd done the right thing. We briefly considered letting the gun get closer to Dwyer's mouth, but decided not to.

We also rejected the idea of freezing the picture of Dwyer at some point and letting the natural sound of the shooting play. Too grotesque.

At no time did we seriously consider going without video. The phones quickly began to ring as people called to thank the station for showing an edited version of the shooting rather than the entire episode. So far as I know, none of the callers questioned our decision to run video.

Many callers, however, complained that WPXI-TV had run the moment of the shooting on its noon news broadcast.

By the end of the week, we had received more than 200 phone calls about our decision from viewers. All but a few were positive. I've never before been in a situation where people called to thank us for *not* doing something.

I did talk to a couple of callers who disagreed with our decision to edit the tape of the shooting; they accused us of "censoring" the news. They didn't accept my explanation of the difference between censoring news and editing it. They were surprised to hear we make decisions like that every day.

Inside our newsroom, most people looked at the unedited video, but a significant number avoided it. Some asked me if I thought it was worth viewing. I told them it was the first time I had ever regretted seeing a piece of tape.

For days after the shooting, we at the station talked about our decision, and we all felt comfortable with it.

I've read that one Harrisburg station refused to run any video of Dwyer's final news conference. I think that was a mistake. Pennsylvanians needed to hear the final arguments of a high-ranking state official who claimed he was railroaded by a defective justice system.

For stations outside the state, I think the decision to use video was less clearcut.

I think seeing the unedited tape has changed me a little bit, though I'm not sure how. Perhaps that is an after-the-fact argument that would have justified showing it, gunshot and all.

But we are in the business of informing people, not changing them through shock therapy. The final news conference was informative. The final gunshot was not.

We made a quick decision—with our hearts rather than with our minds—and judging from community reaction, it was the right one. We've earned some more trust from our viewers. I just hope we live up to it in the next crisis.

To Kill A Messenger: The Ethics of Journalism

Earl R. Hutchison, Sr.

Among the many reasons for my speaking on occasions such as this, is this one: The national polls invariably indicate that American citizens, who, as Ellen Goodman puts it, are "supposed to be the custodians of the ward called democracy" do not know the rights and freedoms guaranteed by the constitution. Failing that constitutional test, of course, citizens can hardly be expected to pass the mass communication role test. Now I know that. Nevertheless, I'm always depressed every time a poll indicates the citizens feel the press should not be attacking policies or actions of Congress or the presidency. And so I take every opportunity to speak on the behavior of the press.

Before advancing on that dark tower on the plain of ethics, however, I should mention what those of us who work and teach in the mass communications area believe the roles and responsibilities of the press to be:

To inform, entertain and instruct. To service our society economically and politically. To keep a surveillance on our environment—a kind of distant early warning system for pollution, civil disturbances, civil liberties, war, etc. To pass on the heritage and values of a democratic society. To embrace a common carriers concept of mass communication. To serve as a watchdog on government and to protect the public's right to know.

Earl R. Hutchinson, Sr., "To Kill a Messenger: The Ethics of Journalism," *Vital Speeches of the Day* (1 July 1987), 572–576. Speech delivered at the Tennessee Technological University, Cooksville, Tenn., April 16, 1987. Reprinted with permission of the author.

As you can see, the responsibilities are awesome. And you'll have to keep in mind that how well we are performing in *some* of these areas is not the thrust of this talk. For example, I deplore as many of you do, such insipid, inane and embarrassing television programs as "The Newly Weds," "The Dating Game" and "Three's Company." And, last year, whenever I inadvertently tuned in on "Family Feud" and caught that odious host kissing his numerous guests, I fervently hoped he would catch herpes from one of them. On the other hand, I take no small amount of joy in being able to watch Masterpiece Theater, Washington Week in Review, and that magnificent McNeil/Lehrer Hour.

Our press *does* keep a surveillance on our environment, but not as well as I would like. Years ago, for example, we should have known about those 239,000 pounds of mercury being emptied into the East Fork of Poplar Creek in Oak Ridge. And the 36 million pounds of uranium released in Oak Ridge between 1944 and 1984. Years ago, we should have been attuned to the dreadful air, water and land pollution taking place. Years ago the ghetto situation should have been on the press agenda so that the city fathers would have been forced to deal with those furies smoldering in the slums. Had the press done so, we might have been spared the city riots of the 'Sixties.

But when the press does hold that surveillance mirror up to society, it suffers because of what it reflects. That happens, for example, whenever the press performs in its watchdog on the government role.

This is the role so misunderstood, not only by the general public, but by the elite in the general public: Doctors, lawyers, business chiefs, and professors. And even Allen Neuharth, who should know better because he is chairman of the nation's largest media company, the Gannett Company, told the Tennessee legislature last week that the press was acting, many times, like mad dogs rather than watch dogs. Now he's on a 50-state bus tour and he'll spread that message throughout this country. It's enough to make a grown man cry. What Neuharth ought to be doing is getting Gannett to divest itself of 91 of those 92 newspapers it owns (Gannett's been collecting newspapers like so many trinkets for a charm bracelet); Gannett should be divesting itself of 17 of the 18 radio stations it owns; and seven of the eight television stations it owns. Neuharth owes this to the journalism profession to help curb the mammoth and debilitating growth of monopoly in the profession.

Among the others who fail to understand this mass communications role of the press, are many of my best friends. One, an English professor, cancelled his subscription to *The Tennessean* because it exposed the corruption and graft taking place in the Blanton administration.

"They ought to leave Blanton alone so he can govern this state!" he said.

I replied, "Looks to me like they're exposing some corruption that ought to be exposed."

"Just because the press says it's happening doesn't mean it *is* happening," he retorted.

And when the *Tennessean* stories proved to be right, and the governor and many of his administrators were sentenced to prison, did that English professor express any appreciation for what *The Tennessean* had done? Did he reinstate his cancelled subscription to *The Tennessean?* No.

He had killed the messenger. And he wasn't about to admit to that human failing.

Why is the watchdog responsibility of the press, its major responsibility, the most misunderstood and disliked of all? Perhaps because that role is a mockingbird role. The press sees and hears and then sings its many songs to the nation and to the world. It is the messenger. But without that role being performed responsibly, we would not have an informed electorate. You and I would not know how to vote in city, state or federal elections. We would not, I believe, have survived these two centuries as a democracy.

But what are the ethics of those men and women in the media who hold the mirror by the roadside of American society? What is the code, the morality, that they operate under?

You and I know what our ethics are supposed to be as students and faculty and how those ethics are formed and being formed, and most of us try to live up to them. But how are the ethics of these messengers who bring the news to our society formed?

Some things you can explain clearly. Some things are not so easily explained. Let me give you two examples:

Jim Shipley is Cookeville's city clerk and finance director. He believes the city's government should operate openly. He believes the public's business should be conducted in public. He has ultimate respect for the role of the press in this regard. "We're just privates in the people's army," he says. He has a degree in accounting from Tennessee Tech.

Lewis Coomer is the Putnam County Circuit Court Clerk. He won the position in an election. He is a high school graduate without previous legal training. He believes that the courts and their decisions and records should be open to public scrutiny. If something happens that tends to jeopardize that mode of operation, he does something about it.

Both of these men strongly believe in the public's right to know. So much so, that I marvel at their commitment. Both, I believe, held these beliefs latent within them. Perhaps it's because they are true Americans. Somehow in the positions they held, those latent beliefs were activated and crystallized and became part of their operational procedure. I believe the same thing works within the journalism profession. With one major difference. The students of journalism are given codes and models to follow—in academe and on the job.

Each practicing journalist has an ethics code developed from a personal code stemming from their individual backgrounds. What happened to me in developing this code happens to most journalists out there:

First of all, I have a low tolerance for social injustice. It probably stems from my family background. Like most of you, I suppose, when I was born there were no silver spoons around. Not even stainless steel spoons. The only spoon I distinctly remember was the one loaded with castor oil being forced through my clenched teeth. My depression days background had a profound influence on me. But perhaps I was prepared for that low tolerance of social injustice by listening to the Lone Ranger on radio—who rode out with his sidekick, Tonto, to mete out justice for all. I even prevailed upon my mother to send away and get a Lone Ranger sweatshirt. I don't really know *all* the influences working on me.

At the University of Missouri School of Journalism, students were forced to memorize the Journalist's Creed, and write it on the final exam in the History of Journalism course taught by Frank Luther Mott. I still remember portions of it. It starts out like this:

"I believe in the profession of journalism. I believe that the public journal is a public trust. That all connected with it are trustees for the public. Acceptance of lesser service than the public service is betrayal of this trust. I believe that a journalist should write only what he holds in his heart to be true."

All that's pretty heavy metal.

Does that creed influence me? Probably more than I know. Ten years later, for example, working on a doctoral dissertation, I was investigating a horrendous censorship program in Milwaukee that was sanctioned by the *Milwaukee Journal*. I asked the *Milwaukee Journal* librarian for the newspaper's file of censorship clippings.

"We don't allow persons to come in here and go through our clippings," she replied, rather haughtily, "we're a private corporation."

Without a thought, I replied, "A public journal is a public trust." There I was, 35 years old, working on a doctoral dissertation, and programmed to respond like a boy scout of America. "If you don't want to let me see those clippings," I continued, "I want to see your editor-in-chief." And when she hesitated, I added, "If the editor feels about this the same way you do, I'll want to see your publisher."

"Just a minute," she said.

She disappeared into a back room and came back three minutes later with the censorship file.

My ethics are tempered also by the history of journalism—by those who came before me in England and in this country and who endured and fought to bring the Fourth estate to its present eminence. And my ethics are tempered by my academic experience. For example, Melvin Mencher of Columbia University, whose text I use in advanced reporting, believes that the journalist must always be wary of concentrations of power and of their possible violations of the rights of individuals. I believed that before I adopted the text. Mencher, however, crystallized those feelings for me and freed me to believe they were something other than biases.

And when I worked as a reporter and in various other editorial capacities on three newspapers, and helped to found a chapter of Sigma Delta Chi, I embraced the press' code of ethics.

Among the twenty odd things the professional journalism code says ought to be done, are these four:

1. To seek truth and to enlighten—as part of the public's right to know.
2. To guard freedom of speech (unpopular opinions, criticism of government) as an inalienable right of a people in a free society.
3. To embrace the common carrier concept of public discussion and information. That is, news and information should flow to the public in the same way public utilities carry water and electricity to the people.
4. To actively censure and try to prevent violations of these standards.

I have major reservations about only one provision of the code. Reporters are encouraged to be objective and fair. To be objective, however, in the sense most persons think of that word, precludes being fair. Being fair precludes being objective. Theodore L. Glasser, a professor at University of Minnesota, has pointed out the failings of "objective" journalism. Objectivity, he says, is biased in favor of the status quo. In favor of leaders and officials, the prominent and the elite. You see, statements made by the ordinary citizen do not make news. Sources supply the sense and substance of the news. And those sources are the prominent and the elite. Objective journalists merely provide a vehicle for these exchanges. A responsible member of the press cannot be objective. Whatever illusions the press had about this kind of objectivity was blown away in the McCarthy era by Senator Joseph McCarthy from Wisconsin, who saw spies, communists and homosexuals under every bed in the State Department and elsewhere.

Well, all of that's well and good. But codes, like talk, are/is cheap. What about the actual performances of the messengers? Let's look at the bad performances first, under the label:

A. Questionable performances—unforgivable acts

(1) A weekly publisher down the road from Cookeville will pull letters to the editor from the editorial page if they are critical of major advertisers.

(2) From conversations I've had and from articles and books I've read, I believe that the *N.Y. Times* can be influenced in its news coverage—especially its coverage of business—by economic factors. And one Denver newspaper, in the past, agreed to write so many column inches of news and

feature stories about a business for every inch of advertising that business paid for. I suspect other newspapers and broadcasting stations are so influenced today.

(3) The stone-walling that *Time Magazine* and CBS did in the libel suits filed against them by General William Westmoreland and Israeli General Ariel Sharon, in light of the editing and sloppy reporting that took place, was despicable.

(4) The fact that the television networks failed to air the Pentagon papers when they were given the opportunity by Ellsberg is indefensible. The networks are, at times, cowardly lions.

(5) The removal of ABC anchorman Frank Reynolds by ABC because the Nixon White House disliked his anti-Viet Nam war stance is not only indefensible but also despicable.

(6) The press has failed in its surveillance of society to warn us of unsafe cars, pollution and Viet Nam.

For those of us who have spent a life "training for the sight," there lies a "grey plain all around." Such a grey plain in fact that it could drive a man to drink. To call for wine, for "one draught of earlier, happier sights."

And I've listed those "happier sights" under:

B. Laudable performances—shining acts.

Let me attempt to set things more right with these examples:

(1) Mary Jo Denton of the *Cookeville Herald-Citizen* has pointed out covert meetings by the City Council and the Hospital Board so that the public's business is, by and large, done in public.

(2) The Ogdensburg, N.Y., *Journal's* late publisher, Frank Little, quickly ushered milk plant owners out of his office when they wanted different coverage of a strike by the farmers.

(3) When a Wisconsin public school teacher was threatened with a suit by the state attorney general if she persisted in telling her state legislator she would campaign for his defeat if he didn't vote for a teachers' pay bill, The Madison, Wis. *Capital Times* publisher of that time, William Evjue, published a telegram with the same message to the teacher's legislator on the front page, and then dared the state's attorney general to sue him. The Wisconsin state attorney general apologized for violating that teacher's freedom of expression.

(4) Certainly *The* (Nashville) *Tennessean* must be cited here for revealing the graft and corruption in the Blanton administration. They have also served the public well by revealing the financial wheeling and dealings of Representative Bill Boner.

(5) And if those Pentagon Papers were refused for publication for television by the television networks, that certainly was not the case with the major newspapers in the country. And we finally found out how we were lead into the disastrous Viet Nam War. The *Washington Post* and *New York*

Times started publishing them. And when the Nixon Administration Justice Department prevailed upon a Supreme Court Justice to exercise prior restraint upon those newspapers, to forbid continued publication of the Pentagon papers, something that had not been done in 300 years, the *Boston Globe* and the *St. Louis Post Dispatch* began their publication. And though the Justice Department wanted those papers restrained also, the Supreme Court was not persuaded it would be in the country's best interest to do so. And so those newspapers continued publishing the Pentagon papers, along with a host of other newspapers throughout the country, while the Supreme Court adjudicated in favor of the *Times* and *Post*.

(6) The *Washington Post* revealed the corruption and miscarriages of justice in the Nixon Administration and brought about the eventual resignation of Richard Nixon.

(7) The television network anchorman who became the first one to call for Richard Nixon's resignation was the man chosen by ABC to replace Frank Reynolds—Howard K. Smith, a former Viet Nam War hawk, who had come to see the error of his beliefs.

(8) The Washington correspondents are now exposing the ineptitude and arrogant excesses of the present Administration.

But all of what I've said about press performances should be placed in an even more proper perspective. What has been happening during this time in other segments and professions of our society:

From 1971 to 1979 Firestone manufactured 20 million Firestone 500 radial tires, and sold them, despite the fact that in 1973 Firestone's director of development reported to top management that the tire was of "inferior quality." In 1975 Firestone ran more tests and found that half failed to pass government high speed tests. The belt separated at high speeds after some 15 or 30,000 miles.

The National Highway Traffic Safety Administration finally forced Firestone, three years later, in 1978, to recall the tire. But Firestone fought it all the way. Meanwhile, some 14,000 tire failures were reported, along with 50 injuries and 29 deaths.

But all of this is nothing compared with what we know the government did at Oak Ridge and in the early atom bomb testing in Nevada.

Or what John Manville and other asbestos companies failed to do in warning their workers and the users of asbestos that asbestos was, indeed, hazardous to their health. As a consequence, some 750,000 persons will die of asbesteosis before the end of this century. Can you imagine that? Some 750,000 persons. And Manville stonewalled it all the way. Just like Bridgestone in Lavergne is now doing.

In the legal profession, fifteen Philadelphia judges were cleared off the bench by the Pennsylvania Supreme Court as a result of a federal probe into cash gifts by a local union. That's the largest number of judges ever suspended at one time. Three of Vermont's five high court justices were accused of numerous violations of judicial ethics. But then scandals have rocked the legal profession from Connecticut to North Carolina, from Operation Greylord in Illinois to California.

In Congress in the last decade, 15 members have been indicted on criminal charges. U.S. Representative Harold Ford is the latest.

Meanwhile, what more need be said about the electronic religion ministers, Oral Roberts and Jim Bakker and the rest?

Besides the recent Wall Street scandals involving investment banker Dennis Levine, speculator Ivan Boesky, and many brokers and brokerage houses, so much corruption has surfaced in New York, that Governor Mario Cuomo has named a Commission on Government Integrity to investigate the corruption in New York State.

But what kind of ethics and arrogance leads presidents to mislead the people? Lyndon Johnson slipped us into a terrible war in Vietnam, denying all the while that he was doing it. Richard Nixon took the war into Cambodia, first bombing there in secret and then invading that country.

And comes now the present Administration. "Disinformation," mining the Nicaraguan harbor, ignoring the World Court on Nicaragua, involved in illegal operations in Iran and Nicaragua and then chastising the press for writing about them.

Just what are the ethics involved in providing arms which will be used to kill thousands of Iraq soldiers and civilians so that some six or eight Americans may be freed?

And if a 51-year-old Californian, Hormos Hezar, is sentenced to three years in prison for setting up a deal to ship 2,000 military radios to Iran (the Justice Department prosecuted him for violating our trade embargo against Iran), who will go to jail in this Administration for selling anywhere from $12 to $40 million in arms to Iran to establish a political foothold or to free hostages?

After noting in his column the incredible number of officials in the present administration being fired, indicted or sent to prison, Carl T. Rowan says he has a feeling that "this country is going through an unprecedented wave of corruption in government, and nobody expects anybody to do anything much to stop it."

And what, finally, in Tennessee, were the ethics of Governor Blanton and his administration? The Butchers and their banking empire?

One of the architects of the Constitution, James Madison, said that "a people who mean to be their own governors must arm themselves with the power knowledge gives."

Thanks to the press, which has fought for more than 300 years to develop something called the right to know doctrine; and thanks to a press which, in the last 35 years, especially, has been evolving into a socially responsible press; the people now have the will and the way to information that enables them to govern more intelligently.

Looking at all that has taken place in our society and in other professions, the journalism profession can feel, overall, right proud that no major incidents have marred the entire profession.

All this tends to make a fellow see the press as a kind of knight in shining armor—although that armor is somewhat scarred, tarnished and smudged. In armor, but still a vulnerable messenger, a national treasure that should be protected, rather than slain.

Now if this vision of the press as a knight in smudged armor is accurate, and I think it is, how can this be? What's working here, I believe, is something akin to what works on the Smucker's Company. (You know—with a name like that, the jelly has to be good.)

What I mean is this: In the journalism and mass communications area, the public is rapidly being educated on what the role of the press should be. The press, itself, is on public display every day. So its ethics have to be good. Otherwise, reporters will know; critics will know; the press, in general, will know; and, finally, the public will know. Having set itself up as the Puritan scaffold of modern-day society, the press simply cannot afford any major ethical lapses.

So every day, the press ventures out across the grey plains and sounds its horn before the dark tower. Which is something quite different from tilting lances at windmills.

DISCUSSION QUESTIONS

1. The media have been criticized for contributing to panic by their coverage of missing children, AIDS, the stock market collapse in 1987, and international terrorism. What stories today are a cause of concern or overconcern to the public because of media "hype"?
2. Do the media have an obligation to expose lies perpetrated by government officials or agencies?
3. Should the press "play vice cop" in political campaigns as von Hoffman portrays them?
4. Is there gratuitous violence in news coverage? Why is there so much emphasis on bad news?

6

ABORTION

Mary Thornberry

Abortion is problematic in our society because people tend to see it as a single issue arguable as black or white, right or wrong. The two factions holding these opposing positions, the pro-choice vs. the pro-life groups, have value systems in conflict.

Pro-choice supporters, insist that a woman's decision whether to bear a child is an intensely personal matter with which the state should not interfere. Often this position is expressed in terms of a "right to privacy." Quality of life, maternal health, family planning, and family size are presented as things about which the mother knows better than any government official. She ought to be left to consult with health professionals and her family on these matters while the government builds roads and worries about national defense. "Freedom of choice" is another value frequently mentioned; quality of life and the capacity of the total family to support and nurture a child may also be stressed. Advocates of this position insist that the decision to seek an abortion is a painful one, made "in necessity and sorrow," but one which ought to be allowed.

Pro-life supporters, insist that the "right to life" is the only real issue. No one ought to have the right to terminate the life of another, they assert, and to take life is to commit murder. Life for them begins at the moment of conception, and the right to life of the potential child overrides all other concerns. Strengthening the home and preserving the family are two secondary concerns frequently voiced by this side.

Thus we have two stances built on two different and perhaps irreconcilable sets of values. The first problem, then, is how to reconcile these extremes. In a democratic society the problem is troublesome because our policy makers want to be responsive to societal wishes. What are they to do when portions of the society want two opposite things?

The second problem is that those who are more ambivalent about abortion, who might want to permit it under certain circumstances but forbid it under others, may hold both sets of values at once but not be able to rank order them in any meaningful way. These people are not used to having to choose between a notion of life, especially as it may appear in a small mass of fetal tissue, and a right to be free of governmental control over family matters. They want both things at the same time.

Laws are a reflection of values held by those in power. Our current legal situation reflects the problems posed by the larger society. Legislatures seem unable to deal with the issue of abortion for fear of angering one of the two groups at the extreme. Courts have intervened and tried to balance rights, making the ranking for those who felt they could not choose. Often the results please almost no one.

A quick review of the legal history of abortion in this country may help us understand the current dilemma better. For many years it was a crime in every state to perform an abortion. Abortion laws were enacted near the end of the last century when the medical profession urged protection for the welfare of the mother. At that time abortion practices were hazardous, and the death rate from abortions was high. By the 1960s advances in medical technology had made abortion less risky than normal childbirth, and some states were revising their laws to allow abortions under state supervision.

States were not concerned about maternal health alone, however. When called upon to justify its abortion laws in the early 1970s, for example, Texas responded that the potential life of the child was an important issue. Many people felt that clearing the way for easy abortions would sanction promiscuous sexual behavior. While some state legislatures (Georgia, New York, California were among this group) rewrote their laws to permit abortion under a variety of circumstances, other states refused to liberalize their laws. Abortion became a political issue. A bitter and divisive state referendum on the matter took place in Michigan in the fall of 1972, and the Mondale campaign for the Presidency was tainted by the charge that the candidate supported "Amnesty, acid, and abortion."

The Supreme Court of the United States stepped into the fray with its decision *Roe* v. *Wade* (410 U.S. 113) rendered in January 1973. In fact, the Court had previously acted in a similar area. It had already made several rulings striking down laws that prohibited the sale or distribution of contraceptive devices. The values expressed in those laws and in those decisions bore a remarkable resemblance to the abortion debate. Proponents of the law urged the Court to uphold the status quo or risk sanctioning immorality. Opponents spoke of the right of privacy and the need to keep the government out of intimate decisions involving the marital bedroom. Yet, the public seemed to acquiesce in those decisions. No great outcry followed *Griswold* v. *Connecticut* (381 U.S. 479, 1965) or *Eisenstadt* v. *Baird* (405 U.S. 438, 1972).

Why, then, did the public react so strongly to *Roe?* The Court itself made a conscious effort to articulate the values involved. The Justices ruled that a balancing of interests recognized in the Constitution forbade states from prohibiting abortions altogether and allowed a woman great freedom to seek an abortion during the earliest stages of her pregnancy. Pregnancy was divided into "trimesters" of three months each, and the legal rights and duties were declared to be separate at each stage. Privacy was the dominant value in the first trimester while the potential life of the viable fetus dominated the last stage. Abortions were declared a matter for the woman and her doctor to decide in the first case; the state could regulate and even forbid abortions in the latter.

Despite the careful attempt of the Court to balance interests and its refusal to confront "the delicate question of when life begins," the public has debated abortion from that day to this. The legal controversy has since moved to the questions of who else has any stake in the abortion decision. Do fathers, parents of pregnant minors, or panels of physicians have any right to block an abortion (*Planned Parenthood of Central Missouri* v. *Danforth,* 428 U.S. 52, 1976)? What is the role of the state? Can it refuse to pay for an abortion, even if the procedure has been termed medically necessary (*Harris* v. *McRae,* 448 U.S. 297, 1980)?

Part of the difficulty lies in trying to sort out the relationship of values to rights. Once the legal arena became the place where abortion was argued most strongly, everyone spoke in terms of the "rights" involved. Yet this approach may mask the fact that rights arise from deeper held sets of values. If those values are in conflict, no right can be absolute.

The readings that follow give various clues as to why this debate is so long lasting. The articles are by three women, each trained in a different academic discipline. Although each has a strong opinion on the matter, they agree that the problem of abortion is a complex one for our society. On what other matters do they agree?

The first article is one of the most widely cited writings in the whole abortion debate. It is by philosopher Judith Jarvis Thomson, who tried to outline the limits of obligation that a mother might experience in seeking an abortion. She wrote just before the 1973 Court decision, at a time when most states still outlawed abortion entirely or allowed abortions only to save the life of the mother. Her perspective was somewhat unusual in that she began by granting—as a point of argument only—that a fetus might be considered as a person. She then attempted to argue that even real persons have only limited claims against us and that there are circumstances in which we may reject such claims even if to do so were to cause the death of another. The perspective is philosophical and logical but not dispassionate.

Mary Segers wrote for a noted Catholic journal and attempted to state the points that might draw the two sides together. She presented an interesting point of view in that she identified herself as both a feminist and a strong Catholic. Although trained as a political scientist, she wrote as a theologian and a woman as well as a social scientist. (Her current post is with the Harvard Divinity School.)

Kristin Luker, a sociologist, did an extensive study of those active in the abortion movement in California. She interviewed many people on both sides of the question and presented a profile of the people and values involved. Note that she stressed the fundamental differences that separate the two camps. Her background as a sociologist led her to examine the ways in which the lifestyles of the activists are reflected in their political stances. She helps us see that value choices are not accidental and may be even more deeply rooted than we thought.

These then are three perspectives on abortion that highlight the problems raised at the outset by the differences in values. Thomson tries to argue that the right to life cannot be absolute and that we need to balance even that value against other claims. Luker highlights the problem of divergent absolute values held by those at the ends of the spectrum. Segers tries to find common values between these two groups. As you read the articles, try to reflect on the source of your own values in relation to abortion and imagine how a societal debate on the matter might come to a solution that could please a majority.

A Defense of Abortion[1]

Judith Jarvis Thomson

...Opponents of abortion commonly spend most of their time establishing that the fetus is a person, and hardly any time explaining the step from there to the impermissibility of abortion. Perhaps they think the step too simple and obvious to require much comment. Or perhaps instead they are simply being economical in argument. Many of those who defend abortion rely on the premise that the fetus is not a person, but only a bit of tissue that will become a person at birth; and why pay out more arguments than you have to? Whatever the explanation, I suggest that the step they take is neither easy nor obvious, that it calls for closer examination than it is commonly given, and that when we do give it this closer examination we shall feel inclined to reject it.

I propose, then, that we grant that the fetus is a person from the moment of conception. How does the argument go from here? Something like this, I take it. Every person has a right to life. So the fetus has a right to life. No doubt the mother has a right to decide what shall happen in and to her body; everyone would grant that. But surely a person's right to life is stronger and more stringent than the mother's right to decide what happens in and to her body, and so outweighs it. So the fetus may not be killed; an abortion may not be performed.

It sounds plausible. But now let me ask you to imagine this. You wake up in the morning and find yourself back to back in bed with an unconscious violinist. A famous unconscious violinist. He has been found to have a fatal kidney ailment, and the Society of Music Lovers has canvassed all the available medical records and found that you alone have the right blood type to help. They have therefore kidnapped you, and last night the violinist's circulatory system was plugged into yours, so that your kidneys can be used to extract poisons from his blood as well as your own. The director of the hospital now tells you, "Look, we're sorry the Society of Music Lovers did this to you—we would never have permitted it if we had known. But still, they did it, and the violinist now is plugged into you. To unplug you would be to kill him. But never mind, it's only for nine months. By then he will have

[1]I am very much indebted to James Thomson for discussion, criticism, and many helpful suggestions.

---

recovered from his ailment, and can safely be unplugged from you." Is it morally incumbent on you to accede to this situation? No doubt it would be very nice of you if you did, a great kindness. But do you *have* to accede to it? What if it were not nine months, but nine years? Or longer still? What if the director of the hospital says, "Tough luck, I agree, but you've now got to stay in bed, with the violinist plugged into you, for the rest of your life. Because remember this. All persons have a right to life, and violinists are persons. Granted you have a *right to decide* what happens in and to your body, but a person's right to life outweighs your right to decide what happens in and to your body. So you cannot ever be unplugged from him." I imagine you would regard this as outrageous, which suggests that something really is wrong with that plausible-sounding argument I mentioned a moment ago.

In this case, of course, you were kidnapped; you didn't volunteer for the operation that plugged the violinist into your kidneys. Can those who oppose abortion on the ground I mentioned make an exception for a pregnancy due to rape? Certainly. They can say that persons have a right to life only if they didn't come into existence because of rape; or they can say that all persons have a right to life, but that some have less of a right to life than others, in particular, that those who came into existence because of rape have less. But these statements have a rather unpleasant sound. Surely the question of whether you have a right to life at all, or how much of it you have, shouldn't turn on the question of whether or not you are the product of a rape. And in fact the people who oppose abortion on the ground I mentioned do not make this distinction, and hence do not make an exception in case of rape.

Nor do they make an exception for a case in which the mother has to spend the nine months of her pregnancy in bed. They would agree that would be a great pity, and hard on the mother; but all the same, all persons have a right to life, the fetus is a person, and so on. I suspect, in fact, that they would not make an exception for a case in which, miraculously enough, the pregnancy went on for nine years; or even the rest of the mother's life.

...[W]e should...ask what it comes to, to have a right to life. In some views having a right to life includes having a right to be given at least the bare minimum one needs for continued life. But suppose that what in fact *is* the bare minimum a man needs for continued life is something he has no right at all to be given? If I am sick unto death, and the only thing that will save my life is the touch of Henry Fonda's cool hand on my fevered brow, then all the same, I have no right to be given the touch of Henry Fonda's cool hand on my fevered brow. It would be frightfully nice of him to fly in from the West Coast to provide it. It would be less nice, though no doubt well meant, if my friends flew out to the West Coast and carried Henry Fonda back with them. But I have no right at all against anybody that he should do this for me. Or again, to return to the story

I told earlier, the fact that for continued life that violinist needs the continued use of your kidneys does not establish that he has a right to be given the continued use of your kidneys. He certainly has no right against you that *you* should give him continued use of your kidneys. For nobody has any right to use your kidneys unless you give him such a right; and nobody has the right against you that you shall give him this right—if you do allow him to go on using your kidneys, this is a kindness on your part, and not something he can claim from you as his due. Nor has he any right against anybody else that *they* should give him continued use of your kidneys. Certainly he had no right against the Society of Music Lovers that they should plug him into you in the first place. And if you now start to unplug yourself, having learned that you will otherwise have to spend nine years in bed with him, there is nobody in the world who must try to prevent you, in order to see to it that he is given something he has a right to be given.

Some people are rather stricter about the right to life. In their view, it does not include the right to be given anything, but amounts to, and only to, the right not to be killed by anybody. But here a related difficulty arises. If everybody is to refrain from killing that violinist, then everybody must refrain from doing a great many different sorts of things. Everybody must refrain from slitting his throat, everybody must refrain from shooting him—and everybody must refrain from unplugging you from him. But does he have a right against everybody that they shall refrain from unplugging you from him? To refrain from doing this is to allow him to continue to use your kidneys. It could be argued that he has a right against us that *we* should allow him to continue to use your kidneys. That is, while he had no right against us that we should give him the use of your kidneys, it might be argued that he anyway has a right against us that we shall not now intervene and deprive him of the use of your kidneys. I shall come back to third-party interventions later. But certainly the violinist has no right against you that *you* shall allow him to continue to use your kidneys. As I said, if you do allow him to use them, it is a kindness on your part, and not something you owe him.

The difficulty I point to here is not peculiar to the right to life. It reappears in connection with all the other natural rights; and it is something which an adequate account of rights must deal with. For present purposes it is enough just to draw attention to it. But I would stress that I am not arguing that people do not have a right to life—quite to the contrary, it seems to me that the primary control we must place on the acceptability of an account of rights is that it should turn out in that account to be a truth that all persons have a right to life. I am arguing only that having a right to life does not guarantee having either a right to be given the use of or a right to be allowed continued use of another person's body—even if one needs it for life itself....

...We surely must all grant that there may be cases in which it would be morally indecent to detach a person from your body at the cost of his life. Suppose you learn that what the violinist needs is not nine years of your life, but only one hour: all you need do to save his life is to spend one hour in that bed with him. Suppose also that letting him use your kidneys for that one hour would not affect your health in the slightest. Admittedly you were kidnapped. Admittedly you did not give anyone permission to plug him into you. Nevertheless it seems to me plain you *ought* to allow him to use your kidneys for that hour—it would be indecent to refuse.

Again, suppose pregnancy lasted only an hour, and constituted no threat to life or health. And suppose that a woman becomes pregnant as a result of rape. Admittedly she did not voluntarily do anything to bring about the existence of a child. Admittedly she did nothing at all which would give the unborn person a right to the use of her body. All the same it might well be said, as in the newly emended violinist story, that she *ought* to allow it to remain for that hour—that it would be indecent in her to refuse.

Now some people are inclined to use the term "right" in such a way that it follows from the fact that you ought to allow a person to use your body for the hour he needs, that he has a right to use your body for the hour he needs, even though he has not been given that right by any person or act. They may say that it follows also that if you refuse, you act unjustly toward him. This use of the term is perhaps so common that it cannot be called wrong; nevertheless it seems to me to be an unfortunate loosening of what we would do better to keep a tight rein on...

A further objection to so using the term "right" that from the fact that A ought to do a thing for B, it follows that B has a right against A that A do it for him, is that it is going to make the question of whether or not a man has a right to a thing turn on how easy it is to provide him with it; and this seems not merely unfortunate, but morally unacceptable. Take the case of Henry Fonda again. I said earlier that I had no right to the touch of his cool hand on my fevered brow, even though I needed it to save my life. I said it would be frightfully nice of him to fly in from the West Coast to provide me with it, but that I had no right against him that he should do so. But suppose he isn't on the West Coast. Suppose he has only to walk across the room, place a hand briefly on my brow—and lo, my life is saved. Then surely he ought to do it, it would be indecent to refuse. Is it to be said "Ah, well, it follows that in this case she has a right to the touch of his hand on her brow, and so it would be an injustice in him to refuse"? So that I have a right to it when it is easy for him to provide it, though no right when it's hard? It's rather a shocking idea that anyone's rights should fade away and disappear as it gets harder and harder to accord them to him.

So my own view is that even though you ought to let the violinist use your kidneys for the one hour he needs, we should not conclude that he has a right to do so—we should say that if you refuse, you are...self-centered and callous, indecent in fact, but not unjust. And similarly, that even supposing a case in which a woman pregnant due to rape ought to allow the unborn person to use her body for the hour he needs, we should not conclude that he has a right to do so; we should conclude that she is self-centered, callous, indecent, but not unjust, if she refuses. The complaints are no less grave; they are just different. However, there is no need to insist on this point. If anyone does wish to deduce "he has a right" from "you ought," then all the same he must surely grant that there are cases in which it is not morally required of you that you allow that violinist to use your kidneys, and in which he does not have a right to use them, and in which you do not do him an injustice if you refuse. And so also for mother and unborn child. Except in such cases as the unborn person has a right to demand it—and we were leaving open the possibility that there may be such cases—nobody is morally *required* to make large sacrifices, of health, of all other interests and concerns, of all other duties and commitments, for nine years, or even for nine months, in order to keep another person alive.

We have in fact to distinguish between two kinds of Samaritan: the Good Samaritan and what we might call the Minimally Decent Samaritan. The story of the Good Samaritan, you will remember, goes like this:

> A certain man went down from Jerusalem to Jericho, and fell among thieves, which stripped him of his raiment, and wounded him, and departed, leaving him half dead.
>
> And by chance there came down a certain priest that way; and when he saw him, he passed by on the other side.
>
> And likewise a Levite, when he was at the place, came and looked on him, and passed by on the other side.
>
> But a certain Samaritan, as he journeyed, came where he was; and when he saw him he had compassion on him.
>
> And went to him, and bound up his wounds, pouring in oil and wine, and set him on his own beast, and brought him to an inn, and took care of him.
>
> And on the morrow, when he departed, he took out two pence, and gave them to the host, and said unto him, 'Take care of him; and whatsoever thou spendest more, when I come again, I will repay thee.'
>
> ***(Luke 10:30–35)***

The Good Samaritan went out of his way, at some cost to himself, to help one in need of it. We are not told what the options were, that is, whether or not the priest and the Levite could have helped by doing less than the Good Samaritan did, but assuming they could have, then the fact they did nothing at all shows they were not even Minimally Decent Samaritans, not because they were not Samaritans, but because they were not even minimally decent.

...After telling the story of the Good Samaritan, Jesus said "Go, and do thou likewise." Perhaps he meant that we are morally required to act as the Good Samaritan did. Perhaps he was urging people to do more than is morally required of them....[I]t is not morally required of anyone that he give long stretches of his life—nine years or nine months—to sustaining the life of a person who has no special right (we were leaving open the possibility of this) to demand it.

Indeed, with one rather striking class of exceptions, no one in any country in the world is *legally* required to do anywhere near as much as this for anyone else. The class of exceptions is obvious. My main concern here is not the state of the law in respect to abortion, but it is worth drawing attention to the fact that in no state in this country is any man compelled by law to be even a Minimally Decent Samaritan to any person;...By contrast, in most states in this country women are compelled by law to be not merely Minimally Decent Samaritans, but Good Samaritans to unborn persons inside them. This doesn't by itself settle anything one way or the other, because it may well be argued that there should be laws in this country—as there are in many European countries—compelling at least Minimally Decent Samaritanism.[2] But it does show that there is a gross injustice in the existing state of the law. And it shows also that the groups currently working against liberalization of abortion laws, in fact working toward having it declared unconstitutional for a state to permit abortion, had better start working for the adoption of Good Samaritan laws generally, or earn the charge that they are acting in bad faith.

...But of course there are arguments and arguments, and it may be said that I have simply fastened on the wrong one. It may be said that what is important is not merely the fact that the fetus is a person, but that it is a person for whom the woman has a special kind of responsibility issuing from the fact that she is its mother. And it might be argued that all my analogies are therefore irrelevant—for you do not have that special kind of responsibility for that violinist, Henry Fonda does not have that special kind of responsibility for me. And our attention might be drawn to the fact that men and women both *are* compelled by law to provide support for their children.

I have in effect dealt (briefly) with this argument...above; but a (still briefer) recapitulation now may be in order. Surely we do not have any such "special responsibility" for a person unless we have assumed it, explicitly or implicitly. If a set of parents do not try to prevent pregnancy, do not obtain

[2]For a discussion of the difficulties involved, and a survey of the European experience with such laws, see *The Good Samaritan and the Law*, ed. James M. Ratcliffe (New York, 1966).

an abortion, and then at the time of birth of the child do not put it out for adoption, but rather take it home with them, then they have assumed responsibility for it, they have given it rights, and they cannot *now* withdraw support from it at the cost of its life because they now find it difficult to go on providing for it. But if they have taken all reasonable precautions against having a child, they do not simply by virtue of their biological relationship to the child who comes into existence have a special responsibility for it. They may wish to assume responsibility for it, or they may not wish to. And I am suggesting that if assuming responsibility for it would require large sacrifices, then they may refuse. A Good Samaritan would not refuse—or anyway, a Splendid Samaritan, if the sacrifices that had to be made were enormous. But then so would a Good Samaritan assume responsibility for that violinist; so would Henry Fonda, if he is a Good Samaritan, fly in from the West Coast and assume responsibility for me.

...First, while I do argue that abortion is not impermissible, I do not argue that it is always permissible. There may well be cases in which carrying the child to term requires only Minimally Decent Samaritanism of the mother, and this is a standard we must not fall below. I am inclined to think it a merit of my account precisely that it does *not* give a general yes or a general no. It allows for and supports our sense that, for example, a sick and desperately frightened fourteen-year-old schoolgirl, pregnant due to rape, may *of course* choose abortion, and that any law which rules this out is an insane law. And it also allows for and supports our sense that in other cases resort to abortion is even positively indecent. It would be indecent in the woman to request an abortion, and indecent in a doctor to perform it, if she is in her seventh month, and wants the abortion just to avoid the nuisance of postponing a trip abroad. The very fact that the arguments I have been drawing attention to treat all cases of abortion, or even all cases of abortion in which the mother's life is not at stake, as morally on a par ought to have made them suspect at the outset....

Abortion Politics & Policy: Is There a Middle Ground?

Mary C. Segers

...At some level other than the legal or the metaphysical, prolife advocates are saying that life is a gift to be welcomed, and that the attitude of welcoming or non-welcoming reflects the innermost judgments of persons and the community as to the worthwhileness of living. Thus the decision to give birth or to abort new life is very much a comment about ourselves and our conception of the good life. Prolifers ask: What kind of society are we that permits abortion on demand, that makes such a decision wholly an individual one and that, to protect individual freedom, tends to minimize the significance of the decision, even to portray it as ethically (or humanly) neutral?

In other words, prolife people are well positioned to mount a thoroughgoing and credible critique of contemporary society as excessively individualized, privatized, non-communitarian, and to show that these characteristics of our society are expressed and enhanced when abortion is portrayed as a matter over which society has no right or need to show concern or exert control. This value orientation is almost completely eclipsed by exclusive reliance on the language of rights. Further, in employing this language, prolife activists are choosing to contest the abortion issue on the home grounds of prochoice advocates; for it is in the political and social theory of liberalism that rights and duties receive greatest emphasis as the framing timbers of society's structure; it is through the dominance of liberalism in our constitutional reflection that the woman's right of privacy with respect to decision over reproduction gained recognition. Relying on this same liberal theory to defend the right to life, prolifers show little awareness that the theory is neither universal, eternal nor immutable; they fail to recognize the historical, time-bound, conditional character of the assertion of such basic "rights" in society.

What I am suggesting is that both sides stop discussing abortion as though it were a conflict between the right to life and the right to reproductive freedom. The vocabulary of rights and the assumptions of liberalism can be useful; they do not suffice to resolve every political dilemma. In the conflict over abortion, broad, phenomenological, experiential characterization

---

Mary C. Segers, "Abortion Politics and Policy: Is There a Middle Ground?" *Christianity and Crisis* 40, no. 2 (18 February 1980), 21–27. Edited version reprinted with permission of Gail Hovey, managing editor, *Christianity and Crisis.*

must replace the relatively narrow legal conceptions of the issue. Having an abortion is not a matter of right(s) in the sense of a positive good to which one is entitled. It is a negative option, an undesirable, unfortunate event in a woman's life, perhaps a desperate measure undertaken "in necessity and sorrow." I suggest that the negative character of abortion is something about which both sides can agree and that this agreement can form the basis for cooperative efforts to enact public policy. The aim of any practical policy on abortion that is politically feasible and minimally acceptable to both sides would be *to reduce the incidence of abortion without coercing women....*

STEPS TOWARD PEACE

How would stressing cooperation rather than conflict change abortion politics? For one thing, both prochoice and prolife groups would have to resist the impulse to push for total victory in the political arena. In a liberal democratic society such as ours, politics is, after all, the art of compromise. What is politically feasible will be what is acceptable to both sides, and this will require flexibility, concessions and the exercise of restraint. It must be stressed that such concessions need not be, in fact are not—denials of ethical principle; when total victory is impossible or will cause disproportionate evils, prudence not only permits but requires compromise.

Second, parties to this controversy will have to assess what public policy is politically feasible and acceptable not only to themselves but to the public at large. This will require fashioning a policy that can accommodate the ambivalent positions of the majority of Americans concerning the morality of abortion and the conditions under which they believe it should be performed.

Third, both prolife and prochoice factions will have to assess what public policies are just and equitable. Here an important requirement is that no policy be unduly burdensome to any single class or group within society.

Assuming agreement between some prolife and some prochoice advocates that the aim of public policy should be to reduce the incidence of abortion without coercing women, how may these criteria for a sound, feasible abortion policy be applied to current policy proposals? In the effort to describe a practical, acceptable abortion policy, it seems easier to begin with the negative—that is, to say what such a policy would *not* be or do.

First, such a policy would not recriminalize abortion. Whatever else one may say about public opinion concerning abortion, it seems clear that a sizable majority of American citizens believe abortion should be legally available under certain conditions; (exactly what those conditions are, of course, is disputed). Moreover, even if a proposal to recriminalize abortion were politically acceptable, it would not survive judicial review by the Supreme Court; given the current composition of the Court, it is unlikely to change its mind on the legality of abortion in the foreseeable future.

Further, even if Congress and Court were somehow to recriminalize abortion, enforcement would pose innumerable problems among doctors, police, prosecutors and women as women. Finally, such a policy making abortion a violation of criminal law would be inconsistent with the stated objective: preventing abortions without coercing women. Outlawing abortion would be coercive of both those women who think they should in conscience terminate a pregnancy and those physicians willing to perform abortions.

The effort to enact a constitutional amendment defining a fetus as a human being with full legal rights from the moment of conception and restricting abortion to life-endangering pregnancies also faces innummerable obstacles. To date, the House and Senate have failed to report a human life amendment out of committee, let alone pass it by a two-thirds vote. The Senate, which has shown itself strongly opposed to severe restrictions on abortion funding, will hardly be more amenable to an almost absolute restriction on the abortion right itself. The alternative method of amending the Constitution—holding a constitutional convention upon the request of two-thirds of the states—seems no more promising for the prolife movement. Apart from the fact that this second method has never been used successfully in American history, it seems highly unlikely that an amendment almost totally prohibiting abortion can collect favorable ratification majorities in the legislatures of 38 states. Moreover, the social cost of securing ratification would be an intolerable increase in political divisiveness. Finally, should a human life amendment ever be ratified, such a policy almost totally prohibiting abortions would meet with the same problems of implementation and the same ethical objections mentioned earlier.

If a human life amendment fails to satisfy our criteria of sound public policy, would a policy of preventing abortions through restricting public funding pass muster? Here I think prochoice advocates must at least recognize the plausibility to prolifers of Hyde amendment type restrictions. Those who believe that abortion is the wrongful taking of human life object to having their tax money spent for purposes they consider gravely immoral. On this and other grounds, they have been able to persuade a sufficient number of legislators at congressional and state levels to support restrictions on Medicaid funding of abortions. In this effort, they have acted in the best traditions of democratic politics. They have mobilized political pressure at the grass roots on an issue about which they have strong moral convictions, and they have cared enough to stay with the issue in the halls of Congress and state legislatures. From a political scientist's viewpoint, those who decry apathy in American politics can only applaud this indication of active citizen participation in the political process. Moreover, in terms of political feasibility, abortion opponents do seem to reflect public opinion, which, for whatever reasons, is generally negative on the issue of Medicaid funding.

LEGISLATING AGAINST THE POOR

However, our criteria as to sound abortion policy include a requirement that public policies be not only politically acceptable to a majority of the American population, but that they be just and equitable. In particular, such policies should not be unduly burdensome to any single social class or group within society. Now it is the poor alone who bear the burden of this type of anti-abortion legislation. It is precisely because indigent women are dependent upon public assistance that the Hyde Amendment is so effective. Because they are poor, their behavior can be controlled in ways that the behavior of wealthy and middle-class women cannot. It seems arbitrary and unfairly discriminatory to single out the medical expense of abortion from a general medical program for the indigent and so make poor women bear the burden of prolifers' opposition to abortion. It would be better, in my judgment, to focus the considerable energy and resources of the prolife movement on policies designed to prevent distressful pregnancies from occurring in the first place rather than on policies designed to prevent one class of the population from choosing in conscience to exercise a legal right which other citizens may exercise because they are financially able.

Apart from the merits or demerits of public funding of poor women's abortions, the Hyde Amendment raises tactical questions concerning the practice in Congress of attaching anti-abortion amendments to major pieces of legislation. Some argue that such riders are legislatively inefficient and inappropriate since they are usually unrelated to the substance of a bill and often result in prolonged conference committee negotiations. I think this critique of prolife political strategy has only partial validity. After all, in the period immediately following the Supreme Court's legalization of abortion in 1973, anti-abortion forces in Congress attached to proposed legislation some restrictive amendments which, on balance, do not seem objectionable and in fact implement the rights so often invoked by abortion rights advocates. I am thinking in particular of the "conscience clauses" enacted by Congress and by 40 states protecting doctors and hospitals from being forced to do abortions against their moral beliefs and the moral beliefs of their trustees. Such conscience clauses are entirely consistent with the pluralism and freedom so heavily stressed in prochoice arguments....

CREATING NEW OPTIONS

A public policy designed to reduce abortions without coercing women would contain positive programs of assistance to women rather than negative prohibitions restricting their options. Such measures would include: comprehensive welfare programs for mothers and children; greater support for childcare, part-time work (with fringe benefits) and flexi-time scheduling to enable mothers to combine childrearing and gainful employment; increased funding of research on more effective contraceptives; better sex education programs; improved adoption services (including government subsidies for foster care and the adoption of hard-to-place children); support for parents raising retarded children; and better all-round programs for teenagers at risk of pregnancy.

I believe that both prochoice and prolife movements could redirect their energies and resources in a cooperative effort to enact public policies of this nature. The general thrust of such policies is to increase the range of women's choices and reduce the need for and the number of abortions.

It would be foolishly optimistic to suggest that prolife and prochoice forces will be able in the near future to opt for détente and work together for public policies such as these. Détente will not come easily; in particular, the developing confrontation over the appeal of *McRae* to the Supreme Court may simply reinforce polarization. In the short run, therefore, and particularly in this election year, abortion politics will probably become more heated and intense, at the risk of undermining long-range possibilities for cooperation. Accommodation will not come about unless partisans on both sides are convinced (1) that they cannot win using the old strategies (at least, not without great damage to the social fabric), and (2) that they can achieve many of their aims more effectively through cooperation rather than confrontation....

Abortion and the Politics of Motherhood

Kristin Luker

...The values that lead pro-life and pro-choice women into different attitudes toward abortion are the same values that led them at an earlier time to adopt different lifestyles that supported a given view of abortion.

For example, pro-life women have *always* valued family roles very highly and have arranged their lives accordingly. They did not acquire high-level educational and occupational skills, for example, because they married, and they married because their values suggested that this would be the most satisfying life open to them. Similarly, pro-choice women postponed (or avoided) marriage and family roles because they chose to acquire the skills they needed to be successful in the larger world, having concluded that the role of wife and mother was too limited for them. Thus, activists on both sides of the issue are women who have a given set of values about what are the most satisfying and appropriate roles for women, and they have made *life commitments that now limit their ability to change their minds.* Women who have many children and little education, for example, are seriously handicapped in attempting to become doctors or lawyers; women who have reached their late forties with few children or none are limited in their ability to build (or rebuild) a family. For most of these activists, therefore, their position on abortion is the "tip of the iceberg," a shorthand way of supporting and proclaiming not only a complex set of values but a given set of social resources as well.

To put the matter differently, we might say that for pro-life women the traditional division of life into separate male roles and female roles still works, but for pro-choice women it does not. Having made a commitment to the traditional female roles of wife, mother, and homemaker, pro-life women are limited in those kinds of resources—education, class status, recent occupational experiences—they would need to compete in what has traditionally been the male sphere, namely, the paid labor force. The average pro-choice woman, in contrast, is comparatively well endowed with exactly those resources: she is highly educated, she already has a job, and she has recent (and continuous) experience in the job market.

Kristin Luker, *Abortion and the Politics of Motherhood* (Berkeley: University of California Press, 1984), 186–191 (chapter 7) and 198–215 (chapter 8). Edited version reprinted with permission of the University of California Press.

In consequence, anything that supports a traditional division of labor into male and female worlds is, broadly speaking, in the interests of pro-life women because that is where their resources lie. Conversely, such a traditional division of labor, when strictly enforced, is against the interests of pro-choice women because it limits their abilities to use the valuable "male" resources that they have in relative abundance. It is therefore apparent that attitudes toward abortion, even though rooted in childhood experiences, are also intimately related to present-day interests. Women who oppose abortion and seek to make it officially unavailable are declaring, both practically and symbolically, that women's reproductive roles should be given social primacy. Once an embryo is defined as a child and an abortion as the death of a person, almost everything else in a woman's life must "go on hold" during the course of her pregnancy: any attempt to gain "male" resources such as a job, an education, or other skills must be subordinated to her uniquely female responsibility of serving the needs of this newly conceived person. Thus, when personhood is bestowed on the embryo, women's nonreproductive roles are made secondary to their reproductive roles. The act of conception therefore creates a pregnant woman rather than a woman who is pregnant; it creates a woman whose life, in cases where roles or values clash, is defined by the fact that she is—or may become—pregnant.

...Pro-choice men and women act on their belief that men and women are equal not only because they have (or should have) equal rights but also because they have substantially similar life experiences. The pro-choice women we met have approximately the same kinds of education as their husbands do, and many of them have the same kinds of jobs—they are lawyers, physicians, college professors, and the like. Even those who do not work in traditionally male occupations have jobs in the paid labor market and thus share common experiences. They and their husbands share many social resources in common: they both have some status outside the home, they both have a paycheck, and they both have a set of peers and friends located in the work world rather than in the family world. In terms of the traditional studies of family power, pro-choice husbands and wives use the same bargaining chips and have roughly equal amounts of them.[1]

[1]There is a long sociological research tradition on the relative power status of husbands and wives and what contributes to their relative power; see Robert Blood and Donald Wolfe, *Husbands and Wives;* Robert Blood and Robert Hamlin, "The Effects of the Wife's Employment on the Family Power Structure," pp. 347–52; Phyllis Hallenbeck, "An Analysis of Power Dynamics in Marriage," *Journal of Marriage and the Family* 27 (1966):200–03; and David Heer, "Measurement and Bases of Family Power: An Overview," *Marriage and Family Living* 25 (1963):133–39. For fundamental critiques of this literature, see Constantina Safilios-Rothchild, "Family Sociology or Wives' Family Sociology? A Cross-Cultural Examination of Decision-Making," pp. 290–301; and Dair Gillespie, "Who Has the Power? The Marital Struggle," pp. 445–58.

Pro-choice women, therefore, value (and can afford) an approach to sexuality that, by sidelining reproduction, diminishes the differences between men and women; they can do this *because they have other resources on which to build a marriage.* Since their value is intimacy and since the daily lives of men and women on the pro-choice side are substantially similar, intimacy in the bedroom is merely an extension of the intimacy of their larger world.

Pro-life women and men, by contrast, tend to live in "separate spheres." Because their lives are based on a social and emotional division of labor where each sex has its appropriate work, to accept contraception or abortion would devalue the one secure resource left to these women: the private world of home and hearth. This would be disastrous not only in terms of status but also in terms of meaning: if values about fertility and family are not essential to a marriage, what supports does a traditional marriage have in times of stress? To accept highly effective contraception, which actually and symbolically subordinates the role of children in the family to other needs and goals, would be to cut the ground of meaning out from under at least one (and perhaps both) partners' lives. Therefore, contraception, which sidelines the reproductive capacities of men and women, is both useless and threatening to pro-life people.

THE CORE OF THE DEBATE

In summary, women come to be pro-life and pro-choice activists as the end result of lives that center around different definitions of motherhood. They grow up with a belief about the nature of the embryo, so events in their lives lead them to believe that the embryo is a unique person, or a fetus; that people are intimately tied to their biological roles, or that these roles are but a minor part of life; that motherhood is the most important and satisfying role open to a woman, or that motherhood is only one of several roles, a burden when defined as the only role. These beliefs and values are rooted in the concrete circumstances of women's lives—their educations, incomes, occupations, and the different marital and family choices they have made along the way—and they work simultaneously to shape those circumstances in turn. Values about the relative place of reason and faith, about the role of actively planning for life versus learning to accept gracefully life's unknowns, of the relative satisfactions inherent in work and family—all of these factors place activists in a specific relationship to the larger world and give them a specific set of resources with which to confront that world.

The simultaneous and on-going modification of both their lives and their values by each other finds these activists located in a specific place in the social world. They are financially successful, or they are not. They become highly educated, or they do not. They become married and have a large family, or they have a small one. And at each step of the way, both their values and their lives have undergone either ratification or revision....

WORLD VIEWS

All [the] different issues that divide pro-life and pro-choice activists from one another—their views on men and women, sexuality, contraception, and morality—in turn reflect the fact that the two sides have two very different orientations to the world and that these orientations in turn revolve around two very different moral centers. The pro-life world view, notwithstanding the occasional atheist or agnostic attracted to it, is at the core one that centers around God: pro-life activists are on the whole deeply committed to their religious faith and deeply involved with it. A number of important consequences follow.

Because most pro-life people have a deep faith in God, they also believe in the rightness of His plan for the world. They are therefore skeptical about the ability of individual humans to understand, much less control, events that unfold according to a divine, rather than human, blueprint. From their point of view, human attempts at control are simply arrogance, an unwillingness to admit that larger forces than human will determine human fate. One woman made the point clearly: "God is the Creator of life, and I think all sexual activity should be open to that [creation]. That does not mean that you have to have a certain number of children or anything, but it should be open to Him and His will. The contraceptive mentality denies His will, 'It's my will, not your will.' And here again, the selfishness comes in."

This comment grew out of a discussion on contraception, but it also reveals values about human efficacy and its role in a larger world. While individuals can and should control their lives, pro-life people believe they should do so with a humility that understands that a force greater than themselves exists and, furthermore, that unpredicted things can be valuable. A woman who lost two children early in life to a rare genetic defect makes the point: "I didn't plan my son, my third child, and only because I was rather frightened that I might have a problem with another child. But I was certainly delighted when I became pregnant and had him. That's what I mean, I guess I feel that you can't plan everything in life. Some of the nicest things that have happened to me have certainly been the unplanned." Another woman went further: "I think people are foolish to worry about things in the future. The future takes care of itself."

Consequently, from the pro-life point of view, the contemporary movement away from the religious stand, what they see as the "secularization" of society, is at least one part of the troubles of contemporary society. By this they mean at least two things. First, there is the decline in religious commitment, which they feel keenly. But, second, they are also talking about a decline of a common community, a collective sense of what is right and wrong. From their viewpoint, once morality is no longer codified in some central set of rules that all accept and that finds its ultimate justification in the belief in a Supreme Being, then morality becomes a variation of "do your own thing."

For pro-life people, once the belief in a Supreme Being (and by definition a common sense of culture) is lost, a set of consequences emerge that not only creates abortion per se but creates a climate where phenomena such as abortion can flourish. For example, once one no longer believes in an afterlife, then one becomes more this-worldly. As a consequence, one becomes more interested in material goods and develops a world view that evaluates things (and, more importantly, people) in terms of what Marxists would call their "use value." Further, people come to live in the "here-and-now" rather than thinking of this life—and in particular the pain and disappointments of this life—as spiritual training for the next life. When the belief in God (and in an afterlife) are lost, pro-life people feel that human life becomes selfish, unbearably painful, and meaningless.

> I think basically a secular nature of our society, that we basically lost our notion of God as being important in our lives...it's hard at times to see that suffering can make you a better person, so people don't want any part of it.
>
> I think there's a decline in our civilization. Bracken, Dr. Julius Bracken, said that the problem used to be why does God allow suffering or pain or things like that, and now the problem is man's own existence, you know, man believes that he's in a circle of nothingness and therefore there is no such thing as a moral or immoral act.

One of the harshest criticisms pro-life people make about pro-choice people, therefore, which encapsulates their feeling that pro-choice people are too focused on a short-term pragmatic view of the present world rather than on the long-term view of a transcendent world, is that pro-choice people are "utilitarian."

In part, pro-life people are right: the pro-choice world view is not centered around a Divine Being, but rather around a belief in the highest abilities of human beings. For them, reason—the human capacity to use intelligence, rather than faith, to understand and alter the environment—is at the core of their world; for many of them, therefore, religious or spiritual beliefs are restricted only to those areas over which humans have not yet established either knowledge or control: the origin of the universe, the meaning of life, etc. As one pro-choice activist, speaking of her own spiritual beliefs, noted: "What should I call it? Destiny? A Supreme Being? I don't know. I don't worship anything, I don't go anyplace and do anything about it, it's just an awareness that there's a whole area that might be arranging something for me, that I am not arranging myself—though every day I do more about arranging things myself."

Whatever religious values pro-choice people have are subordinated to a belief that individuals live in the here and now and must therefore make decisions in the present about the present. Few pro-choice people expressed clear beliefs in an afterlife so that their time frame includes only the worldly dimension of life. Thus, the entire articulation of their world view focuses them once again on human—rather than divine—capacities and, in particular, on the capacity for reason.

There are important implications to the fact that reason is the centerpiece of the pro-choice universe. First, they are, as their opponents claim, "utilitarian." Without explicitly claiming the heritage of the Scottish moralists, utilitarianism is consonant with many of the pro-choice side's vaguely Protestant beliefs and, more to the point, with their value of rationality and its extensions: control, planning, and fairness. Second, as this heritage implies, they are interventionists. From their point of view, the fact of being the only animal gifted with intellect means that humans should use that intellect to solve the problems of human existence. What the pro-life people see as a humility in the face of a God whose ways are unknowable to mere humans, pro-choice people see as a fatalistic reliance upon a Creator whom humans wishfully endow with magical powers. These same values lead pro-choice people to be skeptical of the claim that certain areas are, or should be, sacrosanct, beyond the reach of human intervention. *Sacred* to them is too close to *sacred cow,* and religion can merge imperceptibly into dogma, where the church could persecute Galileo because science was too threatening both to an old way of thinking of things and an established power structure. Truth, for pro-choice people, must always take precedence over faith.

Because of their faith in the human ability to discover truth, pro-choice people are on the whole optimistic about "human nature." While in their more despairing moments they can agree with the pro-life diagnosis of malaise in contemporary American life—that "things fall apart and the center does not hold" in Yeats' terms—they emphatically disagree upon the solution. Rather than advocate what they see as a retreat from the present, an attempt to re-create idealized images of the past, they would argue that "the Lord helps those who help themselves" and that people should rally to the task of applying human ingenuity to the problems that surround us.

In consequence, pro-choice people do not see suffering as either ennobling or as spiritual discipline. In fact, they see it as stupid, as a waste, and as a failure, particularly when technology exists to eliminate it. While some problems are not at present amenable to human control, pro-choice people will admit, they are sure to fall to the march of human progress. Thus, not only can humans "play God," it is, in an ironic sort of way, what they owe their Creator, if they have one: given the ability to alter Nature, it is immoral not to do so, especially when those activities will diminish human pain.

All of these values come home for pro-choice people when they talk about the *quality of life.* By this term they mean a number of things. In part they use this phrase as a short-hand way of indicating that they think of *life* as consisting of social as well as biological dimensions. The embryo, for example, is only a potential person to them in large part because it has not yet begun to have a social dimension to its life, only a physical one. In corollary, a pregnant woman's rights, being both social and physical, transcend those of the embryo. This view is rooted in their values about reason: biological life is physical and of the body. Humans share physical life with all other living beings, but reason is the gift of humans alone. Thus social life, which exists only by virtue of the human capacity for reason, is the more valuable dimension of life for pro-choice people. (This viewpoint explains in part why many pro-choice people find unfathomable the question of "when does life begin?" For them it is obvious: physical life began only once, most probably when the "cosmic soup" yielded its first complex amino acids, the forerunners of DNA; social life begins at "viability" when the embryo can live—and begin to form social relationships—outside of the womb.)

But for pro-life people, this line of reasoning is ominous. If social life is more important than physical life, it then follows that people may be ranked by the value of their social contributions, thus making invidious distinctions among individuals. In contrast, if physical life is valued because it is a gift from the Creator, then no mere human can make claim to evaluate among the gifts with which various individuals are born. A view that the physical or genetic dimension of life is paramount—that all who are born genetically human are, a priori, persons—means that at some level all are equal. A hopelessly damaged newborn is, on this level, as equally deserving of social resources as anyone else. What pro-life people fear is that if the pro-choice view of the world is adopted, then those who are less socially *productive* may be deemed less socially *valuable.* For pro-life people, many of whom have situational reasons to fear how pro-choice people would assign them a social price tag, such a prospect is a nightmare.

The phrase *quality of life* evokes for pro-choice people a pleasing vista of the human intellect directed to resolving the complicated problems of life—the urge for knowledge used to tame sickness, poverty, inequality, and other ills of humankind. To pro-life people, in contrast, precisely because it is focused on the here and now and actively rejects the sacred and the transcendent, it evokes the image of Nazi Germany where the "devalued" weak are sacrificed to enlarge the comfort of the powerful.

Thus, in similar ways, both pro-life and pro-choice world views founder on the same rock, that of assuming that others do (or must or should) share the same values. Pro-life people assume that all good people should follow God's teachings, and moreover they assume that most good-minded people would agree in the main as to what God's teachings actually are. (This conveniently overlooks such things as wars of religion, which are usually caused by differences of opinion on just such matters.) Pro-choice people, in their turn, because they value reason, assume that most reasonable people will come to similar solutions when confronted with similar problems. The paradox of utilitarianism, that one person's good may be another person's evil, as in the case of the pro-life belief that a too-effective contraceptive is a bad thing, is not something they can easily envisage, much less confront.[2]

What neither of these points of view fully appreciates is that neither religion nor reason is static, self-evident, or "out there." Reasonable people who are located in very different parts of the social world find themselves differentially exposed to diverse realities, and this differential exposure leads each of them to come up with different—but often equally reasonable—constructions of the world. Similarly, even deeply devout religious people, because they too are located in different parts of the social world and, furthermore, come from different religious and cultural traditions, can disagree about what God's will is in any particular situation. When combined with the fact that attitudes toward abortion rest on these deep, rarely examined notions about the world, it is unambiguously clear why the abortion debate is so heated and why the chances for rational discussion, reasoned arguments, and mutual accommodation are so slim.

DISCUSSION QUESTIONS

1. Are there some values so fundamental that they should receive special protection and not be subject to majority preference? What should the role of the courts, the legislatures, the press, political action groups, and churches be in debates where policy choices force us to decide between deeply held values?
2. Is Segers correct that the stress on "rights" has undermined the more important debate on values?

[2]For a thoughtful exposition of this and other dilemmas associated with the philosophy of utilitarianism, see Amartya Sen and Bernard Williams, eds., *Utilitarianism and Beyond.*

3. In Luker's essay are there values which both sides hold common? What can be done about the gap between the two world views and lifestyle choices which seem to be the roots from which attitudes on abortion emerge? How do economic choices and values enter here?
4. Is the debate over abortion really a conflict between constitutional rights—those of the fetus versus those of the mother?

7

THE CONSTITUTION AND THE PUBLIC DISCUSSION OF CAPITAL PUNISHMENT

John C. Koritansky

In Chapter 2 the tenuous and yet inseparable relationship in America between moral and legal or Constitutional issues was outlined. The reason for this is not difficult to comprehend. Our Constitutional order rests upon a principled neutrality towards the question of how people ought to live. As a people we Americans tend in public discussion to turn from explicitly moral criteria to issues of procedure and legal form. However, it often happens that discussion of questions of procedure or form are freighted with moral implications. It is a very interesting question whether the tendency to translate moral issues into the judicial language of legal rights does more to inform or to distort our moral discourse.

One consequence of the legalistic character of our moral discourse has been that the issue of capital punishment in America has been discussed largely in connection with the question of the meaning of the Eighth Amendment's prohibition of "cruel and unusual punishments." It would seem that, for us, the two questions pertaining to the constitutionality of capital punishment and its morality are more or less rolled into one. That is, we tend to equate a question of whether or not capital punishment is right or just with the question of whether or not it is permitted by the Constitution. The limiting effect of reasoning from the Constitutional prohibition is clear and disconcerting: The interpretation of the Eighth Amendment seems to depend upon explicit recourse to moral judgment that we must bring to the words "cruel and unusual." Simply redefining this moral question as one of constitutionality does not evade the issues because the terms of the Eighth Amendment itself are unavoidably moral. The Constitution throws us back upon our own resources—it asks us to make a moral judgment we may feel especially nervous about.

In the recent cases involving capital punishment, the Court has risked being especially vulnerable to the charge of reading their own moral values into the business of Constitutional adjudication. The issue is between those justices who argue in effect that capital punishment is unconstitutional because it is wrong and those who believe it improper for a justice to rule on matters of right and wrong on the authority of his own conscience or moral reasoning. Perhaps it is more in keeping with the basic idea of a democratic or self-governing republic that the people should decide for themselves such questions as whether death is a cruel or unusual punishment. Would this mean, though, that the Eighth Amendment's terms would be judicially unenforceable? Do states that enact laws providing for the death penalty establish precedents that might serve to settle the constitutional issue in subsequent adjudication since the citizenry in those state have already decided the issue of "cruel and unusual punishment"? The Court's attempt to steer a middle course between moral imperiousness and concession has met with only partial success.

At whatever level capital punishment is discussed, it is important to consider the legitimate purpose of punishment. For the purposes of rehabilitation, capital punishment is wholly inappropriate, and obviously there are less extreme ways of effectively protecting society from criminals than by inflicting death. The most commonly discussed question is whether capital punishment has any value as a deterrent. Here the question rests precariously in a balance of doubt with credible evidence marshalled by each side. The difficulty arises with the definition of deterrence. If one means that the wrongdoer will be deterred by fear of suffering the gravest consequences if caught in the commission of a capital crime, it may be argued that such fear is not sufficiently reliable. However, if one means to include in the notion of deterrence the moral suasion of the law itself in pronouncing certain crimes so heinous as to call for an ultimate punishment of death, then the argument may be stronger.

This last point leads directly to the question whether it is appropriate or constitutional that retribution be considered one of the purposes of punishment. Here one finds common ground between the competing camps. As an opponent of capital punishment, Justice Brennan has stated that this is precisely what the Eighth Amendment ought to be understood to prevent. Punishment thus understood is vengeance and vengeance is but a species of cruelty. However, others, like Walter Berns, are not calling for retribution itself but rather for retributive justice. For while justice mitigates retribution, Berns fears justice may become diluted if it is wholly sanitized of retribution.

In any case, the Court has ruled through Justice Stewart that retribution is an element of punishment that states have traditionally been allowed to exercise and that retribution is by itself not unconstitutional.

Finally, there is the question of discrimination and racial prejudice in the application of capital punishment. Opponents of capital punishment claim that the death penalty is meted out more often to the poor, disadvantaged minorities. Supporters answer this criticism with their own claims that members of poor and disadvantaged minorities also commit a higher percentage of capital crimes. In a recent case the Court refused to declare that capital punishment is presumptively unconsitutional for violating the equal protection clause because of any lack of even-handedness in its application.

The Court has, in the past, required that capital crimes be defined in state law with great precision. Moreover, the Court requires the state courts to be scrupulous about procedures whereby juries will not abuse their discretion and will understand the extraordinary seriousness of a conviction for a capital crime. In spite of their precautions the issue of capital punishment remains one that divides states, communities, and even families. It touches the heart of American ideals that value life as well as justice.

Gregg v. *Georgia*

Justice Potter Stewart

...As we have seen, however, the Eighth Amendment demands more than that a challenged punishment be acceptable to contemporary society. The Court also must ask whether it comports with the basic concept of human dignity at the core of the Amendment. *Trop* v. *Dulles,* 356 U.S., at 100 (plurality opinion). Although we cannot "invalidate a category of penalties because we deem less severe penalties adequate to serve the ends of penology," *Furman* v. *Georgia, supra,* at 451 (POWELL, J., dissenting), the sanction imposed cannot be so totally without penological justification that it results in the gratuitous infliction of suffering. Cf. *Wilkerson* v. *Utah,* 99 U.S., at 135–136; *In re Kemmler,* 136 U.S., at 447.

Excerpts from the majority opinion, Justice Potter Stewart, *Gregg* v. *Georgia,* 428 U.S. 153 (183–89, 206–7).

The death penalty is said to serve two principal social purposes: retribution and deterrence of capital crimes by prospective offenders.[1]

In part, capital punishment is an expression of society's moral outrage at particularly offensive conduct.[2] This function may be unappealing to many, but it is essential in an ordered society that asks its citizens to rely on legal processes rather than self-help to vindicate their wrongs.

> The instinct for retribution is part of the nature of man, and channeling that instinct in the administration of criminal justice serves an important purpose in promoting the stability of a society governed by law. When people begin to believe that organized society is unwilling or unable to impose upon criminal offenders the punishment they 'deserve,' then there are sown the seeds of anarchy—of self-help, vigilante justice, and lynch law. *Furman* v. *Georgia, supra,* at 308 (STEWART, J., concurring).

"Retribution is no longer the dominant objective of the criminal law," *Williams* v. *New York,* 337 U. S. 241, 248 (1949), but neither is it a forbidden objective nor one inconsistent with our respect for the dignity of men. *Furman* v. *Georgia,* 408 U. S., at 394–395 (BURGER, C. J., dissenting); *id.,* at 452–454 (POWELL, J., dissenting); *Powell* v. *Texas,* 392 U. S., at 531 535–536 (plurality opinion). Indeed, the decision that capital punishment may be the appropriate sanction in extreme cases is an expression of the community's belief that certain crimes are themselves so grievous an affront to humanity that the only adequate response may be the penalty of death.[3]

Statistical attempts to evaluate the worth of the death penalty as a deterrent to crimes by potential offenders have occasioned a great deal of debate.[4] The results simply have been inconclusive. As one opponent of capital punishment has said:

> [A]fter all possible inquiry, including the probing of all possible methods of inquiry, we do not know, and for systematic and easily visible reasons cannot know, what the truth about this 'deterrent' effect may be....

[1]Another purpose that has been discussed is the incapacitation of dangerous criminals and the consquent prevention of crimes that they may otherwise commit in the future. See *People* v. *Anderson,* 6 Cal. 3d 628, 651, 493 P. 2d 880, 896, cert. denied, 406 U. S. 958 (1972); *Commonwealth* v. *O'Neal,* supra, at ———, 339 N. E. 2d, at 685-686.

[2]See H. Packer, Limits of the Criminal Sanction 43-44 (1968).

[3]Lord Justice Denning, Master of the Rolls of the Court of Appeal in England, spoke to this effect before the British Royal Commission on Capital Punishment:...

[4]See, *e. g.,* Peck, The Deterrent Effect of Capital Punishment: Ehrlich and His Critics, 85 Yale L. J. 359 (1976); Baldus & Cole, A Comparison of the Work of Thorsten Sellin and Isaac Ehrlich on the Deterrent Effect of Capital Punishment, 85 Yale L. J. 170 (1975); Bowers & Pierce, The Illusion of Deterrence in Isaac Ehrlich's Research on Capital Punishment, 85 Yale L. J. 187 (1975); Ehrlich, The Deterrent Effect of Capital Punishment: A Question of Life and Death, 65 Am. Econ. Rev. 397 (June 1975); Hook, The Death Sentence, in The Death Penalty in America, 146 (H. Bedau ed. 1967); T. Sellin, The Death Penalty, A Report for the Model Penal Code Project of the American Law Institute (1959).

> The inescapable flaw is...that social conditions in any state are not constant through time, and that social conditions are not the same in any two states. If an effect were observed (and the observed effects, one way or another, are not large) then one could not at all tell whether any of this effect is attributable to the presence or absence of capital punishment. A 'scientific'—that is to say, a soundly based—conclusion is simply impossible, and no methodological path out of this tangle suggests itself. C. Black, Capital Punishment: The Inevitability of Caprice and Mistake 25–26 (1974).

Although some of the studies suggest that the death penalty may not function as a significantly greater deterrent than lesser penalties,[5] there is no convincing empirical evidence either supporting or refuting this view. We may nevertheless assume safely that there are murderers, such as those who act in passion, for whom the threat of death has little or no deterrent effect. But for many others, the death penalty undoubtedly is a significant deterrent. There are carefully contemplated murders, such as murder for hire, where the possible penalty of death may well enter into the cold calculus that precedes the decision to act.[6] And there are some categories of murder, such as murder by a life prisoner, where other sanctions may not be adequate.[7]

The value of capital punishment as a deterrent of crime is a complex factual issue the resolution of which properly rests with the legislatures, which can evaluate the results of statistical studies in terms of their own local conditions and with a flexibility of approach that is not available to the courts. *Furman* v. *Georgia, supra,* at 403–405 (BURGER, C. J., dissenting). Indeed, many of the post-*Furman* statutes reflect just such a responsible effort to define those crimes and those criminals for which capital punishment is most probably an effective deterrent.

In sum, we cannot say that the judgment of the Georgia Legislature that capital punishment may be necessary in some cases is clearly wrong. Considerations of federalism, as well as respect for the ability of a legislature to evaluate, in terms of its particular State, the moral consensus concerning the death penalty and its social utility as a sanction, require us to conclude, in

[5]See *e. g.*, The Death Penalty in America, *supra*, at 258–332; Report of the Royal Commission on Capital Punishment, 1949–1953, Cmd. 8932.

[6]Other types of calculated murders, apparently occurring with increasing frequency, include the use of bombs or other means of indiscriminate killings, the extortion murder of hostages or kidnap victims, and the execution-style killing of witnesses to a crime.

[7]We have been shown no statistics breaking down the total number of murders into the categories described above. The overall trend in the number of murders committed in the nation, however, has been upward for some time. In 1964, reported murders totaled an estimated 9,250. During the ensuing decade, the number reported increased 123%, until it totaled approximately 20,600 in 1974. In 1972, the year *Furman* was announced; the total estimated was 18,520. Despite a fractional decrease in 1975 as compared with 1974, the number of murders increased in the three years immediately following *Furman* to approximately 20,400, an increase of almost 10%. See FBI, Uniform Crime Reports, for 1964, 1972, 1974, and 1975, Preliminary Annual Release.

the absence of more convincing evidence, that the infliction of death as a punishment for murder is not without justification and thus is not unconstitutionally severe.

Finally, we must consider whether the punishment of death is disproportionate in relation to the crime for which it is imposed. There is no question that death as a punishment is unique in its severity and irrevocability. *Furman* v. *Georgia,* 408 U. S., at 286–291 (BRENNAN, J., concurring); *id.,* at 306 (STEWART, J., concurring). When a defendant's life is at stake, the Court has been particularly sensitive to insure that every safeguard is observed. *Powell* v. *Alabama,* 287 U. S. 45, 71 (1932); *Reid* v. *Covert,* 354 U. S. 1, 77 (1957) (HARLAN, J., concurring in result). But we are concerned here only with the imposition of capital punishment for the crime of murder, and when a life has been taken deliberately by the offender,[8] we cannot say that the punishment is invariably disproportionate to the crime. It is an extreme sanction, suitable to the most extreme of crimes.

We hold that the death penalty is not a form of punishment that may never be imposed, regardless of the circumstances of the offense, regardless of the character of the offender, and regardless of the procedure followed in reaching the decision to impose it.

...While *Furman* did not hold that the infliction of the death penalty *per se* violates the Constitution's ban on cruel and unusual punishments, it did recognize that the penalty of death is different in kind from any other punishment imposed under our system of criminal justice. Because of the uniqueness of the death penalty, *Furman* held that it could not be imposed under sentencing procedures that created a substantial risk that it would be inflicted in an arbitrary and capricious manner. MR. JUSTICE WHITE concluded that "the death penalty is exacted with great infrequency even for the most atrocious crimes and...there is no meaningful basis for distinguishing the few cases in which it is imposed from the many cases in which it is not." 408 U. S., at 313 (concurring). Indeed, the death sentences examined by the Court in *Furman* were "cruel and unusual in the same way that being struck by lightning is cruel and unusual. For, of all the people convicted of [capital crimes], many just as reprehensible as these, the petitioners [in *Furman* were] among a capriciously selected random handful upon whom the sentence of death has in fact been imposed....[T]he Eighth and Fourteenth Amendments cannot tolerate the infliction of a sentence of death under legal systems that

[8]We do not address here the question whether the taking of the criminal's life is a proportionate sanction where no victim has been deprived of life—for example, when capital punishment is imposed for rape, kidnaping, or armed robbery that does not result in the death of any human being.

permit this unique penalty to be so wantonly and so freakishly imposed." *Id.*, at 309–310 (STEWART, J., concurring).[9]

Furman mandates that where discretion is afforded a sentencing body on a matter so grave as the determination of whether a human life should be taken or spared, that discretion must be suitably directed and limited so as to minimize the risk of wholly arbitrary and capricious action.

...The basic concern of *Furman* centered on those defendants who were being condemned to death capriciously and arbitrarily. Under the procedures before the Court in that case, sentencing authorities were not directed to give attention to the nature or circumstances of the crime committed or to the character or record of the defendant. Left unguided, juries imposed the death sentence in a way that could only be called freakish. The new Georgia sentencing procedures, by contrast, focus the jury's attention on the particularized nature of the crime and the particularized characteristics of the individual defendant. While the jury is permitted to consider any aggravating or mitigating circumstances, it must find and identify at least one statutory aggravating factor before it may impose a penalty of death. In this way the jury's discretion is channeled. No longer can a jury wantonly and freakishly impose the death sentence; it is always circumscribed by the legislative guidelines. In addition, the review function of the Supreme Court of Georgia affords additional assurance that the concerns that prompted our decision in *Furman* are not present to any significant degree in the Georgia procedure applied here.

For the reasons expressed in this opinion, we hold that the statutory system under which Gregg was sentenced to death does not violate the Constitution. Accordingly, the judgment of the Georgia Supreme Court is affirmed.

It is so ordered....

[9]This view was expressed by other Members of the Court who concurred in the judgments. See 408 U. S., at 255–257 (Douglas, J.); *id.*, at 291–295 (BRENNAN, J.). The dissenters viewed this concern as the basis for the *Furman* decision: "The decisive grievance of the opinions...is that the present system of discretionary sentencing in capital cases has failed to produce evenhanded justice;...that the selection process has followed no rational pattern." *Id.*, at 398–399. (BURGER, C. J., dissenting).

Gregg v. *Georgia*

Justice William Brennan

...This Court inescapably has the duty, as the ultimate arbiter of the meaning of our Constitution, to say whether, when individuals condemned to death stand before our Bar, "moral concepts" require us to hold that the law has progressed to the point where we should declare that the punishment of death, like punishments on the rack, the screw, and the wheel, is no longer morally tolerable in our civilized society.[1] My opinion in *Furman* v. *Georgia* concluded that our civilization and the law had progressed to this point and that therefore the punishment of death, for whatever crime and under all circumstances, is "cruel and unusual" in violation of the Eighth and Fourteenth Amendments of the Constitution. I shall not again canvass the reasons that led to that conclusion. I emphasize only that foremost among the "moral concepts" recognized in our cases and inherent in the Clause is the primary moral principle that the State, even as it punishes, must treat its citizens in a manner consistent with their intrinsic worth as human beings—a punishment must not be so severe as to be degrading to human dignity. A judicial determination whether the punishment of death comports with human dignity is therefore not only permitted but compelled by the Clause. 408 U. S., at 270.

I do not understand that the Court disagrees that "[i]n comparison to all other punishments today...the deliberate extinguishment of human life by the State is uniquely degrading to human dignity." *Id.*, at 291. For three of my Brethren hold today that mandatory infliction of the death penalty constitutes cruel and unusual punishment. I perceive no principled basis for this limitation. Death for whatever crime and under all circumstances "is truly an awesome punishment. The calculated killing of a human being by the State involves, by its very nature, a denial of the executed person's humanity....An executed person has indeed 'lost the right to have rights.' " *Id.*, at 290. Death is not only an unusually severe punishment, unusual in its pain, in its finality, and in its enormity, but it serves no penal purpose more effectively than a less severe punishment; therefore the principle inherent in the Clause that prohibits pointless infliction of excessive punishment when

[1]Tao, Beyond *Furman v. Georgia:* The Need for a Morally Based Decision on Capital Punishment, 51 Notre Dame Law. 722, 736 (1976).

Excerpts from the dissenting opinion, Justice William Brennan, *Gregg* v. *Georgia*, 428 US 229–31.

less severe punishment can adequately achieve the same purposes invalidates the punishment. *Id.*, at 279.

The fatal constitutional infirmity in the punishment of death is that it treats "members of the human race as nonhumans, as objects to be toyed with and discarded. [It is] thus inconsistent with the fundamental premise of the Clause that even the vilest criminal remains a human being possessed of common human dignity." *Id.*, at 273. As such it is a penalty that "'subjects the individual to a fate forbidden by the principle of civilized treatment guaranteed by the [Clause]."[2] I therefore would hold, on that ground alone, that death is today a cruel and unusual punishment prohibited by the Clause. "Justice of this kind is obviously no less shocking than the crime itself, and the new 'official' murder, far from offering redress for the offense committed against society, adds instead a second defilement to the first."[3]

The Death Penalty in America, What the Record Shows

Watt Espy

I appreciate having the opportunity of testifying before you during your deliberations on this human piece of legislation which seeks to abolish capital punishment in our state—something which has been done in practically every civilized country, with the notable exception of certain states in the United States and the Government of the Republic of South Africa.

By way of introduction I would like to tell you something of my research for the past seven years which, I believe, qualifies me to discuss the subject now being considered by your distinguished committee. My work entails research into the history of capital punishment in our country and hopefully will culminate in the publication of a series of volumes that will contain listings of all legal executions that have taken place in the United States, including as many documented facts as possible on those executed and their crimes.

[2] *Trop* v. *Dulles*, 356 U. S., at 99 (plurality opinion of Warren, C. J.).

[3] A. Camus, Reflections on the Guillotine 5–6 (Fridtjof-Karla Pub. 1960).

Watt Espy, "The Death Penalty in America, What the Record Shows," *Christianity and Crisis* 40 (23 June 1980), 191–195. Reprinted with permission of Gail Hovey, managing editor, *Christianity and Crisis*.

My work is entirely objective and does not seek to present a brief for or against capital punishment. Indeed, when I started it some seven years ago, I had personally formed no fixed opinions on the subject. However, as my research progressed and certain facts, inequities and injustices became obvious to me I became convinced that I am unalterably opposed to it. In addition to the moral repugnance that all civilized men have towards the taking of human life, even under the most aggravating of circumstances, the death penalty has always been used in a discriminating and unfair manner and has never served its avowed purpose of being a deterrent to other acts of violence.

Indeed, I am convinced, to some extent at least, that the exact contrary is true, that it actually increases violence in that it is a demonstration, condoned by the executing governmental authority, of a depressing lack of appreciation for the intrinsic value of all human life that has a naturally demoralizing effect on the population in general.

At this time I have confirmed a total of 11,334 legal executions that have taken place in the geographical area now comprising the United States of America since the first, which was that of Daniel Frank who was hanged in the Colony of Virginia on March 1, 1622, for stealing a calf and other chattels belonging to Sir George Yeardley. This work is far from complete as I would estimate that there have been between 18,000 and 20,000 human beings who have paid the supreme penalty during the ensuing 357 years. I would also like to add that such important information as races, ages, educations, occupations, etc., have not yet been obtained on all of the 11,334 confirmed executions. But this information has been obtained on a sufficient number for certain observations and conclusions to be formed on a tentative basis. Let me begin those observations and conclusions by addressing the issue of the death penalty as a deterrent.

The argument we most often hear in favor of capital punishment is that it is a deterrent to crime. In my opinion the only person who it really deters is the man who is executed. Certainly he will never sin again. There are simply too many cases of persons who knew the awful fate prescribed by the law in capital cases but who, nonetheless, committed crimes that resulted in their being put to death themselves.

J. Samuel McCue was a prominent attorney in Charlottesville, Va., who, in addition to serving as the Mayor of Thomas Jefferson's hometown, had also served as an attorney in many capital cases, both as a prosecutor and as defense counsel. He well knew the penalty for murder and yet, on February 10, 1905, he was hanged in Charlottesville for the murder of his wife.

During his tenure as Sheriff of Allegheney County, Md., George Swearingen had hanged several convicted felons. He certainly knew the terrors of the gallows where, in most instances, persons were not spared by the merciful death of having their necks broken but instead slowly strangled to death—in some instances for as long as thirty minutes, retaining consciousness until almost the very end. In spite of this knowledge of the consequences of murder, George Swearingen was, himself, hanged in Cumberland on October 2, 1829, for having murdered his wife.

Charles Justice, an inmate electrician at the Ohio State Prison around the turn of the century installed the electric chair at that institution. Released on parole, he killed a policeman, was tried, convicted and on October 27, 1911, he expiated his crime in the very chair he had constructed and wired.

On October 8, 1875, a black man named George Speer was legally hanged at Fayetteville, Ga., for the rape of a white girl. Among witnesses of this execution was Speer's [sic] names results from the fact that, prior to emancipation, they belonged to different owners). Four days after Speer's execution, Edmundson raped a white woman, was captured and lodged in the Fayetteville jail from whence he was taken by a mob on the night of October 17 and hanged from the same gallows from which his brother had been executed nine days earlier.

I shall burden you with but one other example of one who knew the awful penalty for murder but was not deterred, though there were hundreds of others. On August 24, 1827, a man named Jesse Strang was publicly hanged in Albany, N.Y. Among the witnesses was Levi Kelley, a prosperous farmer from Cooperstown. The execution made such a strong impression on Mr. Kelley that, after returning home, he remarked to a number of his neighbors that he did not believe that anyone who ever witnessed an execution could commit a murder through fear of being hanged himself. Ten days later this same Kelley shot and killed one of his tenants. This man on whom the execution of August 24 had made such a profound impression was then tried and condemned to die. On December 28, 1827, just four months after he had traveled to Albany to witness Strang's execution he was hanged himself. A tragic aftermath of the Kelley execution was the fact that, during the proceedings, one of the platforms erected so that witnesses could have a good view, collapsed and two persons were killed. Additionally, a neighbor and friend named Cooke became so depressed following the execution that one week later he committed suicide by hanging himself.

Thank God we have gotten away from public executions, but if they are really intended to be deterrents to crime then it seems as though we should want to make them as public as possible. Public executions, with their grim, carnival horror, continued right on up until this century in some jurisdictions. The last two that I have recorded were those of Rainey Bethea, a black man, in Kentucky and Roscoe "Red" Jackson, a white man, in Galena, Mo.

Bethea was convicted of the rape-murder of an aged white woman and on August 14, 1936, he paid with his life in a public spectacle at Owensboro, Ky. Thousands upon thousands of persons arrived from several states, and their drunken decorum was so disgusting that the condemnation of the civilized world was brought down on the Commonwealth of Kentucky. It rapidly changed its law to read that future hangings should take place in private.

Missouri allowed public hangings up until 1937 when it passed a bill providing for the asphyxiation of those condemned to die at the State Prison. Roscoe Jackson, a 36-year-old drifter who claimed to be a great-nephew of General Stonewall Jackson and who had murdered a friendly motorist who had given him a ride, had been sentenced under the old law, and he thus goes down as the last man publicly hanged in a legal manner in the United States.

There were tragic aftermaths to virtually every public execution. On May 9, 1879, two black men, Tom Jones and Henry McLeod, were hanged at Appling, Ga. Some white citizens of McDuffie County who had traveled to Appling to join the festivities got into a brawl immediately after the execution and 25 shots were fired. One man was fatally wounded and three others injured less seriously.

In June 1889, a man named Alex Henderson was hanged at Bainbridge, Ga. Henry Lindsey took his two young sons, one 10 and the other 13, to witness the execution, no doubt believing that it would have some salutory effect. The youngest son, highly impressionable and religiously inclined, afterwards improvised a crude gallows in the cow pen by placing a plank at an angle to represent the scaffold and suspending a plowline from a scantling to serve as a noose. For several days he spent much of his time on this makeshift scaffold, repeating the religious services held at Henderson's execution, singing the hymns, and playing a game which he called "Henderson's hanging." On July 20, 1889, he did not return home for supper, and when his mother went to the cow pen searching for him, she found his lifeless body hanging from the plowline.

NO ROOM FOR ERROR

While it is quite clear to me that the death penalty does not deter violent crime and cannot be proven to do so and may in many cases foster violent behavior, there are other aspects of capital punishment that, to my way of thinking, make it an unacceptable form of punishment. Perhaps the most obvious aspect is that the death penalty is bound to be applied to innocent people no matter what our safeguards against such mistakes are.

I concede that most of the people who have been executed in this country have been guilty of the crimes for which they were convicted. However, there also have been plenty of innocent people, subsequently proven innocent beyond a shadow of a doubt, to have been deprived of their lives by due process of law. In addition to those proven innocent after their execution there are others, I am sure, who were innocent but have never been proven to be so, because law enforcement officials and prosecutors will not investigate a case once an execution has been held. The case is closed for them, and it is probably too much to expect them to go out and try to prove that they have executed an innocent person, no matter what the evidence.

To my way of thinking nothing can be more horrible or repugnant than that the state, with all its power for good or evil, should deprive one of its citizens of life for a crime committed by another. The examples are many. The father of Supreme Court Justice Lucius Quintius Cincinnatus Lamar, himself a brilliant Milledgeville, Ga., jurist, once sentenced a Methodist minister to hang for the rape-murder of his sister-in-law. The judgment of the court was duly carried out, and several years later Judge Lamar was in his office when he was informed that a message had just arrived from Mississippi that a man, hanged there for another crime, had confessed from the gallows to the crime for which the minister had been executed. So hurt was the judge that he locked his office, walked to his home, kissed the members of his family, including the future Supreme Court Justice, who was then but a small child, goodbye, and shot himself through the head.

January 7, 1898, was hanging day in Greenfield, Mass. On that day Jack O'Neill became one of the last persons to be hanged in the Bay State, which was soon to provide for the electrocution of its condemned. O'Neill was an Irishman, one of the immigrants hated in that state at that particular time, the same Irish strain that was later to give our country President John F. Kennedy. O'Neill, who maintained that he was innocent and was a victim of bigotry, had been convicted of the rape-murder of Hattie Evelyn McCloud at Buckland on January 8, 1897. His last words were: "I shall meet death like a man, and I hope those who see me hanged will live to see the day when it is proved that I am innocent—and it will some day." These prophetic words came true shortly afterwards when a soldier from Shelburne Falls, a member of the Sixth Massachusetts Militia, dying of wounds received in Cuba during the Spanish American War, confessed that he and not O'Neill had murdered Miss McCloud, furnishing details and information that only the actual killer could have known.

In Dutchess County, N.Y., in 1806, there was a drunken brawl at the home of Jesse Wood, a farmer, in which the participants were Wood and his two sons, Joseph and Hezekiah: A shotgun was fired and Joseph Wood fell dead. Hezekiah swore that his father had fired the gun, and Jesse was duly arrested and convicted on Hezekiah's testimony. The old man claimed that he was too drunk to remember what had happened, and he went to his death saying that while he might have killed Joseph, he did not recall it. Ten years later, as he lay dying, Hezekiah Wood confessed that he had fired the shot that killed his brother and admitted that he had perjured himself against his father to save his own life.

Of all the countries on the face of the earth, I feel that we have more safeguards to prevent the conviction of the innocent than probably any other, but this is not enough as the innocent are, on occasion, convicted. I cannot imagine any human being, who is not a perfect monster himself, viewing with unconcern the prospect of an innocent man being executed, but that possibility always exists where the death penalty is available.

Along with the execution of innocent people we must consider the execution of the insane. During the nightmare regime of Adolf Hitler in Germany, the Jews were not the only persons to be liquidated. The insane and those who suffered from various mental and physical disorders were also shot, hanged, gassed and used for medical experiments. The civilized world recoiled in horror at this excessive use of death as an instrument of state policy. The argument will be advanced by those who advocate capital punishment that this has not and cannot happen in this country, where statutes forbid the execution of those who are not mentally responsible for their acts of violence.

Yet insane persons have been executed in the United States. Where the man whose life is in jeopardy is penniless and friendless with no funds with which to employ adequate alienists to examine him and to testify for him, the only psychiatrists available have generally been those from state hospitals who, in all too many instances, have given only perfunctory examinations, frequently for periods as short as 15 minutes in the cell of the accused and who, in practically every instance, have served as an extension of the prosecuting arm of the state, certifying a man to be sane enough to be executed.

A CASE OF TOTAL INSANITY

One of the most celebrated cases in American history of an obviously insane person being executed is the case of Albert Fish who was electrocuted by the State of New York on January 16, 1936. Fish, a 65-year-old house painter, was a member of a distinguished family that had furnished a Secretary of State of the United States, a United States Senator and several members of Congress. A religious fanatic, he was in and out of mental institutions for all of his adult life but nonetheless managed to father and raise a large family of children. At the time of his arrest for the murder of an 11-year-old girl, Grace Budd, he admitted to having eaten her flesh for a period of several days after he had killed her. He then calmly related that over the course of 20 years he had murdered and cannibalistically feasted off the bodies of numerous children of both sexes.

This grandfatherly-appearing old man was x-rayed and found to have no less than 30 needles of various sizes, including a large sailing needle, totally imbedded in his body in the region of his abdomen and scrotum. Many of these needles had been inserted for so long a time that they had calcified. Thoroughly examined by the eminent alienist, Dr. Frederic Wertham, he was declared totally insane. In fact, Dr. Wertham said that there was no known perversion that Fish had not practiced at one time or another, and Wertham presented a long list of these perversions which, in addition to the most extreme forms of sadism and masochism, included the fact that he had, supplemented his diet with human feces.

The state presented analysts from the state hospitals that had held Fish on numerous occasions, including twice after he had killed and eaten Grace Budd, and they all said that they had released him after short periods of confinement because, while he was peculiar and eccentric, he was not insane. They testified that he was perfectly sane at the time of his crime and perfectly sane then. His conviction was affirmed on appeal and then a strong plea for executive clemency was made to Governor Herbert H. Lehman. Lehman, an avowed liberal who did much to further progressive causes in this country during a long and useful life, listened to the evidence. He then made a startling statement in which he expressed the opinion that Fish was insane but said that so horrible was his crime that he saw no alternative to allowing the law to take its course.

This pathetic, sick old man went to the electric chair with an air of exhilaration, actually helping to strap himself to the instrument of death and explaining that he looked forward to the charge of electricity as being the most powerful sexual stimulation that he had ever received.

I would also like to cite to you the case of Elmer N. Arrant, who was the local manager for one of Alabama's major utility companies in Fort Deposit. Arrant had a long record of mental instability and had, at one time, been a patient in a private sanitorium. Subject to delusions, he became convinced that one of his neighbors, John E. Norman, was having an affair with Mrs. Arrant. On the evening of June 20, 1935, he telephoned Norman and asked that he and Mrs. Norman step over to his house. When the Normans entered his yard, he shot and killed both of them from a place of concealment behind a tree. His defense was one of insanity, but he was nonetheless convicted and the sentence of death pronounced. After the conviction had been affirmed, a strong effort was made to have the sentence commuted on the grounds of mental incompetency, but Governor Bibb Graves declined to do so. The Governor conceded that Arrant was insane, but he said that he had been in that condition for years and yet had been accepted as a leader of his community. On June 19, 1936, while murmuring a prayer, Elmer N. Arrant was electrocuted at Kilby Prison.

As long as the death penalty remains on the statutes there is always the possibility that people who are not responsible will be put to death by the state, which has an obligation to take care of them and to protect them from themselves and others. In so many cases the execution of the insane is the expedient and popular thing to do, but it is never the right thing to do. If the state can kill an Albert Fish, the state can close down its mental hospital and set up a crematorium on the grounds, or a gas chamber, as Hitler did. I have only used these two illustrations for the sake of brevity. Hundreds of other insane persons also have been executed.

CAPITAL CHARGE/POLITICAL CONTROL

As Americans we are all indignant and condemnatory of the death penalty being used as a political tool in other countries. We consider it an abhorrent and barbaric practice. We say that it can never happen here, but it has in the past and, as long as it remains an accepted form of punishment, it can happen again.

In the very early days of the colonies, the Puritans in Massachusetts passed a law, on October 19, 1658, which provided that every person of the "cursed sect of the Quakers" found within the colony "should be immediately imprisoned without fail and, being convicted to be of the sect of Quakers, should immediately be banished on pain of death." We know that at least four persons were hanged in the Massachusetts Bay Colony because of the fact that they were Quakers.

On May 4, 1884, a labor rally was held in Chicago's Haymarket Square that was addressed by a number of labor organizers, some of whom were avowed anarchists. The meeting was heavily patrolled by policemen, which was highly and rightly resented by the workers who had gathered peacefully. Toward the conclusion of the rally a bomb was exploded; one policeman was instantly killed and six others subsequently died of their wounds. Albert Parsons and other leaders were arrested, and four of them, Parsons, August Spies, George Engel and Adolph Fischer, were hanged on November 11, 1887, after having been tried and convicted. Others were sentenced to varying prison terms, though it was never proven that any of those convicted had any prior knowledge of the bomb.

There are many other examples of the death penalty having been used in our country as a means of political control. The case of Johnny Harris here in Alabama is presently being discussed the world over as one having political overtones. Personally I have not studied this case or the facts surrounding it to any extent, my work being primarily one of studying cases where the death penalty has actually been exacted, and I do not feel qualified to express any sentiments on it. However, rather than see the good name of Alabama criticized in such a fashion I would hope that some legislative group would make an impartial study of the circumstances of the entire affair.

Certainly wherever the death penalty is condoned and is recognized as a legitimate form of punishment, the potential is present for its misuse as a political weapon when placed in the wrong hands. This, of course, includes many overzealous prosecutors and other politicians who have used the death penalty as a means of seeking higher political office. These men, generally speaking, are not necessarily bloodthirsty but they are inordinately ambitious. In many instances they have succeeded temporarily, but their constituents have usually seen through their lust for office and their successes have been short lived. Governors Whitman of New York (the Becker case) and Dorsey of Georgia (the Leo Frank case) have met with such fate. Others have failed to obtain their highest ambitions because of their vigorous espousals of the death penalty, even in states where capital punishment is an accepted fact. There can be but little doubt that his hardened attitude was partially responsible for the defeat of Attorney General Shevin in the Florida gubernatorial primaries last year by the more moderate Bob Graham, who, nevertheless, now has the dubious distinction of having consented to the first nonconsensual execution in this country since 1967.

There are those who argue for the death penalty on the grounds that mercy should not be shown to one who has shown no mercy. These advocates of using the law as a means of of vengeance instead of punishment are saying, in essence, that law and government, which should be the most exalted expression of man's noblest and most merciful thoughts and ideals, actually should reflect man's basest instinct—the desire and will to kill. Punishment for crime must be exacted, certainly and surely—about that there can be no doubt—but is the death penalty a fit and rational punishment? I say no, it is not. It does not restore life to the victim, nor does it restore the husband to the widow nor the parent to the orphan. The ends of justice are far better served, the sacredness of life affirmed instead of denied by the state, and the possibility of some form of restitution remains with the abolition of capital punishment and the substitution of greater safeguards in the pardoning and parole process.

SOME ARE MORE EQUAL THAN OTHERS

Perhaps the most disturbing aspect of the death penalty is that it is discriminately applied. There has always been discrimination in the application of capital punishment, and as long as death penalty laws remain on the statutes there always will be. With but a few exceptions, members of minorities, the poor, the friendless, the uneducated and, if you will pardon the expression, "the different," are the ones who pay with their lives for their crimes.

The black man who killed the white man has always been more likely to pay with his life than the white man who has killed the black man. This has been universally true in every state in this Union, not just the South. In my research, that is in over 11,000 cases, I can recall only two where white men were hanged for murders of black men. One occurred in the state of Georgia in the 1870's and the other in the state of Mississippi in the 1890's. Both of these white men were more or less outcasts, thoroughly despised by their white neighbors, one because he was a gambler and whiskey dealer, the other because he was considered a rogue in general, and both because they chose blacks for their closest friends.

My work has shown me fairly conclusively that economics enter into the application of the death penalty. Only rarely has a man been executed for the murder of someone belonging to a lower social or economic order. However, where one has killed his social or economic superior, he has practically been assured of atoning for his transgression with his life. The poor, of course, suffer most in this situation, having to rely on court-appointed attorneys for their defense. Once they are convicted they have not the means to afford a prolonged fight for life. Generally the poor do not have powerful and influential friends to seek executive clemency for them. They are simply forgotten except for their family whose suffering is, of course, intense. I have found cases where loved ones have died of grief or have committed suicide.

Let me conclude my comments on the discriminatory nature of the death penalty by mentioning a contemporary case. We are all familiar with the case of Dan White, the former San Francisco policeman and city councilman, an accepted member of the "establishment," who entered the San Francisco City Hall through a back window with a loaded revolver and shot Mayor George Moscone and Councilman Harvey Milk to death. White promptly surrendered himself to the police at the station where he had previously been employed, wept and pleaded insanity, claiming that he had not meant to kill but offering no reason for sneaking into the offices armed. He was convicted of manslaughter and received a seven-year sentence after entering a plea of insanity.

The same week that he was convicted, in the same state of California, another killer—a drifter who had killed several people and drank their blood—also pleaded insanity but was convicted of first-degree murder and sentenced to be executed in the gas chamber. To my way of thinking, White's crime was one of premeditated murder if there ever has been one. Also, to my way of thinking, one who drinks human blood, believing himself to be some sort of vampire or Dracula, is obviously insane and not a fit candidate for the gas chamber.

No other illustration could more dramatically show the injustice of the death penalty even today when we have the most stringent safeguards possible ordered by the Federal courts and written into law by the various legislatures. Different juries try different cases, and, being different, they weigh the evidence with different sets of scales. Different judges decide on degrees of mitigation and they "march to the tune of different drummers." I would like to echo a statement attributed to the Marquis de Lafayette who is reported to have said, "I shall ask for the abolition of the penalty of death until I have the infallibility of human judgment demonstrated to me."

To summarize, I would urge you to report from your committee this bill to abolish capital punishment in our state. I would do so because the death penalty, a throwback to a less enlightened era, serves no useful purpose. It is not a deterrent to crime nor does it restore life to the victim. It is demoralizing to the population in general in that it shows a lack of regard for the sanctity of human life by the state itself. Finally, the possibility of error exists and I am certain that each of you will agree with me that nothing can be more terrible or more reprehensible than for the state to unjustly take the life of one of its own.

Someday the death penalty will be eradicated in the United States, and we will look back on it as a part of our Dark Ages just as we now look back on the hanging of witches at Salem as an abomination we can no longer tolerate. If mankind is to survive on this planet, we must learn to live together and be civilized. The death penalty is not civilized. Let its demise begin with us.

For Capital Punishment: Crime and the Morality of the Death Penalty

Walter Berns

CONCLUSION

...There is a sense in which punishment may be likened to dramatic poetry or the purpose of punishment to one of the intentions of a great dramatic poet (and Shakespeare is clearly the greatest in our language). The plots of Shakespeare's tragedies involve political men—Caesar the emperor, Coriolanus the general, Lear the king, Hamlet the son of a king, and others, including, of course, Macbeth who would be king—and this is not fortuitous, nor does it represent the prejudices of a poet who lived in an aristocratic age. He chose to write about such men because the moral problems can be made fully intelligible only in what they do or do not do and in the consequences of what they do or do not do. Dramatic poetry depicts men's actions because men are revealed in, or make themselves known through, their actions; and the essence of a human action consists in its being virtuous or vicious.[1] Only a ruler or a contender for rule can act with the freedom and on a scale that allows the virtuousness or viciousness of human deeds to be fully displayed. Macbeth was such a man and in his fall, brought about by his own acts, and in the consequent suffering he endured, is revealed the meaning of morality. In *Macbeth* the majesty of the moral law is demonstrated to us; as I said, it teaches us the awesomeness of the commandment, thou shalt not kill. In a similar fashion, the punishments imposed by the legal order remind us of the reign of the moral order; not only do they remind us of it, but by enforcing its prescriptions, they enhance the dignity of the legal order in the eyes of moral men, in the eyes of those decent citizens who cry out "for gods who will avenge injustice."[2] Reenforcing the moral order is especially important in a self-governing community, a community that gives laws to itself.

That the American legal order must, in the eyes of its citizens, have this dignity is the substance of Madison's argument in the Forty-ninth *Federalist.*

[1]Aristotle, "Poetics" 1448 A-1.

[2]Thomas L. Pangle, "The Political Psychology of Religion in Plato's Laws," *American Political Science Review* 70 (Dec. 1976):1062.

In it he was responding to Jefferson's suggestion that there be conventions of the people whenever "any two of the three branches of government," by extraordinary majorities, shall concur in the opinion that the Constitution should be amended. Madison opposed this suggestion; he saw that these appeals, especially if they were to be frequent, would "deprive the government of that veneration which time bestows on everything, and without which perhaps the wisest and freest governments would not possess the requisite stability." Government rests on opinion, he went on, and the strength of opinion in each individual depends in part on the extent to which he supposes others to share it and in part on its venerableness. Such factors would not matter in a "nation of philosophers"; among such a people a "reverence for the laws would be inculcated by the voice of enlightened reason." But there can be no nation of philosophers, or even one governed by philosophers, and any real government, even "the most rational" government, "will not find it a superfluous advantage to have the prejudices of the community on its side."

I can illustrate Madison's point, and show its relevance to capital punishment, by saying first that if the laws were understood to be divinely inspired or, in the extreme case, divinely given, they would enjoy all the dignity that the opinions of men can attach to anything and all the dignity required to insure their being obeyed by most of the men living under them. Like Duncan in the opinion of Macduff, they would be "the Lord's anointed," and they would be obeyed even as Macduff obeyed the laws of the Scottish kingdom. Only a Macbeth would challenge them, and only a Meursault would ignore them. But the laws of the United States are not of this description; in fact, among the proposed amendments that became the Bill of Rights was one declaring, not that all power comes from God, but rather "that all power is originally vested in, and consequently derives from the people"; and this proposal was dropped only because it was thought to be redundant: the Constitution's Preamble said essentially the same thing, and what we know as the Tenth Amendment reiterated it.[3] So Madison proposed to make the Constitution venerable in the minds of the people, and Lincoln, in the Lyceum speech referred to above went so far as to say that a "political religion" should be made of it. They did this not because the Constitution and the laws made pursuant to it could not be supported by "enlightened reason," but because they feared enlightened reason would be in short supply; they therefore sought to augment it. The laws of the United States would be obeyed by some men because they could hear and understand "the voice of enlightened reason," and by other men because they would regard the laws with that "veneration which time bestows on everything."

[3]U. S. Congress, "The Debate and Proceedings In the Congress of the United States, 1789–1824," 42 vols., known as "The Annals of Congress" (Gales & Seaton, 1834–56), vol. 1, pp. 451, 790.

But, as our history attests, this is only conditionally true. The Constitution is surely regarded with veneration by us—so much so that Supreme Court justices have occasionally complained of our habit of making "constitutionality synonymous with wisdom,"[4] or wisdom synonymous with constitutionality—but the extent to which it is venerated and its authority accepted depends on the compatibility of its rules with our moral sensibilities, for the Constitution, despite its venerable character, is not the only source of these moral sensibilities. There was even a period before slavery was abolished by the Thirteenth Amendment when the Constitution was regarded by some very moral men as an abomination: William Lloyd Garrison called it "a convenant with death and an agreement with Hell," and there were honorable men holding important political offices and judicial appointments who refused to enforce the Fugitive Slave Law even though its constitutionality had been affirmed.[5] In time this opinion spread far beyond the ranks of the original Abolitionists until those who held it comprised a constitutional majority of the people, and slavery was abolished. But Lincoln knew that more than amendments were required to make the Constitution once more worthy of the veneration of moral men. This is why, in the Gettysburg Address, he made the principle of the Constitution an inheritance from "our fathers," and asked the living generation to dedicate themselves to the cause that the Gettysburg dead had left "unfinished," so that generations yet unborn might enjoy a "new birth of freedom." For the same reason, in his Second Inaugural he called upon the nation to see in the Civil War the expiation demanded by a just God for the sin of slavery. As Harry V. Jaffa has shown,[6] the Constitution had not only to be cleansed of its aspects of slavery, but, if it were once again to be an object of veneration, it would have to be exalted, its dignity enhanced. This Lincoln sought to do and this, I think, he accomplished. That it should be so esteemed is, as I said before, especially important in a self-governing nation that gives laws to itself, because it is only a short step from the principle that the laws are merely a product of one's own will to the opinion that the only consideration that informs the law is self-interest; and this opinion is only one remove from lawlessness. A nation of simply self-interested men will soon enough perish from the earth.

It was not an accident that Lincoln spoke as he did at Gettysburg or that he chose as the occasion for his words the dedication of a cemetery built on a portion of the greatest battlefield of the Civil War. Two and a half years earlier, in his First Inaugural, he had said that Americans, north and south,

[4]West Virginia State Board of Education v. Barnette, 319 US 624, 670. (1943). Dissenting opinion.
[5]Ableman v. Booth, 21 Howard 506 (1859).
[6]Jaffa, "Crisis of the House Divided," chap. 9, esp. pp. 225–32.

were not enemies but friends, and must not be enemies. Passion had strained but must not be allowed to break the bonds of affection that tied them one to another. He closed by saying this: "The mystic chords of memory, stretching from every battle-field, and patriot grave, to every living heart and hearthstone, all over this broad land, will yet swell the chorus of the Union, when again touched, as surely they will be, by the better angels of our nature." The chords of memory that would swell the chorus of the Union, when touched by a Lincoln, could be touched, even by a Lincoln, only on the most solemn of occasions, and in the life of a nation no occasion is more solemn than the burial of patriots who have died defending it on the field of battle. War is surely an evil, but as Hegel said, it is not an "absolute evil."[7] It exacts the supreme sacrifice, but precisely because of that it can call forth the sublime rhetoric of a Lincoln. His words at Gettysburg serve to remind Americans in particular of what Hegel said people in general needed to know, and could be made to know by means of war and the sacrifices demanded of them in wars, namely, that their country is something more than a "civil society" the purpose of which is simply the protection of individual and selfish interests.

Capital punishment, like Shakespeare's dramatic and Lincoln's political poetry (and it is surely that, and was understood by him to be that) serves to remind us of the majesty of the moral order that is embodied in our law and of the terrible consequences of its breach. The law must not be understood to be merely statute that we enact or repeal at our will and obey or disobey at our convenience, especially not the criminal law. Wherever law is regarded as merely statutory, men will soon enough disobey it, and they will learn how to do so without any inconvenience to themselves. The criminal law must possess a dignity far beyond that possessed by mere statutory enactment or utilitarian and self-interested calculations; the most powerful means we have to give it that dignity is to authorize it to impose the ultimate penalty. The criminal law must be made awful, by which I mean, awe-inspiring, or commanding "profound respect or reverential fear." It must remind us of the moral order by which alone we can live as *human* beings, and in our day the only punishment that can do this is capital punishment.

That was not always the case. In the beginning, banishment was considered the equal to the death penalty in severity and significance: Cain was not put to death but, instead, was banished "from the presence of the Lord" to become a "fugitive and vagabond" on the earth, unfit to live in the human community—or, as Justice Felix Frankfurter once said respecting certain

[7]G. W. F. Hegel, "Philosophy of Right," Trans. T. M. Knox, (London: Oxford University Press, 1967), sec. 324 (pp. 209–10).

American criminals, unfit "to remain in the communion of our citizens."[8] But he said that in a dissenting opinion; the Court's majority said that Americans may no longer be banished or punished by being deprived of their citizenship. They may voluntarily renounce their citizenship, but imposed as punishment, expatriation is unconstitutionally cruel and unusual.[9] Citizenship, said Chief Justice Warren, is the right to have rights, and Congress may not deprive anyone of that right, no matter what duties he shirks or what crimes he commits. Even a traitor who levies war against the United States is entitled to remain a citizen of the United States if, for some reason (perhaps because he is uncertain who is going to win that war), he wishes to do so. The essence of American citizenship, as the Warren Court saw it, consists in the right to keep one's options open, so to speak, rather like Meursault (except that Meursault would regard loss of citizenship as no punishment at all). The justices may not know it, but this understanding of the rights and duties of American citizenship owes much to Beccaria, who devoted the chapter following his chapter on the death penalty to "banishment and confiscations," and in the course of it said that the "loss of possessions is a punishment greater than that of banishment."[10]

Beccaria opposed both banishment and capital punishment because he understood that both were inconsistent with the principle of self-interest, which was the basis of the political order he favored. If a man's first or only duty is to himself, of course he will prefer his money to his country; he will also prefer his money to his brother. In fact, he will prefer his brother's money to his brother, and a people of this description, or a country that understands itself in this Beccarian manner, can put the mark of Cain on no one. For the same reason, such a country can have no legitimate reason to execute its criminals, or, indeed, to punish them in any manner. What would be accomplished by punishment in such a place? Punishment arises out of the demand for justice, and justice is demanded by angry, morally indignant men; its purpose is to satisfy that moral indignation and thereby promote the law-abidingness which, it is assumed, accompanies it. But the principle of self-interest denies the moral basis of that indignation.

Not only will a country based solely on self-interest have no legitimate reason to punish; it may have no need to punish. It may be able to solve what we call the crime problem by substituting a law of contracts for a law of crimes. According to Beccaria and Hobbes's social contract, men agree to yield their natural freedom to the "sovereign" in exchange for his promise

[8]Trop v. Dulles, 356 US 86, 122 (1958). Dissenting opinion.

[9]Affroyim v. Rusk, 387 U. S. 253 (1967). Expatriation and banishment are not equivalent terms. "Expatriation" means loss of citizenship but not necessarily expulsion from the country.

[10]Cesare Beccaria, "On Crimes and Punishment," Trans. Henry Paolucci (Indianapolis: Bobbs Merrill, Library of Liberal Arts 1963), p. 53.

to keep the peace. As it becomes more difficult for the sovereign to fulfill his part of the contract, there is a demand that he be made to pay for his non-performance. From this come compensation or insurance schemes embodied in statutes whereby the sovereign (or state), being unable to keep the peace by punishing criminals, agrees to compensate its contractual partners for injuries suffered at the hands of criminals, injuries the police are unable to prevent. The insurance policy takes the place of law enforcement and the *posse comitatus*, and John Wayne and Gary Cooper give way to Mutual of Omaha. There is no anger in this kind of law and none (or no reason for any) in the society. The principle can be carried further still. If we ignore the victim (and nothing we do can restore his life anyway), there would appear to be no reason why—the worth of a man being his price, as Hobbes put it—coverage should not be extended to the losses incurred in a murder. If we ignore the victim's sensibilities (and what are they but absurd vanities?), there would appear to be no reason why—the worth of a woman being *her* price—coverage should not be extended to the losses incurred in a rape. Other examples will, no doubt, suggest themselves.

This might appear to be an almost perfect solution to what we persist in calling the crime problem, achieved without risking the terrible things sometimes done by an angry people. A people that is not angry with "criminals" will not be able to deter crime, but a people fully covered by insurance has no need to deter crime: they will be insured against all the losses they can, in principle, suffer. What is now called crime can be expected to increase in volume, of course, and this will cause an increase in the premiums paid, directly or in the form of taxes; but it will no longer be necessary to apprehend, try, and punish criminals, which is now costing Americans more than $1.5 billion a month (a cost that is increasing at an annual rate of about 15 percent),[11] and one can buy a lot of insurance for $1.5 billion a month. There is this difficulty: as Rousseau put it, to exclude anger from the human community is to concentrate all the passions in a "self-interest of the meanest sort,"[12] and such a place would not be fit for human habitation.

When, in 1976, the Supreme Court declared death to be a constitutional penalty, it decided that the United States was not that sort of country; most of us, I think, can appreciate that judgment. We want to live among people who do not value their possessions more than their citizenship, who do not

[11]U.S. Department of Justice, Law Enforcement Assistance Administration, National Criminal Justice Information and Statistics Service, "Expenditure and Employment Data for the Criminal Justice System," 1974. (Washington, D.C.: U.S. Government Printing Office, 1976), p. 2. The 1974 total was $16,279,000,000 broken down as follows: Federal, $2,603,000,000; State, $4,546,000,000; and Local, $9,130,000,000.

[12]Jean Jacque Rousseau, "Emil," in *Oeuvers Complètes*. (Dijon: Pleiades, 1969), vol. 4, p. 633 (footnote at the end of the Savoyard Vicar section).

think exclusively or even primarily of their own rights, people whom we can depend on even as they exercise their rights, and whom we can trust, which is to say, people who, even in the absence of a policeman, will not assault our bodies or steal our possessions, and might even come to our assistance when we need it, and who stand ready, when the occasion demands it, to risk their lives in the defense of their country. If we are of the opinion that the United States may rightly ask of its citizens this awful sacrifice, then we are also of the opinion that it may rightly impose the most awful penalty; if it may rightly honor its heroes, it may rightly execute the worst of its criminals. By doing so, it will remind its citizens that it is a country worthy of heroes.

DISCUSSION QUESTIONS

1. What is the legitimate purpose of punishment?
2. Some claim that in this country we execute old or sick pets more humanely than we do criminals. If we have capital punishment, shouldn't it be carried out as humanely and painlessly as possible?
3. Does capital punishment, as Berns maintains, "serve to remind us of the majesty of the moral order that is embodies in our law and of the terrible consequences of its breach"?
4. Could you sit on a jury and vote guilty if the death penalty were the mandatory sentence?

8

EVOLUTION AND CREATION IN THE PUBLIC SCHOOLS: A DURABLE CONTROVERSY

Bernard K. Duffy

Apart from Gallileo's sun-centered theory of the universe, few scientific developments have sparked such controversy as Darwin's theory of natural selection. Hotly debated since the latter half of the nineteenth century, Darwin's theory has posed a considerable threat to religious denominations that espouse belief in a literal Bible. In 1925 the nation witnessed the dramatic confrontation between the evolutionists and the Biblical literalists in Dayton, Tennessee. The prosecution argued that John Scopes, a biology teacher, had violated the state's ban on the teaching of evolution, as indeed he had. The nation's newspapers covered the trial in detail and, despite the fact that Scopes was found guilty, the national public found against the fundamentalists, whom they regarded as erecting a barrier of religious prejudice in the path of scientific progress. The battle was then, and continues to be, much more encompassing than the mere dispute over whether or not a particular doctrine, evolution, should be taught. It strikes at the core of public morality, for it concerns whether or not what children learn about religion at home shall be contradicted by what they learn at school. The undermining of parental values by teachers, from Socrates to Scopes, has been a perpetual source of public indignation.

The Scopes trial raised the question of whether the prevailing religious beliefs of the electorate could be used to determine what should and should not be taught in the public schools. In Dayton, Tennessee, as in the rural South generally during the 1920s, fundamentalists were no doubt in the majority. Why should their religious values not be reflected in the public school curriculum? In almost every matter, except the teaching of religion, school boards may follow their own inclinations regarding what shall be in the curriculum. Furthermore, community standards are used to govern what movies can be shown in theatres and what books and magazines can be sold. Why should the public school curriculum be different?

To answer this question we must turn to the United States Constitution, which in its First Amendment prohibits the establishment of a state religion. When the Tennessee legislature voted to outlaw the teaching of evolution, it did so to protect a religious belief, and thus took a step toward establishing a state religion. Evolution is a perceived threat, not just to any item of public conscience, but to a religious belief championed by certain denominations. In Dayton, Tennessee, it might have seemed that the entire community believed with the prosecution counsel, William Jennings Bryan, when he told the jury that the world was created in exactly six twenty-four-hour days, but there was doubtless a minority, even in Dayton, who saw the matter differently. If the degree to which a scientific theory, a novel, a poem, or a work of history violates the religious beliefs of the majority were to become a legitimate criterion for eliminating it from the school curriculum, the floodgates would be opened to all kinds of religiously supported reforms of the public school curriculum. There is little taught in the public schools that cannot be shown to influence religious belief. In Tennessee, fundamentalists recently objected in court to a Holt, Rinehart and Winston reading series that they alleged was anti-Christian because in their view it endorsed such positions as feminism, humanism, and pacificism. It is little wonder that textbook publishers have been accused of self-censorship—of failing to incorporate or diluting material in school textbooks that might make them objectionable in populous states, such as Texas, where fundamentalist religious groups would be apt to take exception.

With the advent of the Moral Majority and the so-called New Religious Right, fundamentalists have taken a new interest in evolutionary theory. Their reasons are much the same as those expressed in the Scopes trial—that the public schools threaten the religious beliefs with which they would like their children inculcated. But there is a new wrinkle in the argumentation that represents an ingenious adaptation to the failure of fundamentalists to exclude evolution from the biology curriculum, particularly in the face of the 1968 Supreme Court decision making laws banning the teaching of evolution unconstitutional. The new mission of the fundamentalists is to have the story of creation taught side-by-side with the theory of evolution. The tact the Religious Right has taken is twofold. First, it wishes to show that evolution is merely a theory, whose acceptance relies on a kind of faith somehow equatable with religious faith; second, it presses the point that creation is also a theory, and one that can be supported scientifically. Thus, when the

Religious Right speaks with seeming contradiction of "creation science," its intention is to place the theory of creation on the same footing as the theory of evolution.

In one of the essays in this chapter, the microbiologist Duane Gish of the Institute for Creation Science calls into question the scientific validity of evolutionary theory. However, as Havard paleontologist Professor Stephen Gould argues in his essay, there are theories of evolution, such as Darwin's theory of natural selection, but there is also the fact of evolution, shown in such material evidence as fossils and extant species of animals, like tree moths, that have shown a pattern of rapid evolution. Even ignoring the fact of evolution, it is difficult to see how a theory of evolution requires faith of the same sort needed to believe the story of Genesis in the Bible.

Equally interesting as a persuasive strategy is the Religious Right's attempt to identify evolution as the central doctrine of secular humanism, which fundamentalist leaders wish to regard as a religion. The Religious Right speaks of secular humanism, a philosophy originated in the early part of the twentieth century by a small group of educators, philosophers, and scientists, as if it were a well-organized and well-financed religion whose goal is to remove the influence of Christianity from society. If secular humanism is a religion, as the Religious Right adamantly asserts, then its doctrines, including evolution, ought not to be taught in the public schools; teaching them would violate the Constitutional prohibition against the establishment of a religion. In fact, secular humanism is a convenient scapegoat, a representation of all who do not agree with the religious, political, and social values of the Religious Right.

It is worth noting the differences in style between the two essays in this chapter. Professor Gould's essay is written in a manner that might tax the average reader less than Dr. Gish's article, which is written more in the style of a scientific paper. The absence of footnotes in Gould's chapter and the extensive documention in Gish's can be accounted for in part by their authors' perceptions of the audiences who would read the essays. On the other hand, it certainly does Gish's case no harm to use the mechanics of scholarship, for it lends an aura of scientific objectivity that helps him take his opposition of evolution beyond the point of simple religious conviction. Gish's use of scientific evidence and objective reasoning to discredit evolution speaks to the potency of such evidence and argumentation in a society dominated by science. Note that Gish uses the statements of evolutionary theorists to discredit evolution. Gould, who says his own theories have been turned against evolution by the anti-evolutionists, criticizes his opponents for using the controversy among evolutionary theorists to discredit the fact of evolution.

In the Scopes trial sixty years ago, the prosecution bitterly opposed efforts by the defense to introduce evidence concerning the fact of evolution.

Although the written statements of scientists were incorporated into the trial transcript, the Court denied the defense the opportunity to call scientific witnesses. The prosecution wanted the case decided on the simple basis of whether or not Scopes violated the law by teaching evolution, but the real issue was who had the right to decide what should be taught, the public or the scientists. In a nation less influenced by fundamentalism than in the 1920s, and more influenced by science, it is interesting that the fundamentalist case against evolution should now be couched in the language of science.

The new strategy for bringing religion into the schools, by insisting that so-called creation science be taught together with evolution, has not persuaded the U.S. Supreme Court. The Court recently ruled that a Louisiana law mandating the teaching of creation science together with evolution violated the establishment clause of the Constitution. Justice Brennan held for the majority that the intent of the law was to foster religious belief and to cast doubt on evolution, and not, as the state maintained, to provide for a "balanced treatment" of creation and evolution.

Thus far fundamentalists have failed to make religion into science by devising the tendentious notion of "creation science," or to make science into religion, by claiming that evolutionary theory relies on faith or is a tenet of secular humanism as a religion of science. Evolution will undoubtedly continue to be a cause célèbre for fundamentalists and others who see the public schools as threatening religious values. Just as school prayer has remained controversial long after the Supreme Court prohibited it nearly thirty years ago, so the teaching of evolution will remain a key issue in the battle to keep religion in the classroom.

Creation, Evolution and Public Education

Duane T. Gish

It is commonly believed that the theory of evolution is the only scientific explanation of origins and that the theory of special creation is based solely on

---

Duane T. Gish, "Creation, Evolution and Public Education," in *Evolution versus Creationism: The Public Education Controversy,* ed. J. Peter Zetterberg (Phoenix, AZ: Oryx Press, 1983), 175–191. Edited version reprinted with permission of the author.

religious beliefs. It is further widely accepted that the theory of evolution is supported by such a vast body of scientific evidence, while encountering so few contradictions, that evolution should be accepted as an established fact. As a consequence, it is maintained by many educators that the theory of evolution should be included in science textbooks as the sole explanation for origins but that the theory of special creation, if taught at all, must be restricted to social science courses.

As a matter of fact, neither evolution nor creation qualifies as a scientific theory. Furthermore, it has become increasingly apparent that there are a number of irresolvable contradictions between evolution theory and the facts of science, and that the mechanisms postulated for the evolutionary process could account for no more than trivial changes.

...Creation has not been observed by human witnesses. Since creation would have involved unique, unrepeatable historical events, creation is not subject to the experimental method. Furthermore, creation as a theory is non-falsifiable. That is, it is impossible to conceive an experiment that could disprove the possibility of creation. Creation thus does not fulfill the criteria of a scientific theory. That does not say anything about its ultimate validity, of course. Furthermore, creation theory* can be used to correlate and explain data, particularly that available from the fossil record, and is thus subject to test in the same manner that other alleged historical events are subject to test—by comparison with historical evidence.

Evolution theory also fails to meet the criteria of a scientific theory. Evolution has never been witnessed by human observers; evolution is not subject to the experimental method; and as formulated by present-day evolutionists, it has become non-falsifiable.

It is obvious that no one has ever witnessed the type of evolutionary changes postulated by the general theory of evolution. No one, for example, witnessed the origin of the universe or the origin of life. No one has ever seen a fish evolve into an amphibian, nor has anyone observed an ape evolve into a man. No one, as a matter of fact, has ever witnessed a significant evolutionary change of any kind.

The example of the peppered moth in England has been cited by such authorities as H. B. D. Kettlewell[1] and Sir Gavin de Beer[2] as the most striking evolutionary change ever witnessed by man. Prior to the industrial revolution in England, the peppered moth, *Biston betularia,* consisted predominatly of a light-colored variety, with a dark-colored form compris-

*An idea or set of ideas may be called a theory even though it does not qualify as a *scientific* theory. The term "model" is, however, a better expression than "theory" for the concept of creation or evolution, although "theory" and "model" will be used interchangeably in this paper.

[1]H. B. D. Kettlewell, "Darwin's Missing Evidence," *Scientific American* 200 (3) (1959): 48–53.

[2]Gavin de Beer, "Review of Everett C. Olson, *Evolution of Life*, 1965," *Nature* 206 (1965): 331–32.

ing a small minority of the population. This was so because predators (birds) could more easily detect the dark-colored variety as these moths rested during the day on light-colored tree trunks and lichen-covered rocks. With the on-set of the industrial revolution and resultant air pollution, the tree trunks and rocks became progressively darker. As a consequence, the dark-colored variety of moths became more and more difficult to detect, while the light-colored variety ultimately became an easy prey. Birds, therefore, began eating more light-colored than dark-colored moths, and today over 95% of the peppered moths in the industrial areas of England are of the darker-colored variety.

Although, as noted above, this shift in populations of peppered moths has been described as the most striking example of evolution ever observed by man, it is obvious that no significant evolutionary change of any kind has occurred among these peppered moths, certainly not the type required to substantiate the general theory of evolution. For however the populations may have shifted in their proportions of the light and dark forms, all of the moths remained from beginning to end peppered moths, *Biston betularia*. It seems evident, then, that if this example is the most striking example of evolution witnessed by man, no real evolution of any kind has ever been observed.

The world-famous evolutionist, Theodosius Dobzhansky, while endeavoring to proclaim his faith in evolution, admitted that no real evolutionary change has ever been observed by man when he said, "...the occurrence of the evolution of life in the history of the earth is established about as well as events *not witnessed by human observers can be*."[3] It can be said with certainty, then, that evolution in the present world has never been observed. It remains as far outside the pale of human observation as the origin of the universe or the origin of life. Evolution has been *postulated* but *never observed*.

Since evolution cannot be observed, it is not amenable to the methods of experimental science. This has been acknowledged by Dobzhansky when he stated, "These evolutionary happenings are unique, unrepeatable, and irreversible. It is as impossible to turn a land vertebrate into a fish as it is to effect the reverse transformation. The applicability of the experimental method to the study of such unique historical processes is severely restricted before all else by the time intervals involved, which far exceed the lifetime of any human experimenter. And yet it is just such *impossibility* that is demanded by antievolutionists when they ask for 'proofs' of evolution which they would magnanimously accept as satisfactory."[4]

[3]T. Dobzbansky. "Evolution at Work." *Science* 127 (1958): 1091.

[4]T. Dobzbansky, "On Methods of Evolutionary Biology and Anthropology: Part 1, Biology," *American Scientist* 45 (1957): 388.

Please note that Dobzhansky has said that the applicability of the experimental method to the study of evolution is an impossibility! It is obvious, then, that evolution fails to qualify as a scientific theory, for it is certain that a theory that cannot be subjected to experimental tests is not a scientific theory.

Furthermore, modern evolution theory has become so plastic, it is non-falsifiable. It can be used to prove anything and everything. Thus, Murray Eden, a professor at Massachusetts Institute of Technology and an evolutionist, has said, with reference to the falsifiability of evolution theory, "This cannot be done in evolution, taking it in its broad sense, and this is really all I meant when I called it tautologous in the first place. It can, indeed, explain anything. You may be ingenious or not in proposing a mechanism which looks plausible to human beings and mechanisms which are consistent with other mechanisms which you have discovered, but it is still an unfalsifiable theory."[5]

...[E]volution has never been observed and is outside the limits of experimental science. Evolution theory is, therefore, no more scientific than creation theory. That does not make it necessarily false, and it can be tested in the same way that creation theory can be tested—by its ability to correlate and explain historical data, that is, the fossil record. Furthermore, since evolution is supposed to have occurred by processes still operating today, the theory must not contradict natural laws.

Evolutionists protest, of course, that these weaknesses of evolution as a theory are not necessarily due to weaknesses of the theory, per se, but are inherent in the very nature of the evolutionary process. It is claimed that the evolutionary process is so slow that it simply cannot be observed during the lifetime of a human experimenter, or, as a matter of fact, during the combined observations of all recorded human experience. Thus, as noted above, Dobzhansky is incensed that creationists should demand that evolution be subjected to the experimental method before any consideration could be given to evolution as an established process.

It must be emphasized, however, that it is for precisely this reason that evolutionists insist that creation must be excluded from science textbooks or, for that matter, from the whole realm of science, as a viable alternative to evolution. They insist that creation must be excluded from possible consideration as a scientific explanation for origins because creation theory cannot be tested by the experimental method. It is evident, however, that this is a characteristic that it shares in common with evolution theory. Thus, if crea-

[5]M. Eden, "Inadequacies of Neo-Darwinian Evolution as a Scientific Theory," in *Mathematical Challenges to the Neo-Darwinian Interpretation of Evolution*. ed. by P. S. Moorehead and M. P. Kaplan (Philadelphia: Wistar Institute Press, 1967), p. 71.

tion must be excluded from science texts and discussions, then evolution must likewise be excluded.

Evolutionists insist that, in any case, the teaching of the creation model would constitute the teaching of religion because creation requires a Creator. The teaching about the creation model and the scientific evidence supporting it, however, can be done without reference to any religious literature. Furthermore, belief in evolution is as intrinsically religious as is belief in creation.

If creation must be excluded from science in general and from science textbooks and science classrooms in particular because it involves the supernatural, it is obvious that theistic evolution must be excluded for exactly the same reason. Thus the only theory that can be taught according to this reasoning, and in fact, the only theory that is being taught in almost all public schools and universities and in the texts they use, is a purely mechanistic, naturalistic, and thus atheistic, theory of evolution. But atheism, the antithesis of theism, is itself a religious belief.

The late Sir Julian Huxley, British evolutionist and biologist, has said that "Gods are peripheral phenomena produced by evolution."[6] What Huxley meant was that the idea of God merely evolved as man evolved from lower animals. Huxley desired to establish a humanistic religion based on evolution. Humanism has been defined as "the belief that man shapes his own destiny. It is a constructive philosophy, a *non-theistic religion*, a way of life." This same publication quotes Huxley as saying, "I use the word 'Humanist' to mean someone who believes that man is just as much a natural phenomenon as an animal or plant; that his body, mind, and soul were not super-naturally created but are products of *evolution*, and that he is not under the control or guidance of any supernatural being or beings, but has to rely on himself and his own powers."[7] The inseparable link between this non-theistic humanistic religion and belief in evolution is evident.

George Gaylord Simpson, Professor of Vertebrate Paleontology at Harvard University until his retirement and one of the world's best-known evolutionists, has said that the Christian faith, which he calls the "higher superstition" (in contrast to the "lower superstition" of pagan tribes of South America and Africa) is intellectually unacceptable.[8]

...[A]ccording to Simpson, man is alone in the Universe (there is no God), he is the result of an impersonal, unconscious process (no one directed his origin or creation), and he is his own master and must manage his own

[6]J. Huxley, *The Observer*, July 17, 1960, p. 17.

[7]*What is Humanism?* The Humanist Community of San Jose, San Jose, CA 95106.

[8]G. G. Simpson, "The World into which Darwin Led Us," *Science* 131 (1960): 966.

destiny (there is no God to determine man's destiny). That, according to Simpson and Huxley, is the evolutionist's view of man. That this is the philosophy held by most biologists has been recently emphasized by Dobzhansky. In his review of Monod's book, *Chance and Necessity*, Dobzhansky said, "He has stated with admirable clarity, and eloquence often verging on pathos, the mechanistic materialist philosophy shared by most of the present 'establishment' in the biological sciences."[9]

No doubt a majority of the scientific community embraces the mechanistic materialistic philosophy of Simpson, Huxley, and Monod. Many of these men are highly intelligent, and they have woven the fabric of evolution theory in an ingenious fashion. They have then combined this evolution theory with humanistic philosophy and have clothed the whole with the term "science." The product, a non-theistic religion, with evolutionary philosophy as its creed under the guise of "science," is being taught in most public schools, colleges and universities of the United States. It has become our unofficial state-sanctioned religion.

Furthermore, a growing number of scientists are becoming convinced that there are basic contradictions between evolution theory and empirical scientific data as well as known scientific laws. On the other hand, these scientists believe special creation provides an excellent model for explaining and correlating data related to origins which is free of such contradictions. Even some evolutionists are beginning to realize that the formulations of modern evolution theory are really incapable of explaining anything and that an adequate scientific theory of evolution, if ever attainable, must await the discovery of as yet unknown natural laws.

The core of modern evolution theory, known as the neo-Darwinian theory of evolution, or the modern synthetic theory, is the hypothesis that the evolutionary process has occurred through natural selection of random mutational changes in the genetic material, selection being in accordance with alterations in the environment. Natural selection, itself, is not a chance process, but the material it must act on, mutant genes, is produced by random, chance processes.

It is an astounding fact that while at the time Darwin popularized it, the concept of natural selection seemed to explain so much, today there is a growing realization that the presently accepted concept of natural selection really explains nothing. It is a mere tautology, that is, it involves circular reasoning.

[9]T. Dobzhansky, "A Biologist's World View: Review of Jacques Monod, *Chance and Necessity: An Essay on the Natural Philosophy of Modern Biology*," *Science* 175 (1972): 49.

In modern theory, natural selection is defined in terms of differential reproduction. In fact, according to Lewontin, differential reproduction *is* natural selection.[10] When it is asked, what survives, the answer is, the fittest. But when it is asked, what are the fittest, the answer is, those that survive! Natural selection thus collapses into a tautology, devoid of explanatory value. It is not possible to explain *why* some varieties live to reproduce more offspring—it is only known that they do.

...According to modern evolutionary theory, ultimately all of evolution is due to mutations.[11] Mutations are random changes in the genes or chromosomes which are highly ordered structures. Any process that occurs by random chance events is subject to the laws of probability.

It is possible to estimate mutation rates. It is also possible to estimate how many favorable mutations would be required to bring about certain evolutionary changes. Assuming that these mutations are produced in a random, chance manner, as is true in the neo-Darwinian interpretation of evolution, it is possible to calculate how long such an evolutionary process would have required to convert an amoeba into a man. When this is done, according to a group of mathematicians, all of whom are evolutionists, the answer turns out to be billions of times longer than the assumed five billion years of earth history.[12]

One of these mathematicians, Murray Eden, stated, "It is our contention that if 'random' is given a serious and crucial interpretation from a probabilistic point of view, the randomness postulate is highly implausible and that an *adequate scientific theory of evolution must await the discovery and elucidation of new natural laws—physical, physico-chemical, and biological.*"[13] What Eden and these mathematicians are saying is that the modern neo-Darwinian theory of evolution is totally inadequate to explain more than trivial change and thus we simply have no basis at present for attempting to explain how evolution may have occurred. As a matter of fact, based on the assumption that the evolutionary process was dependent upon random chance processes, we can simply state that evolution would have been impossible.

...There is a natural tendency,...for all observed natural systems to go from order to disorder, towards increasing randomness. This is true throughout the entire known universe, both at the micro and macro levels.

[10]R. C. Lewontin, "Selection in and of Populations," in *Ideas in Modern Biology* (Garden City, NY: Natural History Press, 1965), p. 304.

[11]See, for example, G. L. Stebbins, *Processes of Organic Evolution* (Englewood-Cliffs, NJ: Prentice-Hall, 1971), p. 3; E. Mayr, *Animal Species and Evolution* (Cambridge, MA: Harvard University Press, 1966), p. 176.

[12]R. Bernhard, "Heresy in the Halls of Biology: Mathematicians Question Darwin," *Scientific Research* 2 (November, 1967): 59–66; P. S. Moorehead and M. P. Kaplan. eds., *Mathematical Challenges to the Neo-Darwinian Interpretation of Evolution* (Philadelphia: Wistar Institute Press, 1967).

[13]Eden, 1967, p. 109.

This tendency is so invariant that it has never been observed to fail. It is a natural law—the Second Law of Thermodynamics.

On the other hand, according to the general theory of evolution, as defined by Huxley, there is a general tendency of natural systems to go from disorder to order, towards an ever higher and higher level of complexity. This tendency supposedly operates in every corner of the universe, both at the micro and macro levels. As a consequence, it is believed, particles have evolved into people.

It is difficult to understand how a discerning person could fail to see the basic contradiction between these two processes. It seems apparent that both cannot be true, but no modern scientist would dare challenge the validity of the Second Law of Thermodynamics.

The usual, but exceedingly naive, answer given by evolutionists to this dilemma is that the Second Law of Thermodynamics applies only to closed systems. If the system is open to an external source of energy, it is asserted, complexity can be generated and maintained within this system at the expense of the energy supplied to it from the outside.

Thus, our solar system is an open system, and energy is supplied to the earth from the sun. The decrease in entropy, or increase in order, on the earth during the evolutionary process, it is said, has been more than compensated by the increase in entropy, or decrease in order, on the sun. The overall result has been a net decrease in order, so the Second Law of Thermodynamics has not been violated, we are told.

An open system and an adequate external source of energy are necessary *but not sufficient* conditions, however, for order to be generated and maintained, since raw undirected, uncontrolled energy is destructive, not constructive. For example, without the protective layer of ozone in the upper atmosphere which absorbs most of the ultraviolet light coming from the sun, life on earth would be impossible.

That much more than merely an external energy source is required to form complex molecules and systems from simpler ones is evident from the following statement by Simpson and Beck: "...the simple expenditure of energy is not sufficient to develop and maintain order. A bull in a china shop performs work, but he neither creates nor maintains organization. The work needed is *particular* work; it must follow specifications; it requires information on how to proceed."[14]

Thus a green plant, utilizing the highly complex photosynthetic system it possesses, can trap light energy from the sun and convert this light energy into chemical energy. A series of other complex systems within the green plant al-

[14]G. G. Simpson and W. S. Beck, *Life: An Introduction to Biology*, 2d ed. (New York: Harcourt, Brace and World, 1965), p. 466.

lows the utilization of this energy to build up complex molecules and systems from simple starting material. Of equal importance is the fact that the green plant possesses a system for directing, maintaining, and replicating these complex energy conversion mechanisms—an incredibly complex genetic system. Without the genetic system, no specifications on how to proceed would exist, chaos would result, and life would be impossible.

For complexity to be generated within a system, then, four conditions must be met: 1. The system must be an open system. 2. An adequate external energy source must be available. 3. The system must possess energy conversion mechanisms. 4. A control mechanism must exist within the system for directing, maintaining, and replicating these energy conversion mechanisms.

The seemingly irresolvable dilemma, from an evolutionary point of view, is how such complex energy conversion mechanisms and genetic systems arose in the *absence* of such systems, when there is a general natural tendency to go from order to disorder, a tendency so universal it can be stated as a natural law, the Second Law of Thermodynamics. Simply stated, machines are required to build machines, and something or somebody must operate the machinery.

The creationist thus opposes the wholly unscientific evolutionary hypothesis that the natural universe with all of its incredible complexity was capable of generating itself, and maintains that there must exist, external to the natural universe, a Creator, or supernatural Agent, who was responsible for introducing, or creating, the high degree of order found within this natural universe. While creationism is extra-scientific, it is not anti-scientific, as is the evolutionary hypothesis which contradicts one of the most well-established laws of science.

Finally, but of utmost significance, is the fact that the fossil record is actually hostile to the evolution model, but conforms remarkably well to predictions based on the creation model.[15] Complex forms of life appear abruptly in the fossil record in the so-called Cambrian sedimentary deposits or rocks. Although these animals, which include such highly complex and diverse forms of life as brachiopods, trilobites, worms, jellyfish, sponges, sea urchins, and sea cucumbers, as well as other crustaceans and molluscs, supposedly required about two to three billion years to evolve, not a single ancestor for any of these animals can be found anywhere on the face of the earth.[16] George Gaylord Simpson has characterized the absence of Precambrian fossils as "the major mystery of the history of life."[17] This fact

[15]D. T. Gish, *Evolution: The Fossils Say No!* (San Diego: Creation-Life Publishers, 1973).

[16]Gish, 1973; see also Preston Cloud, "Pseudofossils: A Plea for Caution," *Geology* 1, 3 (1973): 123–27; D. Axelrod, "Early Cambrian Marine Fauna," *Science* 128 (1958): 7–9; T. N. George, "Fossils in Evolutionary Perspective," *Science Progress* 48 (1960): 1–5.

[17]G. G. Simpson, *The Meaning of Evolution* (New Haven: Yale University Press, 1953), p. 18.

of the fossil record, incomprehensible in the light of the evolution model, is exactly as predicted on the basis of the creation model.

The remainder of the fossil record reveals a remarkable absence of the many transitional forms demanded by the theory of evolution.[18] Gaps between all higher categories of plants and animals, which creationists believe constituted the created kinds, are systematic. For example, Simpson has admitted that "Gaps among known orders, classes, and phyla are systematic and almost always large."[19] Richard B. Goldschmidt, well-known geneticist and a rabid evolutionist, acknowledged that "practically all orders or families known appear suddenly and without any apparent transitions."[20] E. J. H. Corner, Cambridge University botanist and an evolutionist, stated, "...I still think, to the unprejudiced, the fossil record of plants is in favor of special creation."[21]

Recently, the well-known evolutionary paleontologist, David B. Kitts, stated, "Despite the bright promise that paleontology provides a means of 'seeing' evolution, it has presented some nasty difficulties for evolutionists, the most notorious of which is the presence of 'gaps' in the fossil record. *Evolution requires intermediate forms between species and paleontology does not provide them...*"[22]

Lord Solly Zuckerman, for many years the head of the Department of Anatomy at the University of Birmingham, was first knighted and then later raised to the peerage as recognition of his distinguished career as a research scientist. After over 15 years of research on the subject, with a team that rarely included less than four scientists, Lord Zuckerman concluded that *Australopithecus* did not walk upright, he was not intermediate between ape and man, but that he was merely an anthropoid ape....Lord Zuckerman states his conviction, based on a life-time of investigation, that if man has evolved from an ape-like creature he did so without leaving any trace of the transformation in the fossil record.[23] This directly contradicts the popular idea that paleontologists have found numerous evidences of ape-like ancestors for man, but rather suggests they have found none at all.

The explosive appearance of highly complex forms of life in Cambrian and other rocks with the absence of required ancestors, and the abrupt ap-

[18]See Gish, 1973.

[19]G. G. Simpson in *The Evolution of Life*, ed. by Sol Tax (Chicago: University of Chicago Press, 1960), p. 149.

[20]R. B. Goldschmidt, "Evolution as Viewed by One Geneticist," *American Scientist* 40 (1952): 97.

[21]E. J. H. Corner in *Contemporary Botanical Thought*, ed. by A. M. Macleod and L. S. Cobley (Chicago: Quadrangle Books, 1961), p. 97.

[22]David B. Kitts, "Paleontology and Evolutionary Theory," *Evolution* 28 (1974): 467.

[23]S. Zuckerman, *Beyond the Ivory Tower* (New York: Taplinger Publishing Co., 1970), p. 64; see also *Journal of the Royal College of Surgeons of Edinburgh* 11 (1966): 87–115.

pearance of each major plant and animal kind without apparent transitional forms are the facts of greatest importance derivable from a study of the fossil record. These facts are highly contradictory to predictions based on the evolution model, but are just as predicted on the basis of the creation model of origins.

...In his Presidential Address to the Linnaean Society of London, "A Little on Lung-Fishes," Errol White said, "But whatever ideas authorities may have on the subject, the lung-fishes, like every other major group of fishes I know, have their origin firmly based on *nothing*..." He then said, "I have often said how little I should like to have to prove organic evolution in a court of law." He closed his address by saying, "We still do not know the mechanics of evolution in spite of the over-confident claims in some quarters, nor are we likely to make further progress in this by the classical methods of paleontology or biology; and we shall certainly not advance matters by jumping up and down shrilling 'Darwin is God and I, So-and-so, am his prophet'—the recent researches of workers like Dean and Hinshelwood (1964) already suggest the possibility of incipient cracks in the seemingly monolithic walls of the Neo-Darwinian Jericho."[24] White thus seems to be suggesting that the modern neo-Darwinian theory of evolution is in danger of crashing down just as did the walls of Jericho!

Thus, today we have a most astounding situation. Evolution has never been observed by human witnesses. Evolution cannot be subjected to the experimental method. The most sacred tenet of Darwinism—natural selection—in modern formulation is incapable of explaining anything. Furthermore, even some evolutionists are conceding that the mechanism of evolution proposed by evolutionary biologists could account for no more than trivial change in the time believed to have been available, and that an adequate scientific theory of evolution, based on present knowledge, seems impossible. Finally, the major features of the fossil record accord in an amazing fashion with the predictions based on special creation, but contradict the most fundamental predictions generated by the theory of evolution. And yet the demand is unceasing that evolution theory be accepted as the only scientific explanation for origins, even as an established fact, while excluding creation as a mere religious concept!

This rigid indoctrination in evolutionary dogma, with the exclusion of the competing concept of special creation, results in young people being indoctrinated in a non-theistic, naturalistic, humanistic religious philosophy in the guise of science. Science is perverted, academic freedom is denied, the educational process suffers, and constitutional guarantees of religious freedom are violated.

[24]E. White, "Presidential Address: A Little on Lung-Fishes," *Proceedings, Linnean Society of London* 177 (1966): 8.

This unhealthy situation could be corrected by presenting students with the two competing models for origins, the creation model and the evolution model, with all supporting evidence for each model. This would permit an evaluation of the students of the strengths and weaknesses of each model. This is the course true education should pursue rather than following the present process of brainwashing students in evolutionary philosophy.

Evolution as Fact and Theory

Stephen Jay Gould

Kirtley Mather, who died last year at age ninety, was a pillar of both science and Christian religion in America and one of my dearest friends. The difference of a half-century in our ages evaporated before our common interests. The most curious thing we shared was a battle we each fought at the same age. For Kirtley had gone to Tennessee with Clarence Darrow to testify for evolution at the Scopes trial of 1925. When I think that we are enmeshed again in the same struggle for one of the best documented, most compelling and exciting concepts in all of science, I don't know whether to laugh or cry.

According to idealized principles of scientific discourse, the arousal of dormant issues should reflect fresh data that give renewed life to abandoned notions. Those outside the current debate may therefore be excused for suspecting that creationists have come up with something new, or that evolutionists have generated some serious internal trouble. But nothing has changed; the creationists have presented not a single new fact or argument. Darrow and Bryan were at least more entertaining than we lesser antagonists today. The rise of creationism is politics, pure and simple; it represents one issue (and by no means the major concern) of the resurgent evangelical right. Arguments that seemed kooky just a decade ago have reentered the mainstream.

The basic attack of modern creationists falls apart on two general counts before we even reach the supposed factual details of their assault

---

Stephen Jay Gould, "Evolution as Fact and Theory," in *Hen's Teeth and Horse's Toes, Further Reflections in Natural History* (W. W. Norton & Company,), 253–262 (chapter 19). First published in *Discover Magazine,* May 1981.

against evolution. First, they play upon a vernacular misunderstanding of the word "theory" to convey the false impression that we evolutionists are covering up the rotten core of our edifice. Second, they misuse a popular philosophy of science to argue that they are behaving scientifically in attacking evolution. Yet the same philosophy demonstrates that their own belief is not science, and that "scientific creationism" is a meaningless and self-contradictory phrase, an example of what Orwell called "newspeak."

In the American vernacular, "theory" often means "imperfect fact"—part of a hierarchy of confidence running downhill from fact to theory to hypothesis to guess. Thus, creationists can (and do) argue: evolution is "only" a theory, and intense debate now rages about many aspects of the theory. If evolution is less than a fact, and scientists can't even make up their minds about the theory, then what confidence can we have in it? Indeed, President Reagan echoed this argument before an evangelical group in Dallas when he said (in what I devoutly hope was campaign rhetoric): "Well, it is a theory. It is a scientific theory only, and it has in recent years been challenged in the world of science—that is, not believed in the scientific community to be as infallible as it once was."

Well, evolution *is* a theory. It is also a fact. And facts and theories are different things, not rungs in a hierarchy of increasing certainty. Facts are the world's data. Theories are structures of ideas that explain and interpret facts. Facts do not go away while scientists debate rival theories for explaining them. Einstein's theory of gravitation replaced Newton's, but apples did not suspend themselves in mid-air pending the outcome. And human beings evolved from apelike ancestors whether they did so by Darwin's proposed mechanism or by some other, yet to be discovered.

Moreover, "fact" does not mean "absolute certainty." The final proofs of logic and mathematics flow deductively from stated premises and achieve certainty only because they are *not* about the empirical world. Evolutionists make no claim for perpetual truth, though creationists often do (and then attack us for a style of argument that they themselves favor). In science, "fact" can only mean "confirmed to such a degree that it would be perverse to withhold provisional assent." I suppose that apples might start to rise tomorrow, but the possibility does not merit equal time in physics classrooms.

Evolutionists have been clear about this distinction between fact and theory from the very beginning, if only because we have always acknowledged how far we are from completely understanding the mechanisms (theory) by which evolution (fact) occurred. Darwin continually emphasized the difference between his two great and separate accomplishments: establishing the fact of evolution, and proposing a theory—natural selection—to explain the mechanism of evolution. He wrote in *The Descent of Man:* "I had two distinct objects in view; firstly, to show that species had not been separately created, and secondly, that natural selection had been the chief agent of change....Hence if I have erred in...having exaggerated its [natural selection's] power...I have at least, as I hope, done good service in aiding to overthrow the dogma of separate creations."

Thus Darwin acknowledged the provisional nature of natural selection while affirming the fact of evolution. The fruitful theoretical debate that Darwin initiated has never ceased. From the 1940s through the 1960s, Darwin's own theory of natural selection did achieve a temporary hegemony that it never enjoyed in his lifetime. But renewed debate characterizes our decade, and, while no biologist questions the importance of natural selection, many now doubt its ubiquity. In particular, many evolutionists argue that substantial amounts of genetic change may not be subject to natural selection and may spread through populations at random. Others are challenging Darwin's linking of natural selection with gradual, imperceptible change through all intermediary degrees; they are arguing that most evolutionary events may occur far more rapidly than Darwin envisioned.

Scientists regard debates on fundamental issues of theory as a sign of intellectual health and a source of excitement. Science is—and how else can I say it?—most fun when it plays with interesting ideas, examines their implications, and recognizes that old information may be explained in surprisingly new ways. Evolutionary theory is now enjoying this uncommon vigor. Yet amidst all this turmoil no biologist has been led to doubt the fact that evolution occurred; we are debating *how* it happened. We are all trying to explain the same thing: the tree of evolutionary descent linking all organisms by ties of genealogy. Creationists pervert and caricature this debate by conveniently neglecting the common conviction that underlies it, and by falsely suggesting that we now doubt the very phenomenon we are struggling to understand.

Secondly, creationists claim that "the dogma of separate creations," as Darwin characterized it a century ago, is a scientific theory meriting equal time with evolution in high school biology curricula. But a popular viewpoint among philosophers of science belies this creationist argument. Philosopher Karl Popper has argued for decades that the primary criterion of science is the falsifiability of its theories. We can never prove absolutely, but we can falsify. A set of ideas that cannot, in principle, be falsified is not science.

The entire creationist program includes little more than a rhetorical attempt to falsify evolution by presenting supposed contradictions among its supporters. Their brand of creationism, they claim, is "scientific" because it follows the Popperian model in trying to demolish evolution. Yet Popper's argument must apply in both directions. One does not become a scientist by the simple act of trying to falsify a rival and truly scientific system; one has to present an alternative system that also meets Popper's criterion—it too must be falsifiable in principle.

"Scientific creationism" is a self-contradictory, nonsense phrase precisely because it cannot be falsified. I can envision observations and experiments that would disprove any evolutionary theory I know, but I cannot imagine what potential data could lead creationists to abandon their beliefs. Unbeatable systems are dogma, not science. Lest I seem harsh or rhetorical, I quote creationism's leading intellectual, Duane Gish, Ph.D., from his recent (1978) book, *Evolution? The Fossils Say No!* "By creation we mean the bringing into being by a supernatural Creator of the basic kinds of plants and animals by the process of sudden, or fiat, creation. We do not know how the Creator created, what processes He used, *for He used processes which are not now operating anywhere in the natural universe* [Gish's italics]. This is why we refer to creation as special creation. We cannot discover by scientific investigations anything about the creative processes used by the Creator." Pray tell, Dr. Gish, in the light of your last sentence, what then is "scientific" creationism?

Our confidence that evolution occurred centers upon three general arguments. First, we have abundant, direct, observational evidence of evolution in action, from both field and laboratory. This evidence ranges from countless experiments on change in nearly everything about fruit flies subjected to artificial selection in the laboratory to the famous populations of British moths that became black when industrial soot darkened the trees upon which the moths rest. (Moths gain protection from sharp-sighted bird predators by blending into the background.) Creationists do not deny these observations; how could they? Creationists have tightened their act. They now argue that God only created "basic kinds," and allowed for limited evolutionary meandering within them. Thus toy poodles and Great Danes come from the dog kind and moths can change color, but nature cannot convert a dog to a cat or a monkey to a man.

The second and third arguments for evolution—the case for major changes—do not involve direct observation of evolution in action. They rest upon inference, but are no less secure for that reason. Major evolutionary change requires too much time for direct observation on the scale of recorded human history. All historical sciences rest upon inference, and evolution is no different from geology, cosmology, or human history in this respect. In principle, we cannot observe processes that operated in the past. We must infer them from results that still surround us: living and fossil organisms for evolution, documents and artifacts for human history, strata and topography for geology.

The second argument—that the imperfection of nature reveals evolution—strikes many people as ironic, for they feel that evolution should be most elegantly displayed in the nearly perfect adaptation expressed by some organisms—the camber of a gull's wing, or butterflies that cannot be seen in ground litter because they mimic leaves so precisely. But perfection could be imposed by a wise creator or evolved by natural selection. Perfection covers the tracks of past history. And past history—the evidence of descent—is the mark of evolution.

Evolution lies exposed in the *imperfections* that record a history of descent. Why should a rat run, a bat fly, a porpoise swim, and I type this essay with structures built of the same bones unless we all inherited them from a common ancestor? An engineer, starting from scratch, could design better limbs in each case. Why should all the large native mammals of Australia be marsupials, unless they descended from a common ancestor isolated on this island continent? Marsupials are not "better," or ideally suited for Australia; many have been wiped out by placental mammals imported by man from other continents. This principle of imperfection extends to all historical sciences. When we recognize the etymology of September, October, November, and December (seventh, eighth, ninth, and tenth), we know that the year once started in March, or that two additional months must have been added to an original calendar of ten months.

The third argument is more direct: transitions are often found in the fossil record. Preserved transitions are not common—and should not be, according to our understanding of evolution (see next section)—but they are not entirely wanting, as creationists often claim. The lower jaw of reptiles contains several bones, that of mammals only one. The non-mammalian jawbones are reduced, step by step, in mammalian ancestors until they become tiny nubbins located at the back of the jaw. The "hammer" and "anvil" bones of the mammalian ear are descendants of these nubbins. How could such a transition be accomplished? the creationists ask. Surely a bone is either entirely in the jaw or in the ear. Yet paleontologists have discovered two transitional lineages of therapsids (the so-called mammal-like reptiles) with a double jaw joint—one composed of the old quadrate and articular bones (soon to become the hammer and anvil), the other of the squamosal and dentary bones (as in modern mammals). For that matter, what better transitional form could we expect to find than the oldest human, *Australopithecus afarensis*, with its apelike palate, its human upright stance, and a cranial capacity larger than any ape's of the same body size but a full 1,000 cubic centimeters below ours? If God made each of the half-dozen human species discovered in ancient rocks, why did he create in an unbroken temporal sequence of progressively more modern features—increasing cranial capacity, reduced face and teeth, larger body size? Did he create to mimic evolution and test our faith thereby?

Faced with these facts of evolution and the philosophical bankruptcy of their own position, creationists rely upon distortion and innuendo to buttress their rhetorical claim. If I sound sharp or bitter, indeed I am—for I have become a major target of these practices.

I count myself among the evolutionists who argue for a jerky, or episodic, rather than a smoothly gradual, pace of change. In 1972 my colleague Niles Eldredge and I developed the theory of punctuated equilibrium. We argued that two outstanding facts of the fossil record—geologically "sudden" origin of new species and failure to change thereafter (stasis)—reflect the predictions of evolutionary theory, not the imperfections of the fossil record. In most theories, small isolated populations are the source of new species, and the process of speciation takes thousands or tens of thousands of years. This amount of time, so long when measured against our lives, is a geological microsecond. It represents much less than 1 per cent of the average lifespan for a fossil invertebrate species—more than ten million years. Large, widespread, and well established species, on the other hand, are not expected to change very much. We believe that the inertia of large populations explains the stasis of most fossil species over millions of years.

We proposed the theory of punctuated equilibrium largely to provide a different explanation for pervasive trends in the fossil record. Trends, we argued, cannot be attributed to gradual transformation within lineages, but must arise from the differential success of certain kinds of species. A trend, we argued, is more like climbing a flight of stairs (punctuations and stasis) than rolling up an inclined plane.

Since we proposed punctuated equilibria to explain trends, it is infuriating to be quoted again and again by creationists—whether through design or stupidity, I do not know—as admitting that the fossil record includes no transitional forms. Transitional forms are generally lacking at the species level, but they are abundant between larger groups. Yet a pamphlet entitled "Harvard Scientists Agree Evolution Is a Hoax" states: "The facts of punctuated equilibrium which Gould and Eldredge...are forcing Darwinists to swallow fit the picture that Bryan insisted on, and which God has revealed to us in the Bible."

Continuing the distortion, several creationists have equated the theory of punctuated equilibrium with a caricature of the beliefs of Richard Goldschmidt, a great early geneticist. Goldschmidt argued, in a famous book published in 1940, that new groups can arise all at once through major mutations. He referred to these suddenly transformed creatures as "hopeful monsters." (I am attracted to some aspects of the non-caricatured version, but Goldschmidt's theory still has nothing to do with punctuated equilibrium....) Creationist Luther Sunderland talks of the "punctuated equilibrium hopeful monster theory" and tells his hopeful readers that "it amounts to tacit admission that anti-evolutionists are correct in asserting there is no fossil evidence supporting the theory that all life is connected to a common ancestor." Duane Gish writes, "According to Goldschmidt, and now apparently according to Gould, a reptile laid an egg from which the first bird, feathers and all, was produced." Any evolutionist who believed such nonsense would rightly be laughed off the intellectual stage; yet the only theory that could ever envision such a scenario for the origin of birds is creationism—with God acting in the egg.

I am both angry at and amused by the creationists; but mostly I am deeply sad. Sad for many reasons. Sad because so many people who respond to creationist appeals are troubled for the right reason, but venting their anger at the wrong target. It is true that scientists have often been dogmatic and elitist. It is true that we have often allowed the white-coated, advertising image to represent us—"Scientists say that Brand X cures bunions ten times faster than..." We have not fought it adequately because we derive benefits from appearing as a new priesthood. It is also true that faceless and bureaucratic state power intrudes more and more into our lives and removes choices that should belong to individuals and communities. I can understand that school curricula, imposed from above and without local input, might be seen as one more insult on all these grounds. But the culprit is not, and cannot be, evolution or any other fact of the natural world. Identify and fight your legitimate enemies by all means, but we are not among them.

I am sad because the practical result of this brouhaha will not be expanded coverage to include creationism (that would also make me sad), but the reduction or excision of evolution from high school curricula. Evolution is one of the half dozen "great ideas" developed by science. It speaks to the profound issues of genealogy that fascinate all of us—the "roots" phenomenon writ large. Where did we come from? Where did life arise? How did it develop? How are organisms related? It forces us to think, ponder, and wonder. Shall we deprive millions of this knowledge and once again teach biology as a set of dull and unconnected facts, without the thread that weaves diverse material into a supple unity?

But most of all I am saddened by a trend I am just beginning to discern among my colleagues. I sense that some now wish to mute the healthy debate about theory that has brought new life to evolutionary biology. It provides grist for creationist mills, they say, even if only by distortion. Perhaps we should lie low and rally round the flag of strict Darwinism, at least for the moment—a kind of old-time religion on our part.

But we should borrow another metaphor and recognize that we too have to tread a straight and narrow path, surrounded by roads to perdition. For if we ever begin to suppress our search to understand nature, to quench our own intellectual excitement in a misguided effort to present a united front where it does not and should not exist, then we are truly lost.

DISCUSSION QUESTIONS

1. Do you think the government interfered with religious freedom, thereby violating the First Amendment, when it disallowed the teaching of creation theory in public schools?
2. Should creation theory be taught alongside of evolution?
3. Does belief in evolutionary theory require the same kind of faith as belief in creation theory?
4. Do you think it is misleading to speak of "creation science"?
5. Are there other issues in which religion and science come into conflict in the public schools?
6. Should the public schools promote the religious values of the community even if these values are endorsed only by a minority?

9

HOMOSEXUALITY AND PUBLIC POLICY

Stephen H. Wainscott

Despite its reputation as a nation in which personal freedom flourishes, the United States has had a history marked by outbursts of controversy and intolerance of behavior and lifestyles deemed to be outside the American mainstream. Such is the case today concerning the issue of homosexuality and the question of what rights and protections, if any, homosexuals should possess.

Public attitudes toward homosexuality and those who practice it are wide ranging. To some, homosexuality is a genetically ordered sexual orientation as "natural" as being born left-handed in a predominantly right-handed world. Some see homosexuality as deviant but not necessarily morally depraved, while to others homosexuality is a sinful and conscious choice of a perverted lifestyle.

Recent surveys depict a public with ambivalent—perhaps even confused—feelings about homosexuality. Since 1973, majorities as large as eighty percent have said it is "always wrong" or "almost always wrong" for two adults of the same gender to have sexual relations.[1] Yet, during much of the same period less than half those surveyed expressed approval of making homosexual relations illegal.

While the public mood is characterized by a strong aversion to personal contact with homosexuals, attitudes are mixed concerning the hiring of homosexuals in various professions. In March 1987, the Gallup Poll reported that solid majorities oppose the employment of homosexuals as elementary school teachers. Surprisingly, however, most Americans do not object to the hiring of homosexuals in the armed forces and in the medical profession.[2]

In recent years, increasing numbers of politicans, entertainment celebrities, and other public figures have announced their homosexual tendencies. Revelations of "coming out of the closet" are now so commonplace they no longer make front-page headlines. Perhaps this candor has contributed to a diminished level of prejudice and intolerance directed toward the homosexual lifestyle. In 1978, seventy-two percent of Americans said they would not vote for a homosexual for president, even if the candidate were otherwise well qualified. More recently in 1985, only fifty-six percent said that homosexuality should disqualify a person from the Presidency.[3]

Until the mid-1970s homosexuality generated little public controversy and was an issue to be debated primarily in academic and medical circles. The "gay rights" movement had yet to discover the arena of interest-group politics, and few public sensibilities were aroused when, in 1974, the American Psychiatric Association voted to remove homosexuality from the list of mental disorders. Given the climate of openness in the 1970s, homosexuality was viewed in many quarters "not as mad or bad," but a matter of personal preference.[4]

During this period the U.S. Supreme Court had begun to expound a constitutional right to privacy. In 1965 the Court struck down a Connecticut law that had restricted the sale and distribution of birth-control devices. In the 1973 case of *Roe* v. *Wade* the Court expanded the doctrine of privacy to encompass a woman's right to have an abortion during the first two trimesters of her pregnancy. While these decisions had nothing to do with homosexuality per se, they unwittingly served to politicize the issue of "sexual freedom" generally and perhaps gave the "gay rights" movement a sense of mission and momentum it otherwise might not have had.

Throughout the 1970s and into the 1980s politically active homosexuals banded together in a campaign for what they viewed to be their civil rights. Immediate targets of the gay rights movement were state and local laws, many crafted in the nineteenth century, that made it a crime for two adults of the same gender to have sexual relations. Purging antiquated and, often, unenforceable laws governing private sexual conduct was but one goal. The movement also pressed officials in major cities to enact ordinances banning discrimination in employment and public accomodations on the basis of sexual orientation or "affectional preference." The continuing controversy surrounding one such statute, New York City's so-called "Intro Number Two" law enacted in 1986, is examined in "Intro Two" by Duncan A. MacDonald.

Politically, the gay-rights movement reached a peak in the presidential elections of 1980 and 1984, although the gains for the homosexual community were more symbolic than substantive. In both years the Democratic

National Convention approved platforms committed to the support of homosexual rights. It would be a mistake to conclude that homosexuals constituted a significant voting bloc in these elections. Nor would it be accurate to say that embracing the demands of homosexuals caused the Democrats to lose the presidency in 1984. However, there is some truth to the view that support of gay rights contributed to a negative impression of Democrats as a party subservient to single-issue (and largely unpopular) constituencies. In retrospect, the Democrats' selection of San Francisco, a city with a sizable homosexual community, as its convention site only served to underscore this perception.

In the summer of 1986 the focus on homosexual rights shifted to the courts. On August 3, 1982, an Atlanta, Georgia, resident, Michael Hardwick, was arrested at his home and charged with a violation of a state liquor law. When the police served the warrant and were invited into the house by a guest, they observed Mr. Hardwick engaging in anal intercourse with a third man in an adjoining room. Sodomy was and is against the law in Georgia and in twenty-four other states. Even so, no charges were filed against Hardwick. Instead, Hardwick himself took the matter to federal court in an effort to have the Georgia anti-sodomy statute declared unconstitutional. Following conflicting rulings by the district court and the U.S. Court of Appeals, the case was petitioned to the U.S. Supreme Court. Hardwick's challenge to the Georgia law was supported by several homosexual and civil-rights groups, including the National Gay Rights Advocates, the Lesbian Rights Project, and the Women's Legal Defense Fund.

In a 5–4 decision, the Supreme Court upheld the Georgia law. The Constitution's Fourth Amendment, wrote Justice Byron White, entails no "fundamental right to engage in homosexual sodomy." In effect, the Court declared, it is constitutionally proper for a legislature to enact laws reflecting community standards of morality which oppose homosexual activity.

In 1981, not long before Michael Hardwick's case was docketed in federal court, public controversy over homosexuality entered a new and frightening phase when a team of Los Angeles physicians reported that several homosexual men had mysteriously died from infections and diseases that were not thought to be lethal. The terminal condition came to be called AIDS (acquired immune deficiency syndrome). Thought to be introduced into the human blood stream by way of a virus, AIDS so weakens the body's immune system that an ordinarily treatable illness, such as pneumonia, becomes deadly.

Since its detection almost a decade ago, AIDS has rapidly come to be viewed as the plague of the twentieth century. The U.S. Public Health Service estimates that by 1991 there will be 270,000 diagnosed cases and as many as 179,000 deaths.[5]

While the search for a preventive or curative vaccine has been unsuccessful thus far, medical experts have isolated some of the sources of AIDS. A high incidence of the condition had been found among Haitians and intravenous drug users. However, the largest infected population, accounting for nearly three-fourths of the detected cases, has been homosexual men.

As the *New Republic* editorial "Afraids" explains, calm and rational public discussion of the AIDS threat has at times been overcome by intense emotions and unwarranted fears. Solutions are as varied as they are elusive. Fundamentalist Christians, convinced that AIDS is divine retribution for the sin of homosexuality, lead one anti-homosexual campaign. For them repentance and rejection of homosexual "wickedness" are the only acceptable prophylactics. On the other hand, public health programs encourage the use of condoms and other "safe sex" practices in a campaign which has sparked its own ethical controversies with the free distribution of contraceptive devices at schools and university health centers. The debate continues—drawing into it medical practitioners who refuse to treat AIDS patients in apparent violation of the Hippocratic oath; schools that refuse to admit children carrying the virus through transfusions of infected blood; businesses that dismiss homosexuals who test positive for AIDS; and bureaucrats who call for public disclosure of the names of individuals who test positive for the virus. Just last year, conservative columnist William F. Buckley suggested that the tattooing of AIDS sufferers (on the buttocks in the case of homosexual carriers) might slow the spread of the disease by discouraging homosexual contact.[6]

As these diverse and conflicting perspectives show, until an effective remedy for AIDS can be found, few issues of our times present a more dramatic tension among the needs of public welfare, the need to protect the rights of individuals, and the imperatives of private conscience and morality.

NOTES

1. "Opinion Roundup," *Public Opinion* 10, no. 3 (September/October 1987), p. 26.
2. "Opinion Roundup," *Public Opinion* 10, no. 2 (July/August 1987), p. 27.
3. Ibid.
4. David Robinson, Jr., "Sodomy and the Supreme Court," *Commentary* 82, no. 4 (October 1986), p. 57.
5. Ibid., 58.
6. William F. Buckley, Jr., "Looking Out for Number Two," *National Review* 38 (April 25, 1986), pp. 62–63.

Intro Two

Duncan A. MacDonald

Since 1980, at least 50 places in the United States have enacted laws to ban discrimination against homosexuals in employment, housing and public accommodations. Among them are the State of Wisconsin and a score of large municipalities, including Boston, Philadelphia, Washington, D.C., Detroit, Los Angeles, San Francisco, Minneapolis, Milwaukee and, most recently, New York City.

Virtually all of these laws are written alike. It has been reported that most of them are patterned after a bill that was first submitted to the New York City Council in 1971. Their aim is to prohibit discrimination against people based on their so-called "sexual orientation" or "affectional preference." On their face they seem simple and straightforward, but on a closer reading they are seriously flawed and hold the potential ultimately of achieving results exactly the opposite of the intentions of their drafters, namely, of promoting more sexual bigotry in our society, especially affecting women and homosexuals.

This should come as no surprise to lawyers, especially to the members of the bar who have worked in the civil rights area for the past several decades. Laws do not always "roll-out" the way their drafters wanted. Time and events often play dirty tricks on words supposedly etched in stone. Certainly the late Roy Wilkins of the N.A.A.C.P. never would have imagined that Title VII of the 1964 Civil Rights Act would eventually be used by whites and males to stunt and even reverse America's historical commitment to civil rights justice. Those are the risks, of course, in any piece of legislation, even well-drafted legislation like Title VII.

The trouble with the "sexual orientation" laws enacted thus far is that they are not even minimally well drafted. To prove the point, this article will focus on the model of them all, New York City's so-called "Intro Number Two," which was enacted into law by the New York City Council on March 20, 1986.

The language of Intro Two is surprisingly simple. Aside from excepting religious organizations, small landlords and employers from its coverage, Intro Two contains two key points: 1) it prohibits "discrimination against individuals because of their actual or perceived sexual orientation,"

Duncan A. MacDonald, "Intro Two," *America*, (9 August 1986), 45–49. Reprinted with permission of the author.

and 2) it defines "sexual orientation" to "mean heterosexuality, homosexuality or bisexuality."

Interestingly, the law does not define "heterosexuality," "homosexuality" or "bisexuality." It merely lumps all of them together, in effect signaling among other things that in the eyes of the law they are all equal. In fairness to the drafters of Intro Two, it should be noted that they had to draft the law that way because of the equal protection clause of the U.S. Constitution. The drafters apparently felt that they could not, for example, have written the law only to protect the sexual orientation of homosexuals, because heterosexuals then rightly could have argued that it favored one group of citizens over another in violation of the Constitution.

The Constitution as such can be viewed as both a friend and an enemy to the drafters of any legislation that affects or involves personal behavior. As an example, consider the Racketeer-Influenced Corrupt Organizations Act (RICO). The clear purpose of the law was to hit "organized crime" in the pocketbook by tightening the screws on its illegal business practices. The dilemma for its original drafters was that they knew their law would not pass constitutional muster if it simply went after recognized criminal groups, such as the Mafia or its alleged "crime family" members. No, the law had to be equalitarian: It had to define specifically what was illegal and then punish each violation equally. The unexpected legacy of RICO is that it has opened a Pandora's box upon legitimate businesses, which have been hit with a flood of expensive lawsuits alleging violations under this act. In fact, the major impact of RICO has been against publicly held companies and not against the hoodlums its drafters had set out to control.

The history of RICO and a score of other major pieces of legislation provides an important lesson for those who now must wrestle with the likes of Intro Two. If Intro Two's equalitarian balancing act with respect to sexual orientation predicts any future for itself, it is that it will lead to similar, anomalous results. Instead of liberating homosexuals, it is entirely possible that Intro Two in the long run will lead to a sexual free-for-all that will favor aggressive male heterosexuals over women and homosexuals.

In looking at any law (or any act of public policy, for that matter), it makes sense to speculate about how the law will "roll-out" over time—how it will be interpreted in the future by the plaintiffs who will seek its protection, by the people who will defend themselves under it, by its public enforcers and regulators and by the courts, from the trial courts to the U.S. Supreme Court. How will Intro Two perform over time?

One of the ways to predict a possible future for Intro Two is to look at the history of other civil rights laws. Consider for a moment the "race" provisions of Title VII of the 1964 Civil Rights Act. The word "race" covers everybody—blacks, whites, red-skinned and yellow-skinned people. Although it is a neutral term in the Civil Rights Act, the clear intention of Congress in choosing the word was to benefit blacks, in short, to eliminate the pervasive discrimination that had been practiced against them in this country since the colonial period. By and large, that is what the civil rights movement has been all about.

The early history of Title VII met the expectations of its supporters and drafters. Title VII became the law of the land, and courts throughout our nation generally enforced it to the full. Almost overnight, restaurants, hotels, parks, classrooms, jobs and the like were opened to everybody. That is not to say that blacks immediately attained economic and social equality in America under Title VII—unfortunately they did not. But Title VII at least gave them the tools to effectively fight some of the vestiges of American apartheid.

In the beginning, blacks won an enormous number of important legal battles. However, in successfully challenging the white power structure, black activism set in motion an inevitable counteraction, brought on in part by court decisions that were perceived by many whites as excessive (especially with respect to busing and the enforcement of criminal law) and by the growing concern among many whites that the enforcement of Title VII was doing more than repairing the harm of three centuries of racial exploitation—that it was now favoring blacks at the expense of whites who themselves were no better off economically and educationally than most blacks.

The power of this counteraction is evident everywhere today. Federal and state judges, especially a majority of the U.S. Supreme Court Justices, are far less sympathetic to the claims of racial discrimination than they were 20 years ago. In fact, the bulk of the major race-discrimination decisions today seem to favor individual whites or white-controlled institutions. These decisions, however, are not themselves necessarily racist. The legal philosophy behind them is often very equalitarian. With respect to Title VII, they simply recognize that race protection necessarily also covers whites.

Of course, there is far more complexity to the development of race discrimination laws in the United States than is related in this brief history. Moreover, no one should conclude from reading it that social legislation inevitably returns full circle to the status quo. One thing is certain: Laws in a political democracy are not static—they evolve.

The evolution of Title VII ought to tell us something about the possible evolution of Intro Two. First, assuming Intro Two survives constitutional challenges, the new law probably and rightfully will result in many legal victories for homosexuals—exactly what its drafters want. The fact is homosexuals suffer enormous harm in our society, but receive very little protection from our legal system. Intro Two initially will do much to change that, in good part because the facts will be simple. A landlord, for example, will attempt to evict a homosexual for no other reason than that he is homosexual, and the court will rule in favor of the homosexual. The same will happen to a homosexual employee or homosexual customer in a hotel.

Court decisions like these will mount on top of each other, setting written precedents for future plaintiffs, defendants and courts. As time goes on and as the decisions develop a force of their own, more and more people will test to see how far they can go under the new law to determine its limits. Bad and unreasoned decisions almost certainly will result and will be challenged. The inevitable counteraction will develop its own momentum.

The wording of Intro Two suggests that over the long run it will favor heterosexual males and people whose sexual orientation or behavior can best be described as extreme. Because this unintended result will pose grave risks to women, it is almost certain that it will also lead to difficult conflicts with laws that currently protect women's rights, in particular Title VII of the 1964 Civil Rights Act. To understand how this can happen, let us look not at how Intro Two will affect the rights of homosexuals, but instead at its protection of heterosexuals, in particular with respect to their "sexual orientation."

What exactly is a heterosexual? Intro Two does not define the word. The common dictionary definition describes a heterosexual as someone characterized by sexual desire or feeling for those of the opposite sex. As a legal guideline, however, the dictionary definition is deficient. It is too general. It does not tell if there are limits to the so-called sexual attraction, whether it has definitional boundaries outside of which the person becomes something else.

The failure of Intro Two to define adequately the word "heterosexual" will consequently shift the burden of defining to two groups: the adversaries contesting Intro Two and the courts. In each case all parties, including the judge, will be given an equal opportunity to define what the word means.

Their task will not be easy. Is a heterosexual, for example, just a regular man or woman, a monogamous person who wants only one spouse for a lifetime and a few children to round things out? What about the man who is attracted to many women? Or the adulterer? Or the obnoxious office flirt? And what about the man who is physically attracted to women but who otherwise believes and acts as though they are inferior? Suppose this same man likes to harass women, to intimidate them with sexual innuendos, or is the kind who gets pleasure out of bondage, sadomasochism or other violent sex with women—is not he too still a heterosexual? Cannot his sexual proclivities, however bizarre, be described (or will they be defended?) as merely the signs of his sexual orientation? Because this is certainly a possibility under Intro Two, what else can a court do but treat these manifestations as morally and legally neutral?

Of course, one could argue that what a person does on his or her private time should not be the concern of employers, landlords and the like. The trouble with this position is that it is naive about how people display their sexual orientation.

For example, Intro Two arguably prohibits discrimination at the employment application stage and thereafter if the applicant is hired. Suppose a person named "Mr. Macho Heterosexual" applies for a job and during an interview learns that his boss will be a woman. He comments to the interviewer (say, to a male) that he thinks "women belong in the kitchen" or makes other sexist comments about women. Because of these comments he does not get the job, despite the fact that he is otherwise qualified. Does he have a case under Intro Two?

The answer would have to be yes. Mr. Macho would have as much right under Intro Two as anybody to claim that his comments merely reflect his heterosexuality, his sexual orientation. An employer, a feminist or a homosexual might argue in response that Mr. Macho is not protected because his words reflect an orientation that is bigoted or even pathological—that is, in short, threatening to employers who want to create a nondiscriminatory work environment. This may in fact be correct, but it is exactly the problem with Intro Two: By failing to define or limit the scope of the words "sexual orientation," the new law in effect tells us that a person's sexual orientation is irrelevant.

There is a twisted sort of parallel here to the free speech cases of the past half century. As a rule of thumb, speech cannot be restrained simply because the regulator does not like the speaker, his philosophy or what he says. His speech can be restrained only to prevent an imminent public riot. With respect to Intro Two, the employer is treated somewhat like the free speech regulator: Barring only exceptional circumstances, he cannot assume the worst about his potential employee. Is this fair to the employer, especially in light of his obligations under Title VII? Is it fair to the other employees—do they not have the right to expect the employer to protect them from troublemakers?

The point here is that Intro Two opens the door for the Mr. Machos of the world. In fact, it is possible that in time it will actually encourage people with a strongly held sexual orientation to go public with it. It is even possible that Intro Two will encourage employment and residential applicants to announce their so-called sexual orientation immediately at the application stage just to set up the employer or landlord in the event that they are turned down. That way, if the employer or landlord attempts to deny their application on other legitimate grounds—or to fire or evict them later on—

they will be able to harass the employer or the landlord with an Intro Two lawsuit. Anyone who doubts that this scenario is possible simply does not know New York City or the artful aggressiveness of the members of its legal profession.

Let us look at Mr. Macho from a different angle. He gets a job with XYZ Company. He shares a work area with several homosexuals. He shows contempt for them every chance he gets. How far can he go under Intro Two? When can the employer do anything to stop him? Suppose all he does is ridicule the homosexuals, but in a way that is similar to the way other workers ridicule each other on matters that have nothing to do with sexual orientation. What is his limit, if anything? Intro Two provides no answer, except to suggest that the limit is far, perhaps so far in fact as to have the ironic effect of not being able to control verbal bigotry, and in so doing to promote it.

According to its many well-meaning sponsors, Intro Two wants to liberate homosexuals. But will it not also liberate pent-up male heterosexuals who do not like homosexuals or women? Will it not cause them to argue that Intro Two protects their right to express fully their heterosexuality, even to the extent of allowing them to exploit and intimidate their fellow workers who are homosexual and women?

One of the objectives of the Civil Rights Act of 1964 (Title VII) was to repress certain types of expression or behavior. If you were a bigot or a sexist, this act told you to keep it to yourself—you were prohibited from displaying it in the workplace, as a landlord, etc. If you read the literature in support of Intro Two, the opposite result is intended. It allegedly wants to liberate homosexuals. At the same time, however, it contains language that clearly sends a signal to everyone else that they too ought to become freer with respect to their sexual orientation. In short, it seems to invite a sexual free-for-all. If that is the case, and over time I believe it will be, homosexuals and women will lose under Intro Two.

I have focused on the heterosexual aspects of Intro Two to show how flawed it is. The result is the same when the focus shifts to homosexuals, a protected but undefined group. What exactly is a homosexual? Is it merely a person who is sexually attracted to his or her own gender? Is there any legal boundary under Intro Two to that attraction?

What about homosexuals who are attracted to youngsters, so-called pedophiliacs? Are not they protected under Intro Two? The General Counsel of New York City, F.A.O. Schwartz, says no, but there is not a word in Intro Two to support him. Suppose a landlord or employer learns that a potential (or actual) tenant or employee is practicing pedophilia in one way or another. Can either of them take action? Suppose the employer is a school board and the employee is a teacher? Whatever the case, the language of Intro Two does not support the employer or landlord. All the tenant or employee has to do is say he or she is a protected group: a homosexual whose sexual orientation is pedophilia.

This same argument could be applied in defense of a pornographer against a landlord. Once again, the defense is easy: The pornographer says pornography merely represents his or her sexual orientation. Who can prove otherwise under the enormous umbrella of Intro Two?

All of this may be farfetched, and yet other parts of the so-called sexual revolution did not always go the way its philosophers predicted. Sometimes a revolution opens up a Pandora's box. Consider some of the unexpected excesses of the sexual revolution: more than 10 million abortions in the past decade alone; epidemics of mental and physical diseases, including deaths; increased acts of sexual violence against women (but, ironically, less so against homosexuals); massive disruptions of the family unit; the worst poverty our nation has seen for women and children since the Depression; social alienation, especially as the result of a tidal wave of teen-age pregnancies, with most of the harm falling on the backs of nonwhites; religious, racial, sexual and anti-Semitic bigotry in pornography; a dangerous conservative political backlash; sexual exploitation for profit (with men as almost always the prime beneficiaries); wholesale contempt for traditional moral values—in sum, a revolution with a bitter aftertaste.

Intro Two could be the next unpleasant chapter. The law could make matters worse, unless it is quickly killed by a court on the grounds that it is unconstitutionally vague. It liberates so many people in so many contradictory directions that in the end it liberates no one. It loses all meaning.

Intro Two could be interpreted to require employers and landlords to ignore transvestites, pedophiliacs, pornographers, women haters, homosexual haters and the like. Men who harass women with sexual advances, even insults, will now be able to argue that they are just being heterosexual, which in a way is true. Intro Two seemingly licenses all kinds of so-called sexual orientation.

How else can a court interpret the law? The supporters of Intro Two will say that all the court has to do is to look at the intentions of the drafters. None of them intends it to support sexual extremism. Must the court accept this? The answer is an emphatic no.

The standard, accepted method of interpreting a law by U.S. courts is first to look at its language to see if it covers the facts of the case. Usually this means the court will go no further. However, as time goes on, and depending on the facts of the case, courts will interpret the law in accordance with changes in the cultural and jurisprudential climate, which in the case of Intro Two could go either way (extremely conservative or liberal).

Can the court consider the intentions of the drafters of a law? The answer in general is yes, but usually only as a last-ditch attempt to find some meaning in it. In the case of Intro Two, it is doubtful that a court could discern the original intentions of its drafters, because it is clear that they have not considered its many possible ramifications. In fact, that is exactly why courts are so reluctant to rely on the original intention approach. It is unreliable.

The Attorney General of the United States, Edwin Meese, recently started a national debate on the same issue. Mr. Meese claims that Federal courts should interpret the U.S. Constitution based on the original intentions of its drafters back in 1789. His detractors argue that the drafters could not possibly have intended anything with respect to the many complex legal issues of our technological, trillion-dollar economy and our pluralistic culture. In short, they say the language of the Constitution must speak for itself and to the times in which it is interpreted.

The irony about the Meese approach is that it would probably be impossible to find a single supporter on the New York City Council who would agree with it. They cannot agree because of their legitimate fear of the effect it would have on modern civil rights. To be consistent, however, the drafters of Intro Two would have to concede that their bill should be interpreted based on its wording, not on their limited thinking during the cold spring of 1986. If this is so, Intro Two will be in for a difficult, unpredictable future. What an incredible roll of the dice!

Another irony about sexual orientation laws like Intro Two is that they reflect a kind of laissez-faire attitude toward people's sexual inclinations. They seem to say that such inclinations are legally of no moral consequence, as though all our society has to do to achieve sexual liberation is to create a Darwinian landscape where every sexual arrangement, every sexual style is put on equal footing. They ignore the fact that in our culture men, especially heterosexual men, have an advantage (and the requisite power) over the people whom Intro Two puts into the starting gate with them.

If our nation's experiment with economic Darwinism from the 1860's to the 1920's is any guide, sexual Darwinism will evolve quickly to favor the greedy, the mean-spirited, the exploiters, the bigots—in short, the worst among us. It does not take much to guess who will win and who will lose in this not-so-new evolutionary process.

It therefore seems that the better way to guide ourselves through the confusing modern sexual revolution is not to push it along too quickly, not to experiment with laws to regulate things we simply do not understand, but instead to stop it here and there and prudently reflect in vigorous public debate about what it all means, where it is going, whether it needs a course correction.

Intro Two and laws like it take us in the wrong direction. Intro Two does not work.

Two Doctrines of Privacy

David R. Carlin, Jr.

When the U.S. Supreme Court ruled 5 to 4 on June 30 of this year that a Georgia antisodomy law was not banned by the U.S. Constitution, much weeping and gnashing of teeth were heard across the land.

The decision, we are told, is a great setback for the gay rights movement. True—but only if a failure to take a giant forward step is equivalent to a setback. Had the Court ruled the other way, a great leap forward would have been achieved by the gay rights movement. If the history of abortion in the United States is a reliable precedent, a Supreme Court declaration that homosexual acts (a subclass of sodomistic acts) are constitutionally protected would have enhanced, not just the legal, but also the moral legitimacy of such conduct. Rightly or wrongly, the public believes constitutional rights are grounded on moral rights; so when the Court defines a new constitutional right, the public infers it to be declaring a moral right as well.

But to say, as the Court did in its Georgia decision, that the states have the right to restrict homosexual conduct is not the same thing as to say that it would be right or wise to do so. States having antisodomy statutes on their books are still free to repeal them. And they should. In this nation and at this hour, all parties—ranging from those who hold homosexual acts to be rank in the nostrils of God and nature to those who hold such acts to be as innocent and healthy as drinking a glass of freshly squeezed orange juice—ought to be able to agree that homosexual activity among consenting adults should be of no concern to the criminal law. Such laws are either not enforced at all or are enforced in an excessively selective manner, thus providing opportunity for private blackmail and police oppression.

David R. Carlin Jr., "Two Doctrines of Privacy," *America* (9 August 1986), 50–51. Reprinted with permission of the author.

The critics also tell us that the Georgia decision constitutes a retreat on the Court's doctrine of privacy, being inconsistent with the 1965 Griswold ruling (invalidating laws banning the sale and use of contraceptives) and the 1973 Roe v. Wade ruling (overthrowing virtually all laws restricting abortion). The critics are correct. And that is why the truly significant impact of this decision is likely to be felt, not so much in the gay-rights realm, but in the realm of abortion rights. Logic may not be the life of the law, as Justice Oliver Wendell Holmes long ago reminded us, but even the U.S. Supreme Court is bound to feel the pinch of this logical inconsistency; and the Georgia decision, with its about-face on the privacy doctrine, portends, unless I miss my guess, at least a partial reversal of Roe v. Wade. The anti-abortion folks, it seems, are on the verge of a great victory.

The classic formulation of the doctrine of privacy was given by Justice William O. Douglas in his majority opinion in Griswold. Acknowledging that the right of privacy is not to be found in the letter of the Constitution, he argued that it can be found instead in the Constitution's "penumbra." Now, when so liberal a construer of the U.S. Constitution as Justice Douglas can claim no more for the right of privacy than its being found in that document's penumbra—not even the umbra, mind you, but only the penumbra—then we know we are dealing with a patent, not to say blatant, instance of judge-made law. One need not be a member of the Ed Meese school of jurisprudence, which holds that if the Founding Fathers did not expressly intend to put something into the Constitution then it just is not there, to feel uncomfortable with so imaginative a piece of constitutional exegesis. Aristotle, in a passage St. Thomas Aquinas loved to quote, says that a small error in the beginning produces much greater errors farther down the road. Griswold's strange privacy doctrine, which caused only slight concern at the time of its invention, later produced the legal, moral and social catastrophe of Roe v. Wade. The Georgia decision is a long overdue mid-course correction.

The right of privacy that was recognized from Griswold till just the other day suits well with what may be called, for want of a better name, the conventional liberal theory of individual freedom. (I stress the adjective "conventional," for it is entirely possible, I believe, to find another and better liberal theory of individual freedom.) According to this conventional theory, there is a certain sphere of life that is none of the state's business. Within this sphere are to be found an individual's friendships, religious preferences, sexual practices, medical choices, etc. Provided the individual in question is an adult of sound mind, the state has a strict duty to keep its hands off his activities in this private sphere.

As a war cry against oppression, this theory works fairly well, and I would like to reserve my own right to use it in certain circumstances. But as a sober theory of privacy and freedom, of state power and individual right, it will not do.

First of all, no government can afford to renounce absolutely and as a matter of principle its interest in the private lives of its citizens. So far from the private lives of those citizens being the last and least thing the state has to concern itself with, it is in a certain sense the first of the state's concerns. Upon the quality of the private life of its average member, after all, depends the well-being of society at large; and if government is required to worry about the well-being of society as it is, then it must equally worry about the quality of the private lives of its citizens.

And of course, contrary to the conventional liberal theory, local governments in the United States do in fact concern themselves with the quality of private lives; indeed holders of the conventional liberal theory concern themselves with this, though it may be inconsistent of them to do so. What else, in the last analysis, are government programs such as education, public health, scientific research, the promotion of economic development, to name only a few, but attempts to bring about high-quality private lives?

The criminal law, of course, is an exceedingly blunt instrument to use in attempts to improve the quality of private lives. A government may have an interest, for instance, in promoting sobriety and good manners among its citizens, but it would be unwise to attempt this by making rudeness or the sale of alcohol criminal offenses. Further, the value both to society and to its members of having those members lead their adult lives in a self-reliant manner, free from tutelage and paternalism, is so great that the law, both criminal and noncriminal, ought to leave them free to make their own choices whenever this practically can be done, no matter how foolish these choices may often be. But sometimes it is not practical for the law to maintain a hands-off policy. The criminal law may be able to overlook homosexual conduct, but it will probably be a long time before it can afford to overlook cocaine-using conduct, even though the snorting in question takes place within the sphere demarcated as private by the conventional liberal theory.

Second, to define individual freedom in terms of the right to be left alone is to forget that freedom can also be hindered by poverty, ill health, lack of education, etc. It is to forget, in other words, that negative freedom is not the only kind; there is such a thing as positive freedom as well. Isaiah Berlin once wrote a marvelous essay, "Two Concepts of Liberty," pointing out how dangerous the concept of positive freedom has been historically, in that it has provided theorists of totalitarianism from Rousseau to Mao with an excuse for repressing negative freedom, that is, freedom in its plain, common-sense signification. With all due respect to Berlin (it is a wonderful essay) and in full awareness that the enemies of freedom will seize anything, even freedom itself, with which to strike their blows, nonetheless it cannot be denied that to empower people to lead richer and more creative lives is to enhance, in some very intelligible sense of that word, their freedom.

In regarding individual liberty as an absolute, though limited right, one which can be neither justified nor restricted by any end beyond itself, the conventional liberal theory of freedom remains faithful to the spirit, indeed to the letter, of John Locke's 300-year-old theory of inalienable rights. We could do much worse than to have John Locke as our ideological father; indeed most nations have done much worse. But, after all this time, it ought to be possible to make a few small improvements on our heritage. A more adequate theory of individual freedom—and hence of its subcategory, privacy—would treat freedom not as an absolute and self-contained end, but as an end ordered to further ends, above all to the end of a good human life.

The conventional theory regards privacy as a kind of idol. But it is not an idol. Rather it is an essential condition for the full, rich and creative development of human personality. And while the recent Georgia decision tends to undermine the idolistic notion of privacy, there is no reason that it should injure the more adequate notion.

AFRAIDS

In 1983, the latest year for which statistics are available, 130 people, 55 of them students, died in school bus accidents. In that same year, as in all other years to date, zero students were diagnosed with AIDS infections incurred at school. If you were to stand up at your local school board meeting and demand that school buses be banned on the grounds that "any risk, however small, is too great when children are involved," you would not be treated seriously. Yet that is precisely the logic that is carrying the day in many school districts about letting children with AIDS into the classroom.

It is true that not everything is known about AIDS, and it is understandable that parents wish to take no chances where the welfare of their children is concerned. But contrary to what they have been led to believe by many in the media, the transmission of AIDS is far from an utter mystery. As conservatives often point out in other contexts, the search for a perfectly risk-free environment is not only futile, but it also creates costs of its own. In the case of AIDS, the cost is partly a moral one.

The AIDS issue has now spawned a second epidemic—a wave of hysteria whose symptoms include: ostracism, discrimination, and violence. As with other communicable maladies, we'll give this hysteria a name: Acute Fear Regarding AIDS or, more simply, AFRAIDS. Surveys indicate that whereas AIDS has thus far struck only a small fraction of the population, AFRAIDS has already infected well over a hundred million people. According to a recent *New York Times*/CBS poll, 47 percent of Americans believe it is possible to catch AIDS from a shared drinking glass, 28 percent implicate contaminated toilet seats, and 12 percent consider themselves endangered by a shared office environment or even a carrier's touch. Meanwhile, a *Washington Post* survey found that 34 percent of those polled considered it unsafe to "associate" with an AIDS victim—even when no physical contact was involved—and an additional 22 percent were uncertain.

Thanks to such misconceptions, many unlucky AIDS casualties, already laboring under a death sentence, are victimized a second time—thrown out of jobs, apartments, and schools, harassed and discharged by the military, and rejected by roommates, friends, and family. Worse, patients have been barred from hospitals, denied ambulance services, and refused mouth-to-mouth resuscitation. Organizations and families offering refuge to patients have been greeted with bomb warnings, death threats, vandalism, and assault.

The worst form of the AFRAIDS contagion is transmission of the disease from parents to children. In Queens, fear of an AIDS-afflicted second-grader triggered a boycott in two school districts that kept over a quarter of the area's 47,000 elementary and junior high school students at home on the first day of classes. The September 23 *Newsweek* featured a sickening cover photograph of children carrying placards against other children ("NO AIDS CHILDREN IN DISTRICT 27"). Thirteen-year-old Ryan White, banned from school in Indiana, observed pointedly about this state of affairs, "It stinks."

Since August authorities at the Federal Centers for Disease Control have been trying to arrest the spread of misinformation and panic. In a recent report, the center concluded that "casual person-to-person contact, as among schoolchildren, appears to pose no risk." Again, in a September 13 interview in *The New York Times*, Dr. Martha Rogers, an AIDS epidemiologist at the CDC, assured the public that "we obviously believe the evidence thus far indicates that transmission by casual contact will never occur." Unfortunately, these efforts to alleviate panic have inadvertently backfired: decisive judgments such as "never" and "no risk" have been overshadowed in the public mind by caveats such as "appears," "believe," "thus far," and "indicates." Intended simply as gestures of obeisance to scientific protocol, these formal qualifications have been widely misinterpreted as confessions of general ignorance on the part of the medical profession.

Naturally, this atmosphere of uncertainty has encouraged the casual transmission of AFRAIDS. In July the cover of *Life* magazine alerted readers, "NOW NO ONE IS SAFE FROM AIDS." The word "AIDS," plastered in thick, blood-red letters, covered an area three inches tall and ten inches wide. Inside, the ostensible cause for alarm proved considerably thinner. What the article actually substantiated was that no one is safe from AIDS who has sex with a carrier or receives a contaminated blood transfusion.

Rupert Murdoch's *New York Post* has been at the forefront of the misinformation campaign. On September 12, the *Post's* front page screamed, "SCHOOL COOK DIES OF AIDS." As if the hint of likely contamination weren't clear enough, the next day's cover followed with "Top doc's warning to schools: KEEP AIDS KIDS OUT." "Top doc" turned out to be Ronald Rosenblatt, a Queens internist with neither firsthand nor, apparently, thirdhand knowledge of reliable AIDS research.

The best evidence that AIDS can't be transmitted through casual contact is that not one of the family members of the 13,000 presently known AIDS victims (except for sexual partners and children infected in the womb) has developed AIDS symptoms, and none who has been tested is carrying the virus. As the CDC's Rogers observes, if you can't catch the bug by years of hugging, kissing, touching, and sharing food, utensils, and bathrooms with a carrier, chances are virtually nonexistent that you'll contract it just from sharing a classroom or an office. The AIDS virus has been isolated in saliva, tears, and urine. However, Rogers reports, "not one case of transmission from these fluids has ever been documented."

Skeptics raise two points most frequently in the face of this evidence. First, they note that the source of every AIDS victim's virus is not known. Specifically, ten percent of juvenile cases and six percent of adult cases remain unaccounted for. However, these leftover cases reflect procedural difficulties more than substantive doubts. Many juvenile cases cannot be formally closed simply because the mother, suspected of having passed the virus during pregnancy, is deceased or otherwise inaccessible. As for the adults, their cases will stay open as long as their lips remain sealed. The suspected routes—prostitute contact and homosexual activity—are not the sorts of hobbies a family man wants to reveal to his wife and children. In a recent study, a third of the unclassified adult male victims interviewed confessed to prostitute contact, and researchers hope and expect that further admissions will be forthcoming.

Second, skeptics point out that the incubation period of AIDS is several years. Only recently has there been a significant number of AIDS victims. Who is to say they aren't transmitting the disease in ways that won't become tragically apparent until years from now? In fact, the average time between infection and diagnosis of AIDS is one year for children, two for adults. AIDS has been under study for seven years, and yet not a single case of casual transmission has surfaced so far. What's more, among the 300 family members of AIDS victims who have had blood tests, none has shown the presence of the virus.

AIDS, like other infectious diseases, is transmittable after infection, and not just when the symptoms appear. The people developing AIDS now have been carriers for a long time. If the disease were transmittable in ways other than those that already have been established, this would show up now, not several years from now.

Whether with reckless opportunism or with the best of intentions, many publications—and even some physicians—have underscored routine uncertainties and voiced answerable doubts, falsely portraying this as the standpoint of "caution." The ironic result is the present epidemic explosion of AFRAIDS. Much of the public is now hopelessly confused, skeptical even to the point of questioning the sincerity of medical authorities. Dazed by the flurry of information and misinformation, lay people have simply resigned from the debate, concluding that the doctors don't have satisfactory answers. They await the day when medicine comes forth and declares unequivocally, in the words of President Reagan, "This we know for a fact, that it is safe." But this declaration is not likely to issue from the scrupulously cautious scientific community in this decade, perhaps not even in this century.

The question is, what do we do in the meantime? There is always—on a theoretical level—a risk that the AIDS kid at your local elementary school will engage your seven-year-old son in a fistfight, that both will bleed profusely, and that somehow the dastardly virus will worm its way across. There's even a hypothetical possibility that your child will catch the ailment just by drinking from the same water fountain or sitting in the same classroom. All logic and experience belies these fears, but they cannot be dismissed with absolute certainty. To some parents, landlords, and employers, this doesn't matter: a theoretical risk seems reason enough to exclude the infected individual from public life. Isn't that the counsel of caution? Isn't that the "safe" option?

Unfortunately, there is no safe option. Barring a child from school or excluding an adult from shelter and employment is not cost-free. It involves the expulsion not simply of a virus but of a human being. That must count for something. As a palpable cruelty, it seems a lot to ask for the sake of dispelling the darkest fantasies of the imagination.

DISCUSSION QUESTIONS

1. What are the moral and legal issues involved in identifying individuals who have contracted the AIDS virus?
2. Should one's sexual preference matter when it comes to employment opportunities, holding political office, teaching in the public schools, or holding leadership positions in organized religions?
3. Should homosexuals be considered as another discriminated-against minority group such as blacks, hispanics, women, etc., and therefore have the protection of their rights become an affirmative action issue?
4. As a nation have we become more tolerant or intolerant of gay men and lesbian women in this country? Are we more tolerant or discriminating against one group or another?

10

CENSORSHIP AND OBSCENITY

Stephen A. Smith

Few issues in contemporary society have excited the passions of the public, or done so from such diverse ideological positions, as the controversy over the censorship of obscenity. While many Americans believe it a trivial matter in their daily lives, those who are concerned about the issue argue their cases with such legal, moral, or emotional conviction that the debate frequently enters the public policy arena at national, state, and local levels and involves each branch of government. For that reason alone it is politically important, and it clearly illustrates the clash of values inherent in the policy process.

As a political and legal issue, the criminalization and censorship of pornography is a relatively recent phenomenon in the history of suppression. The early years of that history found the Church more concerned with blasphemy and heresy and the State concentrating on sedition. Obscene libel first moved from a Church-declared sin to a common law "crime" in the 1727 case of *Dominus Rex* v. *Curll,* holding government empowered to control communication which "reflects on religion, virtue, or morality." In the United States, the first successful prosecution for obscenity was the Pennsylvania case of *Commonwealth* v. *Sharpless* in 1815, and Vermont enacted the first state statute against obscenity in 1821. The federal government, although not directly criminalizing erotica, acted to prohibit distribution by the Customs Act of 1842, the Postal Act of 1865, and the Comstock Act of 1873, and the Supreme Court first upheld such legislation in the 1896 case of *Swearingen* v. *U.S.*

Censorship of obscenity has continued to be an issue during this century, and two national commissions have addressed the topic. In 1970, the Commission on Obscenity and Pornography, established when Congress found traffic in obscenity and pornography "a matter of national concern," recommended the repeal of all laws restricting access to pornography by consenting adults. President Richard Nixon called the conclusions "morally bankrupt," Vice-President Spiro Agnew decried the "need to restrain bad taste and outrageous vulgarity," and Attorney General John Mitchell pledged to "open a new front against filth peddlers." Despite history's judgment as to the real moral standards of these men, their remarks did reflect the convictions of some citizens who were sincere in their opposition.

In 1985 to 1986, the Attorney General's Commission on Pornography, created at the request of President Ronald Reagan, began with different assumptions and reached different conclusions. Its Charter ignored the important legal distinction between obscenity and pornography, and it charged its members to find ways of controlling pornography even before the Commission had begun to define such materials or examine any data. The Final Report called for tougher legal action against pornography and recommended extra-legal vigilance groups to suppress erotic materials.[1] It drew the ire of citizens who saw a biased commission advancing the narrow-minded, reactionary political agenda of the Religious Right while ignoring the right of individual privacy and the Constitutional guarantee of freedom of expression.

All political controversies involve a dialectical tension between values, but the difficulty of wisely resolving that between censorship and obscenity is exacerbated by several unique factors. First, there is considerable disagreement over what constitutes obscenity, and the inability to define terms presents serious policy problems. The same verbal or graphic sexual materials that might be thought morally offensive, psychologically revolting, or obviously criminal by some might be thought by others to be sensually pleasing, merely amusing, or just plain boring. While some would classify all sexual expression as obscene, others would include other bodily functions, include some or all forms of violence, or struggle with distinctions of degree. Even learned jurists are frustrated by the task. Justice Potter Stewart claimed that he could not define obscenity but knew it when he saw it. Obscenity, though, is as elusive as truth and beauty, and the courts seldom behold it with unanimous eyes.[2]

Second, the field of argument is mined with conflicting claims about the effects of exposure to pornography, and the available empirical data do not resolve the question.[3] At least part of this dilemma can be attributed to differing definitions of the pornographic, but much of it results from differing points of view. Some have contended that consumption of pornography has a positive cathartic effect in reducing sexual aggression and can serve to enhance traditional marriages. Those favoring censorship argue that pornography leads to violence, degrades humanity, destroys traditional values, and undermines our entire social fabric.

Third, even if obscenity can be clearly defined and its effects determined, there is the question of whether it should be controlled by the state or left to the rational choice of individuals. Fourth, even if citizens believe that obscenity should be censored, there is a constitutional question as to whether government has the power to abridge communication on the basis of content. Finally, even if agreement were secured on the wisdom of and authority to regulate pornography, there remains the question of exactly how to restrict communication in a free society. These are difficult questions—but ones that citizens in a democracy must answer to fashion wise public policy.

The readings in this section illustrate the diversity and intensity of the policy debate. Charles Keating, Jr., founder of Citizens for Decent Literature, represents the traditional religio-moral argument for censorship. Although he states that God's moral code needs no defense, he took 123 pages to attack the fare of theatre, cinema, newsstands, sex shops, and records and charge that pornography leads to venereal disease, illegitimacy, degradation of sex, adultery, divorce, abortion, suicide, and moral anarchy.[4] Andrea Dworkin, noted feminist author and advocate, contends that pornography "is the propaganda of sexual fascism" and "promotes violent contempt for the integrity and rightful freedom of women." Representing the production and sale of pornography as a civil rights violation, she has advocated ordinances against pornography on that basis.[5]

The American Civil Liberties Union, with less emotion but with equal conviction, states the First Amendment case against government censorship of ideas, refutes both religious and feminist arguments on effect and control, and stresses the alternative of promoting individual freedom and responsibility. Professor Robert Staples, a member of the *Penthouse*-sponsored commission to counter the Meese Commission, presents a different perspective on pornography—questioning the importance of the topic, challenging the alleged effects, and suggesting that government could better spend its resources in providing sex education and fighting the real sins of unemployment, poverty, and nuclear madness.

The debate over censorship and obscenity typifies the need for agreement on definitions, valid factual data, clear philosophical analysis of values, and rigorous rhetorical tests of arguments in pursuit of wise public policies that maximize individual freedom and promote the good society.

NOTES

1. *Attorney General's Commission on Pornography: Final Report* (Washington, DC: U.S. Department of Justice, 1986), pp. 215, 1957, 1313–50.
2. For a valuable composite judicial definition, see Thomas L. Tedford, *Freedom of Speech in the United States* (New York: Random House, 1985), pp. 197–98.
3. Edward Donnerstein, Daniel Linz, and Steven Penrod, *The Question of Pornography: Research Findings and Policy Implications* (New York: Free Press, 1987).
4. Other dimensions of this stance are illuminated in Louis A. Zurcher, Jr., and R. George Kirkpatrick, *Citizens for Decency: Antipornography Crusades as Status Defense* (Austin: University of Texas Press, 1976).
5. An Indianapolis ordinance drafted and advocated by Dworkin and Catharine MacKinnon was held unconstitutional in *American Booksellers Association* v. *Hudnut*, 598 F. Supp. 1316 (S.D. Ind. 1984); 771 F.2d 323 (7th Cir. 1985); cert. denied 54 U.S.L.W. 3560 (Feb. 24, 1986). The feminist critique is fully articulated in Laura Lederer, ed., *Take Back the Night: Women on Pornography* (New York: William Morrow, 1980); however, see Varda Burstyn, ed., *Women Against Censorship* (Vancouver, Canada: Douglas McIntyre, 1985).

Report of Commissioner Charles H. Keating, Jr.

...In slightly less than two centuries of existence, the United States has developed from a frontier nation to a position of predominance in the world in commerce and industry, as well as in the arts and sciences. It is no mere coincidence that this period of unparalleled progress was one in which the rule of law prevailed. The fact that we enjoyed a "Government of Laws and not of Men" provided the intellectual and cultural climate in which the American could develop his talents and the resources of his country to their respective peaks. Throughout our history, we have been successful in adapting and shaping our laws to meet the changing circumstances of the times. Our law has been a living thing, a constant companion which has served us well as our nation came into its maturity. Our tradition and, in fact, our genius has been the adaptation of our laws to meet the challenges of the times. To renounce law as a solution is to abandon our heritage.

Against the general background of the history of nations and against the specific background of the history of the United States, it is apparent the laws prohibiting obscenity and pornography have played an important role in the

"Report of Commissioner Charles H. Keating, Jr.," excerpts from *The Report of the Commission on Obscenity and Pornography* (New York: Bantam Books, 1970), 579–583, 609–610, 612–614, 617–618, 622–623.

creativity and excellence of our system and our society—these laws have played an important part in our people coming so far and achieving so much.

Accordingly, it seems incredible to this writer that the majority of the Presidential Commission appointed under Public Law 90–100 opts for a "Danish" solution to the problem of pornography; namely, to remove the controls—to repeal the law.

...Such presumption! Such an advocacy of moral anarchy! Such a defiance of the mandate of the Congress which created the Commission! Such a bold advocacy of a libertine philosophy! Truly, it is difficult to believe that to which the majority of this Commission has given birth.

My Report will go into such detail as is possible on the specifics of the problem, but I cannot undertake consideration of the subject of pornography without commenting on its underlying philosophical and moral basis.

For those who believe in God, in His absolute supremacy as the Creator and Lawgiver of life, in the dignity and destiny which He has conferred upon the human person, in the moral code that governs sexual activity—for those who believe in these "things," no argument against pornography should be necessary.

Though the meaning of pornography is generally understood, reference is seldom made to the root meaning of the term itself. This seems important to me. The Greeks had a word for it, for many "its." And the Greek word for pornography is highly significant. It comes from two Greek words in fact: "prostitute" and "write." So, the dictionary defines pornography as "originally a description of prostitutes and their trade."

Pornography is not merely associated in this historical sense with prostitution, but it is actually a form of prostitution because it advertises and advocates "sex for sale," pleasure for a price.

The use of sexual powers is intimately bound up with both love and life, not merely with the momentary satisfaction of desire. Only a person is capable of love, but any of the lower forms of animal life can experience pleasure as a mere sense reaction. A person is much more than a body, and any form of sexual activity which is impersonal, which uses the body alone for pleasure, violates the integrity of the person and thereby reduces him to the level of an irrational and irresponsible animal.

The traditional Judeo-Christian ethic does not condemn pleasure as an evil in itself; it does condemn the pursuit of pleasure for its own sake, as an end rather than a means, deliberately excluding the higher purposes and values to which pleasure is attached. Everybody knows that the appetite for food makes the necessity of eating more palatable, more pleasurable. To eat to live is rational, sound procedure; to live to eat is an abuse of a basically good thing. The same is true of the sex drive. It serves the individual and the common good of the human race, only when it is creative, productive, when it ministers to love and life. When, however, it serves only itself, it becomes a perversion, actually an anti-social force disruptive and eventually destructive of all love and life. Every word by which the organs of sex are designated bears out this statement: genital, generative, reproductive, procreative. Love is always fruitful of lasting good; mere pleasure is of its nature transitory, barren, the only residue likely to be unhappy, remorseful memories. This thought could be amplified and graphically illustrated. Those who speak in defense of sexual morality are accused of making sex "dirty." It's the other way around. The defenders of pornography are guilty of degrading sex. Marcel Proust, French novelist (*Sodom and Gomorrah*), described the effect of his early reading of erotica upon himself: "Oh scream of hell that undermined my adolescence." Literature is a better reflection of life than is scientific opinion; and I am certain that the testimony of men like Proust could be multiplied if someone took the time to assemble the sources.

No, the state cannot legislate virtue, cannot make moral goodness by merely enacting law; but the state can and does legislate against vices which publicly jeopardize the virtue of people who might prefer to remain virtuous. If it is not the proper function of law to offer citizens such protection, then what is it?

...The Eden Theatre is located in East Greenwich Village. This is a sleazy, disreputable part of New York. The Theatre is old and dilapidated. "Oh! Calcutta!" plays at the Eden Theatre. "Oh! Calcutta!" is pure pornography—a two-hour orgy, principally enacted in the nude. It is not possible to verbally depict the depravity, deviation, eroticism or the utter filth of the play. Male and female players fondle each other, commit or simulate intercourse, sodomy, cunnilingus, masturbation, sadism, *ad nauseam*. This abomination, at the time I write this Report, is proposed to be televised live or by video-tape across the nation via lines of American Telephone and Telegraph and various telephonic communications systems. Never in Rome, Greece, or the most debauched nation in history has such utter filth been projected to all parts of a nation. If there is or ever was any such thing as public decency, these actions offend it. If there is or ever was a constitutional prerogative of the American people to have the exercise of police power in the interests of the public health and welfare, this is it.

...Motion picture theaters are to be found in every nook and cranny of the United States. These theaters today present explicit sexual conduct, more often abnormal than normal, as the principal bill of fare. Thanks to Jack Valenti, we have a condition in the motion picture industry today that literally constitutes a course of instruction in decadence, perversion and immorality. Honored companies as Twentieth Century Fox retain pornographers such as Russ Meyer, and produce obscenities such as "Beyond the Valley of the Dolls". It is a sad and dangerous day in America when an industry with as much influence as the motion picture industry turns its back on responsibility and moral code and permits a man such as Russ Meyer access to their most hallowed circles.

To compete with major studio releases in main-line theaters, sexploitation theaters now deal in hardcore pornography disguised as "documentaries" on Danish "sex fairs" or as marriage manuals depicting various positions of intercourse. The showing of explicit sexual activity on the screen under the "Documentary" guise led to the opening of "mini-theaters" in vacant storefronts in New York, San Francisco, Los Angeles, and other cities, which screen unadulterated, undisguised hardcore stag films depicting every imaginable sexual deviation. At the time of this report, there are over 80 such "mini-theaters" in Los Angeles County alone and new ones are opening at the rate of three per week!

An even more alarming, but nonetheless predictable, progression of this deluge of obscenity is the staging of live sex shows which are now taking place in jurisdictions such as Los Angeles, San Francisco, and New York. These "exhibitions" feature live "actors" in actual acts of "normal" sex, as well as perversions such as homosexuality, bestiality, sadism, masochism, etc. One such "show," written up boldly in the Los Angeles "underground" papers, included audience participation to the extent that patrons are invited to the "stage" where oral sex acts and/or intercourse are performed for the voyeuristic pleasure of the other deviates in attendance.

In obvious anticipation of the "soft-line" recommendations of the Commission majority, hard-core pictorial newsstand obscenity that goes beyond anything available in Copenhagen is being displayed openly in innumerable porno shops throughout the country. Many of the shops have display cases containing artificial sexual devices—penises, vaginas, french ticklers, vibrators, etc., as well as penis-shaped candy and inflatable rubber dolls with built-in vagina, etc. Certainly, ancient Sodom and Gomorrah couldn't have been as obsessed with sex as America is today. What is rotten in Denmark is already positively putrid in this country—and all this only in anticipation of the release of the soft-line Majority Report!

Another fact "overlooked" by the majority is that the adoption of their recommendations would open a new "legal" market for the pornographers wares—the *children* of America. They recommend legislation against the sale of *pictorial* obscenity to children—but specifically exempt printed-word or "textual" materials. Thus, while Danish pornographers suffered a drop-off in sales of "textual" material when pictorial obscenity was legalized, their American counterparts will be able to redirect "textual" obscenity to the juvenile market. Ingenious American pornographers will no doubt be quick to devise new techniques to exploit this juvenile market, including mobile porno shops to visit campuses on a monthly basis.

Another most disturbing aspect of legalized pornography as recommended by the Commission majority, is their utter disregard for the moral degradation of the men, women, and children who are forced by economic necessity, or by use of drugs, or simply by seduction, to pose for pornographic pictures. The sexual aberrations and deviations in pornography go far beyond conventional prostitution, and the Commission majority would allow the pornographer who degrades the participants to be raised to the respectability of a legitimate and legal business. Incredible!

In preparing to write this Report, I requested some 50 persons across the United States to send me the entertainment section of their local newspapers. I had intended to elicit from such pages a representative sample of the filth being fed by the entertainment industry into each and every community of this nation. It became obvious through perusal of these newspaper advertisements that a comprehensive presentation of the moral degradation being presented by "show business" today is not only appalling but virtually indescribable. I can only comment that if the majority of the Commission on Obscenity and Pornography has its way and the laws against the pornographers are repealed, we will witness complete moral anarchy in this country that will soon spread to the entire free world.

...I submit that never in the history of modern civilization have we seen more obvious evidence of a decline in public morality than we see today. Venereal disease is at epidemic proportions and literally out of control in many large urban centers—despite medicine. Illegitimacy statistics are skyrocketing—despite the pill and other contraceptive devices—and despite the relatively easy access to abortion. Both of these social statistics reflect a promiscuous attitude toward sex which is no doubt contributed to by many factors—but certainly one factor has to be the deluge of pornography which is screaming at young people from records, motion picture screens, newsstands, the United States mail and their peer groups.

To say that pornography has no effect is patently ridiculous. I submit that if pornography does *not* affect a person—that person has a problem. Pornography is intended to arouse the sexual appetite—one of the most volatile appetites of human nature. Once that appetite is aroused, it will seek satisfaction—and the satisfaction sought—without proper moral restraints—is often reflected in the social statistics discussed above.

Proponents of legalized pornography claim that pornography is actually good because it protects society from the sex deviate who might otherwise commit anti-social conduct. He can now read dirty books and get his kicks that way. They point to a 31 percent decrease in sex crimes in Copenhagen to support this thesis.

...Denmark is currently experiencing the worst epidemic of venereal disease among young people of any nation in the world.

In addition to the social problems of venereal disease and illegitimacy, it is also of the very nature of obscenity to degrade sex and distort the role that sex plays in a normal life. There is no way to measure the terrible effects that pornography has had and is having on marital infidelity that is reflected in divorce statistics, abortions, suicide, and other social problems that further reflect the decline in public morality.

The effects of obscenity on society can best be summed up by repeating here a quotation written in 1705 by Alexander Pope:

> Vice is a monster of so frightful mein,
> As to be hated, only needed to be seen.
> Yet seen too oft, familiar with her face,
> We first endure, then pity, then embrace.

The majority report of the Presidential Commission on Obscenity and Pornography would have America embrace the monster vice.

...At a time when the spread of pornography has reached epidemic proportions in our country and when the moral fiber of our nation seems to be rapidly unravelling, the desperate need is for enlightened and intelligent control of the poisons which threaten us—not the declaration of moral bankruptcy inherent in the repeal of the laws which have been the defense of decent people against the pornographer for profit.

To deny the need for control is literally to deny one's senses, unless such denial is based upon a conclusion that there is nothing evil or dangerous about pornographic material. For a Presidential Commission to have labored for two years at the expense to the taxpayers of almost two million dollars and arrive at the conclusion that pornography is harmless must strike the average American as the epitome of government-gone-berserk.

Credit the American public with enough common sense to know that one who wallows in filth is going to get dirty. This is intuitive knowledge. Those who will spend millions of dollars to tell us otherwise must be malicious or misguided, or both.

The Congress of the United States created a Presidential Commission on Obscenity and Pornography for the purpose of determining legal and constitutional means to protect the country from what the Congress recognized as a threat. Unfortunately, what was intended to provide to our legislators a blueprint for coping with a problem has been turned one-hundred-eighty degrees into a blank check for the pornographers to flood our country with every variety of filth and perversion.

The Commission majority report can only be described as a travesty, preordained by the bias and prejudice of its Chairman, closely followed by his Staff, who has long advocated relaxation of restraints for the dealers in pornography. The Report of the majority of the Commission does not reflect the will of Congress, the opinion of law enforcement officials throughout our country, and, worst of all, flaunts the underlying opinions and desires of the great mass of the American people. Were we not concerned with the morals and life of a nation, the situation represented by the majority Report would be ludicrous.

Far from needing repeal of legislation controlling pornography, what is called for is a return to law enforcement which permits the American to determine for himself the standards of acceptable morality and decency in his community. Our law enforcement in the area of obscenity has been emasculated by courts, seemingly divorced from the realities of our communities, determining from afar the standards of those communities. The law is capable of coping with the problem of pornography and obscenity, but it must be law, coupled with the logic that an American is innately capable of determining for himself his standards of public decency and, beyond that, he has a right to make that determination.

The words of Alexis de Toqueville (during his American visit, 1835–1840) seem appropriate:

> I sought for the greatness and genius of America in her commodius harbors and ample rivers—and it was not there; in her fertile lands and boundless prairies—and it was not there. Not until I went to the churches of America and heard her pulpits aflame with righteousness did I understand the secret of her genius and power. America is great because she is good—and if America ceases to be good, America will cease to be great.

Pornography: The New Terrorism

Andrea Dworkin

All through human history, there have been terrible, cruel wrongs. These wrongs were not committed on a small scale. These wrongs were not rarities or oddities. These wrongs have raged over the earth like wind-swept fires: maiming, destroying, leaving humans turned to ash. Slavery, rape, torture, extermination have been the substance of life for billions of human beings since the beginning of patriarchal time. Some have fattened on atrocity while others have suffered from it until they died.

Andrea Dworkin, "Pornography: The New Terrorism," *New York University Review of Law and Social Change*, 8 (1978–79), 215–218. First published in *The Body Politic*, August 1978. Reprinted by permission of the author.

In any given time, most people have accepted the cruelest wrongs as right. Whether through indifference, ignorance, or brutality, most people, oppressor and oppressed, have apologized for atrocity, defended it, justified it, excused it, laughed at it, or ignored it.

The oppressor, the one who perpetrates the wrongs for his own pleasure or profit, is the master inventor of justification. He is the magician who, out of thin air, fabricates wondrous, imposing, seemingly irrefutable intellectual reasons which explain why one group must be degraded at the hands of another. He is the conjurer who takes the smoking ash of real death and turns it into stories, poems, pictures, which celebrate degradation as life's central truth. He is the illusionist who paints mutilated bodies in chains on the interior canvas of the imagination so that, asleep or awake, we can only hallucinate indignity and outrage. He is the manipulator of psychological reality, the framer of law, the engineer of social necessity, the architect of perception and being.

The oppressed are encapsulated by the culture, laws, and values of the oppressor. Their behaviors are controlled by laws and traditions based on their presumed inferiority. They are, as a matter of course, called abusive names, presumed to have low or disgusting personal and collective traits. They are always subject to sanctioned assault. They are surrounded on every side by images and echoes of their own worthlessness. Involuntarily, unconsciously, not knowing anything else, they have branded into them, burned into their brains, a festering self-hatred, a virulent self-contempt. They have burned out of them the militant dignity on which all self-respect is based.

Oppressed people are not subjugated or controlled by dim warnings or vague threats of harm. Their chains are not made of shadows. Oppressed people are *terrorized*—by raw violence, real violence, unspeakable and pervasive violence. Their bodies are assaulted and despoiled, according to the will of the oppressor.

This violence is always accompanied by cultural assault—propaganda disguised as principle or knowledge. The purity of the "Aryan" or Caucasian race is a favorite principle. Genetic inferiority is a favorite field of knowledge. Libraries are full of erudite texts that prove, beyond a shadow of a doubt, that Jews, the Irish, Mexicans, blacks, homosexuals, and women are slime. These eloquent and resourceful proofs are classified as psychology, theology, economics, philosophy, history, sociology, the so-called science of biology. Sometimes, often, they are made into stories or poems and called art. Degradation is dignified as biological, economic, or historical necessity; or as the logical consequence of the repulsive traits or inherent limitations of the ones degraded. Out on the streets, the propaganda takes a more vulgar form. Signs read "Whites Only" or "Jews and Dogs Not Allowed." Hisses of "kike," "nigger," "queer," and "pussy" fill the air. In this propaganda, the victim is marked. In this propaganda, the victim is targeted. This propaganda is the glove that covers the fist in any reign of terror.

This propaganda does not only sanction violence against the designated group; it incites it. This propaganda does not only threaten assault; it promises it. These are the dreaded images of terror:

—A Jew, emaciated, behind barbed wire, nearly naked, mutilated by the knife of a Nazi doctor: the atrocity is acknowledged.

—A Vietnamese, in a tiger cage, nearly naked, bones twisted and broken, flesh black and blue: the atrocity is acknowledged.

—A black slave on an American plantation, nearly naked, chained, flesh ripped up from the whip: the atrocity is acknowledged.

—A woman, nearly naked, in a cell, chained, flesh ripped up from the whip, breasts mutilated by a knife: she is entertainment, the boy-next-door's favorite fantasy, every man's precious right, every woman's potential fate.

The woman tortured is sexual entertainment.

The woman tortured is sexually arousing.

The anguish of the woman tortured is sexually exciting.

The degradation of the woman tortured is sexually entrancing.

The humiliation of the woman tortured is sexually pleasing, sexually thrilling, sexually gratifying.

Women are a degraded and terrorized people. Women are degraded and terrorized by men. Rape is terrorism. Wife-beating is terrorism. Medical butchering is terrorism. Sexual abuse in its hundred million forms is terrorism.

Women's bodies are possessed by men. Women are forced into involuntary childbearing because men, not women, control women's reproductive functions. Women are an enslaved population: the crop we harvest is children, the fields we work are houses. Women are forced into committing sexual acts with men that violate integrity because the universal religion—contempt for women—has as its first commandment that women exist purely as sexual fodder for men.

Women are an occupied people. Our very bodies are possessed, taken by others who have an inherent right to take, used or abused by others who have an inherent right to use or abuse. The ideology that energizes and justifies this systematic degradation is a fascist ideology—the ideology of biological inferiority. No matter how it is disguised, no matter what refinements pretty it up, this ideology, reduced to its essence, postulates that women are biologically suited to function only as breeders, pieces of ass, and servants. This fascist ideology of female inferiority is the preeminent ideology on this planet. As Shulamith Firestone put it in *The Dialectic of Sex*, "Sex class is so deep as to be invisible." That women exist to be used by men is, quite simply, the common point of view, and the concommitant of this point of view, inexorably linked to it, is that violence used against women to force us to fulfill our so-called natural functions is not really violence at all. Every act of terror or crime committed against women is justified as sexual necessity and/or is dismissed as utterly unimportant. This extreme callousness passes as normalcy, so that when women, after years or decades or centuries of unspeakable abuse, do raise our voices in outrage at the crimes committed against us, we are accused of stupidity or lunacy, or are ignored as if we were flecks of dust instead of flesh and blood.

We women are raising our voices now, because all over this country a new campaign of terror and vilification is being waged against us. Fascist propaganda celebrating sexual violence against women is sweeping this land. Fascist propaganda celebrating the sexual degradation of women is innundating cities, college campuses, and small towns. Pornography is the propaganda of sexual fascism. Pornography is the propaganda of sexual terrorism. Images of women bound, bruised, and maimed on virtually every street corner, on every magazine rack, in every drug store, in movie house after movie house, on billboards, on posters pasted on walls, are death threats to a female population in rebellion. Female rebellion against male sexual despotism, female rebellion against male sexual authority, is now a reality throughout this country. The men, meeting rebellion with an escalation of terror, hang pictures of maimed female bodies in every public place.

We are forced either to capitulate, to be beaten back by those images of abuse into silent acceptance of female degradation as a fact of life, or to develop strategies of resistance derived from a fully conscious will to resist. If we capitulate—smile, be good, pretend that the woman in chains has nothing to do with us, avert our eyes as we pass her image a hundred times a day—we have lost everything. What, after all, does all our work against rape or wife-beating amount to when one of their pictures is worth a thousand of our words?

Strategies of resistance are developing. Women are increasingly refusing to accept the pernicious, debilitating lie that the sexual humiliation of women for fun, pleasure, and profit is the inalienable right of every man. Petitions, leaf-letting, picketing, boycotts, organized vandalism, speak-outs, teach-ins, letter-writing campaigns, intense and militant harrassment of distributors and exhibitors of woman-hating films, and an unyielding refusal to give aid and comfort to the politically self-righteous fellow travellers of the pornographers are increasing as feminists refuse to cower in the face of this new campaign of annihilation. These are beginning actions. Some are rude and some are civil. Some are short-term actions, spontaneously ignited by outrage. Others are long-term strategies that require extensive organization and commitment. Some disregard male law, and break it with militancy and pride. Others dare to demand that the law must protect women from brazen terrorization. All of these actions arise out of the true perception that pornography actively promotes violent contempt for the integrity and rightful freedom of women. And, despite male claims to the contrary, feminists, not pornographers, are being arrested and prosecuted by male law enforcers, all suddenly "civil libertarians" when male privilege is confronted on the streets by angry and uppity women. The concept of "civil liberties" in this country has not ever, and does not now, embody principles and behaviors that respect the sexual rights of women. Therefore, when pornographers are challenged by *women,* police, district attorneys, and judges punish the women, all the while ritualistically claiming to be the legal guardians of "free speech." In fact, they are the legal guardians of male profit, male property, and phallic power.

Feminist actions against pornography must blanket the country, so that no pornographer can hide from, ignore, ridicule, or find refuge from the outrage of women who will not be degraded, who will not submit to terror. Wherever women claim any dignity or want any possibility of freedom, we must confront the fascist propaganda that celebrates atrocity against us head on—expose it for what it is, expose those who make it, those who show it, those who defend it, those who consent to it, those who enjoy it.

In the course of this difficult and dangerous struggle, we will be forced, as we experience the intransigence of those who commit and support these crimes against us, to ask the hardest and deepest questions, the ones we so dread:

What is this male sexuality that requires our humiliation, that literally swells with pride at our anguish?

What does it mean that yet again—and after years of feminist analysis and activism—the men (gay, leftist, whatever) who proclaim a commitment to social justice are resolute in their refusal to face up to the meaning and significance of their enthusiastic advocacy of yet another woman-hating plague?

What does it mean that the pornographers, the consumers of pornography, and the apologists for pornography are the men we grew up with, the men we talk with, live with, the men who are familiar to us and often cherished by us as friends, fathers, brothers, and sons?

How surrounded by this flesh of our flesh that despises us, will we defend the worth of our lives, establish our own authentic integrity, and, at last, achieve our freedom?

American Civil Liberties Union Policy Statement on Censorship of Obscenity, Pornography and Indecency

The ACLU opposes any restraint on the right to create, publish or distribute materials to adults, or the right of adults to choose the materials they read or view, on the basis of obscenity, pornography or indecency.[1] Freedom of speech and press and freedom to read can be safeguarded effectively only if the First Amendment is applied strictly—to prohibit any restriction on these basic rights. In pursuing this policy, the ACLU emphasizes that it is neither urging the circulation nor evaluating the merit of such material.

Laws which punish the distribution or exposure of such material to minors violate the First Amendment, and inevitably restrict the right to publish and distribute such materials to adults. The complex social problems which prompt such statutes cannot be solved by limiting freedom of speech and press and avoiding the real causes.

The ACLU is well aware of the concern of parents, clergy and community officials about the exposure of children to what many regard as hard-core pornography, whether through its availability at neighborhood stores and newsstands or by its unsolicited dissemination through the mails. However, the Union maintains that a causal relationship between exposure to sexually explicit material and juvenile delinquency has never been carried to the point of definitive proof. As a practical matter it would appear that there can be no substitute for parental responsibility. Inevitably, any legal sanctions would threaten the distribution of non-pornographic materials.

The ACLU has long maintained that all definitions of obscenity are meaningless because this type of judgment is inevitably subjective and personal. Court and juries continue to differ over what constitutes obscenity, often including in that category materials that have won world-wide acclaim.

The standard that to be judged obscene a work must lack "serious literary, artistic, political or social value" is imprecise and uncertain. It is impossible to draw the exact line between "important" and "worthless"

[1]Since these terms are variously defined in different settings by different individuals, it is the intention of this policy to cover all meanings from merely sexually explicit material to constitutionally-defined obscenity to any group or individual's definition of pornography—including violence.

"Policy Statement No. 4: Censorship, Obscenity, Pornography and Indecency," *Policy Guide.* American Civil Liberties Union, 132 West 43rd Street, New York, NY. 10036. Reprinted by permission.

material because the informed, critical community is itself just as often divided on the issue of the social importance as on the "appeal to prurient interest" of any given work. Attempts to define "obscenity" frequently result in condemning most severely expression of a controversial nature—the very kind of speech for whose protection the First Amendment was written.

The ACLU believes that the constitutional guarantees of free speech and press apply to all expression and that all limitations of expression on the ground of obscenity, pornography or indecency are unconstitutional. But so long as courts sustain such limitations in any form, it will also work to minimize their restrictive effect.[2] Under the First Amendment and the due process clause of the Fifth Amendment, such statutes should be required to define precisely the forms of proscribed speech, provide strict procedural safeguards, and choose the least restrictive methods of regulation.

The following safeguards for freedom of expression should be required:

1. Any statutory definition of obscenity must be drawn precisely and narrowly.

2. Creators, publishers and producers, their distributors, exhibitors and retailers, should not be threatened with the sanctions of criminal statutes for distributing or being connected with a work before it has been determined obscene in an adversary civil proceeding with a standard of proof of clear and convincing evidence. The state should be required to select a civil proceeding, as the least restrictive method of censorship.

3. Obscenity statutes should provide for prompt trails, determination and appellate review within specified time periods; and to require proof of scienter under clearly defined and reasonable standards.

4. Obscenity statutes should assure defendants the right to counsel; and if a defendant is acquitted, the defendant should be entitled to recover the costs and reasonable attorney's fees incurred in defending the person's First Amendment rights.

5. Creators, publishers and producers, their distributors, exhibitors and retailers, should not be submitted to harassment by a multiplicity of proceedings. The state should not be entitled to subject a work to more than one civil proceeding to determine its obscenity. This could be accomplished either by requiring that its Attorney General institute such proceeding (or designate a district or county attorney to do so), or by providing that once an obscenity proceeding has been commenced in a state against a work, no other proceed-

[2]Legislators, courts, law enforcement personnel and citizen's groups have over the decades tried to censor materials found to be distasteful or punish those who create or deal in it. Techniques and definitions have changed over the years and this policy reflects responses to the various law enforcement approaches although some may be out-dated and some are in their infancy.

ing may be instituted against the same work in other counties, cities or towns until and unless there has been a final judgment that the work is obscene.

6. Distributors, exhibitors and retailers should not be obliged to risk punishment by misjudging the age of a minor. Such persons should not be required to keep records of evidence submitted by minors; and should be entitled to rely reasonably on a minor's statement of age.

7. There should not be a variable standard of obscenity for minors.

The ACLU opposes all zoning plans restricting the availability of books, movies and other communications media because of their content. The ACLU has long opposed any restraint on the dissemination of materials on grounds of obscenity. It therefore believes that zoning plans designed to regulate so-called pornographic materials comprise another form of restraint that impinges on constitutionally protected speech. The breadth of zoning ordinances inevitably inhibits thc full and free exchange of information and expression.

Statutes that restrict pornography on the ground that it contributes to the subordination of women violate the free press and free speech guarantees of the First Amendment. The ACLU opposes any form of sex discrimination against women or men, but censoring speech will in the end lead to more intolerance, not less.

Proponents of such statutes contend that pornography is a form of sex discrimination because it reinforces an inferior image of women and thus harms women's status. They argue that pornography also leads to physical abuse of women, by increasing male aggression towards them; also that actresses and models are often physically and psychologically abused in the actual production of pornographic movies and photographs, typically by being coerced into sex.

Pornography, however, is speech; it is not conduct. Certain pornographic materials may be offensive to some and perhaps most Americans. Yet many publications and films which broad segments of the public may wish to see or read, ranging from current cultural expression to renowned works of art, could be construed as pornography and face restriction under these statutes.

Some assert that there is "scientific proof" showing an actual causal relationship between viewing of pornography and anti-social behavior. The ACLU believes, however, that no different test of the effects of speech is applicable in this area as in any other area.

Much expression may offend the sensibilities of people and indeed have a harmful impact on some. But this is no reason to sacrifice the First Amendment. The First Amendment does not allow suppression of speech because of the potential harm.

Society, moreover, has ample means other than suppression for dealing with the types of harm that some contend are caused or aggravated by pornography. Enforcement of criminal laws regarding assault, coerced sex, kidnapping and trespassing; strengthening of rape laws including elimination of the "spousal rape" exception under which husbands may not be prosecuted for raping their wives; enforcement of Title VII (of the Civil Rights Act of 1964) and other sex discrimination laws are legitimate remedies. Victims of sexual offenses may also have grounds to sue for damages for torts or contract claims.

The ACLU believes that the First Amendment protects the dissemination of all forms of communication. The ACLU opposes on First Amendment grounds laws that restrict the production and distribution of any printed and visual materials even when some of the producers of those materials are punishable under criminal law.

The ACLU views the use of children in the production of visual depictions of sexually explicit conduct as a violation of childrens' rights when such use is highly likely to cause: a) substantial physical harm or, b) substantial and continuing emotional or psychological harm. Government quite properly has the means to protect the interests of children in these situations by the use of criminal prosecution of those persons who are likely to cause such harm to children.[3]

The Black Response

Dr. Robert Staples

As the black member of the "shadow commission," I am indebted to the opponents of sexual fascism for giving me a chance to express the black view on pornography—an opportunity denied by the government-formed commission. Although we represent 35 million American citizens or one in nine inhabitants of this country, the attorney general did not see fit to include one

[3]Persons who cause such harm to children will usually be those who finance the sexually explicit depictions; those who procure the children; those who engage in sexual activity with the children; and those who otherwise actively contribute on the set to the production. Each situation, however, must be examined to determine a specific individual's participation in the activity.

of us among his carefully selected commission. This is hardly surprising considering that Ed Meese is a known adversary of the black community. Perhaps he thought blacks were too perverse to ever agree that porn debased women, destroyed the family and caused violent rapes and sexual promiscuity. More likely he realized that it would be difficult to find a black representative of his/her community who viewed porn as a major issue. In one sense, we were relieved that Meese's attention was diverted from restoring us to our nineteenth-century status and that instead he had decided to concentrate on regulating what all Americans can do in the privacy of their own homes. To that extent, he has become an equal-opportunity enforcer of the denial of human rights to all members of this society.

Most blacks would agree with Dr. Morris Lipton, one of the experts on the 1970 presidential report on pornography, that "given the major issues of the day, pornography is a trivial issue." Blacks would add to that analysis the caveat that porn is a white man's problem—a particular kind of white man's problem. The presidential commission Dr. Lipton served on found that the typical consumer of porn was a white male and that blacks were underrepresented among the purveyors of erotica. However, blacks were not total abstainers from porn consumerism. Nor did they harbor any particular antipathy toward it. Indeed, many today do buy sex videocassettes, purchase *Penthouse* and enjoy risqué jokes, cartoons, etc. But as a group that earns only 56 percent of the income whites do, they often do not have the discretionary income with which to purchase erotica.

As for the black position on porn, it would certainly differ from that arrived at by the Meese commission. Meese and his minions reflect a particular white worldview that there is something inherently damaging and sinful about sexual activity and interest outside the marital bedroom, and that any participation in other kinds of sexual behavior should produce enormous amounts of guilt in the errant individual. Blacks have traditionally had a more naturalistic attitude toward human sexuality, seeing it as the normal expression of sexual attraction between men and women. Even in African societies, sexual conduct was not the result of some divine guidance by God or other deities. It was secularly regulated and encompassed the tolerance of a wide range of sexual attitudes and behaviors. Sexual deviance, where so defined, was not an act against God's will but a violation of community standards.

Rather than seeing the depiction of heterosexual intercourse or nudity as an inherent debasement of women, as a fringe group of feminists claims, the black community would see women as having equal rights to the enjoyment of sexual stimuli. It is nothing more than a continuation of the white male's traditional double standard and paternalism to regard erotica as existing only for male pleasure and women only as sexual objects. Since that double standard has never attracted many American blacks, the claim that women are exploited by exhibiting their nude bodies or engaging in heterosexual intercourse lacks credibility. After all, it was the white missionaries in fourteenth century Africa who forced African women to regard their quasi-nude bodies as sinful and placed them in clothes. This probably accounts for the rather conspicuous absence of black women in the feminist fight against porn. Certainly black men were unlikely to join with the likes of lunatic feminists such as Catharine MacKinnon and Andrea Dworkin, who treat pornography as discrimination against women. They belong to the same genre of feminists as Susan Brownmiller, whose book *Against Our Will* implied that black men deserve some kind of punishment for even thinking about the sexual possession of white women. She even suggests that Emmett Till, the murdered victim of white men in Mississippi, was engaging in more than innocent flirtation when he whistled at a white woman. In her view, lust in a male's heart translates into the mental rape of women.

The black community represents organic evidence against some of the assumptions of the Meese commission on pornography. If porn is alleged to lead to male sexual aggression, that is, rape, why are the lowest consumers of porn (blacks) so overrepresented among those arrested for and convicted of rape? A porn commission without a political axe to grind might have concluded that when other expressions of manhood such as gainful employment and economic success are blocked, those men will express their frustration and masculinity against women. In other words, it is the denial of economic rights, not porn, that is in large part responsible for rape in this country. Such a conclusion would not go down well with the Reagan administration, whose policies have led to the burgeoning number of unemployed black males.

As for the Meese commission view that porn is related to sexual promiscuity, it is almost a laughable finding in the black community. One man's sexual promiscuity is another man's definition of sexual freedom. In most cases it refers to keeping women in their sexual straitjackets so that sexual pleasure remains a male domain. The black community has exhibited a lusty sexual appetite while obeying certain rules of common sense and propriety in its sexual conduct. The kinds of kinky sex favored by a small minority of whites is almost unknown among the black population. Group sex, and sexual crimes other than rape, were and are rare among us. And a recent survey commissioned by the National Institutes of Health found that sexually active black women were more likely to be involved in long-term "serious" relationships than were sexually active white women, and that their serious relationships lasted longer than the relationships of white women.

Still, it is one of the ironies of American life that the one racial group in the U.S. whose image is so strongly linked to sexuality in the public mind should be excluded from a commission dealing with the sexual aspects of human behavior. Ranging from the thousands of lynchings of black men for the dubious sin of lusting after white women to the segregation of races in the South to prevent interracial sexual contact, we now have the more recent variation on the theme of black immorality.

While there may be cause for concern over the high rate of out-of-wedlock births occurring among black women in their teenage years, the Meese commission refused to endorse the best weapon against teenage pregnancy—sex education. The same National Institutes of Health survey discovered that twice as many single black women as white women are having sex through their 20s without contraceptives. Nationally, a majority of all out-of-wedlock births occur among black women. Ultimately, blacks suffer more and are the chief victims of white sexual guilt. They are denied sex education in the public schools because a white-controlled bureaucracy either denies it to the school system or forces it to contain a largely moral content. However, in those few public schools that have decided to provide contraceptive services to their students, only schools with a predominantly black student body have chosen to do so. Using black high-school students as the first guinea pigs in these experiments is akin to the same kind of white colonialism that tested birth-control products on Puerto Rican women to see if they would be safe for white women.

Teenage pregnancy is a problem in the black community because the unwed mothers keep their children and many become dependent on public assistance. The N.I.H. survey found that half of the white women surveyed and only one-tenth of the black women aborted their first pregnancies. Young black women seldom resort to shotgun weddings, because their pool of potential husbands largely consists of young and unemployed black males. Were they to be provided a sound sex education or safe contraceptives, many would never face this dilemma.

The kinds of morals that Ed Meese and Ronald Reagan understand are related to nineteenth-century notions of sin. Blacks would prefer to see their morality expressed in the provision of jobs for the unemployed, shelter for the homeless and food for the hungry.

Finally, a most important reason why pornography is not a burning issue in the black community is that the morals of Ronald Reagan, Ed Meese and Jerry Falwell are not the morals of the kinds of people with which blacks desire to be associated. Their past record is one of supporting racial segregation and black deprivation. Therefore blacks can only hope they will cease to interfere with the private lives of American citizens and adopt a real moral posture toward the conditions of poverty, nuclear disarmament and the conduct of government. Permitting poverty to exist and escalating the nuclear-arms race are the real sins and major issues of today.

DISCUSSION QUESTIONS

1. What are the ethical issues involved in the debate over pornography and censorship?
2. Should the sale and distribution of obscene material be controlled at the local, state or national level? Should it be controlled at all?
3. Robert Staples contends that the government would allocate its resources more fruitfully if it provided sex education and directed its efforts to the real problems of unemployment, poverty and nuclear war rather than focusing of the role of pornography in society. Do you agree?
4. Do you agree or disagree with the ACLU position opposing "any restraint on the right to create, publish or distribute materials to adults, or the rights of adults to choose the materials they read or view on the basis of obscenity, pornography or indecency?"

11

HUMAN RIGHTS

Peter Augustine Lawler

The idea of human rights is the product of philosophy. It comes from the thought that it is possible to determine through human reason what human beings possess simply by virtue of their humanity. This thought is fully at home only in the West (Europe and America). It has been accepted by the rest of the world only insofar as it has been transformed by the West.

The United States, through its Declaration of Independence, was the first nation founded on abstract or rational principle. What makes an American an American more than culture or religion or tradition is the acceptance of the truth of the Declaration's principles. For the Declaration, the purpose of government is to secure or protect rights, rights which all human beings (not just Anglo-Saxons or males or whites or Christians) share by virtue of their common nature.

The Declaration's doctrine of natural rights is indebted, above all, to the English philosopher John Locke. For Locke, human beings are by nature individuals, each with the right to whatever is necessary to preserve his or her own *life.* Each individual is given by nature the *liberty* to secure him or herself as well as possible. Obedience to government can only be justified by the individual's consent in the service of this self-protection. But mere self-preservation is not enough; individuals naturally want to live well. Each individual, as a result, has the right, insofar as it does not threaten the lives and liberty of others, to the *pursuit of happiness,* as he or she defines it.

Locke's doctrine is rather easily criticized for its selfish materialism. Strictly applied, it would produce a foreign policy in which Americans would use other peoples as tools for their own security and prosperity. But Americans have never been completely satisfied with such an interpretation of the Declaration. They have always been conscious of a moral dimension to the universalism of their principles. They have understood them, in part, to raise America above the ranks of selfish nations and hence to give their nation a global mission on behalf of human liberty. Americans have typically been moralistic and sometimes even selfless when it comes to the rights of oppressed individuals and peoples throughout the world.

The intrinsic idealism of the American interpretation of natural rights opened it to the influence of the thought of the German philosopher Immanuel Kant. Kant redefined the idea of rights to do justice to the human being's freedom from natural or merely bodily concerns. For Kant, rights are the recognition of the dignity of *autonomous* beings. Human beings have rights because they are capable of conceiving rational laws for themselves and obeying them. It makes no sense to speak of natural rights, only of *human* rights.

Kant also taught it was reasonable to hope that the world was being transformed by human freedom. He saw evidence that governments throughout the world were reforming themselves on the basis of a growing recognition of the rights or dignity of all free and rational beings. They would all eventually become liberal democracies. This Kantian optimism found its home in America most eloquently in the rhetoric of Woodrow Wilson, especially in his articulation of his hopes for the League of Nations after World War I.

This optimism concerning the progress of the world toward democracy was exploded in the 1930s by the phenomenon of totalitarianism, particularly Marxist communism in the Soviet Union. No longer could it reasonably be believed that the world's movement away from traditional oppression would inevitably promote human freedom and dignity. The West's future, it suddenly appeared, need not be friendly to human rights. The friends of human rights became "anti-communists"; their new task was to resist rather than to promote revolution.

American policy, in this new light, became rather conservative and negative. It knew what it opposed, but it became vague on what it promoted. Americans lost confidence, as a result, in the universal significance and goodness of their principles and institutions. This uncertainty, more than anything else, was responsible for the perception of America's decline in the sixties and seventies.

The selections in this chapter are representative of recent attempts to reinvigorate America's sense of purpose as the world's leading example of a nation dedicated to the protection of human rights. The first selection is from a speech by President Jimmy Carter in 1977 in which he announced the goals of his foreign policy. His policy was to be a reflection of America's "character." America was to overcome the "moral crisis" of Vietnam and regain its "moral stature" before the world by employing its foreign policy to contribute to the "dramatic, worldwide advances in the protection of the individual from the arbitrary power of the state." The morality-negating "inordinate fear of communism" was to recede with the growth of the awareness that communism is not to be the world's future.

The second selection, from a speech given by Carter's Assistant Secretary of State for Human Rights and Humanitarian Affairs, Patricia Derian, in 1979 states more specifically the premises which guided the formulation and implementation of Carter's human rights policy in reference to individuals who disappear because of political kidnapping. She explains the different kinds of disappearances and how governments can be held accountable.

Perhaps the sternest critic of the Carter policy was political scientist Jeane Kirkpatrick, who became President Reagan's Ambassador to the United Nations. She came to Reagan's attention as a critic of Carter's decisions to ignore or at least downgrade the authoritarian-totalitarian distinction. In this third selection, a speech before the UN, Kirkpatrick demands that rights be defined precisely in terms of the individual's freedom from government, that the connection between democracy and the protection of rights be recognized, and that the UN promote the cause of human liberty against all oppressive governments.

President Reagan, after some hesitation, affirmed Carter's choice of a morally-inspiring, human rights-oriented foreign policy. He also attempted to define the idea of rights more precisely. He returned to a great extent, in opposition to contemporary doctrines expanding and diluting the idea of human rights, to the Lockean doctrine of the American founders. To ennoble that understanding, he has used not so much the utopianism of Kant as the belief of Americans in the biblical, personal God. Reagan said, in his New Year's 1986 Address to the Soviet people, that "[i]t is a sacred truth to us that every individual is a unique creation of God." That uniqueness, properly understood, becomes the strongest foundation for the individual's claims of freedom against government.

The final selection is an excerpt from a careful, subtle effort by Clifford Orwin and Thomas Pangle to interpret the philosophical argument for human rights in a way friendly to the Reagan agenda. The authors propose a combination of Lockean and Kantian individualism to counter Marxian and relativistic doctrines destructive of the idea of rights. They also, on a Lockean basis, distinguish between economic goals and economic rights. They do not follow the Reagan initiative of drawing upon the biblical understanding of the human person, perhaps because they do not view that understanding as a product of philosophy.

Address at Notre Dame, May 22, 1977

President Jimmy Carter

In his 25 years as president of Notre Dame, Father Hesburgh has spoken more consistently and more effectively in the support of the rights of human beings than any other person I know. His interest in the Notre Dame Center for Civil Rights has never wavered. And that concern has been demonstrated again today in vivid fashion by the selection of Bishop Donald Lamont, Paul Cardinal Arns, and Stephen Cardinal Kim to receive honorary degrees. In their fight for human freedoms in Rhodesia, Brazil, and South Korea, these three religious leaders typify all that is best in their countries and in our church. I'm honored to join you in recognizing their dedication, their personal sacrifice, and their supreme courage.

Quite often, brave men like these are castigated and sometimes punished, sometimes even put to death, because they enter the realm where human rights is a struggle. And sometimes they are blamed for the very circumstances which they helped to dramatize, but its' been there for a long time. And the flames which they seek to extinguish concern us all and are increasingly visible around the world.

Last week, I spoke in California about the domestic agenda for our Nation: to provide more efficiently for the needs of our people, to demonstrate—against the dark faith of our times—that our Government can be both competent and more humane.

But I want to speak to you today about the strands that connect our actions overseas with our essential character as a nation. I believe we can have a foreign policy that is democratic, that is based on fundamental values, and that uses power and influence, which we have, for humane purposes. We can also have a foreign policy that the American people both support and, for a change, know about and understand.

I have a quiet confidence in our own political system. Because we know that democracy works, we can reject the arguments of those rulers who deny human rights to their people.

We are confident that democracy's example will be compelling, and so we seek to bring that example closer to those from whom in the past few years we have been separated and who are not yet convinced about the advantages of our kind of life.

President Jimmy Carter, "Address at Notre Dame," excerpts from his Address at the Commencement Exercises at the University of Notre Dame. May 22, 1977.

We are confident of our own strength, so we can seek substantial mutual reductions in the nuclear arms race.

And we are confident of the good sense of American people, and so we let them share in the process of making foreign policy decisions. We can thus speak with the voices of 215 million and not just of an isolated handful.

Democracy's great recent successes—in India. Portugal. Spain. Greece—show that our confidence in this system is not misplaced. Being confident of our future, we are now free of that inordinate fear of communism which once led us to embrace any dictator who joined us in that fear. I'm glad that that's being changed.

For too many years, we've been willing to adopt the flawed and erroneous principles and tactics of our adversaries, sometimes abandoning our own values for theirs. We've fought fire with fire never thinking that fire is better quenched with water. This approach failed with Vietnam, the best example of its intellectual and moral poverty. But through failure we have now found our way back to our own principles and values, and we have regained our lost confidence.

By the measure of history our Nation's 200 years are very brief and our rise to world eminence is briefer still. It dates from 1945, when Europe and the old international order lay in ruins. Before then, America was largely on the periphery of world affairs. But since then we have inescapably been at the center of world affairs.

Our policy during this period was guided by two principles: a belief that Soviet expansion was almost inevitable but that it must be contained and the corresponding belief in the importance of an almost exclusive alliance among non-Communist nations on both sides of the Atlantic. That system could not last forever unchanged historical trends have weakened its foundation. The unifying threat of conflict with the Soviet Union has become less intensive, even though the competition has become more extensive.

The Vietnamese war produced a profound moral crisis, sapping worldwide faith in our own policy and our system of life, a crisis of confidence made even more grave by the covert pessimism of some of our leaders.

In less than a generation we've seen the world change dramatically. The daily lives and aspirations of most human beings have been transformed. Colonialism is nearly gone. A new sense of national identity now exists in almost 100 new countries that have been formed in the last generation. Knowledge has become more widespread. Aspirations are higher. As more people have been freed from traditional constraints, more have been determined to achieve for the first time in their lives, social justice.

The world is still divided by ideological disputes, dominated by regional conflicts and threatened by danger that we will not resolve the differences of race and wealth without violence or without drawing into combat the major military powers. We can no longer separate the traditional issues of war and peace from the new global questions of justice, equity, and human rights.

It is a new world, but America should not fear it. It is a new world, and we should help to shape it. It is a new world that calls for a new American foreign policy—a policy based on constant decency in its values and on optimism in our historical vision.

We can no longer expect that the other 150 nations will follow the dictates of the powerful but must continue—confidently—our efforts to inspire, to persuade, and to lead.

Our policy must reflect our belief that the world can hope for more than simple survival and our belief that dignity and freedom are fundamental spiritual requirements. Our policy must shape an international system that will last longer than secret deals.

We cannot make this kind of policy by manipulation. Our policy must be open; it must be candid, it must be one of constructive global involvement, resting on five cardinal principles.

I've tried to make these premises clear to the American people since last January. Let me review what we have been doing and discuss what we intend to do.

First, we have reaffirmed America's commitment to human rights as a fundamental tenet of our foreign policy. In ancestry, religion, color, place of origin, and cultural background, we Americans are as diverse a nation as the world has ever seen. No common mystique of blood or soil unites us. What draws us together, perhaps more than anything else is a belief in human freedom. We want the world to know that our Nation stands for more than financial prosperity.

This does not mean that we can conduct our foreign policy by rigid moral maxims. We live in a world that is imperfect and which will always be imperfect—a world that is complex and confused and which will always be complex and confused.

I understand fully the limits of moral suasion. We have no illusion that changes will come easily or soon. But I also believe that it is a mistake to undervalue the power of words and of the ideas that words embody. In our own history, that power has ranged from Thomas Paine's "Common Sense" to Martin Luther King, Jr.'s "I Have a Dream."

In the life of the human spirit, words *are* action, much more so than many of us may realize who live in countries where freedom of expression is taken for granted. The leaders of totalitarian nations understand this very well. The proof is that words are precisely the action for which dissidents in those countries are being persecuted.

Nonetheless, we can already see dramatic, worldwide advances in the protection of the individual from the arbitrary power of the state. For us to ignore this trend would be to lose influence and moral authority in the world. To lead it will be to regain the moral stature that we once had.

The great democracies are not free because we are strong and prosperous. I believe we are strong and influential and prosperous because we are free.

Throughout the world today, in free nations and in totalitarian countries as well, there is a preoccupation with the subject of human freedom, human rights. And I believe it is incumbent on us in this country to keep that discussion, that debate, that contention alive. No other country is as well-qualified as we to set an example. We have our own shortcomings and faults, and we should strive constantly and with courage to make sure that we are legitimately proud of what we have....

Missing and Disappeared Persons

Patricia M. Derian

I welcome this opportunity to appear before you and your colleagues and commend the committee for its initiative in conducting these hearings on missing or disappeared persons. We consider this problem to be one of the most serious human rights issues confronting the world today, necessitating attention and action not only by the United States but by all members of the international community. This was the view expressed by the U.S. Representative to the Human Rights Commission to Committee III of the United Nations last December and reiterated by him at the U.N. Human Rights Commission earlier this year. It remains our view today.

In your previous hearings, distinguished witnesses from a variety of nongovernmental human rights organizations have provided considerable detail on the disappearance phenomenon. We believe their accounts were carefully researched and accurate. I do not intend to rehearse those details at any great length. Previous testimony has made them painfully familiar to all of us.

Patricia M. Derian, "Missing and Disappeared Persons." Statement before the Subcommittee on International Organizations of the House Foreign Affairs Committee, October 18, 1979. Reprinted from *Department of State Bulletin* (February 1980), 37–39.

What I should like to do today, in accordance with your letter to Secretary Vance requesting my appearance, is to:

- Provide you the Administration's views and response to this relatively new violation of human rights;
- Discuss some of the remedies being proposed both on the bilateral and multilateral levels; and
- Examine the role of our embassies and human rights officers in those countries where disappearances are reliably reported.

Finally, I shall give you a status report on our efforts to give effect to U.N. Resolution 33/173 on disappeared persons adopted by the General Assembly on December 20, 1978.

VIEWS ON AND RESPONSE TO DISAPPEARANCES

As I stated at the outset, the United States views the use of officially sanctioned political kidnappings as one of the most serious problems confronting the international community. Disappearances have become one of the more tragic and insidious instances of human rights abuse occurring in today's world. Coupled with the failure of governments to account for those missing, this disturbing development has been causing intense anguish and suffering for countless individuals and families in many parts of the world. As you know, the word "disappeared" itself has become a euphemism for what often appears to or does amount to political murder, preceded by intensive interrogation and torture of those not charged with any crime.

FORMS OF DISAPPEARANCES

I would like to review very briefly the forms that disappearances take. In one, governmental policy directs the security forces, military, and/or police to round up all persons suspected of subversion to get them out of circulation, to obtain information, to halt specific acts, and to demoralize the "opposition." There are no constraints of any kind placed on those charged with the roundup.

In another, security or police forces operate "unofficially," generally in civilian clothes, with the tacit approval or acquiescence and under the umbrella of protection from the state.

In a third, groups of "civilians," often with official urging or approval, operate their own terrorist forces. (When "unauthorized" groups bring too much embarrassment to the government or when the government wishes to end their actions, it often finds that is has set in motion a force which eludes its control. They are then faced with the problem of trying to contain a group which is nominally its own.)

In all forms, people are abducted from their homes, offices, or while moving about in public. Sometimes operations are strictly clandestine—no one sees the pickup, no phone calls or messages are delivered; people simply vanish. On other occasions, a street or an area is blocked off by unmarked cars, a force of armed men—nearly always in civilian clothes—storms a building or house and emerges with the person or persons who are taken away. Or a group of armed men stops their car in traffic, leaps onto the street with drawn guns, and wrestles the victim into a car and speeds away.

The victims are taken to secret places of detention, often military installations, and tortured for periods ranging from hours to months. Sometimes they die as a consequence of torture, sometimes they are killed in detention, and sometimes they are set up for death in a flamboyant and public way. They may be loaded into a car or van, told to drive away after being given arms without ammunition, followed, and killed in a "shootout." A few endure and eventually find themselves in a regular place of detention. These people may be held indefinitely without trial or charges or they may be charged, tried, and sentenced to official jail terms by military or civilian courts. A miniscule number are released at some stage of the process.

At no point do any parts of the system of justice or the rule of law or due process operate on behalf of the disappeared. They disappear not only literally but also as legal entities.

They do not disappear from the thoughts of their families, however. And what becomes of them? Sometimes they are too frightened to take any action or tell anyone what has happened; this is often the case in the first period of disappearances.

Sooner or later, though, an inquiry is made to some official unit. They are told that there is no record of an arrest; there is no information. Occasionally, the family will receive an anonymous phone call which might say that the disappeared person will be released soon, is all right, or if an infant or child has been taken, might request some item for the child or tell where the child can be picked up if the child is not to be held. But the search is fruitless unless a body is found or the person finally surfaces in prison. Otherwise, the family members wait in tense anguish for months or years. For some there will probably never be an answer.

Responsibility for remedying the tragic phenomenon of disappearances rests with the government which shuts its eyes to or colludes in or engineers disappearances. Whether these disappearances are the result of authorized actions, unauthorized excesses by law enforcement and security agencies, paramilitary or private groups, governments are responsible for bringing them under control, even in times of emergency. In confronting domestic violence or terrorism, there is no justification under domestic or international law for such violations.

Governments furthermore cannot argue that they do not know. Governments are custodians of the law. When they engage in their own campaign of terror, they jeopardize the rule of law and their right to govern. They are no different at those times than the worst of their opponents.

International law, as set forth in the International Covenant on Civil and Political Rights (article 4), the European Convention for the Protection of Human Rights and Fundamental Freedoms (article 15), and the American Convention on Human Rights (article 27) prohibits states, even in times of public emergency, from abandoning certain fundamental guarantees afforded the individual.

Under no circumstances can a state arbitrarily deprive its citizens of their lives or subject them to torture or cruel, inhuman, or degrading punishment. Death sentences can be imposed only in accordance with due process of law. Governments are responsible for the safety and protection of those detained. They are also responsible for rendering an accounting of the whereabouts and fate of those apprehended.

There is now available a well-developed body of human rights standards and precedents. It is up to individual countries to realize them. The United States tries to influence other nations to live up to common international obligations. In the final analysis, the decision to comply with international law—and to do what is right—rests with the individual country. While our ability to influence other nations' human rights performance varies from country to country. I can assure you we are assiduous in our efforts to persuade governments to halt disappearances and accompanying excesses and to insure that those guilty of such practices must be punished in accordance with law.

We urge all governments in whose countries there are disappeared persons to release prisoners arbitrarily detained, to provide the guarantee of fair trial, to publish lists of those missing, and to provide death certificates for those known to be killed. We also urge that they return remains to relatives and establish governmental mechanisms, together with the courts, to trace missing people and clarify their status for their relatives.

In my discussions with the families of the disappeared—both here in Washington and abroad—they emphasize that it would be easier for them to suffer the knowledge of the death of their relatives than to suffer continuous uncertainty about their fates. In most countries, this would represent an act of strength and courage on the part of the government and indicate a desire for national reconciliation, peace, and return to the rule of law.

In our discussions with a variety of governments, we have pointed out that ample precedents exist in international law for dealing with the problem of accounting for those taken prisoner as a result of domestic and international conflicts. During periods of armed conflict and occupation, the 1949 Geneva Convention Relative to the Treatment of Prisoners of War and the 1949 Geneva Convention Relative to the Protection of Civilian Persons in Time of War require parties to implement a variety of reporting and other mechanisms to account for prisoners of war and "protected persons."

More recently in July 1977, additional protocols to the Geneva conventions set forth, in the context of armed conflict, even more detailed provisions for tracing the missing and the dead and for protecting the human rights of those held in captivity.

Protocol I asserts "the right of families to know the fate of their relatives," requires governments to gather and transmit all relevant information concerning persons reported missing by an adverse party, and imposes several obligations concerning the remains of all persons who have died for reasons related to hostilities. These legal requirements make available to countries standards and procedures for dealing with prisoners of war and other detained or interned persons and for handling the problem of missing persons in a humane manner.

Let me digress for a moment and explain a dilemma with which we are sometimes faced. In certain countries there have been efforts by some authorities to eliminate the disappearance phenomenon. The numbers of disappeared may decline dramatically. The question then arises of how the United States should respond. Quite clearly, even one person disappearing is one too many. But if we elect not to recognize this "progress," we may perhaps run the risk of strengthening the hands of individuals in or outside a repressive government who may argue that the U.S. human rights appetite is insatiable. If, on the other hand, we choose to recognize the "progress" that has been made, certain governments may incorrectly conclude that we are reconciled to some irreducible minimum of disappearances or other human rights violations. These are not easy questions to resolve. Difficult judgments and hard choices are required. We confront such problems every day, and in almost every case there are honest differences of opinion on how we can best resolve them.

It is also appropriate to note here that this, like other forms of official human rights violations, is not endemic to any country and is not an inevitable concomitant of political unrest or instability. Some of today's worst offenders have long previous histories of high respect for individual rights, even in times of crisis, which gives us hope that they can return to their best traditions. And in recent times, some whose practices have been most deplored have, indeed, done so and thereby not only regained the respect of the world community but also set an example for others.

ROLE OF EMBASSIES AND HUMAN RIGHTS OFFICERS

Permit me now to speak about the role of our embassies and the human rights officers in embassies in countries where disappearances take place.

Each embassy has a human rights officer usually in the Political Section whose responsibility is to report on human rights conditions and to present the U.S. Government's views to the host government. Our Ambassadors are charged with human rights responsibilities as personal representatives of the President. They are deeply conscious of the priority he has assigned to human rights in our foreign policy. As the President noted in his remarks to the Hispanic Caucus on September 13th: "From the day that I took office, I have sought to place at the top of my agenda and to awaken the conscience of the world and to bring that conscience about human rights to bear on the world's leaders."

An important part of a human rights officer's responsibilities is to maintain contact with individuals and groups most aware of human rights conditions in the country in which he/she works. He or she must be active and energetic in seeking out these contacts. These include private human rights groups; representatives of the religious community, the legal profession, political opposition, and dissident groups; and the families and friends of victims of human rights abuses including the disappeared. Often as important, but sometimes more difficult to manage, are contacts with government agencies responsible for the judicial system, the management of detention centers, and the general administration of justice.

In countries where disappearances have been commonplace, we have registered our disapproval of this phenomenon in the strongest possible terms, emphasizing as well the damage it does to our bilateral relationship and the negative effects it may have on all aspects of our relationship including the assistance we provide.

We talk on two levels; one on the principles concerned [with] the problem itself, clearly and specifically, and we make formal and informal representations about the disappeared on our own initiative and at the behest of the families and friends of the disappeared. Members of the Congress, private citizens, and human rights organizations. We present representation lists containing the names of the disappeared.

The sad reality is that even when a repressive government reaches a stage of willingness to look for certain of the disappeared, or when an individual official is disposed to be helpful in such a search, it is often unable to determine the whereabouts of an individual who may have been picked up by security agencies operating without the knowledge of other agencies or operatives acting independently without the knowledge of their superiors.

In some instances, during the early stages, our representations are disparaged. We are told that the disappearances, while unfortunate, are the unavoidable byproduct of the "war" against subversion or terrorism. We are asked why we are interested at all since the disappeared are not U.S. citizens but terrorists and criminals. It is suggested to us, and not obliquely, that we have no business meddling in another nation's internal affairs. As we enter the third year of this policy, however, these efforts to escape discussion of the issue have by and large been abandoned.

Needless to say, we reject categorically such self-serving and fundamentally erroneous distortions of the international human rights obligations of all countries. We are prepared to demonstrate, and indeed have demonstrated, our concern on this issue in a tangible way using the variety of foreign policy instruments provided by law and policy to the conduct of our foreign affairs.

U.S. SUPPORT FOR U.N. RESOLUTION 33/173

There is much the United States can and does do bilaterally in our efforts to attenuate and eventually eliminate this problem. Our efforts are enhanced when other states join in our representations and express concerns similar to our own.

At times world public opinion may seem ephemeral, but no country—no matter how unenlightened or repressive its regime—enjoys being the target of international scorn and obloquy. In nations where disappearances occur, we have joined with like-minded friends and allies to urge an end to this dreadful human rights violation. We work closely with other free nations to foster our international human rights objectives. There still is no more appropriate forum for such cooperation than the United Nations.

On December 20, 1978, the U.N. General Assembly adopted Resolution 33/173, on disappeared persons. Its genesis can be found in a growing awareness that in various parts of the world, enforced or involuntary disappearances of persons, as a result of excesses by law enforcement or security authorities, unhappily had become a common phenomenon. The resolution called upon governments to search for missing persons, hold law enforcement and security authorities fully accountable for disappearances, and to cooperate with other governments in locating or accounting for persons who disappear. The resolution also requested the U.N. Human Rights Commission to consider the question of the disappeared. It urged the U.N. Secretary General to use his good offices in disappearance cases and to draw the concerns expressed in the resolution to the attention of governments with a view toward disinterested humanitarian action.

The United States strongly supported this resolution, and is working to insure that it is implemented in the spirit which animated its adoption. In late August of 1979 in Geneva, the Subcommission on the Prevention of Discrimination and Protection of Minorities discussed the human rights of detained persons with special emphasis on the disappeared. The outcome of this discussion was a resolution adopted by the subcommission on September 5.

The subcommission considers that the resolution in question places not merely a legal but also a moral obligation, based on the principles of elementary humanity which inspire the international community on all those participating in U.N. activities. Nations are asked to take account at every appropriate opportunity of disappearances brought to their knowledge and to combine their efforts to try to locate the missing and disappeared persons.

The subcommission also proposes for Human Rights Commission approval the creation of a group of experts who would be given all the information available for locating disappeared and missing persons in various regions of the world and who would make necessary contacts with government and families concerned.

The subcommission also transmitted to the U.N. Secretary General several lists of missing persons with a view toward his exercising the good offices role urged in the General Assembly resolution of last December.

Finally, the subcommission suggests that if the disappearance phenomenon continues, its extreme gravity would justify some form of emergency remedy based on the notion of *habeas corpus* designed to induce governments to search for the disappeared.

What is striking about the subcommission's actions is that we are witnessing the beginning of the forging of machinery and procedures within the U.N. system to handle the disappearance phenomenon. The U.N. Human Rights Commission will consider the subcommission's recommendations at its meeting in Geneva in early 1980. I promise you the United States will do all it can to insure constructive action on the subcommission's proposals.

Let me conclude by reiterating my appreciation for the opportunity to appear before your committee, my admiration for the tremendous international public service this forum provides, and my assurances that this Administration remains totally committed to finding ways to mitigate and eliminate the egregious violation of human rights that "disappearances" represent.

Double Standards in Human Rights

Jeane J. Kirkpatrick

The Government of the United States was founded squarely and explicitly on the belief that the most basic function of government is to protect the rights of its citizens. Our Declaration of Independence states, "We hold these truths to be self-evident, that all men are created equal, that they are endowed by their creator with certain unalienable rights, that among these are life, liberty, and the pursuit of happiness." It adds, "To secure these rights, governments are instituted among men, deriving their just powers from the consent of the governed."

These notions—that the individual has rights which are prior to government, that protection of these rights is the very purpose of the existence of government, that the just powers of government depend on the consent of the governed—are the essential core of the American creed. That being the case, we naturally believe that the United Nations has no more important charge than the protection and expansion of the rights of persons. The charter commits the United Nations to this task; several bodies in the United Nations are explicitly devoted to it.

My government stands always ready to join other nations in any serious effort that will expand the perimeters of liberty, law, and opportunity. We believe that the rights of individuals are most effectively promoted and expanded by and through democratic political institutions—where governments are elected through periodic competitive elections, elections that feature freedom to criticize government, to publish criticisms, to organize opposition, and compete for power. Human rights violations may occur even in such systems, but they are relatively few and readily corrected. The reason that popular governments protect human rights best is that people do not impose tyrants upon themselves. Tyrants impose themselves upon people.

There would be no serious human rights abuses if all peoples enjoyed self-government and democracy. The dynamics of freedom and political competition could be relied upon to work to protect minorities, dissenters, and critics against the arbitrary use of governments' powers against them.

Jeane J. Kirkpatrick, U.S. Ambassador to the United Nations, "Double Standards in Human Rights." Statement before the Third Committee of the United Nations General Assembly, New York, 24 November 1981. Reprinted from *Department of State Bulletin* (February 1982), 65–67.

But, unfortunately, many—perhaps even most—people do not live in democracies but live instead under rulers whom they have not chosen and who cannot be counted upon to respect their rights.

Governments, moreover, are not the only source of oppression and tyranny. Serious political philosophers such as Thomas Hobbes, John Locke, Baron Montesquieu, Rousseau, and their medieval predecessors, among others, understood that human rights exist independently of government and that human rights violations exist independently of government as well; that human rights can be and are violated by private violence as well as by public coercion. A government of laws protects and expands rights because it protects individuals against private violence.

Because human rights can be violated by individuals and groups as well as by governments, the protection of human rights should necessarily have a double focus. It should take account of all major sources of abuse: violations by government and violations by private violence, including organized private violence. Tyranny and anarchy alike are incompatible with freedom, security, and the enjoyment of opportunity.

FAIR AND REASONABLE JUDGMENT

It is, of course, not enough for the partisans of freedom to define the character and identify the sources of human rights violations. A serious commitment to human rights by this or any group also requires that one's judgment be fair and reasonable. Fair judgment of a country's human rights practices would judge all by the same moral standards. A reasonable judgment requires that all nations be judged by criteria relevant to their specific character and situation. Thus, it is not fair to judge one nation or group by the Sermon on the Mount and all other nations on the curve; it is not reasonable to judge peaceful countries with a long experience of self-government by the same standards as strife-torn countries with weak legal and political institutions. And it is neither fair nor reasonable to judge the human rights violations of some nations harshly, while ignoring entirely the gross abuses of other peoples.

Although these principles would appear to be almost self-evident, some curious practices have grown up in recent years around the standard of human rights, as some persons and some governments have attempted to use human rights less as a standard and a goal than as a political weapon; less to expand the domains of freedom and law than to expand the scope of their hegemony.

To bring about this transformation of function, an effort has been mounted to deprive the concept of human rights of specific meaning by pretending that all objects of human desire are "rights" which can be had, if not for the asking then at least for the demanding. The proliferation of "rights"—to a happy childhood, to self-fulfillment, to development—has proceeded at the same time that the application of human rights standards has grown more distorted and more cynical.

No aspect of U.N. affairs has been more perverted by politicization of the last decade than have its human rights activities. In Geneva and in New York, human rights has become a bludgeon to be wielded by the strong against the weak, by the majority against the isolated, by the blocs against the unorganized. South Africa, Israel, and the non-Communist nations of South America have been the principal targets of U.N. human rights condemnation—South Africa on grounds of apartheid, Israel on grounds of alleged practices in the West Bank and in the territories occupied in the 1967 war, and assorted non-Communist Latin American countries because, in addition to being nondemocratic, they have been unorganized and unprotected in this body in which from time to time moral outrage is distributed much like violence in a protection racket.

My government believes that apartheid is a morally repugnant system which violates the rights of black peoples and colored who live under it. It is one system through which the inhabitants of one country are denied equal access to freedom, economic opportunity, and equal protection of the laws. It is one system by which one ruling minority refuses to share power and profits from its possession of monopoly power. As such, it is reprehensible. It cannot be condoned by governments and people who believe in government based on the consent of the governed, freely expressed in competitive elections in which all citizens are permitted to participate.

But let us be clear, apartheid is not the only system for denying people the enjoyment of freedom, the right to choose and criticize their rulers, the rule of law, the opportunity for a good job, a good education, a good life. There are other grounds on which other regimes in the last decade have denied their citizens dignity, freedom, equal protection of the law, material well-being and even life; other regimes that have more cruelly and more brutally repressed and slaughtered their citizens.

In my government's view, it is entirely appropriate that the agencies of the United Nations should condemn the spirit and the practice of apartheid and deplore its human consequences, providing, of course, that the same bodies of the United Nations demonstrate a serious moral concern for freedom...

The human rights agencies of the United Nations were silent while three million Kampucheans died in Pol Pot's murderous utopia; the human rights agencies of the United Nations were silent while a quarter of a million Ugandans died at the hands of Idi Amin. The human rights organizations of the United Nations have been silent about the thousands of Soviet citizens denied equal rights, equal protection of the law, denied the right to think, write, publish, work freely, or to emigrate to some place of their own choosing. As we meet here, Andrey Sakharov, one of the world's most distinguished physicists and bravest men, who has been confined to exile in Gorky, has entered upon a hunger strike to protest the refusal of the Soviet Government to allow his daughter-in-law to emigrate. But the United Nations is silent.

VIOLATIONS IN CUBA

The activities of the United Nations with respect to Latin America offer a particularly egregious example of moral hypocrisy. Four countries of Latin America were condemned for one or another human rights violation during the last General Assembly; resolutions condemning El Salvador, Guatemala, Chile, and Bolivia were voted last winter in Geneva during the sessions of the Human Rights Commission. Doubtless, some of these countries, some of these governments were guilty as charged.

But the moral standing of their judges is undermined by their studious unconcern with the much larger violations of human liberty elsewhere in Latin America by the government of Cuba. That government has driven over one million of its citizens into exile. It has incarcerated more political prisoners than any other Latin American nation. It has repressed freedom, denied equality and, incidentally, deprived its citizens of what is termed here the right to development—a talent for which Cuba had demonstrated a large capacity, prior to Fidel Castro's "liberating" revolution.

An especially instructive example of the quality of human rights in Cuba is the fate of Cuba's poets—virtually all of whom are in exile or in jail. Among the former are Heberto Padilla, winner of the National Union of Writers and Artists of Cuba (UNEAC) prize for poetry in 1968; Reinaldo Arenas, author of the novel *Hallucinations,* which was a best seller in Europe; Rogelio Llopis, whose short stories have been translated into English, German, Polish and Hungarian; Edmundo Desnoes; Antonio Benitez Rojo, whose stories won a UNEAC prize in 1968 and who, until he sought asylum in Paris in mid-1980, was the director of publications for Casa de las Americas; Jose Triana, recipient of a Casa award for his play *La Noche de los asesinos* (1965).

Less fortunate even than the poets who have been driven from their native land are those who rot in jail. Two of these cases are known and discussed all over the world by those who value freedom and respect human creativity. Angel Cuadra is an internationally celebrated poet whose works have been translated into English, German and Russian. He was arrested and charged with conduct "against the security of the state" after having unsuccessfully sought permission to emigrate from Cuba in 1967. Having served two-thirds of a 15-year sentence, he was paroled in 1976; but then an anthology of his elegiac, apolitical poetry was published in the United States and, as a result, his parole was revoked. From prison, Angel Cuadra wrote to the exiled poet Juana Rosa Pita in May 1979, "There was no legal basis for this new reprisal against me. Only that I am a poet; that the world speaks my name; that I do not renounce my song. I do not put it on bended knees, nor do I use it for other political or partisan ends, but only literary, universal, timeless ones." After participating in prison "rehabilitation programs," Cuadra was to be released again in July 1979. However, when the authorities learned that he had managed to smuggle out the manuscript of a new collection of his poetry which appeared in English translation under the title *A Correspondence of Poems*, they transferred him to Boniato prison instead of releasing him. Under a constitutional provision giving retroactive effect to penal laws favoring prisoners, Cuadra is entitled by Cuba's own laws to be set free; according to their constitutional norm, he has served his sentence. Nonetheless, his attempts to secure a court order for release have failed.

One of the most pathetic cases of all is that of the poet Armando Valladares, whose case, by the way, was described in length in *Le Monde* November 13. At the time of his arrest in 1960, Mr. Valladares was 23 years old. He was already writing poetry and painting, but at this young age he was not as yet published. After his incarceration, he continued to write and to draw, wherever possible. His poetry has been published in several languages in two volumes, the first entitled *From My Wheelchair*, the second, *The Heart With Which I Live*. His book, *Prisoner of Castro*, was published in both Spanish and French.

In recognition of Mr. Valladares' writing and his talent as a poet, the French PEN Club invited Mr. Valladares to become a member in 1979, and in the following year, 1980, awarded Mr. Valladares its "Liberty Prize." As a reprisal for the publication of these works, in 1979 Mr. Valladares was moved to the remote prison of Boniato, and deprived of his possessions, including all his books and his Bible. He is currently confined at Combinado des Este prison. As further reprisals for having written his book and poetry, his elderly parents and sister, having received permission to emigrate, were told that they would be allowed to leave only if Valladares were to write a letter to the foreign press denouncing the publication of his work. In a letter sent to PEN in 1980, Valladares wrote that such a letter would be the equivalent to "committing moral and spiritual suicide," and he refused to write it.

Mr. Valladares has never had specific charges brought against him. He has not violated any of Cuba's laws or regulations. He did not participate in any terrorist activities; no munitions, arms, or explosives were ever found in his home or in his possession. The sole reason for his 20 years of imprisonment is that he did not share the Cuban Government's ideology and, furthermore, that he refused to submit to its rehabilitation programs. In August 1974, the prison director ordered that no food be given to Mr. Valladares and, after 49 days of such imprisonment and punishment, he was left a total invalid. This is, of course, a direct violation of Article 5 of the Universal Declaration, regarding cruel punishment.

Armando Valladares has been officially adopted by Amnesty International as a prisoner of conscience and Amnesty International has submitted numerous appeals on his behalf. The International PEN Club has also appealed for his release, as well as the London-based Writers and Scholars International and many other human rights organizations all over the world. On November 12, 1980, the French PEN Club wrote to the Cuban ambassador in Paris but received no reply.

The Venezuelan Government has repeatedly asked for the release of Mr. Valladares. In 1979, a Venezuelan official met with Carlos Rafael Rodriquez, Vice Prime Minister of Cuba, to ask for Valladares' release. During the nonaligned conference held in Havana during the fall of 1979, the same official met with Fidel Castro and pleaded again for Valladares' release on humanitarian grounds. Since then, the President of Venezuela, Herrera Campins, has also explored the possibility of gaining Valladares' release through various Cuban Government channels. But all attempts have failed.

CONCLUSION

What are we to think of defenders of human rights who ignore the victims of major tyrants and focus all their ferocity on the victims of minor tyrants? Nothing is more necessary with respect to the treatment of human rights questions in the United Nations than to affirm and to adhere to a single standard. For if we do not have a single standard, then our resolutions and recommendations are merely tendentious political statements without moral content. Either we consistently uphold the right of all people to be free, regardless of the kind of system they live under, or we do not, ourselves, have the right to talk about human rights and to make recommendations that we expect others will follow.

In a word, nothing less than the moral integrity of the United Nations is at issue in our deliberations here. Nothing less than the commitment of this organization to its own reason for being is at stake.

The Philosophical Foundation of Human Rights

Clifford Orwin and Thomas Pangle

...Today we find ourselves in a situation for which the twofold [Lockean and Kantian] philosophic tradition underlying human rights does not offer unambiguous guidance. As a composite of different stages of Western thought, it is often at tension with itself, its two strands sustaining contradictory political conclusions. But far graver is the fact that the entire complex tradition has been superseded, in the predominant intellectual circles, by two newer understandings of politics that are hostile to the very notion of permanent, universal, and inviolable individual rights. One such understanding is Marxism, and the other is moral relativism.

If only for the sake of argument or because their opponents force them to it, Marxist and quasi-Marxist regimes have also taken to talking of human rights. For Marx himself, it must be noted, the rights of man offered a typically insidious example of "bourgeois formalism." They were the deceitful and self-deceiving veil behind which the bourgeois minority hid its exploitation of the proletarian majority. It is not only that these principles did not tend to the equal economic benefit of all—something, of course, that they had never pretended to do—but that they expressed, in their focus on the individual, an outmoded and perverted view of man. Self-concern, competitiveness, the family, and private property—all these must be dissolved in the cauldron of human "species-being" and by the abolition of the division of labor.

It is no wonder, then, that contemporary Marxist regimes greet criticism stated in terms of human rights with a collectivist reinterpretation of these that utterly transforms their original meaning. Sometimes, to be sure, they merely lie. Honoring the imposing example of Stalin's Constitution of 1935, they claim to extend to the individual a wide range of rights that they in fact deny him. Even in so lying, however, they assert that possession of such rights is contingent upon respect for collective interests. Insofar as Marxists will speak of sacrosanct human rights, they will vest them not in

Clifford Orwin and Thomas Pangle, "The Philosophical Foundation of Human Rights," in *Human Rights in our Time*, ed. Marc Plattner (Boulder, CO: Westview Press, 1984), 12–21. Originally published in *This World*, Fall 1982. Edited version reprinted with permission of Westview Press.

the individual but in the proletariat as a class, in the Marxist state, or the party—or, in the case of Third World pseudo-Marxists, in the popular or national will as divined by the nation's leaders. Rather than protecting the individual, "human rights" thus understood provide an unfailing excuse for ignoring and oppressing him. Hence that combination of surly contempt and aggrieved self-righteousness with which Marxist countries greet Western sallies in support of human rights.

The impact of moral (or historical or cultural) relativism on human rights is something to which we alluded in the first pages of this essay. Relativism makes human rights impossible in theory and so has confused and eroded commitment to them in practice. If there are no permanent, universal, and knowable standards of good or bad for human beings (whether founded, as Locke thought, in nature or, as Kant believed, in reason and history), there can be no authoritative enumeration of human rights. Like everything else in the moral realm, human rights become historically or culturally relative, or a matter of individual preference. No rational defense of human rights is possible, whether of the notion in general or of any particular version of it. This is a far cry from the "self-evident truths" that once presided over liberal democracy, as it is also from a Kantian faith in a rational historical process of which liberal society is the culmination. It means that however deeply we may happen to cherish our Western heritage of human rights, we have no rational ground for complaint if somebody thumbs his nose at them or is pleased to insist on an alternative list. For such a person rejects them with either more nor less right than we cherish them.

ECONOMIC, SOCIAL, AND CULTURAL RIGHTS?

All of these confusions, and the diffidence stemming from them, converge on the issue of "economic, social, and cultural" rights. These are rights that, as their names imply, know how to keep their distance from civil and political ones. They include such things as a right to health, to housing, to education, to employment, and to many other goods. Separate United Nations covenants deal with each of these two "baskets" of rights, political and non-political. This implicit recognition of the parity of the two has rightly been viewed as a victory for the Soviet Union as the patriarch of every society that underwrites, widely if not well, many of the rights just listed while quashing civil and political ones. Because there are now so many such societies, however, actual or merely aspiring, the victory is not that of the Russians alone, and it is no accident that in recent decades it has been this newer set of human rights that has tended to dominate international public discourse. The argument is often heard, and most of the nations of the world act as though they accept it, that nations must crawl before they can walk and that "economic, social, and cultural" rights are both more basic than, and a prerequisite of, civil and political ones.

At least as far as certain fundamental economic and social rights are concerned, there is some sense to this position. Nobody would deny that some degree of safety, health, and prosperity comprise the most urgent requirements of human beings. Nor may we doubt that civil and political freedoms will not long survive, nor easily come into being, where the longings for these basic goods are frustrated. Precisely because nobody would deny these things, however—least of all the founders of the original human rights tradition, so insistent on civil and political rights—we must attend to what may be lurking behind the current stress on these obvious points.

The notion of subpolitical rights is not in itself novel; Locke, it will be remembered, argued for natural rights to life, liberty, and property. What he meant by the last of these, however, was not a claim against society for any fixed degree of property, but the freedom or opportunity for all, within reasonable limits of law, to endeavor to acquire property and, having acquired it, to dispose of it. This right he presented as a natural and necessary extension of the right to endeavor to preserve oneself. And he went on to argue that in order for an individual to enjoy it in security, civil and political rights are required as well. Hence that venerable Lockean slogan, "no taxation without representation," which also implies the gamut of liberties needed to insure that representation is more than merely nominal.

In urging economic freedom for all under law as the crucial economic right, and in insisting on civil and political rights as its indispensable handmaidens, Locke articulated two of the cardinal premises of modern liberal democracy. He was also the proponent of a third, the truth of which has now been established for Western and non-Western societies alike: the efficacy of the combination of economic, civil, and political freedoms in fostering economic growth. In all of these respects, however, "economic rights" a la the United Nations present a rather different picture.

The ultimate primacy of economic concerns over political ones—the point of agreement between Locke and today's proponents of economic rights—is rarely used today as he used it, to argue vigorously for political rights. Instead the assumption seems to be that the two are commonly in tension and that the less-urgent political rights must wait—or be expressed only "collectively"—pending the achievement of "development." Economic needs serve to explain away, minimize, or detract attention from the widespread denial of political rights.

But are these economic goals properly awarded the honorific title "rights"? The striking fact is that today's fashionable "economic rights" are not necessarily either economic *freedoms* or economic claims *vested in dividual.* They are instead universal claims to the satisfaction of aggregate societal needs (housing, sanitation, education, etc.); as demands on the economy rather than rules for the protection of individuals, they lend themselves to justifying the suppression of economic freedoms and individual rights in the name of meeting the demands (or demonstrating statistical progress in meeting them). Moreover, the list of economic demands posing as ultimate, universal human rights tends to multiply, for no clear standard informs them, and no great reflection produced them. They are merely things that most people want, and that the poorer countries wish they could persuade the richer ones to give them. They are open-ended and hence often unreasonable. There is no way, for example, that an underdeveloped country can provide adequate education or medical care for all of its citizens. By proclaiming these as universal human rights, however, such countries arm themselves with the most respectable of reasons for pressing for the global redistribution of wealth. No one can blame them for that; but we can question the status as "human rights" of what are, in a sense, letters to Santa Claus. Meanwhile, it is sobering to observe that neither the United Nations International Covenant on Economic, Social, and Cultural Rights nor the Charter of Economic Rights and Duties of States so much as recognizes the individual's right to property or the state's duty to protect such a right.[1]

Right-wing regimes, to be sure, rarely succeed in dazzling the forums of international opinion by invoking collective and nonpolitical rights. Right-wing collectivism is not much in demand. Besides, to liberals there is something transparent about citing economic freedom in defense of oligarchies that deliberately regulate property to prevent rather than to promote the diffusion of economic opportunity. But "progressive regimes"—one swallows hard at that term—by dint of their "progressiveness," do manage to fool a lot of the people a lot of the time, as they brandish many fine paper rights, primarily of the shiny, recently devised sort. It would be unpleasantly ironic if the rhetoric of human rights, having begun by staunchly propounding the freedoms of the individual, political and subpolitical, should come in the end to align itself against them.

The great practical achievement of the older human rights tradition, in establishing the "inalienable rights" of the individual, was precisely to

[1]Contrast the United Nations Declaration on the Elimination of Discrimination Against Women (1967), Article 5, section 1, subsection a. The United Nations Declaration of the Rights of the Child (1959) upholds no right of the child to own any property, including a home, or to have any property held for the child by guardians; furthermore, it upholds no right of the child to have any precedence in inheriting the home or any of the property of the child's parents; contrast the enormously greater rights of children insisted on by Locke, *Two Treatises of Government*, First Treatise, sections 88–90. Observe, in this connection, the dilution of Article 17 of the Universal Declaration of Human Rights (1948) in Article 17 of the later United Nations International Covenant on Civil and Political Rights (compare Article 17 of the Declaration of the Rights of Man and Citizen [1789]...

deprive despotism of theoretical or philosophical respectability. There was no right, individual or collective, however derived, whether of a majority or minority, in the name of which any individual could be deprived of his rights unless he had voluntarily transferred or forfeited them. The newer tradition threatens to reverse this result. By transferring the focus of human rights away from the individual and his various freedoms, it takes the formerly inalienable and makes it hostage to other concerns. It has thus become easier to justify, harder to protect against, assaults upon the individual.

THE PRIMACY OF THE INDIVIDUAL

We have already made it abundantly clear where we would turn to discover the theoretical foundation for a viable U.S. human rights policy. The place to begin is with the first and most basic—also by far the solidest—stratum of the modern human rights tradition. That is the one proclaimed by the Declaration of Independence and given its finest elaboration in the thoughtful rhetoric of Abraham Lincoln. More than any other, this aspect of the tradition is our own and remains embodied in the institutions of both our government and our society. It is the only version of human rights viable in the world today that focuses inequivocally on the individual and his basic freedoms. This is crucial in a world in which, as one careful surveyor of the state of human rights has concluded, "more and more the individual stands alone in the face of an all-pervading State."[2] If this focus on the individual can no longer bear, as it once seemed to do, the stamp of theoretical certainty, its practical urgency—and so, one may hope, its moral appeal—remains, to put it mildly, undiminished. Finally, this stratum of the human rights tradition is the least dogmatic or parochial and the most politic one.

This point is worth emphasizing. We are all used to hearing how the attempt to apply U.S. notions of human rights in milieux unreceptive to them smacks of naivete or even "cultural imperialism." Complacency and high-handedness do exist, and Americans have displayed their share of them. But the better we understand our tradition, the more it will impress us by its inherent resilience and adaptability. To further the principles of human rights that underlie U.S. institutions is not necessarily to strive to export the institutions themselves, let alone to demand of other nations that they swallow them whole or as a whole. For these institutions are merely the adaptation, to conditions peculiar to the United States, of an understanding that originated in Europe and has become the common heritage of the West. To

[2]John P. Humphrey, "The International Law of Human Rights in the Middle Twentieth Century," in M. Box, ed., *The Present State of International Law and other Essays* (Kluwen, the Netherlands: 1973), p. 105.

renew this understanding on the level of human rights policy need amount to nothing more parochial than this: to champion the cause of the priority, dignity, and liberties of the individual human being.

We have already suggested the relatively undogmatic character of that stratum of the human rights tradition that inspired the founders of the United States of America: By presenting this understanding in the form of a structure resembling a pyramid, we tried to indicate the order and relative priority of the different human rights. All the human rights merit protection, but not all are strictly absolute: What is required is respect for the edifice of human rights as a whole. Some rights are more urgent than others because the others depend on them, and their violation entails more lasting and destructive consequences. Thus any government may in a moment of crisis suspend civil and political liberties in order to maintain the prepolitical rights to life, private liberty, and property—such being also the only way of preserving the prospects of the liberties suspended. (Witness, even within the rights-loving Anglo-Saxon tradition, wartime censorship of the press and suspension of habeas corpus.)

Thus, also, verdicts as to the relative legitimacy of regimes in terms of human rights must attend not just to the rank of the rights that may be neglected, but to the rank and scope of such as may be protected. In such cases (it may be conceded) respect for the rights that are acknowledged will almost always suffer because of the neglect of those that are not: The different levels of rights, when in place, mutually reinforce one another. It may nonetheless be stated that in practice the protection of human rights need not be a matter of all or nothing. In addition, the concrete political situation and the viable alternatives open to the ruling body must be taken into account; nor is it merely the degree of the violation that is pertinent, but also its duration and the prospects for redress.

It follows that a reasonable policy of advancing human rights involves complex and cautious, if ultimately stern, moral judgment. It hardly helps to draw up lengthy lists of rights without indication of their justification, derivation, and ranking. This is another reason to be leery of the elaborate pronouncements of the United Nations, which prove to be less declarations of human rights than enumerations of ultimately desirable goals to be achieved universally in some world more fortunate than our own. When the permanent core of human rights is thus gift-wrapped in gossamer, the basic rights are obfuscated, their urgency diluted. Indeed the very disproportion between utopian goals, propounded as absolute rights, and the capacity or willingness of most regimes to meet them is a loud and clear invitation to cynicism and hypocrisy. Where standards are hopelessly out of line, reality cuts them down to size, and the very notion of human rights is liable to fall into contempt.

It thus becomes important to gain greater clarity about the limits of what can properly be demanded in the name of human rights, and here we would emphasize two points. First, there is no human right to an equality of conditions, results, or outcomes in life. The idea of human rights implies that men are equal in a very precise sense: They are equal inasmuch as they are all endowed with the inalienable rights described above, and not in any other way.[3] What they make of life on the basis of these rights, together with their other distinct endowments (and what life makes of them), is not determined by the rights. The doctrine of human rights begins from awareness of, and strives to maintain respect for, human inequality and diversity; human rights are intended to foster the conditions within which individuality, creativity, and excellence can become manifest. None of this is to deny that a strong democratic bias is implicit in the political rights and the principle of government by consent. To quote Locke, there is to be "one Rule for Rich and Poor, for the Favourite at Court, and the Country Man at Plough"; for it is "the interest, as well as the intention of the People, to have a fair and *equal Representative,* " by which means "every single person becomes subject, equally with other the meanest men, to those Laws, which he himself, as part of the Legislative has established."[4] This means that according to Locke's teaching political authority rests finally with the majority; but the distinguished or unusual individual and minority has as much right to the protection of life, liberty, and property from the tyranny of the majority as from any other tyranny—and the most astute philosophic schemes for balancing governmental power keep this right squarely in view.

The second point is really another aspect of this concern for individuality: Human rights belong to all people *as individuals,* not as members of any economic class, religion, race, or nation. Groups, other than the family, have no rights as such. "Group rights" are at most the expression of the rights of the individuals who comprise the groups, and no group may pursue its rights at the expense of the rights of any individual or any other group. One generation may not be forced to forego its rights for the sake of later generations or be deprived of its rights because of the supposed crimes of its forefathers; one class may not have its rights protected at the expense of another class's rights; an individual's belonging to any race or religion cannot disqualify him from equal protection of his rights; and so on.

[3]Cf. Locke, *Two Treatises of Government,* Second Treatise, section 54.

[4]Locke, *Two Treatises of Government,* Second Treatise, sections 94, 142, 158 (italics in the original).

FROM PRINCIPLES TO POLICY

An intelligent application of the principles that we have expressed as a pyramid of rights would take note of those facts of life that currently surface under the names of collective, economic, and social rights. The fact is, such attention to harsh political realities is implicit in the principles themselves. Where a regime can make a powerful case for suspending or deferring less urgent rights for the sake of maintaining more urgent ones, we should hear it out, although not by any means uncritically. We should, accordingly, give credit where it is due to regimes that, unable for convincing reasons to implement the full range of human rights, display the most thorough commitment to those feasible under the circumstances. This we should do even where the rights protected are only subpolitical ones. We would not be true to our own tradition if we undervalued such solid goods as peace, order, and prosperity; economic and religious freedoms and the right to emigrate; the existence of an independent judiciary. At the same time neither would we be true to it if we did not insist on the incompleteness and precariousness of such goods where the other civil and political freedoms are lacking.

Here indeed our metaphor of the pyramid requires some correction. For it is not only the case that the lower freedoms must be present if the loftier ones are to be secured. The reverse is substantially true as well. Political and civic freedoms thus resemble the keystone of the arch of human rights. Comprising its highest point, they at the same time cement the whole, which without them must always threaten to collapse.

But besides emphasizing self-government as a means to securing subpolitical rights, we must also stress its intrinsic dignity. In this we would ratify in theory what has been amply established in practice: the extraordinary moral power of the appeal to political freedom. This, in other words, is the place to acknowledge the thought of Rousseau and Kant, with its emphasis on political freedom as a crucial aspect of moral freedom. In order to be satisfying, whether to ourselves or others, any human rights policy must attend to political rights not only as instrumental but as the culmination of the whole edifice—as neither the most urgent nor the least difficult, as the rarest but at the same time the finest rights of which human beings are capable. A unified and integrated structure of individual rights, worth preserving even when unfinished but achieving completeness only in free self-government limited by nothing but these rights themselves—such is the vision that we would offer over against the current ones. In short, we Americans should do whatever is feasible to reestablish ourselves as the party of freedom in the world.

The principles that we suggest represent a kind of synthesis of two successive stages of the Western human rights tradition, and a foreign policy informed by them would combine elements of the policies corresponding to each. Because, however, our synthesis of principle is an unequal one, drawing more heavily upon the cautious and flexible principles of the earlier human rights tradition, so too will the synthesis of policies be unequal. Just as every government is primarily responsible for protecting the human rights of its own citizens, the chief and overriding U.S. policy objective must remain the security of the United States—and such security cannot be maintained primarily by talk of human rights. Yet within the limits imposed upon it by this overriding objective, the United States should do its best to further human rights elsewhere in the world, relentlessly bringing the civil and political rights to the foreground of public attention.

Such a policy is all the more defensible in that the United States and its closest allies—Canada, Western Europe, Israel, Japan—which its own interest bids it defend, are also almost the only places where human rights, culminating in free self-government, have come into their own. The defense of the existing liberal democracies—and who can doubt that they are on the defensive?—is the real cornerstone of any grand strategy for the support of human rights. We must be clear on this: This is the cake; everything else, however worthy, is frosting.

But beyond this realm of our alliances, interest and principle are certain to diverge frequently, presenting policymakers with dilemmas that they will have to resolve as best they can. Because the countries that respect the whole range of human rights are so few, their defense will necessarily involve arrangements with countries that do not. It is now unfashionable to speak of the totality of anti-Communist nations as the "Free World," and in truth the "Free World" always harbored regimes to which freedom was only a euphemism. But if not all of the countries that belonged to the Free World were free, all of the free countries belonged to the Free World. So did most of the less free ones that were on the way to becoming freer. At some point it becomes necessary to weigh the exigencies of preserving human rights where they exist against those of extending them to places they do not.

Of such dilemmas there can be no theoretical resolution. Again we recall that, according to the original human rights understanding, national interest is by no means divorced from principle. The connections are two, however, and they may tend in opposite directions. On the one hand, a state is in principle a sovereign unit, and the primary obligations of its governors are to their own citizens and to their state's treaty allies. On the other, a state founded on the principles of human rights has also a powerful interest in the dissemination of those principles: There has never been a war between two liberal democracies. What is more, there can be no doubt that success at furthering human rights elsewhere would greatly boost the morale and prestige of the Western alliance—as failure to maintain them in any place where they presently exist would deliver a shattering blow to it.

With these considerations in mind, we have proposed a modified version of the original American human rights tradition as the one most appropriate to the current situation. In theory our policy combines a commitment to the dignity of the individual with an appreciation of the other solid if less sublime blessings of the human rights tradition. In practice it encourages attention to the rank order of the various rights and to the exigencies of particular situations—encourages, but cannot insure; and this final point is worth stressing. For the human rights policy has not been invented that can substitute for the good sense of those called upon to implement it.

DISCUSSION QUESTIONS

1. What are the values that underlie present foreign policy?
2. Should the United States resume aid to a country because it takes fewer political prisoners in any given year?
3. Should the United States supply military technology to a "humane" dictator whose repression does not include torture?
4. In the interest of "peace" should the United States overlook human rights violations in a nation of strategic importance to our defense?
5. Discuss the differences outlined by Orwin and Pangle of economic, social and cultural rights when compared to political rights.

12

NUCLEAR ARMS

Bernard Schechterman

Analyses, as well as reactions, to nuclear weapons technology developments and strategies are largely a reflection of intellectual perceptions of the nature of international politics, and particularly of the American relationship with the Soviet Union. On a broadly conceived continuum, from one extreme to the other, three general viewpoints have evolved since the end of World War II—a predominantly idealistic left, a predominantly idealistic right, and a *realpolitik,* anti-idealist position. Although oversimplified, all three categories embody moralistic outlooks as part of their rationales in public debate over nuclear arms and strategies. Unfortunately, however, lack of consistency, combinations, and variations contribute to the confusion among respective viewpoints as each specific debate arises.

IDEALISTIC LEFT POSITION

At the conclusion of World War II, a wide consensus existed in American society that the world had entered a new historical epoch—"the nuclear age." Hiroshima and Nagasaki conveyed the message that the nuclear age included a military as well as a possible peaceful use of nuclear energy. The advantage in the initial perception of the nuclear issue lay with the traditional anti-power, anti-violence idealists and moralists. Revulsed at the use of American nuclear power in the concluding stages of World War II, their thought pattern invoked "the necessity principle"—the moral imperative and urgency to denuclearize (eliminate the capability) and simultaneously to universalize the governance or control of mankind's political relations. The explicit inference was that human evolution had reached a critical juncture where man's innovative capabilities *would* lead to the destruction of the entire human race—the ultimate immoral act.

This assumption and the sequentially derived views have operated as a continuous thread of ideas and beliefs throughout the entire post-World War II period. The particulars, tactics, and special pleadings have varied according to circumstances—technological developments and political crises in Soviet-American relations. From the initial abhorrence of the late 1940s that led to a "banning the bomb" advocacy, the late 1950s and early 1960s moved towards "the necessity principle" that surfaced as Bertrand Russell's epithet, "better Red than dead." In the 1970s and 1980s, a similar view emerged among groups associated with the *Bulletin of Atomic Scientists* (the Hans Bethe group) and the Union of Concerned Scientists. The chief fear in the 1980s has been that of "a nuclear winter," especially as it is outlined by Carl Sagan, and vehemently espoused by the Physicians for Social Responsibility (Bernard Lown and others) and their counterparts in the health (Helen Caldicott) and environmental (Paul Ehrlich) fields. The legal and academic communities' counterpart of concern was expressed by the late Grenville Clark, whose position is today championed by Saul Mendlovitz and Richard Falk.

Summarily, among these varying interest groups and factions can be found ideological pacifists, unilateral disarmamentalists, and those simply seeking constant and/or consistent U.S. initiatives for nuclear negotiation with the USSR to fulfill the moral imperative of disarmament. In most instances, the demand for disarmament usually assumes, stated or unstated, that America is guilty of failing to pursue this needed policy and the Soviets are open to, or will be cooperative, in this objective. The clamor for total denuclearization remains an unswerving goal since the issue is seen in moral absolutes, right being on their side and wrong on the opponents' side.

IDEALISTIC RIGHT POSITION

The tradition of the American Right vis-à-vis international affairs has historically been one of isolationism, often based on the supposition that American society, being morally superior to its antecedents (especially Europe), ought to have little to do with them. A foreign policy of non-involvement after 1945 became rapidly impractical for at least two reasons: the decline of distances due to the acceleration of the communication and transportation revolution and the appearance of the Soviet Union as a second nuclear superpower.

The Soviets (communism) represented an immoral set of values (an evil system) in ethical conflict with the United States (free world) and its democratic and moral goodness. Given this polarized characterization of systems and ideas, early Rightists moralized the use of nuclear weapons in a "preemptive or preventive war" to expunge the ultimate evil, the USSR, from world politics.

Greater subtlety emerged on the Right in the 1950s and 1960s under the name of "protracted conflict" (Robert Straus-Hupé, Stefan Possony, etc.), which suggested a mirror-imaging response policy for the United States. Accepting the view that the Soviets were in a "battle to the death" with the Americans, a battle that employed every possible means to win, the United States was counseled to respond in kind. Under the influence of these academics and publicists like James Burnham, a strategy that placed heavy priority on nuclear weapons, even at the expense of conventional modes of war preparedness and other instruments of foreign policy, came to dominate the Eisenhower Years (1953–1961). The morality of the nuclear option, though not preemptive, but as a threat or "massive retaliation doctrine," was emphasized and pursued as morally necessary to achieve complete victory. Even though the policy was not implemented effectively, the United States sought and hoped to sustain a "superiority" over the Soviets and maintain a strategic nuclear threat.

The latest resurgence of this viewpoint has taken place in the Reagan Administration. The focus in the 1980s of the American position, based on the assumption of a " window of vulnerability," has been to expand U.S. nuclear capabilities with a trillion dollars allocated disproportionately to nuclear weaponry in a five-year military build-up. Defense Secretary Weinberger (1981–1987) raised the question of renewed American efforts to obtain superiority over the Soviets with the Strategic Defense Initiative and he sought to uphold the possible use of nuclear weapons to defeat the "evil empire." The most extreme version of confronting the Soviets (Colin Gray) accepted both the viability and morality of fighting "a limited nuclear war" to either deter or defeat the Soviet Union. Confusion reigned in the last years of the Reagan Administration because of the failure to either attain nuclear superiority or achieve an overall arms reduction agreement.

REALPOLITIK POSITION

This viewpoint recognizes the basic alternatives in the nuclear arms controversy: the inability, if not undesirability to abolish nuclear weapons altogether, and the potential for both sides to cut back or manage existing arms capabilities. The realpolitik position acknowledges that, given the record of man's past history, total abolition is unrealistic. Nuclear weapons are looked on as "necessary evil" in this particular technological age and are seen as a vital part of protecting a society from external threats. Nuclear weapons, among other capabilities, stand as the guarantors of the highest moral goal in the conduct of foreign relations: national independence and survival.

Considerable disagreement exists over the quantity and quality of nuclear weapons needed to maintain a nation's security. This leads to the realpolitik's second position that accepts the feasibility of controlling and/or reducing the weaponry by tacit and formal efforts of the superpowers. Such efforts include deterrence theory and arms control negotiations, and non-nuclear proliferation. Although mutual interests exist and serve as a basis for American and Soviet cooperation, they cannot be guaranteed in a world of egocentrism and dogmatic ideologies.

The primary post-World War II nuclear debate has taken place within the realpolitik arena with the idealistic left and right exerting pressure on the realpolitiks to skew in their direction. Incremental changes have occurred at each end of the continuum: There have been new nuclear buildups as well as arms cutbacks and anti-nuclear agreements. The realpolitik view insists that the post-war history has been a "managed success" since nuclear war and devastation have been avoided despite continual international conflict. There remains no other option than to continue the nuclear arsenal. At the same time the effort continues to decrease it and simultaneously sustain the balance of power between the superpowers and the politico-military blocs they represent.

New Views Behind Moscow's Flexible New Diplomacy

Michael Forrestal and Allen Lynch

The dramatic series of foreign policy initiatives launched by Mikhail Gorbachev—ranging from arms control to human rights—has left many in the West wondering about the deeper motivations. Many have dismissed them as simply "tactical" adjustments, the pursuit of age-old objectives under new names.

Michael Forrestal and Allen Lynch, "New Views Behind Moscow's Flexible New Diplomacy," *Christian Science Monitor,* 13 October 1987, 15. Reprinted with permission of The Institute for East-West Security Studies.

The analysis of Soviet foreign policy always warrants the greatest caution. Yet there is equal if not greater danger in underestimating the extent of movement in Soviet international policy, as the United States debacle at the Reykjavik summit and the self-inflicted allied paralysis on the intermediate-range nuclear forces issue convincingly illustrate.

The key changes in Soviet perspectives on international affairs have been identified by a bipartisan task force on Soviet foreign policy convened under the auspices of the Institute for East-West Security Studies. The group's report highlights five areas in which the Soviets have reevaluated orthodox positions:

The Soviet leadership has concluded that the Soviet Union's international relationships should be subordinated to the prime task of economic modernization at home. Mr. Gorbachev's desire for domestic reform has led him to search for structures of stability in critical areas—in arms control, most visibly—which would provide a durable and predictable framework for the resource choice that must be made. The need for such stability assumes double importance for Gorbachev, since instability in the USSR's foreign relations could affect not only the politics of resource allocation but the viability of Gorbachev's own political position.

The Gorbachev leadership has concluded that favored international environment can be created only on the basis of *political* accommodation with the leading industrial powers—above all with the US, still the focal point of Soviet attention in foreign affairs. The Soviet choice for accommodation thus represents more than a "tactical" adjustment to shifting circumstances, the "breathing spell" that some in the West have detected. Rather, it reflects a strategic reevaluation of the international environment and of the factors affecting the USSR's global position.

There has been a major reexamination of security issues. Top Soviet officials, including military officials, stress that a nuclear war cannot under any circumstances be won. As a corollary, the leadership now argues, with implicit criticism of Soviet security policy under Leonid Brezhnev, that security cannot be obtained by military means alone. Security in the nuclear age is said to be mutual in character and, because of the destructive potential modern weaponry, a common concern of all countries. Relatedly, Soviet policy analysts and Gorbachev himself claim to reject nuclear weapons as a durable guarantor of peace. They assert that even nuclear parity, which they continue to regard as a major historical achievement of communism, could cease to be capable of enduring stability in the face of unregulated arms competition between East and West. Nuclear arms control thus assumes priority as a means of reducing the external threat, limiting resource requirements for the military, and establishing a framework of stability in East–West strategic relations.

The Soviet concept of peaceful coexistence is being revised. Key Soviet policy analysts now interpret peaceful coexistence less as a form of class struggle—the traditional Soviet viewpoint—and more as long-lasting condition in which states with different social and political systems will have to learn how to live with each other for the indefinite future. As Yevgeny Primakov, a close adviser to Gorbachev, recently noted in a key article in *Pravda*, peaceful coexistence is no longer regarded "as a breathing space" by the Soviets. "Interstate relations," he emphasized, "cannot be the sphere in which the outcome of the confrontation between world socialism and world capitalism is settled."

The Gorbachev leadership evidences increasing recognition of the multipolar and interdependent character of contemporary international relations. This view is reflected in a growing tendency on the part of the USSR to deal directly with key regional actors, such as China and Japan in the Far East, Egypt and Israel in the Middle East, and Mexico in Central America. The main goal has been to reduce the USSR's diplomatic isolation, which was increasingly evident in the last Brezhnev era, and to multiply Soviet options.

The report thus indicates that behind Gorbachev's tactical ingenuity lies a far more sophisticated view of international politics and foreign policy than we have come to expect of Soviet leaders.

A more subtle and flexible Soviet diplomacy requires the West to develop a broader and more active policy toward the USSR, including standards to define and meet common security requirements in a rapidly changing international environment. Failure to do so would sacrifice the initiative to the USSR and forfeit opportunities to encourage the further adaptation of Soviet power. It would also mean abdicating the West's responsibility to future generations to pursue improved relations between East and West.

A Way Out of Reykjavik

Brent Scowcraft, John Deutch and R. James Woolsey

...In the current environment, there are doubtless some senior officials who regard the Administration's zero ballistic-missile proposal at Reykjavik as a

---

sincere effort to establish a radically new basis for United States-Soviet relations. But there are others for whom tactics are paramount, and this can produce extreme demands.

In any negotiations, there is an imprecise border between mere tough bargaining and an intentional thwarting of an agreement by the statement of wholly unacceptable terms. If you cross the border you may lose the deal. In bartering to buy something, you often have nothing to lose by taking a tough stance; perhaps you were ambivalent about the purchase anyway. The best way to get a good price from a rug merchant may cut the price just as you're walking out. [sic]

But in strategic-arms negotiations, there is a symmetry to most agreed upon limitations. If Washington proposes that Moscow have zero intermediate-range missiles in Europe, or zero mobile ICBM's or zero ballistic missiles, it can expect the same demand in return. Tough bargaining proposals here should be ones that you are prepared to live with, because you can lose not just the deal itself but—by undermining public support for your programs—also lose what you already have.

Tough bargaining helped lead to the "zero option"—the proposal to deploy no American or Soviet intermediate-range missiles in Europe. When it was first proposed, in 1981, this may have seemed unacceptable to the Russians; it had some attractive features for Americans, however, since the United States had not yet deployed intermediate-range missiles and would have been trading potential United States systems for existing Soviet ones.

Now, however, the Russians have agreed to a version of the zero option, and it is a very different matter. Today, zero intermediate-range on each side in Europe means completely withdrawing the intermediate-range missiles that the United States and its allies have recently worked hard to deploy. The current zero option would leave Western Europe naked to the 600 or so Soviet shorter-range missiles that are essentially unmatched by United States systems. A sounder American proposal—for each side to keep 100 intermediate-range warheads in Europe (in addition to a similar number in Asia and the United States)—was apparently scrapped and the zero option for Europe resuscitated in the heady atmosphere of Reykjavik.

Another, more troubling United States position is the proposal—set forth in Reykjavik, and now tabled in Geneva—to ban all ballistic missiles within 10 years. This proposal would mean that the United States, in order to maintain a deterrent, would have to rely solely on its bombers and cruise missiles to penetrate the numerous Soviet radar installations, surface-to-air missiles and fighter interceptors that constitute the world's most massive air-defense network.

Underlying this tactical negotiating approach is the view of some Administration officials that the American people cannot be counted on to support reasonable modernization of strategic forces for offensive use and careful, gradual arms control. This fear, which may in part be based on the unwise but temporary efforts by Congress to restrict United States strategic programs in the mid-1970's following SALT I, is overblown.

Admittedly, politicians need to do a better job explaining major strategic notions—the degree to which NATO rests on nuclear deterrence, for instance, and the fact that modernization is needed to improve the survivability of weaponry and to deter Soviet conventional and nuclear attack—not to add to the size of our arsenal. Explanations are harder when events—Vietnam, Watergate, the Iran-contra imbroglio—disrupt executive-legislative and Republican-Democratic cooperation. But Americans are generally far more willing to support sensible strategic programs and careful arms-control talks than some would suggest.

In addition to domestic politics, sincere beliefs and negotiating tactics, another factor contributing to the Administration's trashing of deterrence has been a propensity for flashy, staged public events and for proposals that attract television news cameras. There is certainly nothing wrong with presenting national strategy in a favorable light, but if one begins and ends strategic planning with an eye to the next evening's news and polls, one courts eventual disaster—especially considering that the opponents, the current world chess champions, plan many moves ahead.

For all these reasons, there is now a great deal of uncertainty about our nation's strategic policy. It is unclear whether the Administration has fundamentally undermined the country's ability, and the public's support of that ability, to maintain nuclear deterrence. It is also unclear whether it is too late to drop back into a more modest, careful, gradual approach toward strategic modernization. It is clear, though, that thus far S.D.I. has already protected the United States, by preventing an agreement at Reykjavik that would have destroyed the American ballistic-missile deterrent within a decade, left American bombers and cruise missiles facing extensive air defenses and the Russians facing essentially none; weakened the announced S.D.I. rationale (because it would become only an "insurance policy"); removed United States intermediate-range forces from Europe and left some 600 Soviet shorter-range missiles unopposed; allowed the Russians to maintain their advantage in conventional and chemical forces, and undercut the West's support for maintaining its defenses.

The Reykjavik proposals may well have set back the cause of responsible arms control by many years. Since the early 1970's leaders of both parties (when not running for office or addressing blatantly antinuclear groups) have been urging a more realistic approach to arms negotiations. While recognizing the understandable public urge for a dramatic and simple agreement that would transform the nuclear competition, most leaders have urged more modest expectations for formal agreements should focus on stabilizing measures that reduce the probability of nuclear war and not an expected earthshaking breakthrough between two competing superpowers. The Administration's initiative at Reykjavik has now been seized upon by both the right and the left, for different reasons, as demonstrating that it is possible for the leaders of East and West, merely by signing the right paper, to bring lasting peace.

One of the many unfortunate aspects of this illusion is that it could undermine the willingness of many in the West to be patient about deterrence just as patience is beginning to pay off. The Soviet Union faces many problems, which should lend us some reasonable hope, firmness, strength, and careful arms-control proposals could help produce a positive trend. Under Mikhail Gorbachev, there have been some signs of change in Russia. Information on disasters and riots has been provided more openly than in the past, and a few prominent dissidents have been freed. But we must be cautious here.

From Peter the Great to Nikita Khrushchev, Russian leaders who have been domestic reformers have often been the most aggressive in foreign policy. Moreover, leaders who dare to sponsor bold changes can be busted if internal reaction is strongly negative; this happened to both Georgi Malenkov and Khrushchev. If domestic reform or—less likely—both domestic reform and foreign-policy retrenchment should be on Gorbachev's mind, this could happen to him as well—and happen faster than we could rebuild an abandoned deterrent. Further by undermining the care for modernizing and making more survivable our offensive weaponry, the Administration has risked creating an unstable environment for its successor. A later President who might want to return to a policy of careful negotiation and strategic-force modernization—whatever his policy on S.D.I. to be something more than an insurance policy, could find his hands tied.

In spite of this, it may not be too late for the center to hold, for the restoration of an intellectual basis for a system of credible deterrence, strategic stability and step-by-step arms control. A bipartisan consensus can be rebuilt for such an approach.

Strategic stability can be enhanced by insuring the survivability of our strategic weaponry, and not locking ourselves into systems such as silo-based ICBM's, even if that means not using arms control to block Soviet survivability improvements, such as a shift to mobile forces. But within a framework of defending Western values, stability must also mean that the United States continue to support NATO by holding Soviet military forces at bay with nuclear weapons when it cannot effectively do so with conventional ones.

Such an approach would require some modernization of American offensive forces—including the development of a small mobile ICBM. It would also require continuing improvement in American ability to put Soviet ICBM's at risk—with Trident II, and accurate small mobile ICBMs and the MX. Together, these efforts might encourage the Russians to agree to arms reductions emphasizing cuts in large ICBM's equipped with MIRV's.

Work on defensive systems should also continue. However, if major reductions in large Soviet ICBM's with MIRV's were carried out under an arms-control agreement, more attention could be paid to aspects of the S.D.I. program other than the boost-phase intercept, which is useful principally against such ICBM's. A defense against tactical ballistic missiles could be undertaken with European and other allies, such as Israel. Defense against Soviet cruise missiles and depressed-trajectory ballistic missiles carried by submarines could be given a higher priority. The anti-tactical defense would protect European-based United States forces from conventional as well as nuclear attack. The defense against cruise missiles, and perhaps against some ballistic missiles, would protect our bomber bases and at least some command and control sites from sudden attack from close-in submarines.

There is clearly a role for research and development on spaced-based and exotic S.D.I. technology, including an orderly testing program. The Soviet program alone requires such an American effort. But it should be scientifically sound—a work horse, not a show horse—and realistic in its content, size and growth.

Efforts should also be maintained to negotiate an agreement on intermediate-range missiles with the Russians that would allow some relatively small number of such missiles to remain in Europe. A move away from battlefield nuclear weapons and toward modern conventional weapons to combat Soviet tank concentrations would further reduce reliance on nuclear weapons without abandoning their deterrent value. Some modernization of NATO's chemical-warfare capability is required to deter Soviet use of chemicals in wartime. Agreed restraints on nuclear tests would help reduce reliance on nuclear weapons without crippling the safety improvements that only some types of testing can provide, and would complete a plausible package.

It is time to regroup. The United States can ill afford suddenly to cast off the strategy that has, however precariously, preserved peace for 40 years. Congress must have a central role in any effort to return to moderation. Because of its structure and organization, however, Congress has no naturally coherent view of defense and arms-control policy. It is currently divided among those who passionately believe that the military competition between the United States and the Soviet Union is a ghastly mistake; those who support realistic policies to deal with difficult defense questions, and those who—like the Administration—have great faith in single solutions. There is considerable strain among these groups, notwithstanding the fact that some Congressmen are at various times adherents of more than one of them.

It is, of course, in the executive branch that foreign policy and national-security policy should be crafted. But when the executive branch proposes to cripple the nation's deterrent, as it did at Reykjavik, the security of the nation, indeed of the world's democracies as a whole, demands the Congress demonstrate great responsibility and exert its constitutional powers wisely and carefully. This is no time to try to take advantage of the apparent confusion in the executive branch or to impair even further America's deterrent posture. It is time, rather, for Congressional statesmanship of the highest order to repair the damage already done. There is a core of members from both political parties who understand these issues and who can contribute to a policy of maintaining nuclear deterrence, strengthening conventional forces and conducting responsible arms-control negotiations. In the 100th Congress, they have their work cut out for them.

The decision to undercut the revenue base in 1981 and the decision to trash deterrence in 1986 had certain features in common. Both leave the country now with huge deficits—political and financial—and require dedication and rebuilding so that the nation can merely return to where it once was. Such rebuilding, and even progress, is not beyond us. But we must begin. Now.

Nuclear Strategy: A Case for a Theory of Victory

Colin S. Gray

...Counter-military targeting is not, of course, even close to being a novel idea in U.S. war planning. Indeed, one may speculate to the effect that counter-military targeting already comprises the lion's share of strategic resource allocations in SIOP planning—a thought supported amply by the bevy of official commentaries offered in 1974–75 in support of the "Schlesinger shift" in targeting, largely following the guidance provided by NSDM 242 (of 1974). *If* there is a shift impending in favor of (still more) large counter-military strike options in the SIOP, one can speculate that such a shift might imply the paying of heavier attention to Soviet projection forces

---

Colin S. Gray, "Nuclear Strategy: A Case for a Theory of Victory," *International Security* 4, no. 1 (Summer 1979), 54–87.

or, at a more basic level, a commitment to purchasing the ability to neutralize a far higher fraction of really hard Soviet military (and political) targets than is the case at present.

For the U.S. Government to endorse a full-fledged war-fighting doctrine in the strategic realm would constitute a doctrinal revolution. Such a doctrine would deny the validity of the stability theory that has informed U.S. defense and arms control policy since the mid-1960s. Strategic stability, in the standard formula, requires that societal assets (people and industry) be near totally vulnerable, while strategic weapons be invulnerable. The Soviet Union has always believed in the value of the assured destruction option vis-à-vis the United States, but not in *mutual* assured destruction. It is too early to be certain, but even if the United States under President Carter *might* be willing to shift its declaratory focus (and eventually its actual targeting plans)—and to invest in actual military capability—more toward military targets than is the case at present, it is unlikely that it will be able to overcome its fundamental skepticism over the wisdom of approaching a central nuclear war as one should approach (or did approach, in pre-nuclear days) non-nuclear war. Pending the occurrence (and resolution in favor of change) of a sophisticated debate over the worth of still-fashionable ideas concerning crisis and arms race instability, American strategic policy will be shifted at the margin rather than rewritten. Also, a particular strategic posture, even one as large as that to be maintained in the 1980s by the United States (with the blessing of SALT II), is not omni-competent.

At the present time the United States does not have a strategic posture capable of seeking a military outcome to a war in which Western political authorities could place any confidence. Moreover, on the record extant, the interest of the Carter Administration in purchasing such a posture rapidly has to be judged to be distinctly lukewarm. Carter's record on the character and timing of the MX ICBM program, on the B-1 bomber (aborted), and on civil defense, would have to fuel incredulity over the likely postural matching for any proclaimed new strategic doctrine with a war-waging, as opposed to a pre-war deterrent, orientation. If, as (almost certainly over-) reported, the U.S. Government should inch towards a very heavily counter-military strategic nuclear employment doctrine, it will need to understand the requirements and limitations of such an approach. A non-defense professional might be somewhat puzzled by this discussion. As a general rule, he might observe, U.S. war planning surely has *always* been oriented most heavily towards Soviet military targets (strategic forces, projection forces, command and control targets, and war-supporting industry and transport networks)–so what is new? The answer lies in the scope of the military targeting, in its ability to cope with a much harder target set than before, and in its design for separation from civil society. Anybody who sought to argue that the United States suddenly had discovered counter-military targeting as an interesting option, would of course be guilty of misleading his audience. For example, Richard Burt of *The New York Times* wrote recently that:

> The Carter Administration has revised the United States strategy for deterring nuclear war by adopting a concept that would require strategic forces to be capable of large-scale precision attacks against Soviet military targets as well as all-out retaliatory blows against cities.
>
> The new strategy, which has emerged after months of debate in the Pentagon, represents a significant departure from the long-held concept that the United States needs only to threaten all-out retaliation against Soviet cities to deter Moscow from launching a nuclear attack.[1]

Clausewitz wrote of war that "[i]ts grammar, indeed, may be its own [i.e., war should be waged in a way that makes military sense, given its unique dynamics], but not its logic."[2] A U.S. SIOP oriented towards different kinds of military targets should be guided by a political logic—what are our war aims? A rewriting and recomputing of the SIOP in an even more heavily counter-military direction than is the case at present could place the United States in a somewhat worse position than that occupied by the (major) allied politicians of World War I—there could be a determination to do *military* damage to the enemy (which is very sensible), but a lack of commitment to the idea of prosecuting the war to the point where the enemy is defeated militarily (unlike World War I). The question of just how the military damage to be wrought is to be translated into political advantage could easily be evaded.

It may be ungenerous to proffer such a negative (or, at least, skeptical) verdict, but it does seem that the official (at least in the Department of Defense) redirection of U.S. strategic nuclear targeting preferences continues to neglect factors that bear upon the issue of desired war outcomes. As noted earlier, a counter-political control strategy cannot succeed unless a Soviet military offensive, at the theater and/or intercontinental levels, is thwarted. However, it would be foolish to wage the military war without taking proper prior account of the Soviet perspective upon Soviet vulnerabilities. There is considerable danger that the United States, looking to the damage promise of an inventory of cruise missiles and (much later) MX ICBMs, will neglect the very important political criteria for strategic targeting. A theory of victory over the Soviet Union can be only partially military in character—the more important part is political. The United States and its allies probably should not aim at achieving the military defeat of the Soviet Union, con-

[1] "Carter Shifts U.S. Strategy for Deterring Nuclear War", *op. cit.*

[2] *On War, Op. Cit.*, p. 605.

sidered as a unified whole; instead, it should seek to impose such military stalemate and defeat as is needed to persuade disaffected Warsaw Pact allies and ethnic minorities inside the Soviet Union that they can assert their own values in very active political ways. It is possible that a heavily counter-military focused SIOP might have the same insensitivity to Soviet domestic fragilities as may be found in the counter-economic recovery orientation of the 1970s.

In important respects, a heavily counter-military SIOP would be the kind of war plan that the Soviet Union is well equipped to counter. Notwithstanding its apparent war-waging focus, the American authors and executors of such a doctrine would be unlikely to have considered the conduct of war as a whole: really they would still be seeking, very substantially, to be responsive to pre-war deterrence needs. With a clear political war aim—to encourage the dissolution of the Soviet state—much of the military war might not need to be fought at all. The apparently resolute determination of the American defense community not to think through its deterrence needs, which would involve addressing the question of war aims, promises to produce yet another marginal improvement in doctrine (after all, U.S. strategic forces have always been targeted against Soviet military power—whatever annual Posture Statements may have said).[3] It may be worth reminding American policy makers in 1979 that the United States had a counterforce doctrine in Vietnam. A focus upon counter-military action, bereft of an overarching political intent, save of the vaguest kind, is unlikely to serve American interests well, except by unmerited luck.

The war-fighting theme which now has limited, though important, official support in Washington, comprises no more than half of the change in thinking that is needed. It is essential for pre-war deterrent effect that Soviet leaders not believe they could wage a successful short war. But, for reasons that none could predict in advance, war might occur regardless of the pre-war theories and the postures of the two sides. In that event, it will be essential that the United States has a theory of war responsive to its political interests.[4] Because a counter-military focus in the SIOP is not informed by a clear goal of political victory against the Soviet state, the United States is un-

[3]In his valuable study of the counterforce debate of the early 1970s, Desmond Ball quotes an Air Force general as claiming (in February 1973) that the SIOP was "never reworked under (President) Johnson. It is still basically the same as 1962." *Déjà Vu: The Return to Counterforce in the Nixon Administration, op. cit.*, p. 17.

[4]Such a war might not be tripped by a military accident that related to political intention on neither side. It might pertain to matters of vital interest to both sides. In short, the U.S. defense community might discover that it did have political goals that far transcended Brodie's prediction that the earliest possible war termination would likely be the superordinate objective (see Footnote 54).

likely to be able to wage an intercontinental nuclear war in a very intelligent fashion. In World War II, American wartime leaders declined to attempt to look beyond the battlefield, so long as the war was still in progress, with results of impressive negative educational value for succeeding generations. How much more intelligent it would be to have explicit war aims that should, in and of themselves, have considerable pre- and intra-war deterrent value.

One hesitates to criticize the reported current trend in official thinking, so healthy a change is it in its war-waging focus from the murderous and impolitic counter-economic themes of the 1960s and (most of the) 1970s. Nonetheless, the point has to be made that there continues to be an absence of political judgment overseeing U.S. strategic nuclear employment policy and, *ergo,* there is a neglect of strategy. A possible change in the 1980s in strategic employment orientation towards the counter-military, is fully compatible with a U.S. defense community which would not be able to bring itself to think of thermonuclear war in terms of victory or defeat. The U.S. defense community, substantially coerced in its thinking by the adverse trends in the major East-West military balances, has progressed from a counter-economic, to a counter-military focus in its nuclear employment reasoning (although the mechanical details of war planning may well have focused more upon Soviet military assets than the U.S. defense community generally understood to be the case), but it has yet to accept a *strategic* focus and advance to a counter-political control thesis. Unlike Soviet defense analysts, Western commentators continue to be bemused by the reality-numbing concept of "war termination." Wars are indeed terminated, but they are also won or lost. Moreover, if the U.S. defense community envisages (as it must, realistically) the sacrifice (presumably unwilling) of tens of millions of Americans in a thermonuclear war, that sacrifice should be undertaken only in a *very* worthwhile cause. If there is no theory of political victory in the U.S. SIOP, then there can be little justification for nuclear planning at all.

STABILITY AND THE NEED FOR DEFENSE

The principal intellectual culprit in our pantheon of false strategic gods is the concept of stability. For more than fifteen years, influential members of the U.S. defense and arms control community have believed that it is useful, or even essential, that the Soviet Union has guaranteed unrestricted strategic access to American societal assets. Such unrestricted access *was* believed to have a number of stabilizing consequences. In and of itself it should limit arms competitive activity (such activity as remained would stem from "normal" modernization and from efforts to offset counterforce-relevant developments on the other side),[5] while—more basically—it should promote some relaxation of tension, in that the Soviet Union would, belatedly, be assured of its ability to deter (through punishment) the United States.[6] (This theory has some features in common with the view that the four-fold rise in oil prices in 1973–74 was "good for us"—compelling us to confront the implications of our own profligacy in the energy consumption field.)

Analysts of all (or perhaps most) doctrinal persuasions have come at last to accept the view that the Soviet Union does not relax as a consequence of its achieving a very high quality assured destruction capability: the excellent reason for such continued effort is that the assured destruction of American societal assets plays no known role in Soviet deterrent or wartime planning—save as a threat to deter American counter-economic strikes. In addition, Soviet planners probably see considerable political coercive value for a post-war world in a very large counter-societal threat. Backward though it has seemed to some, the Soviet Union has provided unmistakable evidence of believing that wars, even large nuclear wars, can be won or lost. The mass-murder of Americans makes a great deal of sense in terms of the authority structure of a post-war world (since the Soviet Union cannot consummate a victory properly through the physical occupation of North America), but such a grisly exercise has little or nothing to do with the prosecution of a war (save as a counterdeterrent threat).

American strategic (and arms control) policy, since the mid-1960s, has been misinformed by stability criteria which rested (and rest) upon a near-total misreading of Soviet phenomena. Soviet leaders are opportunists with a war-waging doctrine as their strategic *leitmotiv.* Supposedly sophisticated self-restraint in American arms competitive activity, designed so as not to stimulate "destabilizing" Soviet responses, has simply presented the Soviet Union with an upcoming period of strategic superiority of uncertain duration. The American stability theorem held only for so long as both sides endorsed it. There is legitimate dispute today over the quality of Soviet strategic

[5]Classic "period-piece" statements of the arms-race stability thesis were George W. Rathjens: *The Future of the Strategic Arms Race: Options for the 1970s* (New York: Carnegie Endowment for International Peace, 1969); and "The Dynamics of the Arms Race," *Scientific American*, Vol. 220, No. 4 (April, 1969), pp. 15–25.

[6]Strange to note, the theory of arms race dynamics that featured as its centerpiece the proposition that each side acts and reacts in a fairly mechanistic fashion in pursuit of a secure assured destruction capability, has now been discredited pretty well definitively by the historical facts, but the strategic policy premises that flow from that flawed theory have not been overhauled thoroughly. Since virtually all U.S. commentators agree that the Soviet Union is not attracted to MAD reasoning, the long-familiar "instability" case against urban-area BMD and non-marginal civil defense provision, is simply wrong. We are still in search of an adequate explanatory model for the strategic arms competition. See Colin S. Gray, *The Soviet-American Arms Race* (Lexington, Mass.: Lexington, 1976).

programs, but no one, to the knowledge of this author, disputes the contention that the Soviet Union is seeking both to protect its societal assets (assured survival, not mutual assured destruction) and to pose the maximum threat to American strategic forces, compatible with the adequate manipulation of Western hopes and fears for the future for the purpose of discouraging a strong American competitive response. Unlike the Soviet Union, the United States has declined to recognize (courtesy of its still-authoritative stability theory) that an adequate strategic deterrent posture requires the striking of a balance between offensive and defensive elements. There is a painful irony of several dimensions in this American intellectual failing.

First, among the more pertinent asymmetries that separate the U.S. from the Soviet political systems, is the acute sensitivity of the former to the *personal* well-being of its human charges. It is little short of bizarre to discover that it is the Soviet Union, and not the United States, that has a serious civil defense program.[7] Second, potentially the strongest element in the overall Western stance vis-à-vis the Soviet Union is its industrial mobilization capacity. Reasonably good American BMD carries healthily terminal implications for Soviet opportunism or adventure. A BMD system that works well enables the United States to wage a long war and to mass produce the military means for eventual victory. So great is American mobilization potential, vis-à-vis the extant strategic posture, that U.S. defense policy, logically, should endorse a defensive emphasis. Such an emphasis is the guarantor of strategic forces in overwhelming numbers *tomorrow*.

Third, if U.S. strategic nuclear forces are to be politically relevant in future crises, the American homeland has to be physically defended. It is unreasonable to ask an American President to wage an acute crisis, or the early stages of a central war, while he is fearful of being responsible for the loss of more than 100 million Americans. If escalation discipline is to be imposed upon the Soviet Union, even in the direst of situations, potential damage to North America has to be limited. Damage-limitation has to involve both counterforce action and active and passive defenses. The claim that actually to protect (even very imperfectly) Americans and their industry would be destabilizing, is a doctrinal cliché whose shallowness merits uncompromising exposure. Since virtually all Western commentators recognize that the Soviet Union is not moved in its strategic policy by assured destruction criteria, and since no one can deny that an American President could not threaten, or implement, even highly intelligent strikes against the Soviet body politic if American society is totally open to Soviet retaliation, the stability concept is in need of fundamental redefinition. As long as American

[7]To have a serious civil defense program does not mean that a country is preparing for war, any more than equipping a ship with lifeboats means that the shipping line is preparing to operate the ship in a dangerous manner.

society is essentially unprotected by BMD, air defense, and civil defense, the United States will have to lose any process of competitive escalation against the Soviet force posture anticipated for the 1980s.

Fourth, even if the arms controllers' argument were correct, that a defensive emphasis would stimulate the Soviet Union into working harder so as to be able to overcome it through offensive force improvement,[8] so what? Generically, the claim that this or that American initiative will catalyze Soviet reactions tends to be accorded far too respectful a hearing. Certainly it is sensible to consider adversary reactions and to take a full systemic look at possibilities, but a country as wealthy (and as responsible for international security) as the United States should not be deterred by the mere prospect of competition from undertaking necessary programs. (For example, an MX ICBM, deployed in a multiple protective structure [MPS] mode, will certainly have some noteworthy impact upon Soviet arms competitive activity, but such recognition does not constitute proof of the folly of deploying MX/MPS).[9] Crude though it may sound, the United States would probably achieve more in the field of arms control if it decided to achieve and sustain a politically useful measure of strategic superiority,[10] than if it continues its endorsement of the elusive quality known as essential equivalence.

SUPERIORITY FOR STABILITY

If it is true, or at least probable, that a central war could be won or lost, then it has to follow that the concept of strategic superiority should be revived in popularity in the West. Superiority has a variety of possible meanings, rang-

[8]An argument central to the case against urban-area ABM defense was that its banning by treaty would break the action-reaction cycle of the arms race: the Soviet Union would not need to develop and deploy offensive forces to overcome such an American deployment (in order to preserve their assured destruction capability). It is a matter of history that the ABM treaty banned the ABM defense of U. S. cities, but Soviet offensive force improvements have marched steadily onward. The action-reaction thesis was logical and reasonable; it just happened to be wrong (it neglected the local color, the domestic engines of the arms competition).

[9]If U.S. MX/MPS should induce the Soviet Union to proceed down a similar path, then stability (by anyone's definition) would be promoted. Rubles spent on MPSs are rubles not spent on missiles and warheads. It is true that an MPS system in place might attract the Soviet Union to producing large numbers of missiles, undetected, to be surge-deployed in a period of acute need. However, the Soviet Government can produce ICBMs secretly now—in the absence of an MPS system they could be fired from pre-surveyed "soft" sites. The verification argument against MX/MPS is not a telling one, but—as a hedge—deployment of a fairly thin (preferentially assigned) ballistic missile defense system around the MPS could purchase an extraordinary degree of leverage vis-à-vis any secretly (or suddenly) deployed Soviet missiles. See Colin S. Gray, *The MX ICBM: Multiple Protective Structure (MPS) Basing and Arms Control*, H1-2977-P (Croton-on-Hudson, New York: Hudson Institute, February, 1979).

[10]On the political meaning of strategic power, see Edward N. Luttwak, *Strategic Power: Military Capabilities and Political Utility, The Washington Papers*, Vol. IV (Beverly Hills, California: SAGE, 1976).

ing from the ability to dissuade a putative adversary from offering resistance (i.e., deterring a crisis), through the imposition of severe escalation discipline on opponents, to a context wherein one could prosecute actual armed conflict to a successful conclusion. There is certainly no consensus within the United States defense community today over the issue of whether or not any central war outcome is possible which would warrant description as victory. However, a consensus is emerging to the effect that the Soviet Union appears to believe in the possibility of victory, and that the time is long-overdue for a basic overhaul of our intellectual capital in the nuclear deterrence field.[11] At the very least, most defense analysts would endorse the proposition that it is important for the United States to be able to deny the Soviet Union victory on its own terms.

There is a need for Western strategic thinkers to address and overcome the emerging tension between the (probable) requirements of high-quality deterrence, and the still-authoritative and inhibiting ideas of crisis and arms race instability which have directed the U.S. defense community away from programs that speak to Soviet reality. A false choice has misinformed the structure of our thinking. The historical record of the arms competition since the mid-1960s shows that the choice has not been between, on the one hand, a measure of U.S. restraint which would facilitate Soviet acquisition of an assured destruction capability—an achievement that would promote the prospects of arms control negotiations intended to codify a more stable strategic environment—and, on the other hand, an absence of American restraint which would serve to stimulate Soviet countervailing programs and which would be doomed to failure anyway. Instead, the choice has been between a measure of American restraint which facilitated the Soviet drive to achieve a not implausible war-winning capability, and a relative absence of restraint which would greatly complicate the life of Soviet defense planners. Overall, the evidence suggests that the Soviet Union has not been seeking a deterrent, as that concept and capability has been (mis?)understood in the West for nearly twenty years. The choice the United States confronts today is whether or not it will tolerate Soviet acquisition, unmatched, of an emerging war-fighting capability which might, with some good judgment and some luck, produce success in crisis diplomacy and in war.

[11]Noteworthy endeavors since the mid-1970s include: Robert Jervis, "Deterrence Theory Revisited," *World Politics*, Vol. XXXI, No. 2 (January, 1979), pp. 289–324; Patrick Morgan, *Deterrence: A Conceptual Analysis* (Beverly Hills, California: SAGE, 1977); and Richard Rosecrance, *Strategic Deterrence Reconsidered, Adelphi Paper* No. 116 (London: IISS, Spring 1975). Even well-considered judgments published as recently as 1975 can look a little fragile in 1979. Consider these words of Professor Rosecrance: "Thus it is possible to say that although the deterrent requirements that were deemed necessary to protect Europe in the 1950s are probably not currently being met, they may not have to be met. An improvement in the Soviet-Western relationship makes them less necessary now than they were then." *Ibid.*, p. 36.

The instability arguments that are leveled against those who urge an American response (functionally) in kind are somewhat fragile. For example, there is good reason to believe that the Soviet Union would be profoundly discouraged by the prospect of having to wage an arms competition against an American opponent no longer severely inhibited by its long-familiar stability theory. In addition, an American war-fighting-oriented strategic posture, if well-designed, should not contribute to crisis instability. The fact that the United States might pose a theoretical first-strike threat to much of the Soviet strategic posture, should not give aid and comfort to the "use them or lose them" argument. A central purpose informing U.S. strategic posture would be its denial of any plausible Soviet theory of victory. Why the Soviet Union would be interested in starting a war that it would stand little, if any, prospect of winning is, to say the least, obscure.

The contemporary debate over strategic doctrine, whatever its eventual effect may be upon U.S. war planning and declaratory policy, has registered a qualitative advance over most of the strategic thinking of the past fifteen years. The debate has focused upon what might be needed to deter *Soviet* leaders, *qua* Soviet leaders, and some (still unduly limited) attempt has been made to consider operational, as opposed to pre-war declaratory, strategy. Theories of pre-war deterrence, however sophisticated, cannot *guarantee* that the United States will never slip into an acute crisis wherein a president has to initiate strategic nuclear employment or, *de facto*, surrender. In such a situation, a president would need realistic war plans that carried a vision of the war as a whole and embodied a theory of how military action should produce desired political ends. In short, he would be in need of strategy. Fortunately, still orthodox wisdom notwithstanding, there is no necessary tension between a realistic wartime strategy (and the posture to match) and the pre-war deterrence of undesired Soviet behavior.

DISCUSSION QUESTIONS

1. Discuss the underlying ethical/moral positions espoused by proponents of the "idealistic left," "the idealistic right," and those in the "realpolitic" camp concerning nuclear arms.
2. Discuss the controversy inherent in national monies being spent to bolster defense programs to the detriment of social service programs.
3. Investigate the American apprehension of "the bomb" in the 1950s and 1960s when people were building bomb shelters in their back yards, and American attitudes today.
4. Speculate on whether there is a Soviet equivalent of left, right, and realism.

13

IN SEARCH OF FRIENDS: DEMOCRACIES, DICTATORS, AND THE UNITED STATES

Loch Johnson

The United States exists in a world with some 178 other nations—some as friendly as Canada, others as hostile as Libya. Of these nations, only eighteen by one recent count are democracies.[1] The rest are ruled by one form or another of dictatorship—one-man rule or, at best, a small oligarchy. Democracies can be identified as those nations that permit parties or groups to compete for office in relatively free elections; another hallmark of democracy is the presence of a free press.

In contrast, dictatorships permit neither free elections nor a free press. These "closed" societies are often placed, for analytical purposes, into one of two categories: authoritarian or totalitarian. The authoritarian dictatorships are anti-communist and "right-wing," and are led by a military or civilian oligarchy, at the head of which may be a charismatic "strong man." Ferdinand E. Marcos, president of the Philippines until he was ousted in 1986, is an example. The totalitarian dictatorships are communist and "left-wing," and are led by a communist party or Marxist group. Fidel Castro, premier of Cuba, is an illustration of this type—another charismatic strong man whose views on how to organize society are quite different from Marcos'.

Another key attribute distinguishing authoritarian from totalitarian regimes—and central to this selection of readings—is the degree to which each influences (or "penetrates") the organizations of society. Some scholars argue that authoritarian dictators are content to control the political aspects of power. They wish to enjoy the fruits of high office but show little interest in forcing citizens to adopt their particular religious, social, or even political views. As long as citizens refrain from challenging their control over political office—that is, as long as they eschew demands for free elections or the right to criticize the regime—the authoritarians are content to give their people some latitude in their private lives. The totalitarian regimes, in contrast, are accused of a compulsion to dominate every aspect of society, from the family to the church to the schools and every group in between. Every mind must give its full allegiance to the state, the new opium of the masses—or so the leaders hope.

Viewed from the vantage point of this last distinction, the authoritarian regimes become more tolerable morally for the United States, argue some observers, because their behavior is less obtrusive against their own citizens, their grip less tight on their throats. Moreover, their philosophy is free of a missionary zeal to convert other nations to the "religion" of communism and is, therefore, less dangerous to U.S. foreign policy interests; indeed, democracies and authoritarian regimes are, in a sense, joined by this common threat of communist global expansion. The merits of this distinction are a central focus in this section of the book.

Whatever the differences between authoritarian and totalitarian regimes, one conclusion is indisputable: Both have political systems anathema to the values and traditions of the United States. Beyond their rejection of free elections and open discussion lies an even more chilling record. Many of these regimes have a history of savage brutality toward their own citizens. The communist totalitarian Joseph Stalin of the Soviet Union (who died in 1953) was, for example, an infamous mass murderer. So, more recently, was Pol Pot, the despotic ruler of Cambodia (a nation in Indochina which he and other communists call Kampuchea) during the late 1970s. Stalin ordered the deaths of several million people who resisted his program of forced collectivization, striking particular hard during the 1930s against the "kulak" class of prosperous and capitalist-oriented peasants. Pol Pot, a radical communist-agrarian and—astonishingly—an ally of the United States, similarly (if even less subtly) was responsible for the murder of over a million "bourgeoise"—practically anyone living in the country's cities who exhibited "suspious contacts" with the West or who seemed "intellectual" (even if their only sins were to know some French, read books, or wear glasses)—and the forced evacuation of cities to recapture a more pure rural existence. The recent film "The Killing Fields" portrays the horror of the Pol Pot reign of terror, which ended in most parts of the country when he was driven from the capital by invading communist Vietnam forces in 1979 (the same army that drove the United States from Vietnam).

The record for authoritarian regimes is unpleasant, too. President Augusto Pinochet's regime in Chile has a reputation for torturing political dissidents, many of whom have disappeared without a trace after their capture. Amnesty International, winner of the Nobel Prize for Peace in 1977, and other human-rights groups have documented such practices in Argentina and the Philippines (before their recent turns toward democracy), Panama, Haiti, Guatemala, the Soviet Union, Rwanda, Syria, and scores of other chiefly military oligarchies around the world. In all, torture has been practiced in some sixty-five countries—or more than one-third of the nations on this planet.[2]

In a word, this globe is composed of nations that few Americans would warmly embrace as friends with common values. Yet, the United States must live in the world it finds, not one it might wish for. This means choosing friends and allies from a list that is short on appeal. Not all dictators are a venal as Stalin, Pol Pot, and Pinochet, but the selection remains one of many bads and only a few goods—though, happily, there is nothing irreversible about dictatorships and occasionally a repressed people are able to throw off the bonds of tyranny and establish a democracy, as witnessed recently in the Philippines. Unfortunately, democracies too can be reversed.

And choose America must among these poor choices, for this country cannot stand alone in the world or even rely solely on the other handful of democracies. Oil, bauxite, magnesium and other resources are vital to American industry and defense; often they are available only through countries ruled by dictators and oligarchies. The United States must have markets for its goods, too; a steadily rising portion of U.S. foreign trade is conducted with nations whose internal political practices most Americans would find repugnant. Moreover, as we have learned from two world wars, the United States must have military allies to protect itself against powerful adversaries. Sometimes in order to guard the security interests of this nation, U.S. leaders have had to join arms with dictators. A classic illustration is the U.S.–Soviet alliance against the Axis powers in World War II—an unsavory but necessary choice made as a means to defeat what at the time was an even more dangerous threat: the Nazi war machine.

At the heart of the readings in this section are several vital normative questions, among them: What nations of the world should the United States support or shun? What criteria should be used to make this often difficult judgment? Before turning to the readings, it may be useful to examine briefly the empirical question: What nations has the United States displayed an affinity toward in the recent past?

Data on U.S. ties with other nations through formal agreements (treaties and other international commitments) provide an important index of America's associations abroad. An examination of these agreements for the three decades following World War II (from the Truman through the Ford Administration) reveals that 58 percent were signed with democratic regimes, 37 percent with authoritarian regimes, and only 5 percent with totalitarian regimes.[3] Since the Kennedy Administration (1961–1963), the proclivity of the United States to select authoritarian states as international partners has begun to rival, in number, U.S. pacts with democracies.

Throughout this period, with few exceptions, America has kept Marxist regimes at arm's length. Despite the low percentage of U.S. agreements with totalitarian regimes, however, the United States did sign sixty-four international agreements with the Soviet Union during this period; and, today, America carries on trade arrangements with the USSR, sells IBMs and other goods to the world's largest communist state (the People's Republic of China, PRC), and even engages in brisk commerce with Angola—a Marxist regime which is at the same time the target of CIA-sponsored paramilitary warfare!

Overall, though, in its selection of international partners the United States has shown a decided preference for its neighbors in the western hemisphere and for nations on the perimeter of the communist Eurasian land mass—a combination of democratic and authoritarian regimes. In the postwar period, the United Kingdom, Canada, and Japan topped the list of America's agreement partners. Among the "top twelve" appear, as well, three other members (to join Canada) of the North Atlantic Treaty Alliance (NATO, the chief western defense pact signed in 1949)—France, West Germany, and Italy—revealing the strong U.S. affinity for Western European democracies. At the same time, two other key regions are represented on the list: Latin America (with Mexico and Brazil) and the Far East (with, in addition to Japan, the Philippines, the Republic of China, the Republic of Korea, and Pakistan). The order is:

1. United Kingdom
2. Canada
3. Japan
4. Philippines
5. Mexico
6. Brazil
7. Republic of China
8. South Korea
9. France
10. West Germany
11. Italy
12. Pakistan

The purpose of the readings that follow is to encourage thought about the "rightness" of these and other U.S. alignments since World War II. The selections offer a range of views from three individuals who have given a good deal of thought to this subject. In the first selection, entitled "Doctrine of Moral Equivalence," Dr. Jeane J. Kirkpatrick, a political scientist and former U.S. ambassador to the United Nations during the early years of the Reagan administration, advances a theme for which she has become well known: The United States must resist totalitarian regimes without exception, because of both their inherently repulsive characteristics and their ties to the Soviet Union. Her fear of totalitarian regimes in the western hemisphere—more Cubas, and perhaps more Cuban missile crises—overmasters any concern she might have about fate of Latinos languishing under the more common authoritarian rule found south of the border.

For Michael Walzer, a political philosopher, all tyrannies—authoritarian and totalitarian—remain an object of scorn. In his "Totalitarianism vs. Authoritarianism," he rejects the Kirkpatrick thesis that of the two forms of repression, authoritarianism is the more benign, and that it will always be better for the United States to stand apart from the totalitarians. He prefers to examine the merits of U.S. ties abroad on a case-by-case basis, holding his nose when America must associate with unsavory regimes and always looking for opportunities to encourage democratic principles within other nations. Above all, his anguish goes out to the victims of repression, regardless of whether the heavy hand is right or left.

The third selection is by the late Senator Frank Church (D., Idaho), former chairman of the Senate Foreign Relations Committee (1978–1980). He believed that a major mistake of American foreign policy was to assume automatically that left-wing, Marxist revolutions could be resisted only by U.S. military intervention—either overtly as in Vietnam or covertly as in Nicaragua. For Church, a better response was to employ the power of diplomacy and the lure of economic inducements, especially trade incentives that would improve the living standards of poor nations and reduce the appeal of Marxist rhetoric. Further, in his view, sometimes the best response was a "hands off" policy which would allow the developing nations to work out their own problems, free from interference by the United States.

Each of these selections requires the reader to weigh in his or her mind important issues of conviction and morality. Which nations should we deal with as friends and allies? Should the United States ever interfere in the affairs of other countries? What should be the U.S. response when nations trammel the rights of their own citizens? These are enormously difficult questions. The advice of John Quincy Adams 150 years ago (in his Inaugural Address) was for America to be the friend of all the liberties in the world, but the guardian of only her own. How well does this advice hold up today? Can the United States honor its cherished ideals and succeed in a world where most nations reject these principles? The verdict is still out.

NOTES

1. Arendt Lijphart, *Democracies* (New Haven, CT: Yale University Press, 1984), p. 8.
2. Juan Mendez, Newsletter, Amnesty International USA, New York (September 1987), p. 2.
3. Loch Johnson, *The Making of International Agreements: Congress Confronts the Executive* (New York: New York University, 1984), p. 33.

Doctrine of Moral Equivalence

Jeane J. Kirkpatrick

...But even if our whole policy is not governed by obsession with East-West rivalry, and even if we do not have an uncontrollable desire to impose military solutions everywhere, surely in Central America the United States reflects, in purest form, all the worst tendencies of U.S. foreign policy: seeing communist influence where there are only indigenous social and economic factors; attempting military solutions where only reforms are appropriate.

Once again, I respectfully dissent. The government headed by Ronald Reagan has not the slightest tendency to imagine that the political turmoil in Central America has no roots in social and economic problems. We know the people of El Salvador, Honduras, Nicaragua, and Costa Rica have been ill fed, ill housed, ill clothed, and illiterate for centuries. We know they have generally been governed by bad governments, one-party systems as under Somoza or military dictatorships as in El Salvador before 1979. We know that there existed in both countries neglect, unmet needs, unfulfilled hopes, and that these gave rise to movements for reform and revolution. We understand, broadly speaking, how it happened.

In both Nicaragua and El Salvador, three political currents existed:

First, the traditional oligarchs who had most of what there was to get;

Second, a large group of middle class, farmers, trade unionists, businessmen, who wanted to get rid of the dictator and establish a democratic government; and

Third, a small group of Marxist-Leninists tied to Havana and Moscow, trained, as they themselves have told us, in Havana, in the Middle East with

---

Jeane J. Kirkpatrick, "Doctrine of Moral Equivalence," *Department of State Bulletin* 84 (August 1984), 59–60.

the PLO, or elsewhere in the Soviet block; armed and advised by their Soviet sponsors.

In Nicaragua, these two groups, the democrats and Leninists, joined in a broad-based popular front to overthrow Somoza. Their program was democracy, but once in power, the Leninists forced out the democrats and betrayed the promises of democracy made to the Organization of American States (OAS) and the Nicaraguan people. Most of the democrats are now in exile; many are with the Contras, still fighting for a democratic Nicaragua. The Leninists, meanwhile, have consolidated one-party control.

In El Salvador, where the same three-sided contest existed, no popular front was formed. Instead, after a coup overthrew General Romero in October 1979, the democratic forces came to power in the administration of Napoleon Duarte, who immediately undertook to democratize the government, nationalize credit, and instigate sweeping land reforms; the guerrillas and the traditional armed right took up armed struggle against the government—one operating out of Managua; the other, it is said, out of Guatemala.

The stakes are high. The Soviet Union understood the strategic importance of the region, through which most sealanes pass with most of the oil and other strategic materials the United States would supply to Europe in case of an emergency. By 1967 the Soviets were writing in theoretical journals about opportunities for tying down the United States in the Western Hemisphere and rendering us less able to act in such remote places as Europe and Asia. The United States, finally, has also understood the stakes and the challenge and believes that challenge must be met.

Here, concerning U.S. policy in Central America, the charge of obsessive concern with East-West relations melds imperceptibly into an argument that there is no significant moral difference between Soviet policy in Eastern Europe and U.S. policy in Central America. This position was put with clarity during the Oxford Union debate by a questioner who asked:

> It is not true that your country controls in, for example, the whole of Latin America, many corrupt and puppet governments—and surely the question we are asking you to address yourself tonight is what is the difference, if any—and I suspect there is no difference—as do many, many people in this country—what is the difference between your puppet regimes and the puppet regimes of the Soviet Union?

In a followup exchange the questioner charged Central American governments, supported by the United States, with "terrorizing, torturing, killing."

The first striking fact about views such as those of the questioner is that the level of outrage far exceeds the level of information. The charges do not square with the facts. The United States does not, repeat not, support dictatorships in Central America. Let me be specific. It is not generally understood in Europe that the United States tried hard to encourage and help develop a democracy in Nicaragua:

- By supporting the efforts to replace Somoza and helping to negotiate his departure—supporting the OAS resolution that called for his ouster;
- By providing $25 million in emergency food and medical aid in the first week the Sandinistas came to power and $115 million in generous, prompt economic aid; and
- By offering assistance of diverse kinds relevant to the development of democratic institutions, even though the Sandinista junta gave early signs of claiming a monopoly of power and imposing censorship. We also supported, inside the international fiscal institutions such as the Inter-American Development Bank, Nicaraguan loan applications enabling it to secure from these institutions more assistance than the Somoza regime had received from international fiscal institutions in the previous 20 years.

The United States remains hopeful that Nicaragua's government will decide to cease destabilization of its neighbors, relax repression, and expand freedom in Nicaragua.

In El Salvador it is well known that the United States supported the coup that brought down General Romero in October 1979, installed Napoleon Duarte and his Christian Democrats in office, and sponsored the land reforms which were designed by AFL-CIO specialists. From that time forward, the United States has encouraged and assisted a process of democratic development in El Salvador, which has been warmly supported by the Salvadoran people—who walk for miles, stand for hours, braving bullets and threats to cast their votes in favor of democracy in El Salvador. In a hundred ways, the people of El Salvador continue to demonstrate their lack of support for the guerrillas whose violence has not won the hearts or minds of the Salvadorans. Violent minorities—relying on revolution and not persuasion—can devastate the economy, terrorize families and villages. But in more than 4 years of trying, they have not prevented the great majority of Salvadorans from showing their opposition to politics of violence and extending their support for democratic politics.

It is true that the United States has strategic goals in Central America. We believe it would be bad for the people of the region and bad for the United States for there to be installed one-party, Marxist-Leninist states integrated into the Soviet bloc and willing to have their territory serve as bases for the projection of Soviet military power in the hemisphere. That is the strategic basis of our policy. We also have serious political and moral grounds for this position.

• We do not think it is moral to leave small countries and helpless people defenseless against conquest by violent minorities which are armed and trained by remote dictatorships. The amount of Soviet-bloc arms funneled into El Salvador is staggering. So is the sophistication of the guerrilla command and control system, including a special communication system that guides the insurgency from outside Managua.

• We believe our political goal, a more democratic and stable hemisphere, requires building democracies, not the multiplication of dictatorships.

The U.S. Government warmly supports the democratic governments of Costa Rica and Honduras and works to further democratic development in Central America. To that end, the recommendations of the Kissinger commission have been translated into a legislative package which has been submitted to Congress. The package calls for a mix of social, economic, political, and security assistance, not unlike the support package that helped to rebuild Europe after World War II.

The U.S. Government agrees with the National Bipartisan Commission on Central America that:

> Central America is both vital and vulnerable and that whatever other cases may arise to claim the nation's attention, the U.S. cannot afford to turn away from that threatened region. Central America's crisis is our crisis.

We do see East-West dimensions to that crisis. We do see external support as well as indigenous social and economic factors. We want to respond to all levels of the problem. We do seek a negotiated diplomatic solution. We support and have supported a wide variety of diplomatic efforts, the most important current one, the Contadora process, to resolve the regional problems within the region. We will continue to do so.

The time has come in this discussion to confront the issue of using force. I am aware that the United States is charged today with displaying a proclivity for the use of force to solve problems, a penchant for military solutions. The proofs cited, as I understand it, are our landing in Grenada, which both we and the Grenadans call a liberation, not an invasion; our military assistance to the Government of El Salvador; our presence, through military maneuvers, in Honduras; and our putative support for Nicaragua's insurgents. Sometimes participation in the multinational force in Lebanon is also adduced to support the view that the U.S. Government is headed by gunslingers who would, in the words of a famous American cigarette advertisement, "rather fight than switch."

I desire to deal forthrightly with these questions....The facts are not really difficult to establish. El Salvador has been the object of unceasing armed attacks by insurgents whose identity, training, supplies, and goals are clear. The leadership of El Salvador's FMLN [Farabundo Marti National Liberation Front] has been open about their commitment to armed struggle and prolonged war. An article by Shafik Handal in the *World Marxist Review* of fall 1980 straightforwardly explains that the FMLN has no interest in a negotiated settlement, being persuaded that full victory is within reach. Since then, certain proposals for what they call "power sharing" have been made—all involve "restructuring" the government; "purging" the armed forces, national guard, and police; and otherwise assuming power over the state. They have continued to this moment to reject utterly "power sharing" based on free elections held in the presence of international observers. The reasons, doubtless, are that they know they do not enjoy popular support; and they do not, in any case, recognize popular sovereignty expressed through free elections as the legitimate basis of a legitimate government.

Confronted with the need to combat the guerrillas and also control violence from other sources, the Government of El Salvador requires arms, training, and communications equipment. Otherwise, it will simply be vanquished by superior force, after which a new dictatorship will be imposed on an unwilling people. There is only one group seeking to impose a military solution in El Salvador; they are the guerrillas. It is all very well to argue that persons of good will ought to be able to find a peaceful solution peaceably. But if one side makes surrender a precondition of peace, then the alternatives are only to surrender or resist. We can, of course, continue to try to persuade the other party to reconsider. And that is precisely what the United States has done and is doing in El Salvador. Meanwhile, however, we believe it necessary and acceptable to supply military assistance needed to permit the government to continue to resist guerrilla attacks. Morality does not, indeed cannot, require that we stand by passively while a small nation—underequipped and unsophisticated—succumbs to well-armed and trained guerrilla forces.

More than El Salvador is at stake. Subversion and violence have already disrupted ordinary life in Costa Rica and Honduras. Do we leave them essentially defenseless against externally supported violence? What of Chad? What of the Sudan? Has the transvaluation of values so far progressed that now, in the West, it is not permissible to help countries help protect themselves against armed subversion and armed aggression?

From our side of the Atlantic, it sometimes seems that in Europe there is more sympathy for the Nicaraguans who threaten the peace, independence, and freedom of all their neighbors than for the neighbors themselves. Sometimes it seems there is more "understanding" of the thousands of Cuban and Soviet-bloc military advisers in Nicaragua—one of whose tasks it is to direct the struggle against El Salvador—than for the 37 or so U.S. military advisers in El Salvador who help that country fend off its would-be conquerers. Sometimes it seems that there is more enthusiasm for Nicaragua's preparations for what gives every evidence of being staged, rigged elections than for El Salvador's earnest efforts to have genuinely free elections under difficult circumstances. Sometimes it sounds as though our friends are as inclined to exaggerate America's minimal use of force for limited, defensive purposes as they are to minimize the Soviet bloc's regular reliance on force to subvert and overwhelm hapless, too often helpless, Third World nations....

Totalitarianism vs. Authoritarianism

Michael Walzer

Every political theorist hopes that his concepts and distinctions will turn, magically, into common currency, so that men and women on the street will talk exactly as he does. And he fears at the same time that his work will be distorted, corrupted, appropriated for partisan uses over which he has no control. Most of the theorists who first worked out the concept of totalitarianism in the late 1940s and the early 1950s lived to see both their hopes and fears fully realized. "Totalitarian" quickly became a cold war tag, our everyday name for the Communist regimes of the East. By contrast, we described ourselves and our allies in those innocent days with words like "free" and "liberal"; our governments were "constitutionalist." The struggle had this form: the free world against communism, limited government against totalitarianism—a fantasy version of what political theory is all about.

Today we are too sophisticated for such simple distinctions, or too cynical. We know that the free world includes a large number of brutal and repressive regimes. These are "our" dictatorships, many of which, to the naked eye, don't look all that different from "theirs." But the new cold war-

---

Michael Walzer, "Totalitarianism vs. Authoritarianism," *The New Republic* (July 4 and 11, 1981), 21; 24–25. Reprinted with permission of *The New Republic.*

riors of the 1980s want to draw the line exactly as it was drawn in the 1950s. So they have dug deeper into the original theory, looking for richer conceptual plunder. And indeed, as the theory was worked out by writers like Hannah Arendt and Carl Friedrich, totalitarianism was not contrasted with freedom. There was, after all, nothing new about unfree government. Most states through most of human history have been unfree; most still are. Totalitarianism was a radically new kind of unfreedom, a new species of the genus "tyrannus," different from all the others. This was the difference on which the theorists focused their attention, and it played a part too in political debates among small groups of leftist intellectuals struggling to understand Stalinist terror. But it was a difference largely ignored in the official ideology of the cold war.

Now, however, it has been taken up by the new cold war ideologists, led, for the moment, by our representative to the United Nations [Dr. Jeane Kirkpatrick]. Yes, they say, many of our allies are tyrants and always have been. But these are ordinary, old-fashioned tyrants. The real enemy, the present danger, is totalitarianism, that is, communism. And for the sake of the struggle against communism, we must make our peace with tyranny. Authoritarian regimes in South Korea or Guatemala or Argentina are not so bad when compared with Russia or North Vietnam or Cuba. (China, with which, it appears, we must also make our peace, tends to get overlooked in these discussions.) We must not allow moralistic qualms about routine oppression—the tyrants ye always have with you—to get in the way of our outrage at what is truly new and truly dangerous. Compared to the cold war rhetoric of the 1950s, this sort of talk represents, I suppose, a more sophisticated appropriation of the original theory. It is not, however, a less corrupt one.

The original theory still has genuine value. Totalitarianism is indeed a new kind of tyranny, not entirely without precedent in the long history of tyranny, but new nonetheless. Partly its novelty consists in nothing more than a radical improvement in bureaucratic and police control, the introduction of a more advanced technology of surveillance: old tyranny with new machinery. One of the most frightening features of Orwell's *1984* was the two-way television screen. But machines are of little use without the will to use them, and what is most novel and most important about totalitarianism is the peculiarly modern ambition of its leaders: to control everything, to wipe out not merely opposition, but every form of difference, recalcitrance, hesitation, private doubt, and caution, to create an entirely new order and even a new kind of human being. Hence the need to penetrate every aspect of social life, religion, culture, and family, to seize every secondary association, to supervise all communication between persons, all movement between places, all thought and all feeling. Older tyrannies were marked by a more limited ambition. Their leaders wanted simply to stay in power, to enjoy the fruits of power for as long as possible. They were a danger to rivals and opponents, but private life, traditional routines, passive minorities were generally (not always) safe from their interventions.

That is the key distinction and it remains, to my mind, a useful guide to 20th-century politics. But it can't just be applied mechanically, dividing the world, for totalitarianism is an "ideal type," a picture of horrifying perfection never quite achieved in fact, while authoritarianism is a catchall category. The idea of totality bears the marks of its discovery in the immediate aftermath of the Holocaust and in the last years of Stalin's personal rule. The concentration camp, Hannah Arendt wrote, is the model of totalitarian control. The Hitler and Stalin regimes come as close as regimes have ever come to realizing that model, but even they realized it for some, not for all, of their subjects. And if we set aside the Soviet Union, where Stalinism remains today a regime-in-reserve, it is clear that all the other examples of post-World War II Communist and fascist governments are failed totalitarianisms. They don't measure up to Arendt's standard, they fall short of Orwell's brilliant science fiction, their terror isn't total. Between these regimes and other sorts of tyranny it isn't easy to draw a sharp line. And it is sheer willfulness, ideological relentlessness, to insist that this line, once it is worked out, will conform to the cold war division between East and West.

Consider now the two major moral/political arguments of the new cold warriors. I'll take them from Jeane Kirkpatrick's *Commentary* article ("Dictatorships and Double Standards," November 1979), a particularly good example of contemporary ideology, even if it isn't, or just because it isn't, a particularly good article. The first of these is an argument about political possibility. Communist totalitarianism brings with it a long, dark night. "There is no instance of a revolutionary 'socialist' or Communist society being democraticized," writes Kirkpatrick. Our own tyrants, by contrast, are sometimes replaced by democratic regimes—though it is always important for the stability of the new democracy that the replacement take place *very slowly*. Kirkpatrick doesn't discuss what might be called the reverse replacement rate. In fact, I'm afraid, the decline of democracy in the free world is rather more noticeable than its slow advance. In any case, this is a false distinction. Hungary, Czechoslovakia, and Poland probably would be democratic states today were it not for the Red Army. The Red Army is a threat to human freedom, but communism, in these states at least, is an ugly but not a powerful political system. There is nothing in its internal mechanics that rules out a democratic transformation. Assuming that the Russians don't intervene—an unlikely but analytically necessary assumption—the prospects for democracy are probably better, certainly no worse, in much of Eastern Europe than, to cite some of Kirkpatrick's odder examples, in Argentina, Brazil, South Korea, and Zaire. In all these cases, social structure and political culture are far more important than the current regime in shaping the long-term evolution.

The second argument is about relative brutality. Old-fashioned tyrannies, according to Kirkpatrick, because they don't set out to transform their societies, do much less damage to them. They tolerate existing patterns of misery and injustice, but at least they don't create new ones. And their subjects are accustomed to the old patterns, have long ago adjusted to them and learned how to survive. Hence "such societies create no refugees." This is the "damning contrast" between Communist regimes and "other autocracies." The massive refugee population of the modern world is largely a creation of Communist totalitarianism. It would be nice—not for the refugees but for the ideological peace of mind of the rest of us—if this were true. But it isn't true. The refugees who fled Hungary in 1956 or Afghanistan in 1980 were fleeing the Red Army, not domestic oppression. The million Cubans who have reached our shores since the 1960s probably could be matched by a million Haitians, were the latter given a comparable welcome. And the largest single group of refugees since World War II was produced by Pakistani repression in East Bengal, which was nothing if not old-fashioned. Certainly there are Communist states that fit Kirkpatrick's account. East Germany and Cambodia are different but equally clearcut examples. But the line she draws is a fabrication.

The contrast between totalitarian and authoritarian regimes is a conceptual contrast, not a practical one. It doesn't conform to, nor does it justify, our actual alliances. It doesn't make Kissinger's Pakistani "tilt" of 1971 smell any better. It doesn't rule out economic (or even military) cooperation with Communist China. One can't pull politics or morality out of a theoretical hat. That sort of thing is always a trick. Theory, *once we have it right,* does nothing more than shape our perceptions, guide our understanding; within the framework it provides, choices still have to be made.

The hardest choice, and the one for the sake of which the new cold war ideology has been worked out, is simply this: an authoritarian regime, old-fashioned, brutal, repressive, allied to the West, is threatened by a revolutionary movement some of whose leaders have totalitarian ambitions and/or Russian connections. What should we do? The claim of the new cold warriors is that the liberal impulse in all such cases is to support the revolutionaries or at least to desert at the first opportunity the authoritarian regime. And what they want instead is the opposite policy, a steadfast commitment to the regime, because totalitarianism is the greater danger, the irreversible transformation and so on.

But this is to turn policy into a reflex of ideology (disguised as theory). There just isn't going to be one answer in cases like the one I've described, and to act as if there is one answer—we get it right or wrong, we win or lose—is the beginning of political disaster. Often we can't do anything at all. Or rather, our choice is the same choice that the Russians have faced again and again in Eastern Europe: send in the troops or let the local conflict take its course. But let's assume that there is room, some limited room, for political maneuver (economic aid, military supply, diplomatic pressure, and so on). Then, obviously, the direction of our maneuvers will have to be determined by the shape of the terrain. How much popular support does the regime have? How much capacity for change? Who are the rebels and what is their "cause"? What sorts of alliances have they already made and how stable are those alliances? What are our own strategic interests in the area? That last question is generally taken to mean we should align ourselves with the established regime. In fact, however, if there really are strategic interests, and if we take them seriously, then it would seem to follow that we should line up as early as possible with the side most likely to win, so long as there is a real chance of keeping the winners out of the Russian camp. It is characteristic of the new cold warriors that they would support authoritarian governments both when it is in our interests to do so and also when it isn't—so that one is led to suspect that they just support authoritarian governments. In any case, there probably are such governments that we ought on balance to help. Otherwise, we could hardly have any relations at all with third world states. And there probably are oppositionists and revolutionaries whom we ought on balance to help too.

Rarely, however, in any part of the third world, are there going to be old or new regimes, governments, or movements to which we should be ideologically committed. We don't have to become apologists for the internal policies of our allies. What we owe them at most is critical support. Foreign policy is always a double business: we have to pursue our interests and we have to defend our values. In the long run, we hope that these two efforts come together, but at any given moment there are conflicts and contradictions. Maybe it is in our interest to support, say, the present South Korean regime. But we must also, for the sake of our values, maintain some critical distance from it. And that kind of argument doesn't work only for right-wing regimes. After 1960, it was in our interest that Cuban communism develop in, say, a Yugoslav rather than a Bulgarian direction, and we might have accomplished that, or at least assisted in it, through some sort of economic cooperation. But cooperation would have been no excuse for a failure to criticize Castro's dictatorship, the repression of dissidents, the campaign against homosexuals, and so on.

A policy of this kind assumes that there is no long, dark night, no thousand-year Reich, no totalitarian transformation that is proof against political opposition and social change. That has to be, I think, the working assumption of any sane diplomacy. The new cold warriors exploit what we might think of as the apocalyptic features of the theory of totalitarianism. And in the 20th century it is difficult to avoid some engagement with, some hard contemplation of, apocalypse. In political terms that means that there have been and will be again regimes so evil that the only moral stand one can adopt toward them is absolute opposition. But what policies follow from that moral stand? Surely Stalin's was one such regime, and yet we fought with Stalin against the Nazis. Even evil has its degrees. We must hope—we can reasonably believe—that it also has its duration.

In the third world, at any rate, there is not likely to be much permanence—no sustained development toward modernity and liberty, but also very few stable or solidly established tyrannies. No doubt many of the tyrants will have totalitarian ambitions; the rhetoric of revolution is now the *lingua franca* of the third world. But that only means that there will be many failed totalitarianisms. Whether these failures will be bloodier than the "other autocracies" is a question unlikely to find a yes or no answer. Some of them will and some won't. For our part, we can and should maintain a steady hostility toward every sort of totalitarian ambition. But that is no reason for supporting the "other autocracies" or excusing their bloodiness. We can make the alliances we have to make on both sides of this shadowy line, and we can condemn when we must the internal policies of our allies. I understand, of course, that there are serious diplomatic difficulties involved in any such policy—much discussed and never overcome during the Carter years. But it is a worse policy to refuse altogether to confront those difficulties. The real danger, *the present danger*, of the new cold war ideology is that it will drive us into alliances that our material defense does not require and rule out the outspokenness that the defense of our values does require. And all this for the sake of a misunderstood and badly applied political theory!

But perhaps I overestimate the power of theory (it is a common professional mistake). One might detect among contemporary cold warriors a sneaking sympathy for "traditional autocrats [who] leave in place existing allocations of wealth, power, status, and other resources...." On the far left, there is often similar sympathy for revolutionaries who upset those allocations, even if they do so only in order to establish a new tyranny—and this view, too, has its theoretical rationale. But I would propose a different sympathy: for the tortured dissidents, the imprisoned oppositionists, the threatened minorities, all the "disappeared" and murdered men and women of all the tyrannies, old and new. And we don't need a political theory to explain why we should keep these people always in the forefront of our consciousness, their names on the tip of our tongues.

We Must Learn to Live with Revolutions

Frank Church

America's inability to come to terms with revolutionary change in the Third World has been a leitmotif of U.S. diplomacy for nearly 40 years. This failure has created our biggest international problems in the post-war era.

But the root of our problem is not, as many Americans persist in believing, the relentless spread of communism. Rather, it is our own difficulty in understanding that Third World revolutions are primarily nationalist, not communist. Nationalism, not capitalism or communism, is the dominant political force in the modern world.

You might think that revolutionary nationalism and the desire for self-determination would be relatively easy for Americans—the first successful revolutionaries to win their independence—to understand. But instead we have been dumbfounded when other peoples have tried to pursue the goals of our own revolution two centuries ago.

Yes, the United States generally has supported political independence movements, as in India or later in Africa, against the traditional colonial powers of Europe. Those situations were easy for us—we've never been nationalists. But where a nationalist uprising was combined with a Marxist element of some kind or with violent revolutionary behavior, Americans have come unhinged.

This happened most dramatically in the biggest tragedy of American diplomacy since World War II, Vietnam. But it has happened repeatedly in other countries as well, most recently in Nicaragua and El Salvador.

Given the size and the seriousness of our failures to deal successfully with nationalistic revolutions, you might think we'd be busy trying to figure out why we've done so badly, and how we could do better in the future. But on the contrary, we simply stick to discredited patterns of behavior, repeating the old errors as though they had never happened before.

The latest example is the report of the Kissinger Commission on Latin America which painted events in Central America in ominously stark colors. The commission said that in principle America can accept revolutionary situations, but in Nicaragua and El Salvador we cannot. Why? Because of Soviet and Cuban involvement.

But the sad fact is that the Soviets will always try to take advantage of revolutionary situations, as will the Cubans, particularly in this hemisphere.

Frank Church, "We Must Learn to Live with Revolutions," *The Washington Post*, 11 March 1984, C1, C4. Reprinted with permission of Bethine Church.

To solve our problem we have to learn to adapt to revolutions even when communists are involved in them, or we will continue to repeat the errors of the last four decades.

Revolutionary regimes are not easy to live with—particularly for a country as conservative as the United States has become. As Hannah Arendt—no Marxist herself—noted in her classic work, "On Revolution," the United States has made a series of desperate attempts to block revolutions in other countries, "with the result that American power and prestige were used and misused to support obsolete and corrupt political regimes that long since had become objects of hatred and contempt among their own citizens."

Why does America, the first nation born of revolution in the modern age, find it so difficult to come to terms with revolutionary change in the late 20th century?

One answer involves the nature of our own revolution. It was essentially a revolt against political stupidity and insensitivity. With sparsely populated, easily accessible and abundant lands, the restless and dissatisfied in early America had an outlet for their discontent. The young United States never had to deal with the limitless misery of an impoverished majority.

In the first half of this century, when the country faced sharpened class conflict as a result of the excesses of an unbridled capitalism, we were blessed with patrician leaders, Theodore and Franklin Roosevelt, who had the foresight to introduce needed reforms. An intelligent, conservative property-owning class had the sense to accept them.

But our experience is alien to other countries which do not share our natural wealth. In poor countries a desperate majority often lives on the margin of subsistence. A selfish property-owning minority and, often, an indifferent middle class intransigently protect their privileges. Dissidence is considered subversive. It isn't surprising that those who seek change resort to insurrection.

They take their lead not from the American, but from the French revolutionary tradition where, in Arendt's phrase, the "passion of compassion" led the Robespierres of the time to terrible excesses in the name of justice for the impoverished masses.

The spectacle of violent, sometimes anarchic revolutionary activity combined with an obsessive fear that revolutions will inevitably fall prey to communism has led us to oppose radical change all over the Third World, even where it is abundantly clear that the existing order offers no real hope of improving the lives of the great majority. As a result, those who ought to be our allies—those who are ready to fight for justice for the impoverished majority—find themselves, as revolutionaries, opposed not only to the ruling forces in their own societies, but the United States.

I am not arguing that revolutions are romantic or pleasant. History is full of examples, from France to Iran, of revolutions born in brutality and often accompanied by extended bloodbaths of vengeance and reprisal, and which ultimately produce just another form of authoritarianism to replace the old. But the fact that we may not like the revolutionary process or its results is, alas, not going to prevent revolutions. On the other hand, the fact that revolutions are going to happen need not mean disaster for the United States. Our past failures do suggest a way we can adapt to revolutions without fighting them or sacrificing vital national interests.

Consider the case of Vietnam. Our overriding concern with "monolithic" communism led us grossly to misread the revolution in that country. Ignoring centuries of enmity between the Vietnamese and the Chinese, our leaders interpreted a possible victory for Ho Chi Minh's forces as a victory for international communism. The war against the French and then the war among the Vietnamese in our eyes became a proxy war by China and the Soviet Union even after those two powers had split, destroying the myth of "monolithic" communism. Indochina, in the new American demonology, was seen as the first in a series of falling dominoes.

Vietnam did fall to the communists, but only two dominoes followed—Laos and Cambodia, both of which we had roped into the war. Thailand, Malaysia and Indonesia continue to exist on their own terms. The People's Republic of China, for whom Hanoi was supposed to be a proxy, is now engaged in armed skirmishes against Vietnam.

Meanwhile, the United States, having been compelled to abandon the delusion of containing the giant of Asia behind a flimsy network of pygmy governments stretched thinly around her vast frontiers, has at last shown the good sense to make friends with China. American influence, far from collapsing, has drawn strength from this sensible new policy, and has been rising ever since. As for communism taking over, it is already a waning force. The thriving economies are capitalist: Japan, South Korea, Taiwan, Hong Kong, Singapore. You don't hear Asians describing communism as the wave of the future.

If any lessons were learned from our ordeal in Southeast Asia, they have yet to show up in the Western Hemisphere, where our objective is not simply to contain, but to eradicate communism, regardless of the circumstances in each case. In pursuit of this goal, we took heed of one restraint. The legacy of resentment against us still harbored by our Latin neighbors, stemming from the days of "gunboat diplomacy," made it advisable, wherever feasible, to substitute "cloak and dagger" methods—covert instead of overt means.

Hence the American-sponsored coup to oust a democratically elected government in Guatemala in 1954. The ousted president, Jacobo Arbenz, was by American standards, a New Deal liberal. But our cold warriors of that era decided he was a red threat. As U.S. Ambassador John Peurifoy, arriving in Guatemala on his special mission, put it: "If Arbenz is not a communist, he'll do until the real thing comes along."

In Cuba, the United States spared no effort to get rid of Fidel Castro. We financed and armed an exile expeditionary force in an attempted repeat of the Guatemalan coup, only to see it routed at the Bay of Pigs. Then the CIA tried repeatedly to assassinate Castro, even enlisting the Mafia in the endeavor; and the United States imposed against Cuba the most severe trade embargo inflicted on any country since the end of World War II.

Even where the left gained power in fair and open elections, the United States has been unwilling to accept the results. Hence the Nixon administration's secret intervention in Chile aimed first at preventing the election of and then at ousting President Salvador Allende.

Despite these and other efforts by the United States, another Marxist regime did arise in the hemisphere: Nicaragua. And, true to form, the United States has again financed, armed and promoted an exile army whose objective is its overthrow.

After spending billions of dollars, and emptying the CIA's bag of dirty tricks, what do we have to show for our efforts? Obviously, the hemisphere has not been swept clean of communism. Cuba and Nicaragua have avowedly Marxist regimes; in El Salvador, an insurrection gains momentum against an American-trained and -equipped army, despite an American-sponsored agrarian reform program and our hopes for the election of a reformist president and legislature. The result defies our grand design, the army fights indifferently; the agrarian reform is stymied, and the Salvadoran middle class and traditional landed interests remain determined to elect extreme rightists to the important legislative and executive positions.

By our unrelenting hostility to Castro, we have invested him with heroic dimensions far greater than would be warranted by Cuba's intrinsic importance in the world. We are in the process of performing a similar service for the commandantes of Nicaragua and, at the same time, discrediting the legitimate domestic opponents of their political excesses. We have left Cuba no alternative to increased reliance upon Russia, and we now seem determined to duplicate the same blunder with Nicaragua.

So by any standard, American policy has failed to achieve its objective: to inoculate the hemisphere against Marxist regimes. But are we fated to cling to the disproven policy of opposing each new revolution because of Marxist involvement, even though the insurgents fight to overthrow an intolerable social and economic order?

By making the outcome of this internal struggle a national security issue for the United States, as the Kissinger Commission does, we virtually guarantee an American military intervention wherever the tide turns in favor of the insurgents. If this happened in El Salvador, it would be difficult to imagine that the present administration would stop before it had gone "to the source," Nicaragua or even Cuba. In the process, of course, we would fulfill Che Guevara's prophecy of two, three, many Vietnams in Latin America.

We should stop exaggerating the threat of Marxist revolution in Third World countries. We know now that there are many variants of Marxist governments and that we can live comfortably with some of them. The domino theory is no more valid in Central America than it was in Southeast Asia. And it is an insult to our neighbor, Mexico, for it assumes that Mexico is too weak and unsophisticated to look out for its own interests.

We repeatedly ignore the explicit signals from Marxists in Central America that they will respect our concerns. For example, we worry that the commandantes in Nicaragua will invite the Soviets or the Cubans to establish bases in their countries. Yet, the Sandinista government in Nicaragua has explicitly committed itself not to offer such bases to the Russians or Cubans. Instead, they have offered to enter into a treaty with the United States and other regional countries not to do so. And the political arm of the insurgents in El Salvador has also committed itself to no foreign bases on its soil.

Why not take them up on these commitments? The United States, with the help of other regional powers who share our interests, including Venezuela, Mexico, Colombia and Panama, has the means to ensure that the revolutionaries keep their word. If Nicaragua violated its treaty obligation to those states, the United States would have legal grounds and regional sanction for taking action.

If the threat of communist bases is real, then a negotiated agreement precluding them would surely be perceived as a "victory" for the United States and a "defeat" for the Russians. And with a Nicaraguan treaty agreement with the United States and the countries of the region, the Salvadoran insurgents, should they prevail, would surely follow suit.

Although the Nicaraguan revolution has followed classic lines, in comparative terms it has been relatively moderate. There has been no widespread terror, and the regime has shown itself sensitive to international pressure. If we cannot come to terms with the Nicaraguan revolution, then we probably are fated to oppose all revolutions in the hemisphere.

The problem is illustrated in human terms by a vignette of the Kissinger Commission in Nicaragua. According to press accounts, the members of the commission were angered by the confrontational tone of the meetings with the Nicaraguans and their obvious reliance on Soviet and Cuban intelligence.

Imagine the setting: The commission arrives in Nicaragua one week after the *contras*, supported by the United States, blow up a major oil facility.

On the one side, a largely conservative commission led by Henry Kissinger, Robert Strauss, William Clements and Lane Kirkland, men in their late 50s or 60s, expecting to be acclaimed for their willingness to listen to the upstart revolutionaries. On the other side, peacock-proud Nicaraguan *commandames* in their 30s or early 40s, men and women, who had spent years fighting in the mountains, who had seen their friends and comrades die at their side in opposition to the U.S.-supported Somoza dictatorship, and naturally resentful of U.S. support of the counterrevolution. To them, a commission led by Kissinger, architect of the campaign to destabilize Allende, had to be seen as a facade for the American plan to bring them down. Is it a wonder there was no meeting of minds?

Whoever gains power in Central America must govern. And governing means solving mundane problems: the balance between imports and exports, mobilization of capital, access to technology and know-how. The United States, the Western European countries and the nearby regional powers Colombia, Mexico and Venezuela, are the primary markets and sources of petroleum, capital and technology. The social democratic movements in Western Europe are important sources of political sustenance for revolutionary movements in Central America.

If we had the wit to work with our friends and allies rather than against them, the potential abuses and exuberance of revolution in Central America can be contained within boundaries acceptable to this country. There is no reason to transform a revolution in any of the countries of Central America, regardless from where it draws its initial external support, into a security crisis for us.

The objective of U.S. policy should be to create the conditions in which the logic of geographic proximity, access to American capital and technology and cultural opportunity can begin to exert their inexorable long-term pull. Russia is distant, despotic and economically primitive. It cannot compete with the West in terms of the tools of modernization and the concept of freedom.

But if we insist on painting the Cubas and Nicaraguas of this world—and there will be others—into a corner, we save the Russians from their own disabilities. If, on the other hand, we were to abandon our failed policy and adopt the alternative I suggest, pessimism might soon give way to optimism. After a while, democracy may begin to take root again. The wicked little oligarchies, no longer assured American protection against the grievances of their own people, may even be forced to make the essential concessions. The United States and Cuba might be trading again, joined in several regional pacts to advance the interests of both. And Marxist governments, far from overtaking the hemisphere, will be lagging behind as successful free enterprise countries set the standard.

We will marvel at the progress in our own neighborhood, measured from the day we stopped trying to repress the irrepressible and exchanged our unreasonable fear of communism for a rekindled faith in freedom.

DISCUSSION QUESTIONS

1. What nations of the world should the United States support or shun, and what criteria should be used to make this judgment?
2. Should the United States engage in trade arrangements with totalitarian or authoritariam systems or both if there are economic advantages?
3. Should we, as Church maintains, "stop exaggerating the threat of Marxist revolutions in third world countries" and try to accept and respect them as forms of government ideologically different from ours?

14

RICH NATION/ POOR NATION

Martin Slann

Poverty is a definitive economic and social condition for a large proportion of the human race and for a majority of the world's countries. Economic development is uneven at best and in many societies no evidence of it even exists. At the same time there is in several polities unprecedented material wealth. For many in poor countries this is an incongruity devoid of simple justice: The earth's abundance should be shared in a more equitable manner. The rich nations, of course, do not consistently see matters quite this way.

The existence of these rather distinct positions is definitely characterized by political considerations. During the drought and famine period of the middle 1980s African countries such as Ethiopia became dependent upon outside governments and agencies for food shipments. The United States was in a position to help but since Ethiopia was controlled by a radical and Marxist regime there was some debate over the matter. For the American government the moral dilemma was acute: Should humanitarian assistance be given to a nation controlled by an anti-American regime that brutalizes its own citizenry and squanders $250 million to celebrate its tenth anniversary?

There is also a larger question: How much good does foreign aid do when it is given? There is a tendency and an expectation for rich nations to provide assistance to poor ones in the Third World, sometimes without discretion. The Third World is as diverse in culture, religion, ethnicity, and language as North America and Western Europe. Morover, economic development is itself an uneven and uncertain phenomenon. While overall economic growth rates since

1980 have been impressive in Latin America and East Asia, they have been abysmal on most of the African continent. Countries differ in their rates of growth. Often huge discrepancies occur as the economic infrastructure of one country, such as Nigeria, is propelled by exporting a scarce natural resource (oil), while another especially depressing example, such as Haiti, has a stagnating and perhaps deteriorating economy.

It is certainly questionable how much humanitarian and political good, if any, foreign assistance does, particularly if it is given to nations that prove to be ingrates. It should be recognized that the governments of many recipient nations express contempt for western values and official disdain for the West's well known materialism. Does any of this detract from the concept that the giving of aid is a humane and moral gesture? The answer may depend on what the aid is for since different countries have different needs from how the aid donor country sees them.

Foreign assistance has been a cornerstone of American foreign policy since the formation of the Marshall Plan in the late 1940s. It is therefore natural for the government to defend both the existence and continuance of foreign aid as an economic and moral commitment. This defense is succinctly summarized in an address by the department of state undersecretary for political affairs, in which Michael H. Armacost points out that foreign aid, a scant one percent of the annual federal budget, is a bargain. For a few billion dollars a year both underdeveloped economies and political democracy itself are encouraged to grow.

Whether they do or not is debatable. Peter S. Bauer and Basil S. Yamey suggest in "Foreign Aid: What Is at Stake?" that foreign aid may do a great deal of good for the government personnel that receives the assistance. How much of the aid actually benefits the rank and file citizenry is at least open to question. They raise another salient issue: Which foreign aid programs may create an image of a West that is a monolithic entity capable and desirous of dominating the political destinies of the Third World?

If the contrary assumption is made—that foreign assistance is a good thing—its administration may leave a great deal to be desired. American foreign policy priorities are not always consistent with a moral commitment to political democracy. We are not, for instance, as eager to support genuine democracies as the Soviet Union is to support political thugs. A revealing essay in *The New Republic* points out that in 1985 the Soviet Union spent $3 billion to assist Cuba's totalitarian-run economy while the United States could manage only $156 million in assistance to the only authentic democracy in Central America, Costa Rica. American foreign aid is roughly proportional to Ireland's, two-tenths of one percent of the Gross National Product. If the United States considers democracy to be the highest form of political morality, why then are we too miserly to act fully on our conviction?

Of course, any foreign assistance program has its limitations. Some of them are addressed in the following essays. Despite a decreasing share of foreign trade, industrial production, and overall economic influence the United States remains a remarkably wealthy country capable of a far-reaching and sustainable effort to assist less fortunate countries. But such an effort requires more than money. A worthy program of foreign aid must consider the ideological nature of recipient regimes, both their moral and political characteristics, and their sociocultural affiliations. These criteria will determine how aid is allocated.

Foreign Assistance and the U.S. National Interest

Michael H. Armacost

I am delighted to be with you today, and I congratulate you on one of the largest international seminars of its kind ever held in Kansas City. Today, I would like to talk about foreign assistance—an essential and effective tool of American foreign policy.

In these days of budget stringency, you may consider my choice of topic evidence more of "uncommon valor" rather than of good sense. And it is said that fools rush in where angels fear to tread. But, as a well-known commentator is fond of saying, I want to tell you the "rest of the story."

Many well-informed and well-intentioned Americans question the purpose, the size, the extent, or the character of our foreign assistance programs. Perhaps the full importance of our programs is not clearly understood, nor the modest cost we pay to achieve important benefits generally known. I would assert quite unequivocally that, dollar for dollar, our foreign assistance program is a low-cost, high-return means of advancing our national interests abroad.

Michael H. Armacost, Under Secretary for Political Affairs, "Foreign Assistance and the U.S. National Interest." Address to the Regional Foreign Policy Conference, Kansas City, Missouri, 11 September 1985. *Department of State Bulletin* 85, No. 2105 (December 1985), 55–57.

FOREIGN ASSISTANCE AND THE AMERICAN PUBLIC

This judgment is not necessarily reflected, mind you, in some of the letters we receive at the Department of State regarding America's foreign assistance programs. Let me share an example or two to give you a flavor of the attitudes that many people hold toward foreign aid.

- "We have to work 5 months out of every year just to pay our taxes. Are we going to bankrupt the United States so we can support the world?"
- "Why does our country lend millions of dollars to foreign countries at 2.5%–3% interest, yet I have to pay 13% for a VA mortgage on my house?"
- "If I don't pay my debts the stores cut off my credit. But with developing countries, we just keep shoveling the money down the drain."
- "We can't do it all ourselves."

These concerns are legitimate concerns; they are genuine concerns. Yet, we feel they also derive from certain misconceptions, even certain myths, about our foreign assistance programs that are deserving of attention. Let me, therefore, make a few remarks about them.

SOME MYTHS ABOUT FOREIGN AID

First, there is the idea that foreign aid is a huge program that constitutes a significant drain on the Federal budget. In a December 1984 Roper poll, 61% of a representative sample of adult Americans said we were spending "too much" on foreign assistance. And no wonder, when other surveys show that many Americans believe foreign assistance spending amounts to as much as 40% of the Federal budget.

The facts suggest otherwise. During the height of the Marshall Plan days in the late 1940s and early 1950s, foreign economic assistance absorbed roughly 11% of the Federal budget. Today the economic component of our foreign assistance—development assistance, economic support funds (ESF), Food for Peace program (P.L. 480), and the Peace Corps—comprises a total of about $12 billion. That works out to less than 1% of the Federal budget or less than one penny of a tax dollar going to assist America's friends and allies around the world.

I would add that the U.S. share of worldwide assistance of all types is shrinking. In the 1950s, America provided over half of all global assistance. In 1983, while still providing the largest absolute amount of aid, our relative share had fallen to less than 30%. Other OECD [Organization for Economic Cooperation and Development] countries—i.e., other industrial democracies—now provide sizable amounts of assistance, and their rates of increase exceed our own. For example, between 1979 and 1981, Japanese foreign assistance doubled; and between 1982 and 1986, its plans call for doubling their program again. And the Nordic countries, among others, allocate a substantially larger share of their GNP [gross national product] in aid to developing countries than we do.

A second misconception is that foreign aid—whatever the benefits it may confer on others—represents a massive outflow of dollars from the United States. The truth is that 70% of the money appropriated for bilateral foreign assistance is spent in the United States, not abroad. American firms supply commodities, equipment, consulting services, and other expertise to foreign assistance projects, which are then exported.

Of possible interest to this audience, in FY [fiscal year] 1984, the U.S. Agency for International Development (AID) paid some $17.2 million to suppliers of goods and services in Missouri and Kansas. Likewise, the Food for Peace program contributes to the prosperity of the U.S. agricultural sector; last year in Missouri and Kansas, the Food for Peace program spent $158.9 million. Additional sums were spent in support of our security assistance programs.

A third misconception—one with strong emotional appeal—is that aid is a giveaway. We do make grants, of course, and we extend soft loans to some developing countries on easy terms at low-interest rates with extended grace and payback periods. But we do so not out of some misguided sense of altruism but to advance some very specific foreign policy purposes. The sale of American grain at low interest is a case in point. One of every five acres of American farmland produces food for export to the developing world. These sales at favorable interest rates are hastening the development of countries that may someday rank among our best customers. Indeed, already, some of our best customers are developing countries.

Twenty or thirty years ago, Taiwan was struggling to feed its people and was receiving substantial American economic assistance. In 1950, Taiwan's per capita income was less than $100 a year. By 1980, it was $2,200—and Taiwan had become a major purchaser of American grain and other products at market prices and is now our seventh largest trading partner. So I think you can see a hard interest which is served, over time, in generating markets through funds at concessional rates.

A fourth misleading suggestion is that the Third World does not pay its debts. A third of our official economic assistance has been extended on a loan or credit basis. These loans are being repaid with interest. Third World countries know they must make their payments to preserve their credit ratings. It is, thus, not surprising that, overall, the repayment record has been quite admirable, with defaults of all loans extended amounting to only a fraction of 1% since 1946. Commercial banks would envy such a record.

A fifth common misconception is that America carries virtually the whole foreign aid burden itself. People often ask why America's friends and allies don't carry their fair share of helping other countries around the world.

Again, the facts may surprise you. Japan has become the second largest donor of bilateral and multilateral official development assistance worldwide. Japan contributes sizable amounts of aid, not only in its own area but also in Africa, Latin America, the Middle East, and Oceania. It also continues to improve the concessionality of its terms; to diversify the geographic scope of its programs; and to concentrate much of its assistance in countries of strategic consequence to us.

Our European allies are also substantial partners in foreign assistance burdensharing. European military aid to key African countries often helps to offset the destabilizing efforts of the Soviets and their allies.

Moreover, with strong support from the United States, the World Bank and the regional development banks have persuaded donors to pool and coordinate resources for concessional aid for economic development to the poorest nations. For example, the International Development Association (IDA)—the soft loan window of the World Bank which loans to the poorest countries—has contributed over $20 billion to the developing world, with nearly $10 billion more committed to projects and awaiting disbursement.

As IDA has expanded, our share has dropped from an initial 42% of a $1 billion program in 1961–64 to 25% of a $9 billion program for 1984–86. Thus, each $1 of U.S. contributions generates $4 of assistance to the poorest countries in the world. In the International Bank for Reconstruction and Development (IBRD), or World Bank, a U.S. contribution of $1 can produce more than $65 of assistance to recipient countries. So, the burden has been substantially picked up around the world, not only by the Europeans and Japanese in their bilateral programs but also because we have restructured our contributions to the international banks in such a way as to diminish our share while evoking larger contributions from others.

The same is also true in the United Nations. The United Nations is more than political debates in the General Assembly; the UN system is a major provider of important economic and food assistance around the globe. Through it, aid donors provide some $2.5 billion for economic and social development, only one-fourth of which is donated by the United States. The United States and other countries also contribute to UN refugee and humanitarian programs and to peacekeeping operations.

Burdensharing for humanitarian aid requires flexible and prompt means to respond to human crises. Here, we Americans excel. Our food programs, disaster relief mechanisms, and flexibility to mobilize resources give us a capability to respond to human tragedy which is simply unmatched. Witness our response to African hunger. We may carry more than our fair share of the humanitarian relief burden. But generosity in the face of need is an American tradition. The efforts of the Federal Government are supplemented—often exceeded—by private Americans. In 1983, American citizens privately contributed $1.3 billion to developing countries. That was roughly half of total Western private giving. American private giving was made more effective, however, because others gave as well.

Security Assistance

Another damaging myth about our foreign assistance program is that it is skewed heavily in favor of military programs at the expense of development assistance.

There is a direct connection between the success of our defense programs and our foreign assistance effort. To protect American security interests in a timely and cost-effective fashion, we do depend on the cooperation of many countries all around the world. A number of these countries are poor and can meet neither their defense requirements nor their development needs solely from their own resources. Our foreign assistance programs help them, with modest help on the side, to address their security problems through their own efforts. If the President didn't have this tool, then the network of cooperation that underpins our global security effort would be seriously undermined. Indeed, in his most recent State of the Union Address, President Reagan noted that, dollar for dollar, security assistance contributes as much to global security as our defense budget itself.

A few examples will demonstrate my point. When war broke out in the Middle East in 1973, we needed Portugal's cooperation to send emergency assistance. Our C-5A cargo planes had to refuel on the way to Israel, and the only place they could do so was in the Azores. Nor could we protect our interests in the Persian Gulf today without the cooperation of a large number of governments in the area. Our capacity to project our military power in the Pacific and Indian Oceans, likewise, depends heavily on access to key facilities in the Philippines. And we remain attuned to the special needs of countries whose strategic cooperation with us exposes them to great risk—as is the case of Pakistan, which is on the front line of resistance to Soviet aggression in Afghanistan.

I would also underscore a distinction between selling American military equipment to another country at retail prices and transferring real resources from the U.S. Treasury to another country. We don't consider commercial sales as security assistance—though they may certainly advance our strategic interests.

Military assistance refers to our provision to another nation of the necessary funds—frequently in the form of foreign military sales credits—to acquire military capabilities, lending those funds at concessional rates or providing them as a grant. We also provide economic support funds, through which we support the economic stabilization of certain countries of strategic concern to us, though the benefits conferred on other countries are not so much to bolster their military efforts as to strengthen the economies which underpin their security. Tailored properly, ESF is used by recipient nations to help diversify and reform their economies. ESF can also be an essential tool in encouraging the operation of market forces and in dismantling state controls.

At present, the ratio between economic and military assistance is roughly two-thirds to one-third—and, therefore, contrary to the popular impression that most of our foreign aid is military aid. In fact, just the reverse is true. In the case of Central America, to take a specific example, the Kissinger commission stressed the importance of economic as well as military aid programs. In Central America during the last 4 fiscal years, 78% of our total aid has been economic assistance; military assistance accounted for only 22%.

Development Assistance and Economic Growth

Thus far, I have spoken primarily about immediate political and security issues. But one of the greatest threats our children will face is international instability caused by the tragedy of endemic poverty and lack of economic opportunity which exists in much of the Third World. Generous impulses have always been basic in this country. So, no one, I suspect, would begrudge U.S. humanitarian foreign assistance to respond to situations such as the drought in Africa. Nor will you be surprised to learn that American official development assistance is about three times the amount of comparable Soviet programs.

At the same time, I would add that, although the United States recognizes a need to respond to the relief requirements of countries in East Africa, for example, it is not satisfactory for us to be simply responding to relief requirements without addressing underlying problems. Therefore, we have established, in the last year or so, an economic policy initiative for Africa, in which we have put money for the explicit purpose of supporting those governments which are demonstrating a willingness and ability to come to terms with their agricultural productivity problems.

This is also to underscore our experience that foreign assistance is not the principal means of financing development; trade is. On the one side of the coin, developing countries earn more foreign exchange through trade with the United States than through the assistance they receive from all donor countries combined. In 1984, for example, the United States purchased approximately 60% of all the manufactured exports of developing countries, which was worth about $60 billion. This represented almost three times the total amount of foreign aid received by all developing countries that year.

On the other side of the coin, the economic growth of developing countries contributes to our own prosperity. American corporations that profit from exports or foreign investments depend on the stable conditions and economic growth in the Third World that foreign assistance promotes. As developing countries prosper and modernize, our trade with them increases, creating new job opportunities for our labor force. Developing countries already purchase over 40% of all U.S. exports. Thus, for example, when the major Latin American economies faced deterioration in the early 1980s, U.S. exports to that region were cut back $16.3 billion between 1981 and 1983.

We also recognize that foreign assistance compared to equity investment is relatively small. Therefore, the Reagan Administration has directed its efforts at the negotiation of investment treaties and other means of reminding developing countries that if they are to finance their development successfully, they must find means of providing the conditions necessary for inviting equity investment rather than relying upon the official contributions or official transfers from us and other governments.

FOREIGN ASSISTANCE AND CURRENT U.S. PRIORITIES

So far, I have tried to address how foreign assistance advances our national interests and tried to tell the "rest of the story" regarding several popular misconceptions about America's foreign assistance efforts. Now let me outline the five priority areas where most of our official bilateral assistance resources are directed.

First is the achievement of a lasting peace in the Middle East. Israel and Egypt are our principal partners in this quest and, by far, the largest recipients of our foreign assistance. Together, they receive well over 40% of our foreign aid. Our economic and military assistance programs also support Jordan and other moderate Arab nations in their roles in the peace process.

We provide extraordinary assistance to Israel in support of a comprehensive Israeli economic program designed to correct fundamental imbalances in the Israeli economy. Without such a disciplined reform program, additional U.S. assistance could tend to perpetuate rather than to ameliorate Israel's economic problems. The Israeli Government has made considerable progress in developing an adjustment program, which it is now implementing.

A second priority is to secure and maintain access to military bases that are important to free world security. About one-fifth of our assistance goes for this purpose, and the countries that are the primary recipients include Spain, Portugal, Greece, Turkey, and the Philippines. Base rights and access both help to ensure international security.

Third, we support our friends who face Soviet or other communist military threats. Korea, Thailand, and Pakistan receive about one-twelfth of our assistance.

Regional stability and our own security depend on the prevention of North Korean aggression against South Korea. Our assistance helps South Korea improve the capabilities of its combat forces, many of which are stationed with our own forces along the DMZ [demilitarized zone] opposite a formidable North Korean opponent which has forward-positioned troops within 50 miles of Seoul.

Thailand faces serious security challenges as a result of Soviet-supported Vietnamese aggression in neighboring Cambodia. Our security assistance to Thailand supports the government's efforts to improve social and economic conditions in the Thai-Cambodian border areas where thousands of refugees have taken refuge. Our military assistance supports the modernization of Thailand's defense forces to deter further Vietnamese aggression.

Our six-year assistance program in Pakistan helps the government there to face the pressure of the Soviet military presence in Afghanistan and the intimidation that occurs almost daily through the incursion of Soviet or Afghan planes across Pakistan's border. Our assistance program supports Pakistan's economy and development and strengthens its defense through the provision of military equipment and training.

Our fourth priority is economic development and the relief of human misery. In Africa, for example, our economic assistance has nearly doubled since 1981. Our assistance programs attack the basic economic causes of poverty and are directed at dismantling statist policies so that market forces can unleash individual enterprise and improve productivity.

Finally, we seek to help our friends in Central America build democracy while weathering the economic and political crises aggravated by subversive pressures from Nicaragua. To that end, our foreign assistance to Central America comes predominantly as economic development.

In Central America, our friends are significantly stronger than they were a year or more ago. The economies of El Salvador, Honduras, Costa Rica, and Guatemala are improving. Democratic institutions in the region are being given a needed chance. For example, in May of last year, Panamanians went to the polls and elected a president for the first time in 16 years. The process of dialogue and reconciliation Salvadoran President Duarte has championed in El Salvador stands in marked contrast to the Sandinista government's intransigent refusal to talk with the opposition in Nicaragua.

CONCLUSION

I hope this brief description about our foreign assistance efforts may have given a better sense of the priorities which guide these programs and, perhaps, dispelled some misimpressions about their extent and character. I hope you will consider the objectives we are seeking to be worthy ones. I also hope there is a heightened awareness of the importance we attach to having this foreign policy to advance our interests overseas. We believe America's foreign assistance programs enhance regional security, promote economic development, encourage the growth of democratic institutions, stimulate commercial relations with the Third World and alleviate human suffering. They help our friends and allies help us while helping themselves.

In short, we believe the benefits of our foreign assistance programs are disproportionate to their cost. We think we get a good return on each dollar. Perhaps most importantly, our foreign assistance programs give us the opportunity to be creative and helpful in shaping the kind of world we hopefully all want to see: a world in which prosperity is growing, a world in which freedom and human opportunities are expanding, and a world in which we are making our contributions to safeguarding peace.

Foreign Aid: What Is at Stake?

Peter Bauer and Basil Yamey

Mr. Hollis B. Chenery, Vice President of the World Bank in charge of economic research, said last year that "Foreign aid is the central component of world development." How can this be so? Large scale development occurs in many places without foreign aid, and did so long before foreign aid was invented.

Official Western aid has now gone to the Third World for about thirty years, more than a human generation. Over this period major deficiencies, even startling anomalies, have become apparent. These untoward results

---

Peter T. Bauer and Basil S. Yamey, "Foreign Aid: What Is at Stake?" *The Public Interest* 68 (Summer 1982), 53–60.

might not matter much if the policy had served to promote the well-being of the peoples of the Third World, but it has not done so. Only exceptionally and in the most propitious circumstances can aid promote or accelerate economic advance, and then merely to a minor extent.

The effects of foreign aid have been quite different. It is foreign aid that has brought into existence the Third World (also called the South). It thus underlies the so-called North-South dialogue or confrontation. *Foreign aid is the source of the North-South conflict, not its solution.* The paramount significance of aid lies in this very important, perhaps momentous, political result.

A further pervasive consequence of aid has been to promote or exacerbate the politicization of life in aid-receiving countries. This major result has gravely damaged the interests of the West and the well-being and prospects of the peoples of Third World countries.

The money spent by the West in no way measures these crucial sequelae of aid. Whatever percentage of their national incomes aid represents, the donor governments cannot wash their hands of the consequences of their so-called caring.

THE CREATION OF "NORTH" AND "SOUTH"

What is there in common between, say, Thailand and Mozambique, Nepal and Argentina, India and Chad, Tuvalu and Brazil, Mayotte and Nigeria? Public and political discussion nowadays envisages the world as one-third rich—the West—and two-thirds poor or even hungry—the "Third World" or "South." In this picture, extreme poverty is the common feature of the Third World.

This is altogether misleading. There is a continuous range of incomes in the world, both between countries and within them, making the line of division between rich and poor countries quite arbitrary. One could say that the world is two-thirds rich and one-third poor, or one-tenth rich and nine-tenths poor, or choose any other two fractions which add up to one. The size of the celebrated gap between rich countries and poor countries (i.e., the difference in their average incomes) depends on the placement of the arbitrary line of division. The picture is also misleading in that many groups or societies in the Third World—especially in the Far East, the Middle East, Southeast Asia, and Latin America—are richer than large groups in the West.

Nor is the Third World stagnant. In recent decades many Third World countries have grown rapidly, as for instance have South Korea, Taiwan, Thailand, Malaysia, Singapore, Jordan, Guatemala, Venezuela, Colombia, Brazil, Kenya, and the Ivory Coast. Indeed, in so far as global aggregation and averaging of incomes and growth rates make any sense at all, both total and *per capita* incomes in the Third World as a whole have, since 1950, grown no less fast than in the West, and probably have grown faster.

It is, of course, hardly sensible to lump together and average incomes of the very different societies of the Third World or South, which comprise some two-thirds of mankind. These societies live in widely different physical and social environments, display radically different attitudes and modes of conduct, and their governments pursue very different policies.

But the diverse components of the Third World do indeed share one characteristic. This is not poverty, stagnation, exploitation, brotherhood, or skin colour; it is the receipt of foreign aid. *The concept of the Third World and the policy of official aid are inseparable. Without foreign aid there is no Third World.* Official aid provides the only bond joining together its diverse and often antagonistic constituents. This has been so ever since practically all of Asia, Africa, and Latin America came to be lumped together in the late 1940s as the underdeveloped world, and thereafter known successively as the less-developed world, the non-aligned world, the developing world, the Third World, and now the South. These expressions never made any sense except in that they denoted a collectivity of aid recipients.

The creation of the Third World has been the most important and far-reaching result of foreign aid. The Third World is moreover a progeny of the West; the foreign aid that created it did not originate in pressure from the Third World, but rather was introduced and organized by the West. It began with President Truman's Point Four Program of 1949. He urged bold measures to help the underdeveloped countries, in which he said that over half of mankind was living in sickness and wretchedness.

Thus by foreign aid did the West create a Third World, and one hostile to itself. Individual Third World countries are often neutral or even friendly to the West, but the organized and articulate Third World is invariably hostile. Its purpose as a collectivity is to coax or extract money from the West. In view of the loss of poise, wide-spread internal dissension, and feelings of guilt in the West, a hostile stance is appropriate to this purpose.

Foreign aid also gave birth to the notion of the West (or North) as a single economic decision-making entity, as a homogeneous aggregate with identical interests, and as an aggregate capable of imposing its collective will on the Third World. In fact, Western governments do not collude over selling or buying prices. Numerous foreign suppliers compete freely and often fiercely for business in Third World markets. Obvious competitors include, for example, construction companies, engineering consultants, and suppliers of manufactured products such as motor cars, trucks, and chemical products. Manufacturers and commodity traders also compete in the purchase of exports from the Third World.

Thus it is foreign aid which has created two fictions: first, that of the Third World as a substantially uniform collectivity with common interests; and second, that of the West as another substantially uniform collectivity, a powerful decision-making unit or homogeneous aggregate manipulating the world economy to the common advantage of its constituents. These fictions have in turn resulted in the reality of the "North-South" dialogue, confrontation, or conflict. References to the modest proportion of the national income of the donors that foreign aid represents obscure these far-reaching political results.

ANOMALIES OF AID

Foreign aid is the transfer of taxpayers' money to distant governments and to official international organizations. The use of the term "aid" to describe these transfers preempts criticism, obscures issues, and prejudges results.

Who could be against aid to the less fortunate? Aid is good, more aid is better. When aid advocates talk of the disappointing record of aid, they mean not that aid has been ineffective or damaging, but that the amounts of aid have been insufficient. The term aid has enabled supporters of intergovernmental transfers to claim a monopoly on compassion, and to dismiss critics as bigoted or lacking in humanity.

The prevailing uncritical—indeed axiomatic—approach to these official wealth transfers has allowed startling and often bizarre anomalies to flourish.

According to the latest available official information (April 1981), Saudi Arabia, Kuwait, Libya, Iran, Iraq, Bahrain, Vietnam, Cuba, and South Yemen all received official Western aid every year from 1977 to 1979. This was at a time when the surpluses of the OPEC countries were widely regarded as embarrassing or as damaging to Western economies, when the government of Vietnam openly persecuted millions of people, and when Cuba dispatched troops to Africa, again to the embarrassment of the West. The survivors among the large numbers of refugees from the Vietnamese government during this period descended on other aid-recipient countries such as the Philippines, Thailand, Indonesia, and Malaysia. Their arrival inflicted substantial costs on these governments and produced much political tension and conflict. Again, in April 1981, the Secretary General of the United Nations announced special aid of $560 million for African refugees when almost all of these people have fled from governments which continue to receive Western aid.

Substantial Western aid has gone and still goes to governments at war with each other; to governments severely restricting the inflow of capital, the shortage of which is said to be the ground for aid; to governments spending lavishly on obvious prestige projects; and to governments pursuing other policies which retard economic advance and harm the interests of their poorest citizens.

Another anomaly occurs when aid provides for the expansion of output of a product in the recipient country at a time when the donor government is grappling with excess capacity at home, with the resulting unemployment in the industry affected. (U.K. aid to expand steel production in Morocco is a current example.)

AID AND ECONOMIC GROWTH

Although the case for official transfers is largely taken for granted, various arguments or rationalizations are often advanced. These are addressed primarily to audiences not yet firmly committed.

The central argument for foreign aid has remained that without it Third World countries cannot progress at a reasonable rate, or cannot progress at all. But not only is foreign aid patently not required for development, it is, in actual fact, much more likely to obstruct it than to promote it.

It diminishes the people of the Third World to suggest that, although they crave material progress, unlike the West they cannot achieve it without external doles. Of course, large parts of the Third World made rapid progress long before foreign aid—witness Southeast Asia, West Africa, and Latin America. The emergence of hundreds of millions of people, both in the South and in the West, from poverty to prosperity has not depended on external gifts. Economic achievement has depended, as it still does depend, on people's own faculties, motivations, and ways of life, on their institutions and on the policies of their rulers. In short, economic achievement depends on the conduct of people, including governments. External donations have never been necessary for the development of any country, anywhere. There are, of course, a number of Third World countries or societies which have not progressed much in the postwar period. This lack of progress reflects factors which cannot be overcome by aid, and are indeed likely to be reinforced by it.

Governments or businesses in the Third World that can use capital productively can borrow at home and abroad.[1] This is also true for governments borrowing to spend on the so-called infrastructure, i.e., on facilities which do not yield a directly appropriable return. If spending on infrastruc-

[1]Where the political survival of a newly-created country is widely doubted, it may not be able to raise capital even if it can use capital productively. These apparent exceptions to the rule that development does not depend upon external aid are plainly irrelevant to the case for global transfers to the Third World.

ture is productive, it increases taxable capacity so that the governments can readily service the borrowed capital. It follows that the absolute maximum contribution of foreign aid to development, in the sense of the growth of the national income, is the avoided cost of borrowing, i.e., interest and amortization. As a percentage of the national income for large Third World countries, this maximum contribution is at best minute, and is far too small to register in the national income statistics. For India in recent years, the contribution of aid would have been at best on the order of one-quarter to one-half of 1 percent of recorded gross domestic product.

The maximum benefit from foreign aid is thus a modest reduction in the cost of investible funds—a resource which is *not* a major independent factor in economic development. It is evident on reflection that the volume of investible funds is not a critical determinant of economic progress, for, if it were, countless poor individuals and societies could not have advanced rapidly in a very short period, as they have done both in the West and in the Third World. The relative unimportance to material progress of the volume of investible funds has been confirmed by much recent research, including that of Simon Kuznets, Edward Denison, Moses Abramovitz, and Sir Alec Cairncross.[2] It is economic achievement that produces assets and money; it is not assets and money which produce economic achievement.

However, suppose that, contrary to the results of reflection and observation, the volume of investible funds was a critical determinant of economic advance. If it were, then those actions of many Third World governments which restrict the inflow of foreign private capital—a course of action made easier by receipts of aid—would be evidence that these governments gave a low priority to economic development. The same applies also to the practice of several governments, including those of India and Nigeria, of in effect passing on to other governments part of the aid they themselves receive.

Any benefit from the reduction of the cost of investible funds is likely to be small. It is also likely to be much more than offset by the adverse repercussions of official aid. And these repercussions are brought about by amounts of aid which, while small in relation to the national income of recipient countries, are nevertheless often a *significant* part of their government revenues and of foreign exchange receipts. These are the relevant magnitudes in assessing the principal repercussions of these transfers, because

[2]According to Kuznets, the contribution of the increases in material capital (both reproducible and non-reproducible) to the increase of per-capita income over long periods in major developed countries was limited, "ranging from less than a seventh to not much more than a fifth" (S. Kuznets, *Postwar Economic Growth*, Cambridge: Harvard University Press, 1964, p. 41). Much more important were improved efficiency in the use of resources and the movement of resources from less productive to more productive sectors. See also P. T. Bauer, *Dissent on Development* (London and Cambridge, Mass.: Harvard University Press, 1971), ch. 2, and *Equality, the Third World and Economic Delusion* (London and Cambridge, Mass.: Harvard University Press, 1981), ch. 14.

aid goes to governments and it increases both the revenues and the external balances at their direct disposal. In India, for instance, the latest official statistics available show that aid receipts in 1978 were of the order of 1.25 percent of officially calculated gross national product—but were about one-fifth of the country's export earnings. The figure of the government's tax receipts in 1978 is not available to us, but in the mid 1970's aid was of the order of one-fifth of its tax revenues. Thus, according to the latest official statistics, foreign aid to India as a proportion both of export earnings and of tax revenues was about thirteen times as significant as it was as a percentage of recorded gross domestic product.

HOW AID CAN INHIBIT DEVELOPMENT

The adverse repercussions of official aid operate precisely on the personal, social, and political factors which determine economic development.

Most importantly, aid increases the money, patronage, and power of the recipient governments, and thereby their grip over the rest of society. It thus promotes the disastrous politicization of life in the Third World (a subject to which we shall return). When social and economic life is extensively politicized, people's livelihood or even their economic and physical survival comes to depend on political and administrative decisions. This result promotes conflict, especially in the multiracial societies of most Third World countries. This sequence diverts energy and attention from productive activity to the political arena; and the direction of people's activities is necessarily a crucial determinant of economic performance.

There are further untoward implications and repercussions of foreign aid which are far from trivial. Aid enables governments to pursue policies which patently retard growth and exacerbate poverty, and there is a long list of such policies. These include persecution of the most productive groups, especially minorities, and sometimes also their expulsion; restraints on the activities of traders and even the destruction of the trading system; restriction on the inflow of foreign capital, enterprise, and skills; voluntary or compulsory purchase of foreign enterprises (which deprives the country of skills very helpful to development, besides absorbing scarce capital); forced collectivization; price policies which discourage food production; and, generally, the imposition of economic controls which restrict external contacts and domestic mobility, and so retard the spread of new ideas and methods.

Aid also is apt to bias development policy towards unsuitable external models. Familiar examples include steel and petrochemical complexes and official airlines. Moreover, in some instances the adoption of external prototypes has gone hand in hand with attempts at more comprehensive modernization, including attempted transformation of people's mores, values, and institutions. Such policies can have dangerous, even explosive, consequences (as in Iran).

Aid also impairs the international competitiveness of economic activities in the recipient countries by helping to create or maintain overvalued exchange rates or to increase the domestic money supply.[3] (These adverse effects could be offset if the transfers greatly enhanced the productivity of resources, but this is extremely improbable.) Foreign aid also makes it easier for governments to pursue imprudent financial policies. Unless aid is increasingly forthcoming, these policies lead to disruptive domestic inflation and to balance of payments difficulties, which in turn are apt to engender a crisis atmosphere and a flight of capital. This sequence encourages the imposition of specific controls, with adverse economic, social, and political results.

It would be naive to suppose that adverse policies would cease in the absence of aid. What is pertinent is that aid makes it easier to pursue and continue these policies. This is the case because, while it does little or nothing to promote development, aid can relieve immediate shortages, especially of consumer goods and of imports. This makes it easier for governments to conceal temporarily from their populations the worst effects of the damaging policies.

BETWEEN AID AND THE POOR: THIRD WORLD RULERS

Foreign aid does not go to the pitiable figures we see on aid posters or in aid advertisements—it goes to their rulers. The policies of these rulers who receive aid are sometimes directly responsible for conditions such as those depicted. This is notably so in parts of Africa and Southeast Asia. But even where this is not so the policies of the rulers, including their patterns of public spending, are determined by their own personal and political interests, among which the position of the poorest has very low priority.[4] Indeed, to support rulers on the basis of the poverty of their subjects does nothing to discourage policies that lead to impoverishment. Many Third World governments have persecuted and even expelled the most productive groups, such as the Chinese in Vietnam and Indonesia, or the Asians in East Africa. On

[3]This effect of aid is discussed in Hans O. Schmitt's "Development Assistance: A View from Bretton Woods," *Public Policy*, Fall 1973.

[4]This political reality has been recognized by others. Governments "genuinely committed to improving the material standards of life of the mass of their population" are "rare in the Third World." C.H. Kirkpatrick and F.I. Nixson, "The North-South Debate: Reflections on the Brandt Commission Report," *Three Banks Review* (London, September 1981), p. 39.

the criterion of poverty, such governments then qualify for more aid, because incomes in their countries have been reduced.

These anomalies or paradoxes are obscured when it is suggested that giving money to the rulers of poor countries is the same as giving it to poor, even destitute people. Giving money to governments is certainly not the same thing as helping the poor. On the contrary: Western aid to Third World governments, especially in Asia and Africa, has extensively supported disastrous economic policies, which have greatly aggravated the lot of the poorest. Dr. Nyerere of Tanzania has for many years been a much favored aid recipient. Apart from large-scale collectivization of farming, his government has forcibly moved millions of people into so-called socialist villages, often far from their homes. These policies have had devastating effects on food production. President Mobutu of Zaire, another recipient of extensive aid, has expelled large numbers of traders. This had led to enforced reversion to subsistence production over large areas, causing much hardship and deprivation. As is well known, the economic performance of these two countries compares dismally with that of Kenya and the Ivory Coast, where such extreme policies have been avoided.[5]...

Two-Tenths of One Percent

The Senate has reversed an embarrassing "no" vote, and it now seems that Philippine president Corazon Aquino will get the $200 million in economic aid she requested in a speech to Congress last month. There shouldn't have been any argument about it. The United States needs Aquino, and she needs us. Her democratic government is the best hope for the Filipino people. After years of supporting the Marcos kleptocracy, we have an obligation to help his successor replenish the ransacked treasury he left behind. Yet as we go to press, the House and Senate still haven't decided where to get the money for Aquino. The Senate version of the aid bill says it would have to be paid for by snipping other countries' shares. The House doesn't specify.

The debate over foreign aid is almost always agonizing, but this year it is especially so. Under pressure to meet Gramm-Rudman deficit reduction targets, both the House and the Senate have made big cuts in the State

[5]The economic policies and achievements of Kenya and Tanzania, and also official Western attitudes to these countries, are compared briefly in Gunter Krabbe, "East Africa and Double Standards," *Encounter*, October 1981.

"Two-Tenths of One Percent," *The New Republic* 195, no. 17 (27 October 1986), 5–7. Reprinted with permission of *The New Republic.*

Department's Economic Support Fund, the chief source of direct cash aid. But since most of the ESF's roughly three-and-a-half billion dollars is earmarked in advance for a handful of countries (Egypt and Israel mainly, but Pakistan, Ireland, Portugal, Tunisia, and a few others get sizable chunks too), the cuts leave hardly anything for the rest of the world. A long list of worthy countries will have to scramble for a share of the shrinking supply of Yankee dollars. Under the House bill, the ESF for all non-earmarked countries would be cut 40 percent, from last year's $1 billion to $600 million. The Senate would impose a 16 percent cut. Food and development assistance, which comes out of a separate fund, would be cut too.

The Reagan administration complains that the cuts threaten what it has come to rely on as an important means of winning friends and influencing people around the world. But with elections approaching in a few weeks, Congress recognizes that the easiest way to cut the deficit is by taking on the least popular spending program of all. The public doesn't mind helping foreign countries suddenly beset by earthquake or famine. But most Americans think that the foreign aid we supply on a regular basis ends up getting wasted. Why not take care of American citizens first? The temptation to look at foreign aid as an "us v. them" issue has never been greater. Foreign aid, though, should not be seen as a handout to the Third World, but as part of the business of maintaining sensible, mutually beneficial relations with poor countries.

Thus we should pursue trade policies that, at a minimum, do not sabotage the goals of foreign aid programs, and that, ideally, serve those goals. The need to support foreign friends would not be so pressing, for example, if this country practiced the free market principles we so often preach to the rest of the world. Subsidized foreign sales of beef and rice under the current U.S. farm bill take millions of dollars worth of market share from countries such as Uruguay (1986 economic aid: $14 million) and Thailand (1986 economic aid: $31.5 million). (See "Stuffing Farmers, Stiffing Peasants," TNR, August 11 & 18.) The Multi-Fiber Arrangement's "voluntary" import restrictions coddle U.S. textile producers and confer windfalls on countries (mainly relatively advanced ones such as Hong Kong, Taiwan, and South Korea) that are lucky enough to be assigned quotas. The Philippines claims it could supply over ten percent of the U.S. market if these quotas were scrapped, compared to the two or three percent it supplies now. The benefits to the Philippine economy would be both larger and more lasting than the $200 million Aquino got.

The U.S. sugar quota is perhaps the best example of how we undermine our own foreign aid program. Since 1981 the federal government has guaranteed American sugar producers triple the world price for their crop. This consumer rip-off is enforced by means of strict quotas on sugar imports from lower cost foreign producers, many of whom are poor Third World countries. These quotas do help the countries that receive them by permitting them to sell in the U.S. market at an inflated price. But there's a catch. To maintain those high prices, the United States must restrict supply—by reducing the quotas. Since 1982 such cuts have cost Caribbean nations as many as 130,000 jobs and up to $300 million in income. The Dominican Republic alone lost $75 million—meanwhile, it received $104 million in U.S. aid in fiscal 1986. The Caribbean Basin Initiative, a centerpiece of the Reagan administration's foreign aid policy, has been largely undone by the sugar policy.

Exports to the United States are now more critical than ever to the Third World's dollar-hungry debtor nations. Between 1981 and 1984, however, the United States actually closed off more of its markets. It's also worth remembering that, by insisting the Third World repay its commercial bank creditors in full, with interest, the Reagan administration is actually encouraging a massive capital transfer *from poor to rich.* Since 1983 Latin America has been sending out $30 billion more per year than it has received. That's five percent of the region's combined gross product.

But assuming we eliminated trade barriers and gave debtors a break, would there still be a case for bilateral aid? Morally, the answer is yes. The United States is the richest country in the world. We should share some of our wealth with the less fortunate countries, many of which would still need help even with free trade and debt relief. As it stands now, we're by no means excessively generous. Though we gave $9.6 billion in development aid in 1985, that was just over two-tenths of one percent of our GNP, according to the Organization for Economic Cooperation and Development. That tied us with Ireland for last among 18 leading industrial nations—and Ireland receives aid from us!

The United States does supply much of the funding for multilateral agencies such as the International Monetary Fund, the World Bank, and regional development banks. But the IMF, which acts as a collection agency for banks in the Third World, is hardly a charitable venture. All of these agencies provide assistance in the form of loans, some interest-free, most not. Most foreign aid is in the form of grants. The World Bank raises considerably less of its capital in the United States than it does in Japan. It gets about the same amount from the United States as it does from West Germany and Switzerland.

And from a cold political point of view, foreign aid is in our self-interest. That's why it was both right and necessary to give money to the Aquino government. It is the best reason to give so much to Egypt and Israel. That money is the price we pay to keep peace between the two biggest powers in the world's most volatile region, and to support a democratic ally of strategic importance. American money can often do as much or more as American arms to check the spread of Soviet influence. When the Kissinger Commission report on Central America came out back in 1983, there was a lot of talk about a "Marshall Plan" for the region. Now that has been quietly forgotten. Central American countries are facing the possibility of cuts in economic aid. The Soviets pay $3 billion a year to keep Cuba's economy going. But under the proposed cuts for this year, it's likely that we won't be able to repeat the $156 million we spent last year to bail out democratic Costa Rica.

Bolivia recently invited U.S. troops into its territory to help wipe out cocaine production centers. It's the first time anything has shown signs of making a dent in that impoverished Andean country's cocaine traffic. In return for sacrificing a source of dollars reckoned to be worth $600 million a year, the Bolivians are asking $100 million to shore up their Central Bank's reserves. There won't be any room for that if the proposed cuts pass. How can we expect the Bolivians to take our commitment to fighting drugs seriously? Meanwhile, Congress is about to spend $1.5 billion on a drug bill, much of which will go to interdiction on the U.S. border, an enterprise that has already failed.

This journal gave Gramm-Rudman its grudging support: We thought it might serve to spur Congress into the hard job of setting priorities among competing items in the budget. In the case of foreign aid, however, Gramm-Rudman has served as an excuse to abandon setting priorities. Cutting foreign aid self-destructively pits the interests of one U.S. ally against another. Increasing foreign aid is the way to establish it as an indispensable function of the national government. After all, it's not a job that can be left to the states.

DISCUSSION QUESTIONS

1. Do we have a right to encourage, or even impose, cultural changes such as birth control, or political changes such as democracy, on developing nations as a prerequisite for their receiving economic aid?
2. When there are poverty, illiteracy, malnutrition, and streetpeople in the United States, should we be sending millions of dollars abroad to combat the same problems in other countries?
3. Should the United States require foreign governments to implement democratic policies as a requisite for economic or military assistance?
4. Does the United States as the most prosperous nation in history and in the world have a moral obligation to assist other countries?

15

TERRORISM

Richard W. Leeman

The problem of terrorism is inherently a moral one. A fundamental moral question in any society is how violence may be judiciously employed, when it should be used, and, most importantly, by whom. Even in democracies, violence is present in many forms, in its prisons, its police, and its military. Incarceration, arrest, riot control, military action—all are names for kinds of violence sanctioned by society.[1]

Terrorism, in its common usage, is a form of violence not sanctioned by society. No universal definition of terrorism exists, but for our purposes a reasonable definition would be that terrorism is the systematic, illegitimate use of violence or the threat of violence for political purposes. This definition, however, encounters two major difficulties.

First, many individuals customarily called "terrorists" have motives which are only nominally political. Some terrorists expropriate money purely for personal gain, for some terrorism becomes a way of life, still others are drawn by the violence. If no political purpose disturbs these non-political motives, however, such a "terrorist" is better labeled something else. The distinction between a terrorist and a criminal resides primarily in that the former is political while the latter is non-political. Some students of terrorism argue that such a distinction is immaterial; terrorists are criminals and should be treated as such. Although terrorists may properly be *treated* as criminals, in order to understand them, identify them, and even prevent them, their political purpose should be kept in mind. As such, the distinction between the terrorist and the criminal is useful for our discussion, though it may not serve for a court of law.

The political nature of terrorism pervades the question of legitimacy, and so the second major difficulty is less easily settled; namely, how does one distinguish "legitimate" from "illegitimate" force? This simple but perplexing question captures the moral dilemma posed by terrorism, and most of the authors in this section address themselves to that very question. This dilemma emerges clearly in the often repeated cliche that "one man's terrorist is another man's freedom fighter." The cliche connotes a kind of moral relativism, that one person's perspective is as good as another's. If such is the case, then the question of legitimacy is moot; society has no moral force for sanctioning one violent act as legitimate or condemning another as illegitimate. Like Alice's Humpty-Dumpty, the word means exactly what one says it means, neither more nor less.

Most people, including the authors of these essays, do not like to treat language that way. For terrorism to be consistently identifiable, however, the legitimate use of violence for political ends needs to be separable from the illegitimate. Repeatedly, the most salient argument in any discussion about terrorism is this question of legitimacy, and the two most commonly featured words are "civilized" and "barbaric." The "civilized" world is routinely contrasted with the "barbaric" terrorist; or the terrorist is the humane one and the "system" barbaric. Both terms are popular because they imply the role of society in determining acceptability. To be civilized is to be an acceptable member of society; to be barbaric is to live beyond the pale. The essays presented here are representative.

Steven Baer's article "Up in Smoke" frames well the moral dilemma of terrorism. Early in the essay he calls into question our accepted notion of terrorism. The term terrorism is "generally misapplied" to abortion clinic bombers, while the "*routine* violence" of abortion is overlooked. Appearing on *Face the Nation,* conservative columnist Pat Buchanan made much the same point. "You've got 29 buildings bombed, and you've got 15 million unborn children destroyed in this country in the last 10 years. Now what is the terrorism?"[2] George Habash, leader of the Popular Front for the Liberation of Palestine, similarly challenges our definition of terrorism. "After what has happened to us we have the right to do anything, including what *you call* terrorism."[3] Notice that a kind of balancing occurs here. The public is asked to balance 29 buildings against 15 million unborn children, and to weigh what has been done to the Palestinians against what the Palestinians themselves have done. Steven Baer does the same for the abortion clinic bombers, analogizing their actions to the destruction of Dachau or Auschwitz. He, however, condemns the bombers because they have recourse to legislative processes that resistance fighters in Hitler's Germany did not. Not all abortion clinic bombers would accept that moral condemnation, nor the reasoning behind it. Like accused bomber Steven Goldsby, they would argue that saving lives is of greater importance than rigorously following democratic procedures. As he put it, he chose "the quickest route possible to stop abortion—the children did not have twenty years for me to get old and gray and go through legislation."[4]

The speeches of President Reagan and Secretary Shultz reflect pretty accurately the typical American response to terrorism, domestic or international. Legal norms ought to prevail, and so Shultz invokes the Geneva convention and the "rule of law." Their use of language reflects that standard. Terrorists, and their patron Mu'ammar Qadhafi, are brutal, subversive, criminal, and barbaric. Qadhafi runs a regime, not a government, of which the Libyan people are, presumably, "ashamed and disgusted." Reagan likens Qadhafi to Hitler with a reference to appeasement, a reference pointedly directed at the Europeans. In contrast, Americans are "slow to anger," seeking first the "peaceful avenues" before resorting to violence. On two counts, then, the bombing of Libya is legitimated: as self-defense and as a last resort.

Reagan's and Shultz's arguments deserve scrutiny before being accepted wholesale. Are they, perhaps, being too vituperative? British politician Paul Rose suggests that Reagan here is like a "prosecutor in a Soviet show trial."[5] Philip Wander has noted how much of American foreign policy is conducted via slogans, euphemisms, and highly connotative labels.[6] Terrorism seems to encourage that tendency. Steven Piecznik resigned from the state department during the Iranian hostage crisis because of that very problem. "In terrorist negotiations themselves," he wrote, "these senior officials too often showed little patience for the painstaking work involved, relying instead on the instincts that brought them to their positions of power" (politics). Not surprisingly, then, Shultz's language casts the issue as one of character: We must show the "stomach to confront" the challenge, we cannot "shrink" from the dilemma; we must avoid "paralysis" and "tackle the issue head on." Some political scientists have written that war is frequently justified in terms of masculinity; Shultz's language does nothing to refute this.[7] Not only does Shultz note how terrorism challenges our courage, but twice in his speech he warns against American impotence.

Daniel Treisman is one writer who does not fully accept the Reagan and Shultz viewpoint. He accepts their definition of terrorism, but quarrels about who should wear the label. He accuses the administration of hypocrisy, which is generally considered a critical moral error. Treisman's essay clearly focuses on a major facet of the legitimacy question: Who speaks for society?

The editors of *The Spectator* suggest several other difficulties with the American response to Libyan terrorism. Although similarly condemning terrorism and its Libyan sponsors, they argue that the U.S. bombing was "disproportionate." An eye for an eye might acceptably justify the bombing, but in this instance they assert that it is inappropriate, comparing it to a hundred eyes for one eye. They also question the self-defense argument, suggesting that the threat needs to be more serious and immediate in order to sanction bombing. The editors raise a final moral point, one of pragmatics. Although terrorism violates certain societal proscriptions, the U.S. reaction is not justified because it will be ineffective. Reagan partially acknowledges that claim in his speech, but argues that "American tradition" precludes inaction.

The final article moves to a very different, but also important, moral question regarding terrorism. Allowing that terrorists are illegitimate, what interaction can they or should they have with the media? Given the integral role of the media in a democracy, which is more important: informing the citizenry? Or aiding society in tracking down and punishing the terrorists? If, as many scholars claim, publicity is a major goal of terrorism, does the media reward their criminal behavior when it provides them with that publicity? Shortly before NBC's interview of Abul Abbas, the network's president addressed this problem. Using a question and answer format, Lawrence Grossman's speech raises the major questions critics have posed, along with his responses.

Taken together, these six essays represent the major moral questions being discussed regarding terrorism. Terrorism provokes strong reactions around the world, both for and against, for as George Shultz correctly remarks, "The use of force at any level involves moral issues." As he also correctly notes, in the sentence preceding that one: "We cannot walk away from every situation that poses a moral dilemma." Clearly, terrorism is one such moral dilemma.

NOTES

1. Paul Wilkinson illustrates this dilemma when he defines "force" as the legitimate use of coercion and "violence" as the illegitimate use of it. *Terrorism and the Liberal State* (New York: New York University Press, 1979), p. 23.
2. Pat Buchanan, "Face the Nation" television broadcast, 30 December 1984 (transcript p. 7).
3. As quoted in Oriana Fallaci, "A Leader of the Fedayeen," *Life,* 12 June 1970, p. 33. (Emphasis mine.)
4. "Clinic Bombers Discuss Acts," *New York Times,* 7 January 1985, p. A12.
5. Paul Rose, "Terror in the Skies," *Contemporary Review* 248 (June 1986), p. 301.
6. Philip Wander, "The Rhetoric of American Foreign Policy," *Quarterly Journal of Speech* 70 (1984), pp. 339–361.
7. Nancy C. M. Harstock, "Masculinity, Citizenship, and the Making of War," *Political Science* 17 (1984), pp. 198–204.

Up in Smoke

Steven Baer

Braving temperatures indistinguishable from those that gave inaugural parade planners cold feet a day earlier, at least 70,000 undaunted prolife protesters made their annual January 22 descent on Washington and the Supreme Court. They came to mark the twelfth year since the Court declared a constitutional right to abortion—a year of escalating violence at abortion clinics and "family planning" centers.

Episodes of violence were and are justly condemned. But to understand the perpetrators and why the term "terrorism" is generally misapplied to their acts, one must also clearly understand the *routine* violence that occurs daily within abortion clinic walls.

A $500 million-a-year abortion industry has sprung up around *Roe v Wade*—an industry exponentially more violent than any of the attacks to date on its facilities: By seven weeks gestation, about the time most women know they are pregnant, the fetal heart has been beating for a month, and the brain is emitting brain waves. The fetus has a delicate face, and hands are already emblazoned with unique fingerprint patterns. By the end of the first trimester, during which 85 percent of America's 1.5 million annual abortions occur, the fetus is sexually differentiated, her major organ systems are functioning, and ultrasonography reveals that she can suck her thumb and swim almost as freely as a fish within her dark, amniotic confines.

But this is no phylogenetic throwback to the Devonian age—as some abortion rhetoric based on debunked onto-genic theories once suggested. Neither is the fetus a "mere blob," "mass of tissue," or simple "product of conception." For all who have eyes to see, the infant's form is undeniably, unmistakably human.

And to watch her die, as I did in a recent reviewing of a suction curettage abortion via ultrasonography, is a numbing experience. It happens nearly 4,000 times a day in this country, and prudence has not restrained its practitioner from pressing to the limit the expansive legal parameters drawn by the Supreme Court. By 1980, according to the Centers for Disease Control, at least 50,000 abortions annually were occurring in the *fifth and sixth months* of gestation.

Most empathic Americans represented by Washington's prolife marchers express their opposition to abortion's brutality by supporting the ef-

---

Steven Baer, "Up in Smoke," *Christianity Today*, 19 April 1985, 19. Reprinted with permission of the author.

forts of their movement's lobbyists, political action committees, and courtroom activists. Focusing on the *two* lives involved each time a pregnant woman enters an abortion clinic, many attempt to dissuade through sidewalk counseling and offerings of housing and help from a growing network of crisis pregnancy centers. Increasing numbers are picketing abortion clinics and the homes of those who operate them. And on the fringes of a movement frustrated for more than a decade by governmental recalcitrance and 16 million abortion deaths, some are building bombs.

To call them terrorists, at least in most cases, is overboard. Dictionaries define terrorism as efforts calculated to inspire fear. Yet as abortion-rights leaders admit, the clinic assailants have apparently gone to great lengths to ensure that no one is hurt by their actions. Such circumspection runs counter to terrorism's aims. The obvious primary aim of these individuals is not to intimidate abortionists or their often troubled clientele, but to save concrete, individual lives. For this group, letters to Congress and the editor are not enough; the most helpless members of their communities are dying daily with state sanction, and they cannot tolerate it. For them, destroying the local clinic and its suction aspirator with a firebomb simply means no unborn babies will be killed there the next day. It is as justifiable, they would likely say, as destroying a Dachau or an Auschwitz.

Such thinking is, however, short-sighted. It ignores the fact that the totalitarian system that gave rise to Dachau and Auschwitz provided no institutional means for dissenting citizens to alter its violently unjust policies. The American system does provide such means, however slow the processes of change through them may be.

For prolifers to resort to violence before exhausting the alternatives—including nonviolent civil rights movements preceding this one, and lately made chic by proabortion congressmen like Senator Lowell Weicker in the seige of South Africa's embassy—is to jeopardize both the case and the nation. The moment someone the whole country recognizes as human dies in an abortion clinic blast, the battle lines may be drawn irrevocably.

Those on the violent fringe of the movement must realize that America's constitutional democracy and role of law, even when it has dehumanized, is too precious a system to put at risk. Those who defend the Supreme Court's radical decision of taking recision of human rights from the unborn must realize the need for reform. There are millions of lives at stake, on both sides of the womb.

United States Air Strike against Libya

Ronald Reagan

My fellow Americans:

At 7 o'clock this evening eastern time air and naval forces of the United States launched a series of strikes against the headquarters, terrorist facilities, and military assets that support Mu'ammar Qadhafi's subversive activities. The attacks were concentrated and carefully targeted to minimize casualties among the Libyan people with whom we have no quarrel.

From initial reports, our forces have succeeded in their mission. Several weeks ago in New Orleans I warned Colonel Qadhafi we would hold his regime accountable for any new terrorist attacks launched against American citizens. More recently I made it clear we would respond as soon as we determined conclusively who was responsible for such attacks.

On April 5th in West Berlin a terrorist bomb exploded in a nightclub frequented by American servicemen. Sergeant Kenneth Ford and a young Turkish woman were killed and 230 others were wounded, among them some 50 American military personnel. This monstrous brutality is but the latest act in Colonel Qadhafi's reign of terror. The evidence is now conclusive that the terrorist bombing of La Belle discotheque was planned and executed under the direct orders of the Libyan regime. On March 25th, more than a week before the attack, orders were sent from Tripoli to the Libyan People's Bureau in East Berlin to conduct a terrorist attack against Americans to cause maximum and indiscriminate casualties. Libya's agents then planted the bomb. On April 4th the People's Bureau alerted Tripoli that the attack would be carried out the following morning. The next day they reported back to Tripoli on the great success of their mission.

Our evidence is direct; it is precise; it is irrefutable. We have solid evidence about other attacks Qadhafi has planned against the United States installations and diplomats and even American tourists.

Thanks to close cooperation with our friends, some of these have been prevented. With the help of French authorities, we recently aborted one such attack: a planned massacre, using grenades and small arms, of civilians waiting in line for visas at an American Embassy.

Colonel Qadhafi is not only an enemy of the United States. His record of subversion and aggression against the neighboring states in Africa is well-

---

Ronald Reagan, "U.S. Air Strike against Libya." Address to the nation, 14 April 1986. Reprinted from *Weekly Compilation of Presidential Documents* (21 April 1986), 491–492.

documented and well-known. He has ordered the murder of fellow Libyans in countless countries. He has sanctioned acts of terror in Africa, Europe and the Middle East, as well as the Western Hemisphere.

Today we have done what we had to do. If necessary, we shall do it again. It gives me no pleasure to say that, and I wish it were otherwise.

Before Qadhafi seized power in 1969, the people of Libya had been friends of the United States. And I'm sure that today most Libyans are ashamed and disgusted that this man has made their country a synonym for barbarism around the world. The Libyan people are a decent people caught in the grip of a tyrant.

To our friends and allies in Europe who cooperated in today's mission, I would only say you have the permanent gratitude of the American people. Europeans who remember history understand better than most that there is no security, no safety, in the appeasement of evil. It must be the core of Western policy that there be no sanctuary for terror. And to sustain such a policy, free men and free nations must unite and work together.

Sometimes it is said that by imposing sanctions against Colonel Qadhafi or by striking at his terrorist installations we only magnify the man's importance, that the proper way to deal with him is to ignore him. I do not agree. Long before I came into this office, Colonel Qadhafi had engaged in acts of international terror, acts that put him outside the company of civilized men. For years, however, he suffered no economic or political or military sanction; and the atrocities mounted in number, as did the innocent dead and wounded. And for us to ignore by inaction the slaughter of American civilians and American soldiers, whether in nightclubs or airline terminals, is simply not in the American tradition. When our citizens are abused or attacked anywhere in the world on the direct orders of a hostile regime, we will respond so long as I'm in this Oval Office. Self-defense is not only our right, it is our duty. It is the purpose behind the mission undertaken tonight, a mission fully consistent with Article 51 of the United Nations Charter.

We believe that this preemptive action against his terrorist installations will not only diminish Colonel Qadhafi's capacity to export terror, it will provide him with incentives and reasons to alter his criminal behavior. I have no illusion that tonight's action will ring down the curtain on Qadhafi's reign of terror. But this mission, violent though it was, can bring closer a safer and more secure world for decent men and women. We will persevere.

This afternoon we consulted with the leaders of Congress regarding what we were about to do and why. Tonight I salute the skill and professionalism of the men and women of our Armed Forces who carried out this mission. It's an honor to be your Commander in Chief.

We Americans are slow to anger. We always seek peaceful avenues before resorting to the use of force—and we did. We tried quiet diplomacy, public condemnation, economic sanctions, and demonstrations of military force. None succeeded. Despite our repeated warnings, Qadhafi continued his reckless policy of intimidation, his relentless pursuit of terror. He counted on America to be passive. He counted wrong.

I warned that there should be no place on Earth where terrorists can rest and train and practice their deadly skills. I meant it. I said that we would act with others, if possible, and alone if necessary to ensure that terrorists have no sanctuary anywhere. Tonight, we have.

Thank you, and God bless you.

Low-Intensity Warfare: The Challenge of Ambiguity

Secretary George Shultz

...The problem of low-intensity warfare requires us to confront a host of political, military, intellectual, legal, and moral questions. The label, indeed, may be misleading. When they are shooting at you or trying to blow you up, it's pretty high intensity. Nor is low-intensity warfare the same as limited war.

No, it's a more complicated set of new and unconventional challenges to our policy. It is the scourge of terrorism worldwide; the struggle for Nicaragua between the democratic resistance and the communist regime; it is the insurgencies against the Soviet and Cuban intervention in Angola and Ethiopia; the civil war and terrorism in Lebanon; our rescue of Grenada; and the Cambodian resistance against the Vietnamese occupation. It is the heroic struggle of the Afghan people against Soviet aggression and occupation. It is a matrix of different kinds of challenges, varying in scope and scale. If they have a single feature in common, it is their ambiguity: the fact that they throw us off balance, that we grope for appropriate means to respond, and that we as a society even debate sometimes over the need to respond.

George Shultz, "Low Intensity Warfare: The Challenge of Ambiguity." Address to Low-Intensity Warfare Conference, Washington, D.C., 15 January 1986. Reprinted from Current Policy No. 783, U.S. Department of State (15 January 1986), 1–4.

The ironic fact is, these new and elusive challenges have proliferated, in part, *because* of our success in deterring nuclear and conventional war.... Low-intensity warfare is their answer to our conventional and nuclear strength—a flanking maneuver, in military terms. They hope that the legal and moral complexities of these kinds of challenges will ensnare us in our own scruples and exploit our humane inhibitions against applying force to defend our interests. Ambiguous warfare has exposed a chink in our armor.

The Nicaraguan communists, for instance, have done all they can to hide their true ambitions. Some were fooled by this. The Nicaraguans used progressive rhetoric to obscure their totalitarian goals. They imported Cuban experts to construct a totalitarian state, but, at first, only a small number, so as to not attract attention. Then, as the numbers rose, we were told the Cubans were teachers or construction workers (who happen to handle guns quite well, as we learned in Grenada). Now we are told they aren't really organized troops, just advisers—who seem to wander into combat. We warned against the Nicaraguans' import of MiGs and other advanced weapons; so they have brought in powerful weapons below that threshold, like Hind helicopters. They have committed aggression against their neighbors and provided arms to terrorists like the M–19 group in Colombia, but cynically used the International Court of Justice to accuse *us* of aggression because we joined with El Salvador in its defense.

These tactics obviously play on the moral scruples that discipline our power, on the American people's antipathy to violence and desire for peace. Well, the truth—which most of us here long recognized—is now gaining wider and wider acceptance. A consensus is emerging in Congress that the Sandinistas are not reformers—or even Sandinistas—but Leninists who seek a monopoly of power at home and subversion of their democratic neighbors—and who must be stopped.

But look at the time the Nicaraguan communists have gained to consolidate their tyranny. Years in which we have been consumed in acrimonious internal debate have been used by them to tighten their grip and heighten the danger to the whole region.

...Terrorism, of course, is the most striking example of ambiguous warfare. Terrorist acts are a form of criminality, waged by surprise against unarmed men, women, and children in cold blood. Terrorist attacks are sometimes the random, senseless acts of zealots; more often, they are systematic and calculated attempts to achieve political ends. Despite the horror they inflict and the widespread recognition that their acts are criminal, few terrorists are caught, and fewer still are punished to the full extent they deserve. They know we abhor the loss of innocent lives; so they live and train in the midst of their women and children. And we debate among ourselves over the appropriate targets or the foreign policy consequences of a punitive blow. Terrorism is the newest strategy of the enemies of freedom—and it's all too effective.

We are right to be reluctant to unsheath our sword. But we cannot let the ambiguities of the terrorist threat reduce us to total impotence. A policy filled with so many qualifications and conditions that they all could never be met would amount to a policy of paralysis. It would amount to an admission that, with all our weaponry and power, we are helpless to defend our citizens, our interests, and our values. This I simply do not accept.

So we must meet this challenge of low-intensity conflict and ambiguous warfare. We have no choice.

THE INTELLECTUAL CHALLENGE OF AMBIGUOUS WARFARE

Our first task, it seems to me, is to come to grips with the problem intellectually.

For various reasons, at least in this century, we Americans have been uncomfortable with conflicts involving limited uses of force for limited ends. Nor have we had to confront systematic terrorism here at home, as Israel has for almost four decades. We have, sometimes, been slow in confronting dangers from abroad, waiting until a limited or ambiguous challenge has escalated into one of global dimensions. Today, we are faced with demands that we be absolutely certain of the need to act before doing so; that we act openly, swiftly, and conclusively; and that we support only those whose aims and conduct we approve in every way.

We know, today, that such simple clarity in the use of power is often elusive in the modern world. We have seen and we will continue to see a wide range of ambiguous threats in the shadow area between major war and millennial peace. Americans must understand, and I believe most Americans do understand, that a number of small challenges, year after year, can add up to a more serious challenge to our interests. The time to act, to help our friends by adding our strength to the equation, is not when the threat is at the doorstep, when the stakes are highest and the needed resources enormous. We must be prepared to commit our political, economic, and, if necessary, military power when the threat is still manageable and when its prudent use can prevent the threat from growing. We have far less margin for error today than we did even 30 years ago. We cannot afford to be complacent about events around the world in the expectation that, in the end, we will have the strength to overcome any challenge. We do not have the luxury of waiting until all the ambiguities have disappeared.

This is the essence of statesmanship—to see a danger when it is not self-evident; to educate our people to the stakes involved: then to fashion a sensible response and rally support.

Our intellectual challenge is especially to understand the need for prudent, limited, proportionate uses of our military power, whether as a means of crisis management, power projection, peacekeeping, localized military action, support for friends, or responding to terrorism—*and* to coordinate our power with our political and diplomatic objectives. Such discreet uses of power for limited purposes will always involve risks. But the risks of inaction will, in many circumstances, be greater.

Our political analysis must be clear sighted. Allies and friends may object to our action—or say they object. But this cannot be decisive. Striking against terrorism in the Middle East, for example, is bound to be controversial. But the worst thing we could do to our moderate friends in the region is to demonstrate that extremist policies succeed and that the United States is impotent to deal with such challenges. If we are to be a factor in the region—if we want countries to take risks for peace relying on our support—then we had better show that our power is an effective counterweight to extremism.

Among other things, this has to include the military supply relationships we have long had with our friends in the Arab world. This is tangible backing for their security in a dangerous period and an important factor for regional stability.

And we must show staying power. Americans are a nation of problem-solvers, and that is a mark of our greatness. Yet many of the problems we face are not susceptible to a quick fix. Few threats can be dealt with as rapidly as Grenada. Most will require perseverance and a longer term commitment. The struggle against terrorism will not be ended by a few dramatic actions. The safeguarding of fragile democracies and vulnerable allies against subversion and covert aggression, in Central America or elsewhere, will require more than brief and quickly completed uses of American power.

Our objective in these situations will always be to prevail. Sometimes, as in the case of Grenada, success will take the form of a total military victory and the removal of foreign troops. In other cases, success will consist of denying victory to the adversary so that political solutions become possible.

We must avoid no-win situations, but we must also have the stomach to confront the harder-to-win situations that call for prudent involvement, even when the results are slow in coming. Steadfastness and endurance are the keys to success; our adversaries notice when we are impatient, uncomfortable, or vacillating. Thus, we lose our leverage, and we *make* the problem more prolonged and more difficult to resolve.

THE POLITICAL, LEGAL, AND MORAL CHALLENGES

Unfortunately, in the wake of Vietnam our endurance against any kind of challenge has been open to question.

Recent decades have left a legacy of contention between the executive and legislative branches and a web of restrictions on executive action embedded in our laws. The result has been a loss of coherence and recurring uncertainty in the minds of friend and foe about the constancy of the United States. The War Powers Resolution sets arbitrary 60-day deadlines that practically invite an adversary to wait us out, that invariably send signals that the United States, despite all our power, may be "short of breath." That description—"short of breath"—was offered by a Syrian, 2 years ago, who watched our congressional debates and concluded that we lacked staying power; this undercut the prospects for successful negotiation. The rationale of our diplomacy—that the May 17 agreement was the way to bring Israeli withdrawal—was itself undercut when Israel pulled back. This problem can recur as we seek to meet other challenges.

We must tackle this political dilemma head on. Recently, a legislator criticized us for not consulting with the Congress before our interception of the airliner carrying terrorists who had killed an American. But if we delayed acting in order to consult, the terrorists would surely have escaped. I have no doubt that the American people want to see their President acting flexibly, effectively, and decisively against the terrorist menace to defend our citizens. Surely there can be accountability without paralysis.

The fact is, we will never face a specific threat that does not involve some hard choices that are difficult for democracy. The simple, tragic truth about many low-intensity challenges is that the "rules of the game" are often blurred, at best. Terrorists do not abide by the Geneva convention. They place a premium on the defenselessness and helplessness of their victims. The more heinous the crime, the more attention terrorists attract to their "cause."

The same is true of communist guerrillas, whose fundamental tenet is that the goal of seizing power justifies any method that comes to hand—urban terrorism or waging war on the civilian economy, as in El Salvador. They believe, as Castro once said, that history will absolve them. In the Philippines, the communist guerrillas are men of extraordinary brutality; they have been compared to the Cambodian communists, and this is not a wild comparison.

In the wake of the recent attacks at the Rome and Vienna airports, we have heard it asserted that military action to retaliate or preempt terrorism is contrary to international law. Some have suggested that even to contemplate using force against terrorism is to lower ourselves to the barbaric level of the terrorists. I want to take this issue head on.

Unlike terrorists and communist guerrillas, we do not believe the end justifies the means. We believe in the rule of law. This nation has long been a champion of international law, the peaceful settlement of disputes, and the UN Charter as a code of conduct for the world community.

But the Charter's restrictions on the use or threat of force in international relations include a specific exception for the right of self-defense. It is absurd to argue that international law prohibits us from capturing terrorists in international waters or airspace; from attacking them on the soil of other nations, even for the purpose of rescuing hostages; or from using force against states that support, train, and harbor terrorists or guerrillas. International law requires no such result. A nation attacked by terrorists is permitted to use force to prevent or preempt future attacks, to seize terrorists, or to rescue its citizens when no other means is available. The law requires that such actions be necessary and proportionate. But this nation has consistently affirmed the right of states to use force in exercise of their right of individual or collective self-defense.

The UN Charter is not a suicide pact. The law is a weapon on our side, and it is up to us to use it to its maximum extent. Cooperation in law enforcement, international agreements against hijacking and terrorism, extraditing and prosecuting terrorists when captured—these are indispensable tools. But we can go further.

There should be no confusion about the status of nations that sponsor terrorism against Americans and American property. There is substantial legal authority for the view that a state which supports terrorist or subversive attacks against another state, or which supports or encourages terrorist planning and other activities within its own territory, is responsible for such attacks. Such conduct can amount to an ongoing armed aggression against the other state under international law. As the President said last week:

> By providing material support to terrorist groups which attack U.S. citizens, Libya has engaged in armed aggression against the United States under established principles of international law, just as if [it] had used its own armed forces.

Think about the practical and strategic implications of allowing a state to evade responsibility for the acts of its terrorist surrogates: a nation like Qadhafi's Libya would acquire immunity while carrying on the secret or ambiguous warfare which poses such a threat today to the security and well-being of free nations. And to let ourselves be deterred by Qadhafi's threats from doing what is needed to stop him will only establish in his mind, and in the minds of other fanatics, that the scheme has worked. State-supported terror will increase through our submission to it, not from our active resistance.

The future will be grim, indeed, if we permit this. The potential gravity of terrorist acts is certain to increase as terrorists obtain the means to use weapons far more destructive and harmful than guns, grenades, and bombs. In fact, state support will probably be the single most important factor in enabling terrorists to acquire such weapons, which may well include nuclear devices small enough for terrorists to assemble but devastating enough to destroy a government's leadership and a nation's morale. We must use the law to preserve civilized order, not to shield those who would wage war against it.

The armed ideologues of the world may believe that our devotion to international law will immobilize us abroad, just as they may believe our political system will immobilize us at home. As we have shown in response to Nicaragua's hypocritical suit in the World Court, we will not permit our enemies—who despise the rule of law as a "bourgeois" notion—to use *our* devotion to law and morality as a weapon against us. When the United States defends its citizens abroad or helps its friends and allies defend themselves against subversion and tyranny, we are not suspending our legal and moral principles. On the contrary, we are strengthening the basis of international stability, justice, and the rule of law.

Our morality must be a source of strength, not paralysis. We cannot walk away from every situation that poses a moral dilemma. The use of force at *any* level involves moral issues. We should use our military power only if the stakes justify it, if other means are not available, and then only in a manner appropriate to a clear objective. But we cannot opt out of every contest. We cannot wait for absolute certainty and clarity. If we do, the world's future will be determined by others—most likely by those who are the most brutal, the most unscrupulous, and the most hostile to everything we believe in.

A STRATEGY FOR AMBIGUOUS WARFARE

Thus, the United States needs an active strategy for dealing with ambiguous warfare. We must be better prepared intellectually and psychologically as a nation; we must be better prepared organizationally as a government. Many important steps have been taken. But more needs to be done.

...With the necessary will, hard work, and a degree of wisdom, we will prevail over this challenge, as we have prevailed over so many others in our proud history.

Terror Error: The Irony of Counterterrorism

Daniel Triesman

What exactly is terrorism? Administration officials such as Secretary of State George Shultz view it as a malignant strain of geopolitical AIDS, eroding the immune system of the international body politic, inducing confusion and paralysis. In the State Department's official definition, it is "the threat or use of violence for political purposes by individuals or groups whether acting for or in opposition to established governmental authority when such actions are intended to shock, stun, or intimidate a target group wider than the immediate victims." Whatever else, terrorism is violence against innocent non-combatants. Elaborating on such definitions has become one of the thriving cottage industries of academe.

In late July 1984 the elite, U.S.-trained Atlacatl Battalion of the El Salvador army swept through the village of Los Llanitos in the northern mountains of El Salvador. The soldiers smashed the roofs of houses, cut down corn, and then spread out through the surrounding countryside to track down the villagers who had fled. Antonio Lobo was hiding in a ravine with his family and others. "The army descended by the river and got to about five meters from us," he told Tutela Legal, the human rights agency of the Salvadoran Catholic Church. "They did not give us any warning and just shot at us." About 80 civilians were killed in similar incidents around Los Llanitos during the next few days.

In a bizarre development, those who initiated the Los Llanitos massacre may soon receive U.S. funding—in the name of fighting terrorism. A State Department memorandum recently leaked to *The Washington Post* outlines a plan to provide $27 million in military support and $26 million in police training funds to El Salvador, Guatemala, Honduras, Costa Rica, and Panama. The money will go to buy everything from X-ray equipment to Bell 212 helicopters and M-16 rifles. Drafted shortly after the June 19 terrorist attack on a San Salvador café that left four Marines dead, the proposal reflects the administration's determination to fight the "terrorist threat" worldwide. And, by the logic of the State Department, this requires shipping weapons to the raiders of Los Llanitos (and their counterparts in Guatemala). What

---

Daniel Triesman, "Terror Error: The Irony of Counterterror," *The New Republic* (14 October 1985), 16–18. Reprinted with permission of *The New Republic.*

matters to the administration is less the nature of the terrorist act than the political views of its perpetrators.

The U.S. has been training other countries' security forces in antiterrorist operations for 18 months under the Anti-Terrorism Assistance Program. But the State Department's new proposal allocates for Central America alone over five times the 1985 budget for antiterrorist training worldwide. And as well as seminars, the new program would provide arms and advanced security equipment. The $22 million earmarked for El Salvador will presumably add to the $483 million in economic and military assistance already requested by the administration and authorized in the foreign aid bill. Because of Guatemala's history of army brutality, the administration has been unable to persuade Congress to authorize more than the most meager military aid to that country. Counterterrorism is a politically irresistible pretext to reopen the flow of arms.

Aid to Guatemala, the memo says, is needed to "reiterate our support of that government's decision to go forward with elections" this November. Yet the Guatemalan government has made no request for U.S. military aid this year and, according to the Guatemalan Embassy in Washington, does not intend to. The army's heavy hand is already felt guiding the election process, endorsing a candidate, and defining the narrow limits of debate. Last March Guatemala's head of state General Humberto Mejia Victores, declared that the country's only human rights agency, the Mutual Support Group for the Families of the Disappeared, was infiltrated by "subversives." Just a few days later, four armed men kidnapped one of the group's leaders, beat him to death, and cut out his tongue. Another of the group's leaders was found murdered at the bottom of a ravine along with her three-year-old son and younger brother. Overwhelming evidence exists that the army has indiscriminately murdered Indian peasants in rural areas. No member of the armed forces has ever been detained, much less tried or convicted, for such offenses.

In these circumstances, more military aid will hardly strengthen the hand of those committed to the democratic process and a return to civilian rule. And there's little sign that Guatemala's military leaders intend to change their ways. General Mejia Victores persistently denies any army involvement in human rights abuses. Guatemala should not be singled out for criticism, he told a press conference last July. "It seems there is also terrorism in the whole world."

In El Salvador incidents such as the Los Llanitos massacre are the outgrowth of official policy. In order to deny guerrilla forces food and support, peasants in certain areas are driven from their homes with grenades and rifles. In Chalatenango province, Colonel Sigifredo Ochoa has established 12 "free-fire" zones. "In these zones there are no civilians," Colonel Ochoa told

Chris Hedges of *The Dallas Morning News*. "There are only concentrations of guerrillas, so we keep these areas under heavy fire." In fact, according to relief officials Hedges interviewed, these areas *are* populated by civilians.

The Guatemalan government's indiscriminate attacks against unarmed Indian peasants also constitute terror. And an admirably succinct definition of terrorism—"Selective Use of Violence for Propagandistic Effects"—appears as a chapter heading in the manual drafted by the CIA for the Nicaraguan *contras* instruction. If it were serious about its own definition, the State Department would have to include Nicaragua among the recipients of counterterrorism aid. Clearly the administration's position is not entirely ingenuous.

Whatever they may say, administration officials do not consider each act of terror around the world an equal offense to the American way of life. Only those judged to threaten U.S. interests meet with a firm response. The real danger, according to President Reagan, is "terrorism that is part of a pattern, the work of a confederation of terrorist states" whose "goal is to expel America from the world." And in Central America the focal point of this anti-American alliance, in Reagan's view, is Nicaragua.

For a government to ignore its country's geopolitical interests would be a dereliction of duty. But the strategic perspective can be misleadingly seductive. One danger to El Salvador's democracy, according to the State Department's memo, is "leftist-instigated labor and student unrest." In fact, union discontent frequently originates in labor groups that supported Salvadoran president José Napoleón Duarte. For the most part, their demands are neither revolutionary nor antidemocratic, and they pose no threat to U.S. interests. Besides pressing for wage increases to keep up with the cost of living, most want Duarte to fulfill his campaign promises to prosecute political assassins and continue the dialogue with the guerrillas.

The foolishness of responding to labor protest with counterterrorist SWAT teams was amply demonstrated in June. A special unit of the Salvadoran treasury police, trained by the U.S., stormed a hospital in San Salvador to break a month-long strike. Shortly before dawn, over 100 troops occupied the building, streaming in through the basement and from a helicopter on the roof. Patients and medical staff were forced to lie down with their hands tied behind their backs. In the confusion four undercover police officers were killed by the troops.

The counterterrorism proposal is particularly disquieting in view of certain attitudes in the State Department. In recent years senior officials have tried to discredit human rights reporting groups who don't share the administration's selective definition of terrorism. On ABC's "Nightline" last February, former secretary of state for human rights Elliott Abrams flatly denied that the Los Llanitos massacre ever happened: "I'm telling you that there were no significant—there were no massacres in El Salvador in 1984." Not only did *The New York Times, The Boston Globe,* and *The Miami Herald* confirm that the massacre took place, even the Salvadoran government's own Human Rights Commission admitted that 80 civilians were killed there "out of combat." State Department officials who investigated the case say that, although there were casualties at Los Llanitos, there was no evidence to indicate a massacre and much evidence to indicate that the guerrillas stage-managed the incident.

Abrams's denials were part of a larger campaign to discredit anyone who suggests that U.S.-backed military forces in the region have committed abuses that qualify as terrorism. In September 1982 Assistant Secretary of State for Inter-American Affairs Thomas Enders (whose job Abrams now holds) circulated a letter attacking an Amnesty International report on human rights violations in Guatemala. Embassy information, Enders declared, "frequently contrasts sharply with that provided by Amnesty International." This was something of an overstatement: in three of the seven cases Enders cited there was no significant difference between the embassy's and Amnesty's accounts. In the other four cases Amnesty relied on a more stringent standard of evidence than the embassy.

Enders, who allowed the letter to be distributed to the Guatemalan press, had worked on Central American policy long enough to know that such public criticism might be taken by the military as permission to attack the offending organization. Enders's actions, according to a report by the Americas Watch Committee, "contributed to circumstances in which, if Amnesty wished to send a mission to that country, the mission's members—and its sources—would not be safe."

Similarly, the administration has also attempted to discredit Tutela Legal by disputing its connection to the Salvadoran Catholic Church. This puts it strangely at odds with Archbishop Arturo Rivera y Damas, who has issued a statement calling Tutela Legal an "important and close part" of his ministry.

To base Central American policy on strategic interests of the U.S. as well as human rights is only reasonable. But the question of strategy should not be smuggled through Congress behind a screen of metal detectors. By packaging military aid as counterterrorism, the administration hopes to deliver aid Congress might otherwise be reluctant to send. Few members of Congress are naive enough to be taken in by this semantic chicanery. But most can read the political signs. Any measure termed "antiterrorism" is bound to draw a flurry of supportive constituent letters. The bill, which will emerge later this fall, is considered likely to pass with only minor "damage limitation" amendments. "It'll really fly," laments one congressional aide.

Reagan, Thatcher, and the Colonel

Paul O. Gendelman

Our first reaction to the bombing of Libya is that the President of the United States has made a mistake, and that Mrs Thatcher is wrong to have encouraged this mistake.

We make this hard judgment in sorrow not in anger. We do not bask in moral outrage. We do not accuse Washington of a crime. Anger and moral outrage are what we feel at Colonel Gaddafi's crimes. We sympathise deeply with the Reagan administration and the American people in their frustration at seeing innocent Americans killed by acts of terrorism, some of them undoubtedly Libyan-sponsored. We also feel that Western Europe has not done all it might have done to try to deter Colonel Gaddafi from the sponsorship of further acts of terrorism. We recognise that to deter Colonel Gaddafi from such sponsorship was the Reagan administration's good intention. But we do not believe that this end justifies the means used by the United States early on Tuesday morning. We also fear that these means take us further away from the desired end, not closer to it.

Let us suppose, for the sake of argument, that Washington does indeed have irrefutable proof of the direct responsibility of the Gaddafi régime for the bomb-blast which killed one American soldier and wounded others in a West Berlin discotheque a fortnight ago, proof which it cannot reveal publicly for fear of compromising its intelligence sources, but and furnished privately to Mrs Thatcher (although in a Commons answer she talked only of having examined "*our own* intelligence evidence"): Even if this is the case, do the United States' "retaliatory strikes" qualify as "self-defence" in the sense of Article 51 of the UN Charter? We have yet to hear an independent authority on international law say unequivocally that they do. Sir Anthony Parsons must be correct to suggest that those who drew up the UN Charter certainly had something different in mind. The delay between the terrorist deed and the retaliation by the victims' national government further robs it of the instinctive moral plausibility of "an eye for an eye." And anyway, was it not rather "a hundred eyes for one eye?" In other words, were the means *proportionate* to the ends?

These doubts about the moral justification of the attack would matter less if the practical effects were to be those intended. If all Libyan-sponsored

---

terrorism were now to disappear from the face of the earth, and if in a short time Libya were also to be rid of Colonel Gaddafi, then our judgment might swing in favour of the action. We fervently hope that these will indeed be the results. Mrs Thatcher insisted in the House that the American intention was to hit "specific targets demonstrably involved in the conduct and support of terrorist activities." But it is in the nature of terrorist activities (as it is of guerrilla warfare) that such targets are almost infinite, even if your bombers could hit them all, and only them, with perfect accuracy; which of course they could not. When Israeli jets destroyed an Iraqi nuclear power plant, they destroyed Iraq's nuclear arms potential. That was a justified "surgical strike." But terrorists are not nuclear power plants. Almost by definition, you cannot destroy them by "surgical strikes." Politically, moreover, the immediate effect of this attack appears to have been to goad the half-mad dictator to further acts of armed lunacy, such as the attack on an American installation on Lampedusa. The immediate ill-effects also include the temporary rallying of the whole Arab world in condemnation of the American action, and a significant fuelling of anti-Reagan and anti-American sentiment in Western Europe.

In short, at the time of writing the international balance sheet on this action looks little short of disastrous. All these consequences were entirely predictable when President Reagan asked Mrs Thatcher for her permission to fly the mission from American bases in Britain. If she did not foresee them immediately herself, they must very soon have been pointed out to her by her own officials. And these are the reasons why she should have urged him most forcefully to reconsider. We do not suggest that she should have flatly and immediately said "no," as the Churchill-Truman agreement theoretically entitles her to do. This is not an argument about sovereignty. Anyone can appreciate the force of Mrs Thatcher's remark that we should not stop the Americans "using their own planes flown by their own pilots to defend their own people." Moreover, it is mean-minded and short-sighted to support the Americans only when and where they are directly defending us. This is an attitude, quite widespread in Western Europe, which people in Washington very understandably resent. No, it is precisely because we *do* feel a responsibility for what happens in the world outside the NATO area and Western Europe, it is just because we *are* concerned about the future of the whole "free world" (and not least, the free Arab world), that Mrs Thatcher should—to adapt Cromwell's famous words—have beseeched him to think it possible that he might be mistaken. Instead, she encouraged him in his mistake.

That is our critical judgment of the attack's likely result. All we can hope now is that it is we who are mistaken in making it. An hour before we went to press a news flash reached us suggesting that Colonel Gaddafi had fled Libya. But even if we are swiftly and happily proved wrong by events, the Government's role in preparing Monday's EEC position on the Libyan crisis will remain extremely difficult to reconcile with its vigorous unilateral endorsement of Tuesday's American attack. The issue is not "What did Sir Geoffrey know when?" Nor is it "Europe or America?" It is simply: "Where do we really stand?" If the Government genuinely believes that the American military action was the right response to this crisis, then it should never have signed an EEC statement which said—almost in so many words—that military action was the wrong response to this crisis. If the Government believes what it put its name to in the EEC statement, then it should not have endorsed the American action. If there are "two ways about this," we cannot see them.

The Face of Terrorism

Lawrence K. Grossman

Television's role in covering terrorism has provoked sharp criticism and intense international debate. Following the TWA hijacking crisis last summer, Prime Minister Margaret Thatcher, Attorney General Edward Meese, Secretary of Defense Caspar Weinberger, State Department Counselor Abraham Sofaer and Henry Kissinger, among others, accused television of encouraging terrorism by supplying terrorists with "the oxygen" they need (to use Mrs. Thatcher's widely quoted metaphor) for their barbarous acts. A surprising number of American newspapers in their editorial columns also took after the television networks while, at the same time, those same newspapers reproduced on their front pages verbatim transcripts and the most dramatic still photos from television's coverage.

By contrast, public support for the news media reached its highest level during last summer's traumatic TWA hostage crisis, according to a recent Gallup study, with 89% of the nation applauding what television did. And a recent Roper study confirmed that the media's coverage of TWA's Flight 847 hijacking was one of the things the American people felt best about.

Television has examined itself and questioned itself about its own terrorism coverage. At NBC News we have been reexamining our own experience in dealing with the recent spate of terrorist incidents. That examination, I can tell you, has produced no dramatic new theories or spe-

Lawrence K. Grossman, "The Face of Terrorism," *The Quill* (June 1986), 38–41. Reprinted with permission of Lawrence K. Grossman, president NBC News.

cial new insights. Instead, our study has reaffirmed that professionalism, tempered by common sense and good judgment in each case, is the most useful guide to covering such incidents, although the very idea of using the words "common sense" and "terrorism" in the same sentence seems paradoxical. Precise planning and rigid rules serve little practical use when it comes to deciding how to cover each highly emotional, terrifying and unpredictable terrorism episode. Decisions must be made on a case-by-case basis.

Our critics have made the following points:

1. Television should refrain from covering terrorist episodes while they are happening, thereby depriving terrorists of the publicity they seek.
2. Television should at the very least heavily restrain and limit its coverage of terrorist episodes.
3. Television lets itself be "used" by terrorists to promote their own interests.
4. Television's coverage of terrorism puts undue pressure on the government and limits its ability to respond or retaliate.
5. Television presents terrorists in a more favorable light than they deserve. By airing terrorist grievances, television at times may seem to justify their criminal behavior.
6. Television coverage tends to protract each terrorism episode and make it more alarming and important than it deserves to be.
7. Television doesn't just cover the story; too often it becomes the story.
8. Television should never interview hostages in captivity and certainly should not seek out hostage families during their time of crisis.
9. The intense network competition for ratings leads to unsound news judgments and sensationalized reporting.
10. Networks should pool their coverage of terrorist incidents and establish ahead of time a uniform set of reporting standards.

Let me respond to each of those criticisms.

1. Should television refrain from covering terrorist episodes as they happen? The answer to that is no. When people are killed, airports or public institutions bombed, airplanes captured, or hostages taken, there is no choice but to report what is happening. In this age of instant communications by satellite and telephone those stories simply cannot be hidden. Television should report such stories even if it means that it serves the terrorists' cause by giving them the exposure they seek. We recognize that most terrorist acts are aimed not just at the victims, but at a far wider audience. We must also recognize that terrorism feeds on the strongest and most basic emotion, fear. And fear feeds on ignorance and rumor. If television ever failed to report major episodes, we would find terrorists escalating their actions to gain attention, as in a sense they already have by hijacking airliners, attacking airports and kidnapping hostages.

The press cannot treat terrorist kidnappings, murders and bombings as if they have not happened. If television cameras were to be turned away from such news, viewers would no longer trust television journalism. It would lose all credibility. One of the biggest victories terrorists could ever achieve would be to force democracies to adopt the repressive press restrictions of dictatorships, banning coverage of terrorist episodes, as some have urged. In a democratic society, it is the height of arrogance to take the position that the general public should not be permitted to know what reporters on-the-scene know, unless the reporters have confidential information that could jeopardize lives. Our guiding principle should be: It is always better to cover it than cover it up.

2. What kinds of special restraints should television exercise when covering terrorist events? We recognize that there is no absolute right to a free press. The First Amendment to the U.S. Constitution exists not to benefit the press but to protect the public's right to know. There are obvious restraints, which are both appropriate and necessary, that the press itself should impose on its coverage. For example, television should not report information that will endanger either the victims of terrorism or those who are trying to put an end to a terrorist episode. In such instances reporters should without question seek the guidance of authorities. It is also important not to get in the way of efforts to end a crisis. Information about the deployment of forces that would endanger lives if it became known to the terrorists should be withheld. But that is not as simple a decision to make as it sounds.

Most of the time, such information is leaked to reporters by the authorities themselves in an effort to put pressure on the terrorists or to placate the public. That is exactly what happened during last summer's TWA hijacking when information was leaked about the deployment of the Delta Force. The networks reported that the Delta Force was being dispatched, but withheld the information they had about where the Force was going. In fact, I am not aware of any failure by any American television network to withhold information that would damage national security or endanger lives. The television networks never revealed what they knew about the Americans hiding in the Canadian embassy during the Iran hostage crisis, nor did any network broadcast the sensitive security facts it had about several of the TWA hostages who were being held in Beirut last summer. In fact, I do not know of a single instance where the reporting of a hostage situation or a terrorist event has caused the death of an innocent victim. So far, at least, all the killings of hostages have taken place *before* the arrival of television cameras, not after.

The capacity for live coverage in this satellite age puts a special burden on television journalists who now must operate without what T.H. White calls "the consoling filter of time." It is important not to lose perspective, and to provide airtime in proportion to the global and political significance as well as the dramatic intensity of the event. Interruptions of the regular schedule must be done with caution and only when there is something new to report. The common sense rule is to provide credible, factual coverage without endangering life or hampering the authorities. These are the basic restraints that television should exercise.

3. Does television allow itself to be "used" by terrorists and does television coverage, therefore, encourage terrorist acts? The answer is yes to both. Television has unquestionably become a primary vehicle for terrorists in search of an audience. Television coverage gives terrorists status; it enables them, at least briefly, to transcend their underdog role.

Television offers terrorists an initial tactical advantage. They write the script for the opening act. They set the news agenda. Through television, they appeal directly to the people over the heads of the government. As the Rand Corporation's Brian Jenkins has said, "Terrorists want a lot of people watching and listening; not a lot of people dead." The very existence of television undoubtedly bears some responsibility for the "copycat" syndrome of terrorism today. News travels instantaneously from one end of the world to the other. One highly visible action inspires others elsewhere.

Should television permit itself to become a platform for terrorist propaganda? One of the most severe criticisms we get is that television itself is held hostage by terrorists who, in effect, are able to shoot their way onto our air and use this most powerful of all media to deliver their political messages. We worry a lot about that although, I suggest, there really is less to this problem than meets the eye. I have seen no evidence that audiences are ever taken in by the propaganda of terrorists who have blackmailed their way onto the television screen. Terrorists are terrible communicators. The brutal actions they must take in order to be seen on television destroys their ability to get their message across. Clearly, television should never be made easily accessible to the lawless. But it is unrealistic to believe that air time will never be surrendered when lives are at stake. The price of refusal becomes too high whenever enough hostages are taken. The consolation is that viewers do not tend to be persuaded by a message delivered at the point of a gun.

It is important to recognize that television is part of the environment, as are airplanes and automobiles which are also favorite tools of terrorists. We have no choice but to learn to live with them and adapt to them. Coverage of killings, hijackings, bombings and brutal threats delivered by hooded outlaws with guns, is more likely to mobilize public outrage against the terrorists than gain support for them.

4. Does television's coverage of terrorism tie government's hands and unduly limit its ability to respond? The answer is yes. In hostage situations,

when millions get to see and, to some extent, know individual victims, the pressure to free the captives intensifies. The more the people know, the more the authorities feel impelled to act if only to overcome the appearance of impotence. At the same time it is a lot harder to respond or retaliate if the public fears that victims, whose faces have become familiar through television, might get killed. A retaliatory strike is easier to consider if the hostages are anonymous and the facts are not widely known.

Television coverage of a terrorist attack does tend to escalate the crisis. It can impel a frustrated government to act rather than appear weak and temporizing before millions of viewers. Or it can lead to paralysis out of fear that "the whole world is watching." We have seen it happen both ways.

By the same token, the authorities themselves are not without major resources in using television's coverage of terrorist outrages to mobilize public opinion. Witness the Reagan administration's campaign against Moammar Khadafy after the Rome and Vienna airport attacks.

In a democracy, public opinion inevitably must be taken into account by all parties to any action and, depending on how it all comes out, television's role in making people aware of a crisis will be labelled a help or a hindrance. Our general rule in a democracy, especially during a crisis: it is better for the people to be informed than to be kept in the dark. And it is better for the government to operate with a knowledgeable public than an ignorant one.

5. Does television show terrorists in a more favorable light than they deserve? The American public does not think so. As I have already indicated, public support for the news media was at its highest, according to a recent Gallup poll, during the TWA hostage crisis, with 89% of the people favoring the network coverage. And this was confirmed by a recent Roper study which concluded that the media's coverage of TWA's Flight 847 hijacking was one of the things people felt best about. In view of the escalating public hostility towards terrorism, it does not appear that television has helped the terrorists' image any. In fact, the most vivid picture to emerge from the TWA crisis was that of the hooded terrorist with one hand clamped over the mouth of the TWA pilot and the other hand holding a gun, hardly an image calculated to win converts.

The reality is that television journalists largely reflect the same notions of right and wrong as the people who are in their audience. No matter what legitimate grievances terrorists may have, television reporters are not likely to go against the grain and make heroes out of them.

6. Does television tend to protract a terrorism episode and exaggerate its importance? Those who answer yes to that question point out that the destruction and killing by terrorists are miniscule compared to the devastation of wars, revolutions, automobile accidents and natural disasters. Be-

cause terrorism is almost always the last resort of the weak and desperate, television's coverage makes terrorists seem far more powerful than they really are. And yet, the consequences of terrorism can be calamitous. It disrupts normal life, kills innocent people, generates large scale fear, and has the potential of embroiling nations in war. After all, the outbreak of World War I was precipitated by the terrorist assassination of an obscure archduke.

Television coverage may well serve to protract a terrorist incident as the terrorists seek to play to the cameras. But this, too, may not be as bad as it appears. As long as terrorists are talking, they are not killing. The experience of the TWA hostage crisis, the recent Egyptair hijacking to Malta, and the Washington, D.C. B'nai B'rith hostage episode several years ago, suggest that television cameras tend to modify the behavior of terrorists who, as a rule, are not disposed to appear as murderers in full view of the entire world. Murder, torture and cruelty tend to be secret acts carried out in darkness, rather than in the full light of public view.

7. Can television ever avoid becoming part of the story? Probably not. Television today is the stage on which terrorist incidents are played. More often than not, television is also the only link, the prime conduit of information, between the terrorists and the authorities. In the Iran and TWA crises, the American government received much, if not most of its information from watching television's coverage. Terrorists want their cause aired, but not their vulnerability and their inhumanity. Government uses television to transmit its messages to the terrorists, but also wants television to minimize the seriousness of the incident to the public. Hostages want television to communicate their plight to the world and hope they will remain the center of attention until they are freed. One victim of the TWA crisis said his worst moments came when the TWA story was pushed off the front pages by the Air India 747 disaster; he was afraid people would forget them. Families of hostages use television to put public pressure on the authorities to free their loved ones, regardless of global or political considerations. All of the conflicting interests have one thing in common. They make television an unavoidable part of the story.

Television journalists, on the other hand, have the responsibility to serve as credible observers and reporters, not as negotiators or direct participants. Any reporter who takes on the role of negotiator or middleman, as has happened in prison riots and hostage situations, forfeits his role as a reporter. When he becomes a player, he is no longer an observer. Television's role is to cover what is happening and not try to change the event or influence the participants. It is television's job to provide calm, rational, accurate reports; to defuse hysteria, rumor and speculation.

Some have urged television reporters to serve as "citizens first and journalists second," by focusing on the evils of terrorism, by refusing ever to give terrorists a platform, and by emphasizing the failure rate of terrorist actions. But television's job is not to propagandize. It is to report the facts and assure the credibility of its journalism. This is true even though television is not immune from the principle that the process of observing a phenomenon inevitably changes that phenomenon. Which is all the more reason for us to do whatever we can to report the story and not to become a voluntary participant in the story.

8. Should television broadcast interviews of hostages while they are in captivity? Should we interview hostage families? My answer is yes to both. True, nothing was more dismaying than the spectacle of frenzied photographers in Beirut climbing all over tables and chairs, stepping in plates of food and pushing and shoving each other while trying to get pictures of the TWA hostages who were put on display by their captors for the infamous group interview. Still, the opportunity to see hostages first hand, to assess their condition, their attitude and the circumstances of their captivity, must not be overlooked. Should we stop trying to gain access to the American, British and French hostages still held in Lebanon from whom we have had no recent firsthand word? Imagine if we could see and hear from political prisoners now held captive in Soviet labor camps and psychiatric wards. Would they be able to talk freely? Certainly not. Would they be required to say things in captivity that they would never say if they were free? Probably. Would they feel compelled to say things that serve their captors' interest? Very possibly. Even so, we should not ignore or overlook any reasonable opportunity to interview hostages or political prisoners. Nor should anyone doubt the ability of the viewing public to make their own practical judgments about interviews given in captivity, or for the capacity of our reporters to put such interviews in perspective. Certainly, hostages themselves are eager to get their story out, even when they know they are being exploited by their captors. If any of us in this room were taken hostage, would we want the news kept secret? Or would we welcome television cameras to record our plight? We should do all we reasonably can to find the victims of terrorism and interview them.

Nothing has provoked more intense criticism than television's efforts to interview grieving hostage families. No one is comfortable with hordes of prying, insensitive reporters asking prying, insensitive questions of the wives, husbands, parents and children of victims while cameras record their every emotion. There is no defense for stupidity, insensitivity or journalistic excess, and there is no doubt we have been guilty at times of all three, despite our strict network guidelines. But what most critics do not realize is that most interviews take place with people who actually *want* to be interviewed. They are eager to answer questions and make their own comments about the hostages or victims. They look for the chance to call attention to the plight of their family members. They want to appear on television in order to reassure the captives, reach out to the captors and influence the authorities. And if the authorities feel pressured under those circumstances, well that is the price of having to govern in a democratic environment.

I myself flew to Frankfurt last summer as the TWA hostage crisis was ending to be sure that we did not exploit the returning hostages or their families who were there to welcome them. I found that our biggest problem turned out to be the families' eagerness to exploit television, rather than the need to protect them from being exploited by us. Relatives of the Americans still in captivity in Lebanon have organized themselves for the purpose of getting publicity on television and all media so that their plight will not be forgotten. Their major complaint is that they do not get on the air enough, not that they are being pushed by television.

9 & 10. Does the intense network competition for ratings lead to unsound news judgments and sensationalized coverage? Some have urged the networks to pool their coverage of terrorist incidents and agree ahead of time on a single set of standards for responsible reporting. That, in my view, is a terrible idea. It goes without saying that no amount of competition should ever justify shoddy news judgments or sensationalized coverage. And the American television networks, which have a long and proud tradition of traveling the high road in news, are especially sensitive about the quality and integrity of their journalism. One of the great strengths of American network coverage is the stimulus, the goad of competition. It makes for enterprising reporting and increases the penalty of making a mistake. If one news organization misses a story or overlooks an angle, its competitors do whatever they can to fill the gap. Whenever coverage is pooled, as it must be during those few times when there is no room for many cameras or an army of reporters, we live in fear that a mistake once made cannot be found out or corrected. Nothing could be more damaging to a free society. In journalism, as in most other pursuits, competition is far better than collusion.

We at NBC News have our own rather stringent standards and guidelines. Other news organizations, our competitors, have theirs. But when reporting on terrorism, no single set of standards can substitute for common sense, a commitment to professionalism and good judgment each time one of those difficult incidents confronts us.

DISCUSSION QUESTIONS

1. What constitutes terrorism? Who are terrorists?
2. What are justifiable responses to terrorism? Is a violent response to violence ethical?
3. What is the media's ethical responsibility regarding the reporting of terrorism?
4. Is terrorism ever justifiable?

CONTRIBUTORS

Bernard K. Duffy Professor and Chair of the Department of Speech Communication, California Polytechnic State University, San Luis Obispo, teaches courses in rhetorical theory and American public address and has published numerous articles in the fields of rhetorical theory and political rhetoric. With H. R. Ryan, he has edited a two-volume reference work entitled *American Orators of the Nineteenth Century* and *American Orators of the Twentieth Century* and is presently the editor for a series of books on individual American orators.

Susan Duffy Associate Professor of Speech Communication, California Polytechnic State University, San Luis Obispo, teaches courses in mass media criticism, public speaking, and oral interpretation of literature and has published in the fields of theatre history and communication education. She is the editor of *Shirley Chisholm: A Bibliography of Writings by and about Her* (Scarecrow Press, 1988).

Lois L. Duke Assistant Professor of Political Science, Auburn University, teaches courses on the Congress and the American presidency. She has written on women and politics.

Charles W. Dunn Professor and Head, Political Science Department, Clemson University, Clemson, South Carolina, teaches courses in the

American presidency, the Congress and religion and politics. His publications in all three areas include *Constitutional Democracy in America: a Reappraisal* and *American Political Theology: Historical Perspective and Theoretical Analysis.*

Loch K. Johnson Associate Professor of Political Science, University of Georgia, Athens, has been an American Political Science Association Congressional Fellow, an aide to Senator Frank Church, and staff director of the Subcommittee on Oversight Committee on Intelligence, in the House of Representatives. His publications on Senator Frank Church include *The Making of International Agreements: Congress Confronts the Executive* and *A Season of Inquiry: The Senate Intelligence Investigation.*

John C. Koritansky Professor of Political Science, Hiram College, Hiram, Ohio, teaches courses in history of political philosophy, Constitutional Law, and American political thought, and has published in the areas of political philosophy and public administration. He is the author of *Alexis de Tocqueville and the New Science of Politics* (Carolina Academic Press, 1986).

William Lasser Associate Professor of Political Science, Clemson University, Clemson, South Carolina, teaches courses in U.S. politics and public law. His publications include articles in the *Journal of Politics* and *Technology Review.* He is the author of *The Limits of Judicial Power: The Supreme Court in American Politics.* (University of North Carolina Press, 1988).

Peter Augustine Lawler Associate Professor of Political Science, Berry College, Mount Berry, Georgia, teaches in the areas of American politics and political philosophy and has published widely on the moral and religious dimensions of American political life.

Richard W. Leeman Assistant Professor, University of North Carolina, Charlotte. Teaches courses in legal and political communication.

William D. Pederson Associate Professor of Political Science and Director of American Studies at Louisiana State University, Shreveport, Louisiana. He is co-editor of *The Rating Game in American Politics* and has published numerous articles in books and journals. He has also worked in the Operations Center at the U.S. Department of State, and the Program Planning and Evaluation Office at the National Institutes of Health.

Bernard Schechterman Professor of Politics and Public Affairs at University of Miami, Coral Gables, Florida. He has taught and published widely in the areas of international politics, and Middle East politics. Among his more recent works is the co-edited (with Martin Slann) *Multidimensional Terrorism.*

Martin Slann Professor of Political Science, Clemson University, Clemson, South Carolina, teaches courses in politics of the Middle East, politics of the Soviet Union, and political philosophy. He is co-author of *The American Republic: Politics, Institutions, and Policies,* author of *Eight Nations: An Introduction to Comparative Politics* and editor of *The Journal of Political Science.*

Stephen A. Smith Associate Professor of Communication, University of Arkansas, Fayettesville, Arkansas, teaches courses in political communication and freedom of speech. He has been Editor of *Free Speech Yearbook* and *Communication Law Review,* and formerly served as a member of the Judiciary Committee of the Arkansas House of Representatives, Chief of Staff for the Arkansas Attorney General, and Executive Assistant to the Governor of Arkansas.

Mary Thornberry Assistant Professor of Political Science, Davidson College, Davidson, North Carolina.

Stephen Wainscott Associate Professor of Political Science, Clemson University, Clemson, South Carolina, teaches courses in southern politics, political parties, and political methodology. He has written extensively on the process of desegregation in the South.

INDEX